POLICE RESPONSE TO MENTAL HEALTH IN CANADA

POLICE RESPONSE TO MENTAL HEALTH IN CANADA

EDITED BY
Uzma Williams, Daniel J. Jones, and John R. Reddon

CANADIAN SCHOLARS
Toronto | Vancouver

Police Response to Mental Health in Canada
Edited by Uzma Williams, Daniel J. Jones, and John R. Reddon

First published in 2019 by
Canadian Scholars, an imprint of CSP Books Inc.
425 Adelaide Street West, Suite 200
Toronto, Ontario
M5V 3C1

www.canadianscholars.ca

Library and Archives Canada Cataloguing in Publication

Title: Police response to mental health in Canada / edited by Uzma Williams, Daniel J. Jones, and
      John R. Reddon. Names: Williams, Uzma, editor. | Jones, Daniel J., 1974- editor. | Reddon,
      John R., editor.
Description: Includes bibliographical references.
Identifiers: Canadiana (print) 20190125241 | Canadiana (ebook) 20190125330 | ISBN
9781773381459 (softcover) | ISBN 9781773381466 (PDF) | ISBN 9781773381473 (EPUB)
Subjects: LCSH: Police services for the mentally ill—Canada. | LCSH: Mentally ill offenders—
Canada. | LCSH: Mental illness—Canada.
Classification: LCC HV8079.3 .P65 2019 | DDC 363.2/308740971—dc23

Page layout by S4Carlisle
Cover design by Ana Chabrand

Printed and bound in Ontario, Canada

Canada

Dedicated to our students, police personnel, and Canadians who struggle with mental health.

The views expressed in this book are those of the authors and do not necessarily reflect any endorsement by or extant policies of any institutions with which they are affiliated.

This book provides general information and should not be interpreted as medical advice to diagnose or treat any mental health concerns for you or others. Please contact a qualified health professional if you need assistance. The editors and authors hold no legal accountability for the information contained in this book.

CONTENTS

ACKNOWLEDGEMENTS

We greatly thank Lydia Fleming, Dr. David M. Gill, and Dr. Jan E. Reddon for their comments and assistance with the chapters.

We also thank Lauren Kennedy, Elizabeth Kuenzel, Dr. Jana Grekul, Kelsie Herceg, Connor Baker, Selina Verkland, Nick Hilton, Kari Thomason from SNUG Métis Child and Family Services, Kimberly Clark and Becci Watson from the Zebra Child Protection Centre, and Scott Pawluik for their contribution.

ACKNOWLEDGEMENTS

We greatly thank Lydia Fleming, Dr. David M. Gill, and Dr. Jan E. Reddon for their comments and assistance with the chapters.

We also thank Lauren Kennedy, Elizabeth Kuenzel, Dr. Jana Grekul, Kelsie Herceg, Connor Baker, Selina Verkland, Nick Hilton, Kari Thomason from SNUG Métis Child and Family Services, Kimberly Clark and Becci Watson from the Zebra Child Protection Centre, and Scott Pawluik for their contribution.

PREFACE

The intersection of law enforcement and mental health is one of the many facets and intricacies found in police work. When members of law enforcement deal with an individual who is experiencing a mental disorder, including substance abuse or a mental health breakdown, the interaction often occurs in a time of crisis. When this crisis results in use of force, the question of whether the incident could have been handled differently often arises. *Why did the police not realize the individual was in crisis? Was the amount of force necessary?* These are valid questions; however, the role of a police officer is to protect the public, and most decisions need to be made in the blink of an eye. When responding to a call, police often do not have adequate training or time to address mental health during a crisis: they are only able to react reasonably in the moment.

Now more than ever, training is crucial for police officers in understanding mental health, for a majority of police calls involve mental health issues. The response to individuals with mental health concerns during a police call must start in training police professionals in the criminal justice system. A large part of this training must include communication, negotiation, and de-escalation skills that can bring a situation to a successful conclusion without causing harm to anyone involved. Providing police professionals with basic knowledge about mental health and basic skills to manage individuals in crisis, with ongoing training, will greatly assist the law enforcement community in maintaining and increasing legitimacy and trust with the community. The more understanding police professionals have about mental health issues, the better they are equipped to deal with abnormal behaviours.

The other place where mental health interacts with law enforcement is internally. The concept of Post-Traumatic Stress Disorder (PTSD) in law enforcement is real, and it is particularly challenging for many officers to initially acknowledge and seek help. Suicide is one of the most prevalent causes of police fatality, second only to traffic accidents. This is an interesting fact when one looks at the totality of mental health and policing. Police deal with individuals who are experiencing mental health crises and may one day experience their own crisis due to what they see daily while carrying out their duties. This is a concept that I fully understand, as I have my own personal struggles with PTSD. Years ago, when working as a homicide investigator, I was involved in a child homicide investigation. The victims were murdered wearing pajamas that depicted specific cartoon characters. To this day, I suffer a very visceral reaction and am upset for several days when I see these characters.

There are those who think that the only mental health concern in policing is PTSD, but that is definitely false. Law enforcement is a microcosm of society; therefore, everything that happens in the world happens in policing as well. People, no matter what their profession, experience mental health symptoms. I personally know police officers from around the world who have experienced an array of mental health issues; some have dealt with these issues appropriately, via working with mental health professionals, while others have not. Those who do not deal with their issues often encounter problems carrying on with their duties and come to a destructive end. I had two colleagues commit suicide while being active members in law enforcement. I encourage officers to seek assistance when dealing with their mental health concerns so they can overcome their difficulties and manage any ongoing triggers.

Training officers in effective communication strategies with individuals experiencing a mental health crisis will not only assist law enforcement with individuals in the community, but will also help them with their colleagues and friends within their respective police agencies. Knowing when people are experiencing a mental health crisis is one thing; knowing how to reach out to them in a meaningful way is a totally different skill that I hope you learn from this book.

If education and training on the topic of communication between law enforcement and individuals dealing with a mental health crisis can save lives, de-escalate situations, and assist in the concept of early and appropriate intervention, then this education is a must. It is not only education; it is a conversation that must go on well past the content of this book.

Daniel J. Jones

PART I

Mental Health Disorders Commonly Encountered in Policing

The chapters in Part I are an introduction to help facilitate an understanding of the common disorders that are encountered in policing professions for persons, yourself, or your colleagues. Foundational concepts in mental health and crucial components of specific disorders are discussed, such as diagnostic criteria, symptoms, incidence and prevalence, comorbid disorders, prognosis, and treatment that ultimately serves to enhance and manage mental health.

CHAPTER 1

Introduction to Mental Health for Policing Professions

Shea-Lyn Boychuk, *Concordia University of Edmonton*
Uzma Williams, *MacEwan University*

LEARNING OBJECTIVES

1. Understand the historical treatment of people with mental disorders, and the impact of deinstitutionalization and moral treatment
2. Demonstrate an understanding of significant terms used in relation to mental health
3. Describe predisposing, precipitating, and perpetuating factors resulting in mental health disorders
4. Demonstrate a knowledge of biological and psychological treatments for mental health disorders
5. Discuss the relationship between mental health and crime

AN INTEGRATIVE APPROACH FOR POLICE TO RESPOND TO MENTAL HEALTH SITUATIONS

Cases such as Sammy Yatim's bring a lot of questions about police response and training to the forefront. The Yatim case emphasizes the need for police education in identifying mental disorders and appropriate responses in de-escalating mental health crises—including instruction on the effective use of communication to create non-lethal outcomes. This book seeks to address this opportunity in education and training among police professionals with the hope that increased knowledge and skill will assist law enforcement to better deal with adverse issues

Case Study: Sammy Yatim[1]

In the late evening on July 27, 2013, 18-year-old Sammy Yatim brandished a small knife on a streetcar in downtown Toronto. Visibly disturbed, wide-eyed, and yelling, Yatim forced the passengers off the streetcar. Minutes later, Constable James Forcillo, a member of the Toronto Police Service for six years, arrived with his weapon drawn, as he perceived a threat, and yelled for Yatim to drop the knife. Minutes later, Forcillo fired three shots into Yatim, mortally wounding him. Forcillo fired another six shots into Yatim's body, now on the ground, using deadly force against a person posing no imminent threat; this resulted in a six-year jail sentence for Forcillo.

While police officers sometimes have no choice but to take a life in order to protect others, some crises can be resolved through non-lethal tactics. As seen on the video footage that surfaced, Forcillo almost immediately resorted to lethal force, doing very little to de-escalate the situation. What was needed that night was someone trained in crisis de-escalation to assess the situation accurately, slow things down, and try to find a non-lethal way to deal with Yatim. Cell phone and expert evidence in the Sammy Yatim case point to a lack of de-escalation attempts. Had Constable Forcillo identified signs of mental distress and used non-lethal intervention techniques, the situation may have had a positive outcome. Forcillo was initially charged with second-degree murder but convicted of attempted murder on July 28, 2016. Forcillo appealed both the conviction and the six-year sentence but was denied both on April 30, 2018.

Questions

1. What steps should have been taken by James Forcillo to handle this situation adequately?
2. Do you believe the sentence James Forcillo received is justified? Why or why not?
3. What impact does the use of excessive police force have on community trust?

surrounding mental disorders, resulting in positive changes within the justice system and how it is viewed.

As a training tool, this material will help develop a working knowledge of the main mental disorders that affect both police and offenders, provide information on how to understand and appropriately respond to mental health situations in non-lethal ways, and discuss legal and ethical issues and ways to acquire community resources. All the objectives focus on furthering law enforcement as a helping profession through the lens of an interdisciplinary approach. The terms *police* and *police officers* in the book include all law enforcement officers and policing professionals.

SUICIDE BY COP

A growing phenomenon in North America is **suicide by police officer** (also sometimes referred to as **suicide by cop** or **copicide**). Suicide by cop is a suicide method in which individuals deliberately behave in a threatening manner, presenting themselves as an actual or apparent danger to others, to provoke lethal police intervention.[2] The notion of suicide by cop first surfaced in the early 1990s with the work of Geberth,[3] who emphasized persons who pursue suicide by cop. These individuals struggle with mental disorders and seek a means to end their lives without having to kill themselves or deal with the shame of ending their own lives. Suicide by cop is sometimes instigated by a mass shooter or a perpetrator who has taken hostages, and in these situations, suicide by cop is chosen over submission to police orders.[4] Most commonly, however, the provocation of simulated weapon possession or disobedience to direct police orders in the form of confrontation lead to an escalated, extreme response from police.[5] In July 2010, the Royal Canadian Mounted Police (RCMP) in the town of Okotoks, Alberta, responded to a domestic assault call when the perpetrator, a known gun owner, stepped out onto his porch, took a kneeling stance, and raised a silver-tipped, dark object to his shoulder, pointing it at the police. Responding to the threat, a police officer shot and killed the perpetrator; the object he was carrying—duct-taped to his hands—was an umbrella.

Mohandie and colleagues[6] analyzed 707 cases in the United States and Canada, and determined that 36% of officer-involved shootings were classified as suicide by cop, with 14% leaving a suicide note.[6] Motives are incredibly difficult to determine in such cases; however, they are not impossible. Sixty-two percent of people had a history of confirmed or probable mental health issues, 48% of the confirmed depression or some other mood disorder, 17% had a substance abuse disorder, 15% a thought disorder, and 3% a personality disorder;[6] 87% had suicidal communications, with 61% of these cases discussing suicide during the incident and 79% specifically mentioning suicide by cop.[6] One interpretation is that the perpetrators are communicating their need for help and leaving room for non-lethal intervention.[6] That being said, suicide by cop situations are unpredictably dangerous and require the same level of caution, if not more, than any other type of situation.

OVERVIEW

As we work through this chapter, we will be providing an overview of psychological disorders and the history of mental health, of the Diagnostic and Statistical Manual of Mental Disorders, 5th edition (DSM-5),[7] and of treatment, as well as other key concepts that build the foundation for the rest of the chapters in Part I.

WHAT IS A PSYCHOLOGICAL DISORDER?

A **psychological disorder**, or mental disorder, is a psychological dysfunction within an individual characterized by abnormality (that is, not normal or typical) in their behaviour and marked distress or impairment in different areas of life (such as social, emotional, cognitive, or behavioural), which is not culturally expected and results from **biopsychosocial** dysfunction.[8] There are four components to consider in this definition:

1. Psychological dysfunction
2. Personal distress or impairment in different areas of living
3. Not culturally expected
4. Biopsychosocial perspective, which involves exploring biological (hereditary, hormonal, structural), psychological (resiliency, coping mechanisms), and social (family support, poverty) factors that explain dysfunction

When we think of these components, we want to think of them in terms of being harmful to the self or to others. On their own, these components are not sufficient for the diagnosis of a psychological disorder. For example, after warm ups, Wayne Gretzky had to have four beverages in a specific order—Diet Coke, ice water, Gatorade, Diet Coke—before he was ready to play. In the 1990s, the

Red Hot Chili Peppers played a series of concerts completely in the nude. Both of these behaviours would be considered abnormal or atypical; however, these people are productive, not distressed because of their behaviours, and others are not negatively impacted by their behaviours; thus, their abnormal behaviour does not imply they are psychologically disordered.

Mental health is on a spectrum. Individuals may have excellent mental health functions but, due to certain events or circumstances, may experience mental health symptoms from time to time in their lives. Conversely, some individuals may have multiple episodes or breakdowns, and these mental health crises or episodes might occur due to reoccurring symptoms of a diagnosed or diagnosable mental health disorder.

HISTORY

The treatment of individuals with mental health disorders reflects the knowledge and political thought of society at the time. Treatment of mental illness extends as far back as the Stone Age, where **trephination**, drilling holes in the brain, was used to let evil spirits out.[9] Through ancient Egyptian times and the Middle Ages, demonic possession was widely accepted as a cause for mental illness.[9] Conversely, in the Arabic world music was used to treat mental illness.[9] The ancient Greeks and Romans rejected supernatural causes for mental illness and believed it was due to natural causes or socio-cultural influences.[9] One of the distinguished theories of this time was Hippocrates **somatogenic hypothesis,** which posited that mental illness was caused by physical or biological dysfunction.[9] It wasn't until the Renaissance that Europe experienced the golden era of medicine and established mental institutions.[9] Their initial intention may have been compassionate, but the reality was that most asylums were places of torture, cruelty, and appalling living conditions with rare physician care.[9] As they were insufficiently funded, they became nothing more than museums for poking fun at persons with mental illnesses.[9]

During the Enlightenment era of the eighteenth century, pioneers such as Chiarughi, Pinel, and Tuke introduced the concept of "moral treatment," which responded to these appalling living conditions by taking a more humane approach to treating people with mental illnesses thanks to reform efforts led by Dix and Beers.[9] This **mental hygiene movement**, as it was known, was characterized by the desire to protect and provide humane treatment for persons with mental illness and sought to alleviate human suffering.[9] The end of the eighteenth century saw the beginning of what would be considered psychotherapy today, a move towards a thoroughly rational and scientific approach to mental disorders.

DEINSTITUTIONALIZATION

In the 1950s, we see the beginnings of **psychopharmacology** as a treatment for psychiatric disorders, as mental illness results from disordered brain chemistry, a widely accepted view today.[10] Because of the discovery of psychopharmacological drugs, the pharmaceutical industry began producing many neurotransmitter-affecting drugs to treat schizophrenia, mania, and depression, and thereafter stimulants and mood stabilizers.[10] Through the success of antipsychotic medications such as chlorpromazine, the advent of tricyclic antidepressants and anti-anxiety medications, the patients' rights movement, and US president Kennedy's community mental health movement, **deinstitutionalization** was set in motion.[11] Beginning in the 1950s, droves of patients were discharged, and hundreds of psychiatric institutions were shut down.[12] By not strengthening community resources for the influx of persons with mental illness, many of these individuals were homeless and lacked adequate support.[13]

Most recently, a positive psychological approach provides individuals with help in optimizing their health and treatment of mental health concerns, whether they struggle with mild or severe symptoms.[14,15] Aligned with this positive approach, the stigmatizing and marginalizing of persons with mental health disorders must be removed so individuals can feel supported and secure in obtaining mental health services from both health professionals and police professionals.[16,17]

DSM

The DSM was first published in 1952 and is currently in its fifth edition, referred to as the DSM-5. The **DSM-5** contains the current listing of all existing and identified psychological mental disorders.[7] This manual is used by mental health practitioners, such as psychiatrists and psychologists, and is considered the principal guide for mental health diagnoses in North America. **Diagnosis**, which is the process of determining whether the problem afflicting the individual meets the criteria for a psychological disorder, can be mild, moderate, or severe. Each disorder identified in the DSM is accompanied by a description of the disorder as well as key information about each disorder:

- specific **diagnostic criteria** (predominant signs and symptoms that are patterns of the disorder)
- **etiology** (factors that are at the root of the disorder or cause the disorder)
- **prevalence** (the occurrence of a specific disorder in a population within a specified period of time)

- **incidence** (the rate of new cases of a disorder within a defined period of time)
- **differential diagnosis** (alternative diagnoses that can possibly explain the observed symptoms or patterns)
- **comorbidity** (two or more disorders co-existing at the same time with either one of the disorders being more pronounced or multiple disorders having an equal weight of impact)
- **prognosis** (course of the disorder and future outlook)
- possible treatment options

NCRMD

Canadian law assumes that people can think and act in a deliberate and rational manner—that the accused, in legal terms, are sane' unless otherwise indicated as being insane. Moreover, Canadian law recognizes that in some instances, mental disorders may cause cognitive or volitional impairment. **Cognitive impairment** is the inability to perceive accurately or reason correctly, and **volitional impairment** is the inability to exert adequate controls on one's behaviour. Not bound by psychological or medical definitions, the lay person typically defines mental disorder as any impairment of psychological functioning that is internal, stable, and involuntary in nature; thus, legal definitions typically focus on acute and severe disease of the mind affecting thought, affect (mood), or behaviour. Offenders found legally insane receive a finding of **Not Criminally Responsible on Account of Mental Disorder** (NCRMD) according to section 16 of the Canadian Criminal Code (see chapter 15).[18] NCRMD dates to the 1800s, when Daniel M'Naghten attempted to shoot the British prime minister, Robert Peel, and mistakenly killed Peel's private secretary instead.[19] The jury in the case heard evidence that M'Naghten was experiencing persecutory delusions that told him the government was conspiring against him and found him not guilty by reason of insanity. M'Naghten's acquittal sparked public outrage that he got away with murder, and, in an attempt to clarify the law, the **M'Naghten standard** was created. This standard forms the basis for insanity provisions of the criminal codes in most common law jurisdictions around the world. This is similar to the notion of *mens rea*. *Actus reus* establishes the accused action or behaviour in committing an element of a crime, whereas *mens rea* explores the mental intentions of the accused. When a person is found to be experiencing a mental health disorder at the time of the crime, *mens rea* cannot be established, so the person cannot be found guilty of a crime, leading to criminal acquittal on grounds of NCRMD.

MALINGERING

Unsurprisingly, the public typically takes issue with the NCRMD defence, believing it is a "loophole that allows too many guilty people to go free."[20,21] One major contributing factor to the public's negative perception of the NCRMD defence is the presence of malingering. **Malingering** is when one pretends to be ill in order to achieve some specific objective, such as being acquitted of a crime. Malingering is often the faking or gross exaggeration of symptoms, usually to be absolved from responsibility for and sentencing of a crime. For example, individuals may falsely claim they were hallucinating at the time they committed a crime in an effort to enter a NCRMD plea. Researchers have attempted to detect malingering using instruments, such as the Minnesota Multiphasic Personality Inventory (MMPI);[22] however, this is questionable, particularly if the individual has some knowledge about the scale. Despite the possibility of someone faking mental illness to not be held criminally responsible, the NCRMD defence is relatively uncommon and not often ruled by the courts.[23] Most people do not fake their mental illness, but malingering can and does happen.

Case Study: Eric Clinton Kirk Newman[24]

Luka Magnotta, born Eric Clinton Kirk Newman in Scarborough, Ontario, sought attention in any way possible, from claiming to be a famous pornography star to making up stories that he had a relationship with convicted killer Karla Homolka, as well as self-promoting his own videos using a pseudonym. This increasing thirst for attention led Newman to begin making multiple videos of him torturing and killing young kittens through drowning and other forms of asphyxiation. Human rights activists from around the world tried to identify Newman, to no avail. Newman commented in one of his last videos that the next video would involve a person. On May 25, 2012, Newman posted a video online, *1 Lunatic 1 Ice Pick*, showing his stabbing, neck slashing, dismemberment, and necrophilic act on 33-year-old Lin Jun.[11] He mailed Lin Jun's hands and feet to elementary schools and various political offices with a note that he would kill again. By the time Newman was identified by police, he had already fled Canada—evidence of a thought-out murder and escape—but was arrested in Berlin on June 4, 2012. During his investigation and trial, Newman pleaded not guilty by reason of mental disorder, claiming

continued

to be schizophrenic. After interviews with Newman and piles of paperwork pertaining to the crime, two forensic psychiatrists came to the same conclusion: Newman did in fact have psychiatric issues, but that these psychiatric issues did not play a role in the premeditation and execution of the crime. All the video footage, from seeing him bring Mr. Lin back to the apartment, to speaking to taxi-drivers, hotel clerks, and flying to Paris, shows a poised and completely rational Newman. He claimed to have killed Mr. Lin because he thought he was a government agent who was after him, but not once did the footage show a man paranoid about his surroundings or exhibiting other mental health symptoms. The behaviour on the footage simply didn't square with a person experiencing schizophrenia. Moreover, there were notable differences in the stories Newman told each psychiatrist, something that was attributed to traumatic response. He was not deluded, and he was never tested for malingering, as Newman refused to be assessed by the prosecution's psychiatrist. Despite having the support of the forensic psychiatrists, his behaviour in the video footage viewed throughout the trial, his refusal to take the stand, and the holes in the interviews resulted in the jury finding Newman guilty on all counts, and he received the maximum life sentence in prison.

Questions
1. Which personality characteristics describe Newman?
2. While Newman has a history of psychiatric issues, his mental health issues did not play a role in premediating and committing the murder. What other facts disqualify him from NCRMD?

MENTAL DISORDERS DISCUSSED IN THE TEXT

There are several categories of mental disorder discussed in subsequent chapters. The disorders highlighted in table 1.1[7] are discussed throughout Part I of the text and were chosen based on their high incidence or impact on the community. Table 1.2[7] provides a brief overview of other categories of disorders that are not discussed throughout the text but that are still important to know.

Common Mental Disorders among Police Professionals

The mental disorders with the highest prevalence in law enforcement are Post-Traumatic Stress Disorder (PTSD), anxiety disorders, and substance-abuse

Table 1.1: Mental disorders discussed in the text

DISORDER	DESCRIPTION	AVERAGE PREVALENCE RATE	MAIN CAUSES	MAIN TREATMENT
Bipolar	Alternating episodes of mania and depression.	1.5% to 2.5%	Biological	Medication Psychotherapy
Schizophrenia	Symptoms involving delusions, hallucinations, disorganized thinking or speaking, disorganized behaviour or movement including catatonia (extreme rigidness or psychomotor agitation), and negative symptoms.	1%	Biological	Medication Psychotherapy
Substance Use Disorder	Continued use of substance(s) despite significant problems related to legal issues, relationships, and engaging in hazardous behaviour.	2% to 8.5%	Biological Psychological Social	Group supports Inpatient treatment Psychotherapy
Conduct Disorder	Extreme defiance, opposition with adults and authority figures to the extremes of vandalism, callousness, lack of remorse and guilt, volatile criminal behaviour involving physical cruelty to people or animals in childhood.	4%	Biological Psychological Social	Life skills Parenting skills
Antisocial Personality Disorder	Pattern of disregard and violation of rights of others since the age of 15 years old. Marked by failure to conform to lawful behaviours, deceitfulness, manipulation, impulsivity, physical aggressiveness, anger, recklessness and lack of concern for the safety of self or others, irresponsibility, lack of remorse, and callousness.	2%	Biological Psychological Social	Life skills Psychotherapy
Post-Traumatic Stress Disorder	Exposure to traumatic event where person was confronted with death or injury to self or others. Response was of fear, helplessness, or horror. The event is re-experienced persistently, avoidance of triggers, negative emotional states (numbing), changed arousal, and reactivity.	4% to 11%	Psychological Social Trauma	Medication for anxiety and depression Psychotherapy
Paraphilic Disorders	Recurring, intense sexual fantasies, urges, or behaviours involving nonconsenting persons.	1% to 5%	Biological Psychological	Psychotherapy

Table 1.2: Other important mental disorders not discussed in the text

ANXIETY DISORDERS	
Description	Person feels threatened by a potential occurrence of a future negative event and includes some of the following: • excessive worrying, • restlessness or feeling on edge, • easily fatigued, • irritability, • difficulty concentrating, • muscle tension, and • sleep disturbance.
Prevalence Rate	6% to 14%
Key Causes	Biological: genetics, neuroanatomy, neurotransmitters. Psychological: behavioural, cognitive. Social: modelling and parental rearing.
Main Treatment	Medications: Benzodiazepines. Psychological treatments: CBT.
Major Disorders within This Category	Agoraphobia: Fear of situations where escape is difficult and help is not available in the event of a panic attack. Generalized anxiety disorder (GAD): Excessive worrying and anxiety where individuals cannot control their worrying that lasts greater than six months along with restlessness, fatigue, sleep disturbances, difficulty concentrating, and muscle tension. Panic Disorder: Two or more expected or unexpected panic attacks that peak within 10 minutes in which individuals experience intense fear. They are concerned about the panic attack and implications of the panic attack, and change their behaviours because of the attacks. Social Anxiety Disorder (Social Phobia): Exposure to social situations that provoke anxiety. Social situations are endured with intense anxiety, which may cause panic attacks. Specific Phobias: An irrational fear and dread that compels a person to avoid a specific object, situation, or activity, including animals (spiders, sharks, snakes), natural environment (tornadoes, water), blood-injection-injury, situations (heights, flying, enclosed spaces such as elevators), and many other triggers (choking, vomiting, clowns).

OBSESSIVE-COMPULSIVE DISORDERS

Description	Obsessions (i.e., thoughts, ideas, images, or impulses) and/or compulsions (repetitive behaviours or mental acts) involving rituals that consume a large amount of time with immense distress and intrusion in the person's day-to-day living.
Prevalence Rate	2%
Key Causes	Biological: genetics, heritability, neuroanatomy, neurotransmitters.
	Psychological: reinforced and maintained behaviours.
Main Treatment	Medications: Antidepressants.
	Psychological: CBT, Exposure and Response Prevention (ERP).
Major Disorders within This Category	Body Dysmorphic Disorder: Preoccupation with an imagined defect in physical appearance along with obsessive thinking of perceived flaws and repetitive checking or avoiding of mirrors.
	Excoriation (Skin-Picking) Disorder: A recurring, uncontrollable urge and act to pick at skin to the extent of causing discomfort and harm.
	Hoarding Disorder: Difficulty ridding oneself of personal belongings that cause clutter to the point that physical living and working spaces can no longer be used.
	Obsessive-Compulsive Disorder: A recurrent and uncontrollable urge to engage in a specific mental act or behaviour that is an obsession and/or compulsion. Examples include, but are not limited to, washing, checking, ordering, praying, and counting.
	Trichotillomania (Hair-Pulling Disorder): A recurring, uncontrollable urge and act to pull hair out, usually off the scalp.

EATING DISORDERS

Description	Dysfunctional eating behaviours that are often characterized by disturbances in the way individuals perceive and experience their body weight or shape, with lack of consideration for consequences of weight control tactics.
Prevalence Rate	1.6%

continued

Key Causes	Biological: Heritability component, limited knowledge about specific genetic influence, dysfunctional neurotransmitters.
	Psychological: Personality traits such as perfectionism, obsessiveness, negative view of self.
	Social: Increasing pressures to achieve "ideal" form, how family communicates cultural ideal expectations, maturational effects, adverse events.
Main Treatment	Biological: Antidepressants.
	Psychological: CBT, interpersonal therapy, nutritional therapy and meal support, family therapy.
Major Disorders within This Category	Anorexia Nervosa: Significant low weight for age, sex, and height caused by restricted food intake because of distorted perceptions of body image and an intense fear of gaining weight or becoming fat.
	Binge Eating Disorder: Recurring episodes of mass food intake where the person cannot control the urge to stop eating, even when not hungry, followed by guilt or shame.
	Bulimia Nervosa: Recurring episodes of uncontrollable binge eating followed by compensatory purging behaviours such as vomiting or laxatives to avoid weight gain that occurs at least twice a week.

SOMATOFORM DISORDERS

Description	Group of disorders in which patients have or (consciously or unconsciously) feign physical, somatic (body) symptoms that cannot be explained by medical findings. Rather, psychological factors such as excessive worry or stress are responsible for impairments.
Prevalence Rate	Unknown
Key Causes	Biological: No consistent evidence of genetic basis.
	Psychological: Various psychological factors likely play a role, including cognitive factors such as interpretations of the meaning and significance of somatic events.
	Social: Early life experiences and social learning.
Main Treatment	Psychological: CBT.
Major Disorders within This Category	Conversion Disorder: Motor or sensory dysfunctions such as blindness or paralysis, with no medical findings or explanation, are caused by psychological factors. The person is not feigning.

Factitious Disorder: Patient intentionally feigns physical or psychological symptoms to seek attention by being in the sick role. External incentives such as insurance claims or time off work are absent. When factitious disorder involves one person, this is referred to as *Munchausen*. When factitious disorder involves two persons such as a mother and child, this is referred to as *Munchausen by Proxy*. Munchausen by Proxy is when a person, usually a mother or care provider, deliberately fakes or generates the symptoms of an illness or injury to gain medical attention and social support by living vicariously through the child.

Illness Anxiety Disorder: Preoccupation with having a disease and its symptoms despite medical evaluation (formerly known as hypochondria).

Somatic Symptom Disorder: The person experiences somatic symptoms that significantly disrupt functioning. Persistent thoughts, feelings, and behaviours are spent on somatic (body) symptoms for a time greater than six months.

DISSOCIATIVE DISORDERS

Description	Characterized by severe maladaptive disruptions or alteration in identity, memory, and consciousness that are experienced as being beyond one's control.
Prevalence Rate	0.1%
Key Causes	Trauma Model: A result of severe childhood trauma accompanied by personality traits that predispose individuals to employ dissociation as a coping strategy.
Main Treatment	Biological: Mediation can help treat comorbid disorders. Psychological: Psychotherapy.
Major Disorders within This Category	Dissociative Identity Disorder: Two or more distinct identities (alters) that control the behaviour of the primary identity (host). Formerly known as Multiple Personality Disorder.
	Dissociative Amnesia: Inability to recall important personal information in one of two forms: localized (person's memory of certain time frames is lost) or generalized (person's lifetime memory is lost).
	Dissociative Fugue: Involves dissociative amnesia (inability to recall important personal information) in addition to sudden departure from work or home, and the person may adopt a new identity in the new residence.

continued

	Depersonalization/Derealization Disorder: A person's sense of their own reality is temporarily lost due to persistent perception of detachment from one's body, such as being an observer from outside the body (depersonalization) and/or distortion in the perception of the environment, such as feeling that the environment is unreal or distorted, such as a table feeling wet when it's dry (derealization).
NEUROCOGNITIVE DISORDERS	
Description	Impaired consciousness and cognition with fluctuation in severity during the course of several hours or days, including · disturbance in attention, · disturbance developed over a short period of time, and · disturbance in cognition: memory deficit, disorientation, perception.
Prevalence Rate	10% to 30% of people who enter acute care facilities.
Key Causes	Biological: Impairment in brain function, improper use of medication, age, sleep deprivation, immobility, excessive stress, high fever. Social: Modification of environmental factors can result in incorrectly perceiving environmental cues.
Main Treatment	Addressing underlying medical or psychological causes. Inclusion of family members in treatment. Social supports and environmental modification (assistive devices and technologies, removing barriers). Medications: Antipsychotic drugs for those in acute delirium when cause is unknown.
Major Disorder within This Category	Major Neurocognitive Disorder: A severe decline in cognitive functioning where the disorder interferes with independent living, such as dementia. Mild Neurocognitive Disorder: A deterioration in cognitive functioning that is not typical or reflective of normal aging. Delirium: Frequent sudden onset of confusion and lack of knowledge of whereabouts, inability to recognize others, resistance to help, and possible psychotic features such as seeing or hearing things that are not present. Delirium occurs most often as a state and symptom rather than as a disorder.

Note: Neurodevelopmental Disorders, Sleep-Wake Disorders, and Elimination Disorders are discussed in the DSM-5 but are not discussed in this table or book.

Case Study: Robbery, Excited Delirium, and Death

An unidentified man broke into a Mississauga home in June 2013, confused and behaving aggressively. When the homeowner confronted him, an altercation ensued and officers were called to the scene. Despite two officers and the homeowner attempting to apprehend the man, his strenuous resistance made them unable to do so. With the help of a third officer, the group managed to get the man handcuffed and then he fell into acute medical distress and died. The autopsy concluded the man's death was a "sudden death associated with excited delirium and prone restraint." According to eyewitnesses, despite the man's level of aggression and resistance, the police involved did not use their weapons, and it was deemed that they used appropriate force and were not the cause of death. A plethora of research indicates that up to 40% of police custody deaths are due to natural causes such as cardiac arrest,[25] and mental health issues such as excited delirium and substance use as well as physical constraint.[26-28] Because a multitude of factors can exist in the cause of death rather than a single factor,[26,29] it is recommended that officers use particular safe postures that do not compromise breathing and other physiological functions,[27] as well as seek medical advice if the person appears to be in medical distress.[26]

Question

1. How would you respond when dealing with someone presenting signs of delirium, confusion, or bizarre behaviour?

---

disorders.[30,31] Police professionals will inevitably experience anxiety, depression, PTSD, and a host of other mental health concerns during their career. Mental health care becomes a priority for police professionals to decrease burn-out both personally and professionally. Counselling as well as self-work on mental health (social, emotional, cognitive, behavioural dysfunction or impairment) can assist police professionals in identifying triggers, managing on-going issues, and enhancing intra- and interpersonal relationships.

INFLUENCES AND FACTORS

Rarely can causation be determined when it comes to mental disorders; however, we can discuss potential influences, which help guide treatment methods. When we think of influence we must think in terms of predisposing, precipitating, and perpetuating factors.[32-34] **Predisposing factors** are any conditioning factors that influence the type and amount of response, making individuals susceptible to given disorders. These factors may be biological, psychological (emotional, cognitive, behavioural), or sociocultural. **Precipitating factors** are events or situations that trigger a given disorder. **Perpetuating factors** are those that make the condition persist, such as severity of condition, compliance issues, or unresolved predisposing and precipitating factors.

There are many limitations in our ability to determine the level of influence from person to person and context to context. More often than not, the mental disorder is influenced by an interplay of all three influence categories, making treatment difficult. As more research about mental disorders is conducted, it becomes abundantly clear that not one thing alone causes mental disorders; therefore, an interplay of biological, psychological, and social treatments is required to effectively manage symptoms. In other words, not one treatment is fully effective in treating any mental disorder.

BIOLOGICAL OR PHYSIOLOGICAL INFLUENCES AND TREATMENTS

Biological or physiological influences include aspects such as heritability, genetic vulnerability, innate characteristics, hormonal factors, medical deficiencies, and neurotransmitter or structural abnormalities/trauma. Biological theories borrow their model from medicine, which has implications for the way people with problems are treated. The most common treatments for biological influences are medications.[8,35] There are certain medications for certain disorders; however, not all disorders require medication. For example, those diagnosed with mood disorders are often prescribed **selective serotonin reuptake inhibitors** (SSRI) because of their relatively mild side effects, their high safety profile (they are not lethal in overdose), and ease of administration.[36,37] **Tricyclics** (TCA) and **monoamine oxidase inhibitors** (MAOI) were the first antidepressants on the market and are still used in treatment today, but they are highly lethal and can result in an overdose.[36,37] Addiction to certain medication and many aversive side effects are key reasons for low **medication adherence**.[38] For substance use disorders, drugs to help with withdrawal symptoms are often prescribed to help the user manage symptoms and avoid relapse. Success with medications is not always obtained; haloperidol as a treatment for schizotypal personality disorder, for example, is relatively ineffective as a treatment.[39]

Psychological Influences and Treatments

Despite the popularity of biological approaches to treatment, psychological approaches continue to be developed and advanced. Only in recent decades have psychological approaches and biological approaches been viewed as interactive and complementary.[40] Psychological influences include influences on behaviour, cognition, and emotion. Behavioural influences are any type of behaviour by the self or others that influences the person's mental disorder. This includes avoidance of situations, behaviour based on mistaken assumptions, hyperactivity, neglect of appearance, irritability, expression of little emotion, etc. Cognitive influences include things such as poor memory/memory selection bias, inability to concentrate, exaggerated self-blame, overgeneralization, distorted schemas, automatic thoughts, etc. Learning and intellectual issues are another layer that complicates the cognitive influences on mental disorders. Adaptions can also be made because of **neuroplasticity**.[41] Emotional influences are any kind of feelings that perpetuate the disorder—often things such as fear, extreme sensitivity, timidity, emotional flatness or emptiness, etc. Emotional vulnerability—either too much, not enough, or mismanaged emotional functioning—plays a huge role in the perpetuation of mental disorders. Those who experience suffering are often highly vulnerable emotionally or completely incapable of feeling, expressing, and understanding emotions.

In terms of psychological treatment, various approaches with varying efficacy exist.[42] The effectiveness of a treatment often depends on the symptom and the individual's preference for treatment. **Psychotherapy** is a collaborative treatment using scientifically validated procedures that help people develop healthier, more effective habits.[42] The most commonly used psychotherapeutic approaches[8,42] are cognitive-behavioural therapy (CBT), solution-focused therapy, psychodynamic therapy, dialectical behavioural therapy (DBT), and interpersonal therapy. CBT attempts to change maladaptive thoughts and behaviours into adaptive ones through techniques such as journaling, exposure and response prevention, cognitive restructuring, and unraveling cognitive distortions. **Solution-focused therapy** focuses on helping the client develop effective coping skills for future situations while working towards short-term and long-term client-established goals. **Psychodynamic therapy** focuses on unconscious processes as they are manifested in a person's present behaviour. **DBT** is a reflective and educational technique where individuals learn about the disorder and themselves, including triggers and self-management. **Interpersonal therapy** is a variation of psychodynamic therapy that emphasizes the interactions between clients and their social environment. There is a wide array of other effective treatments, such as muscle relaxation and breathing techniques, which alleviate symptoms of mental health concerns.

There is debate on the effectiveness of **mandated** (non-voluntary participation in a treatment where the person must complete the program) versus **non-mandated** (voluntary participation in a treatment) programs. It is agreed that some treatment is effective in helping manage mental disorders; however, motivation and completion rates for offenders mandated to treatment are lower in some studies.[43] What this means is that offenders who are mandated to treatment, rather than voluntarily choosing to seek treatment, are often less motivated to do the work the program requires and may not even complete the program. The differences in findings could be due to the type of disorder.

Social Influences and Treatments

Social influences include anything related to family, culture, society, and environment. Environmental influences, also known as **nurture**, are incredibly important to consider when diagnosing and treating mental disorders. Nurture includes an array of factors, such as traumatic events, gender, socialization, support structures, stigma, **socioeconomic status** (e.g., family occupation, income, work status, and education level), and role expectations. For example, stimulation in early years of infancy optimizes our brain and can counteract negative incidents, such as physical trauma, through neuroplasticity. Our upbringing also greatly affects the way we view and cope with the world around us. Cultural or family taboos on sex, for example, can hinder an individual's sexual, emotional, or **interpersonal development**. Interpersonal development is a key component when thinking about mental health. Often, poor interpersonal relationships or their lack are a strong sign that someone is struggling with mental health. Perceptions and behaviours based on experiences and life dynamics can be vastly different if, for example, a person grows up in a positive home characterized by love, consistency, appropriate discipline, support, financial security, and safety, compared to someone who grows up in a home characterized by violence and high conflict, neglect, and poverty. Research has found a correlation between socioeconomic status and mental health; specifically, the poorer the socioeconomic conditions, the higher the risk for mental illness and psychiatric hospitalization.[44] Socioeconomic status both directly and indirectly impacts the development of mental illness through such means as general economic insecurity, lack of access to resources, and stigma resulting in adverse economic stress, often from a young age. Nonetheless, social influence alone cannot fully shape a person's mental health. That is, someone who grows up in a good home environment may still have strong dispositions towards certain mental health conditions that cannot be buffered by a positive home environment. However, people's resiliency may buffer them to some extent against poor mental health coping mechanisms.

CLINICAL DIAGNOSIS AND ASSESSMENT

Essential to the study of mental disorders (**psychopathology**), and ultimately to the treatment of clients, are the processes of clinical assessment and diagnosis. **Clinical assessment** is the systematic evaluation and measurement of biological, psychological, and social factors to make a diagnosis for an individual presenting with a psychological disorder.[45]

In real-life clinical practice, disorders do not present as textbook versions that you read. If you have ever known anyone with a mental health concern or disorder, or have struggled with your own mental health, you will know that mental health is not clear-cut, but has multiple dimensions and shades of grey. Due to the complexities of human behaviour, the presentation of a disorder may require a clinician to diagnose a person in an "other" or "unspecific" category.[7] Essentially, these categories reflect disorders where there is an overlap of disorders, a mental health issue is clearly occurring but cannot be accurately captured by a specific diagnosis, differential diagnosis is difficult (meaning it is difficult to differentiate a person's presentation of a disorder between two disorders that present similar symptoms or signs), or the disorder has not fully presented itself.[7] As a result, the label of a diagnosis can change, but at that time the diagnosis is best captured by other or unspecified. For example, a person may meet the criteria for a general personality disorder and display symptoms of a number of personality disorders but not meet all the criteria for one specific personality disorder, resulting in a diagnosis of "other specified personality disorder or unspecified personality disorder." It is also important to note that disorders can also develop from general medical conditions or due to substance use for any class of disorders.

Clinicians assess psychological problems by conducting assessments to acquire information about an individual needed to provide assistance. Clinical assessment procedures include clinical interviews, behavioural observation and assessment, and psychological tests if needed. Inventories strive to demonstrate high reliability and validity in order to be trustworthy and credible.[46]

The **clinical interview** gathers information on current and past behaviours, attitudes, and emotions, as well as the patient's interpersonal and family history. **Behavioural assessment** uses direct observation to formally assess an individual's thoughts, feelings, and behaviours in specific situations or contexts. **Psychological tests** include specific tests to determine psychopathology, cognitive, emotional, or behavioural responses that might be associated with a specific disorder or assess longstanding personality traits. Most commonly known are psychopathology and personality inventories and intelligence tests. Intelligence tests may be included within a more extensive battery of neuropsychological tests. **Psychopathology inventories** identify mental health symptoms and behaviours that are abnormal and characterized by specific disorders. **Personality inventories** are based on an objective approach in which data with numerous items (questions) are collected and evaluated. For example, the Psychopathy Checklist Revised (PCL-R)[47] can directly assesses traits and behaviours of criminality by using a 20-item semi-structured interview with the client, along with material from institutional files or significant others. **Intelligence testing** aims to assess intelligence by measuring distinct intellectual abilities such as verbal comprehension, perceptual organization, processing speed, and working memory as measured by the Wechsler Adult Intelligence Scale, 4th edition (WAIS-IV).[48]

Spotlight: Dalton Bellmond

I work as a Peace Officer in a metro transit system in a large municipality. This includes patrolling the bus transit and the Light Rail Train (LRT) stations where I respond to calls for service. As an appointed Peace Officer, my main goal is to increase public safety and security on the transit system. Peace Officers focus on provincial and municipal enforcement and can arrest for criminal offences they observe, but unlike the police, we cannot lay criminal charges. What Peace Officers do and are responsible for is completely based on employers and what they want their focus to be, with guidelines from the province. I do not carry a firearm; I carry intermediate weapons such as a baton and pepper spray. Without a lethal force option, I must remain situationally aware and maintain a high level of officer safety to make it home.

In March 2019, I was conducting patrols of a downtown LRT station and observed a male sitting underneath a stairwell. I approached the male and observed a syringe on the ground. I removed the syringe to reduce any opportunity of physical altercation. I explained the legal aspects and asked him to leave. As he was

packing his personal belongings, I recommended safe injection sites and other community resources. The male stood up and was about to head out. I stopped him and asked, "Why are you here?" To which he responded, "because it's warm." I asked again and said "no, why are you here." He got what I was asking and told me his story. He explained how he had been building houses for 20 years. He was a roofer, framer, tile worker, and everything in between. He told me that he got hurt on a jobsite a couple years ago and had to undergo surgery. The doctors prescribed morphine after the surgery to assist with the pain. After a year, he started using more than the prescription called for in order to feel the same. He became tolerant to the opioid after such long use and required more to get the same effect. The doctor became aware of the male abusing the painkiller and cut him off completely. The male said that he was addicted and should have been weaned off it. Without a medical prescription the male turned to street-level morphine and eventually heroin. He could no longer support his addiction and sold everything he owned for the drug. The male uses fentanyl and any opioid that is available. When he finished his story, he looked at me and said, "thank you, thank you for asking." He left the station and I realized the depth of the current opioid crisis. It's easy to call people junkies and move on. It's difficult to stop and listen to their stories.

Everyone has a story and experiences that we may not relate to, but we can all understand someone's position of desperation. Addiction and mental health are the main causes of homelessness, and each situation is caused by

continued

some underlying issue. The male had an addiction that cost him everything, including almost his life. Talking with him, I understood that he was depressed. He sold his house, car, and belongings to afford the drugs. Going from having a job to living on the streets was not only hard on his physical body, but his mental health had also suffered because of his loss. I can't truly understand what it's like to be in that situation, but I can understand that there are other things going on that may have caused his situation. Self-awareness and professional empathy can help remove the stigma of being called "junkies" and can help move individuals to a position of support while delivering enforcement services. As law enforcement officers, we must remember that we are also susceptible to mental health issues. There are many ways this can happen, and they differ from person to person. A common type of disorder in law enforcement personnel is PTSD. It's a phrase people don't like to hear, but by talking about PTSD and mental health in law enforcement we can break down the communication barrier and reduce the amount of harm its members experience.

MENTAL HEALTH AND CRIME

People experiencing mental disorders are overrepresented among those who are arrested and charged with or convicted of criminal offences. The Correctional Investigator of Canada has commented that the number of offenders with a mental illness in Canada's correctional system currently exceeds the capacity of the Correctional Service of Canada.[49] Moreover, police are recognizing that a high proportion of police time is spent on responding to calls involving persons with mental health problems. While only 1% of all police calls are dispatched to persons for mental health disorders,[50] a mental health issue is apparent in many calls, with estimates on average of 40% to 50%.[50-54] In another instance, 12% of all persons with mental health disorders have contact with the police when obtaining mental health services, and 25% of all persons with a mental disorder are arrested at some point in their lives.[50] Many individuals are apprehended due, in part, to the lack of alternative services in the community. This monumental number poses problems for police and prosecutors who are responsible for deciding when to apprehend, arrest, charge, or convict people who are diagnosed with mental disorders. While criminal law gives the state great power, it does not serve the public good to devote resources to punishing acts that may not deserve punishment. For example, it does not make sense to punish a depressed person for making a public disturbance while attempting to commit suicide, or to charge a man with dementia for public indecency when he is walking naked in public but cannot even remember the date or his name.

The Criminal Code does have provisions for when someone should be held criminally responsible or not; however, a lack of community resources puts the decision in these instances in the hands of responders. The education and training provided in this book and via policing organizations will equip police professionals to better understand and respond. By the end of this book, readers should be able to understand the role that mental health plays personally and professionally, and the importance of appropriate response and intervention to ensure safe outcomes.

Case Study: Paul Boyd[54]

In August 2007, Paul Boyd was shot multiple times after Vancouver police responded to a 911 call about a disturbance. Paul Boyd lived with bipolar disorder and may have been experiencing a full manic episode at the time. Armed with a hammer and a bike chain, Boyd was cooperative with police at first; however, when approached he swung at the officers with the chain. Constable Lee Chipperfield believed Boyd to be armed and potentially wearing body armour—both hunches were incorrect—and fired a total of nine shots, eight of which struck Boyd. Constable Chipperfield believed he was acting in self-defence, according to what he was trained to do; however, a video surfaced showing that Boyd had dropped all weapons while crawling behind a car prior to the fatal shot. Constable Chipperfield was found not guilty of use of excessive force because he believed that resorting to lethal force was necessary to preserve himself and others from death or bodily harm.

Questions
1. Was Lee Chipperfield's use of force appropriate or excessive? Explain why.
2. How would you have handled this situation differently?

SUMMARY

The phenomenon of suicide by police officer is coming to the forefront of policing. With adequate training and knowledge about mental health, police professionals are better equipped to make split-second informed decisions in scenarios using de-escalation techniques rather than weapons in responding to atypical behaviours. Understanding and responding to atypical behaviours can be linked to the early historical treatment of individuals with mental health concerns.

At a time when mental health was not understood, persons with a mental illness were often treated with cruelty because they were considered as manifesting demonic or spiritual possession. Through the work of Chiarughi, Pinel, Tuke, Dix, and Beers, persons with mental health disorders were and continue to be treated with more respect and support. The current trend is to remove the stigma of mental health and provide supports and services.

In addition to biological approaches to treatment, psychological approaches continue to be developed and advanced. In recent decades, psychological and biological approaches have been viewed as interactive and complementary. Section 16 of the Canadian Criminal Code, Not Criminally Responsible on Account of Mental Disorder, recognizes that persons experiencing symptoms of a mental disorder during a crime cannot be convicted of a crime because of the disease of the mind that overtakes and controls their thinking and behaviour, and they are therefore unable to understand or appreciate the consequences of their crime. Individuals from time to time attempt to fake a disorder in order to be acquitted of a crime; this is called malingering. There is a strong intersection between crime and mental health, and police officers are best equipped to uphold the law and interact with persons once they understand mental health and seek appropriate biological and psychological treatments.

REFLECTION QUESTIONS

1. Describe the significant historical trends and milestones in dealing with the treatment of individuals with mental health disorders.
2. What occurred during deinstitutionalization? What events led to deinstitutionalization?
3. What is the Diagnostic Statistical Manual of Mental Disorders? Describe the key aspects of the manual.
4. Define malingering and find a recent example of a legal case where the defendant was malingering.

5. Define predisposing, precipitating, and perpetuating factors.
6. Describe five treatments used for psychological disorders.
7. Describe the relationship between crime and mental health.

REFERENCES

1. The case of *R. v. Forcillo*, 2018 [cited 2018 June 28]. ONCA 402 (CanLII) [Internet]. Available from: http://canlii.ca/t/hrqkb
2. Violanti J, Drylie J. "Copicide": concepts, cases, and controversies of suicide by cop. Springfield: Charles C Thomas, 2008.
3. Geberth V. Suicide by cop. Law and Order. 1993 Jul;41(7):105–9.
4. Van Zandt CR. Suicide by cop. Police Chief. 1993 Jul;60:24–30.
5. Homant RJ, Kennedy DB. Suicide by police: a proposed typology of law enforcement officer-assisted suicide. Policing: An International Journal of Police Strategies & Management. 2000 Sep 1;23(3):339–55.
6. Mohandie K, Meloy JR, Collins PI. Suicide by cop among officer-involved shooting cases. Journal of Forensic Sciences [Internet]. 2009 Mar [cited 2018 Mar];54(2):456–62. Available from: https://www.ncbi.nlm.nih.gov/pubmed/19220654
7. American Psychiatric Association. Diagnostic and statistical manual of mental disorders (DSM-5). American Psychiatric Pub; 2013 May 22.
8. Barlow DH, Durand VM, Hofmann SG, Lalumière ML. Abnormal psychology: an integrative approach. Toronto: Nelson Education; 2018.
9. Farreras IG. History of mental illness. Noba textbook series: psychology. Champaign: DEF Publishers; 2017. Available from: nobaproject.com
10. Akram F, Kawa S, Giordano J. Diagnosis in American psychiatry: a brief history of the diagnostic and statistical manual. In: Handbook of DSM-5 disorders in children and adolescents. Cham: Springer; 2017. p. 3–15.
11. Sussman S. The first asylums in Canada: a response to neglectful community care and current trends. The Canadian Journal of Psychiatry. 1998 Apr;43(3):260–4.
12. Lamb HR, Bachrach LL. Some perspectives on deinstitutionalization. Psychiatric Services. 2001 Aug;52(8):1039–45.
13. Johnson AB. Out of bedlam: the truth about deinstitutionalization. Basic Books; 1990.
14. Rosenbaum P, Gorter JW. The 'F-words' in childhood disability: I swear this is how we should think! Child: Care, Health and Development. 2012 Jul 1;38(4):457–63.
15. Seligman ME, Steen TA, Park N, Peterson C. Positive psychology progress: empirical validation of interventions. American Psychologist. 2005 Jul;60(5):410.
16. Sartorius N. Iatrogenic stigma of mental illness: begins with behaviour and attitudes of medical professionals, especially psychiatrists. British Medical Journal. 2002 Jun 22; 324(7352): 1470–71.
17. Corrigan PW, Larson JE, Michaels PJ, Buchholz BA, Del Rossi R, Fontecchio MJ, Castro D, Gause M, Krzyżanowski R, Rüsch N. Diminishing the self-stigma of mental illness by coming out proud. Psychiatry Research. 2015 Sep 30;229(1):148–54.
18. Criminal Code, R. S. C., 1985, c. C-46.
19. The case of *R. v. M'Naghten*, 1843.
20. Hans VP. An analysis of public attitudes toward the insanity defence. Criminology [Internet]. 1986 [cited 2018 Apr];4:393–415.

21. Knopp E. Psychopathy and the insanity defense: a grounded theory exploration of public perception (doctoral dissertation, California Baptist University).
22. Helmes E, Reddon JR. A perspective on developments in assessing psychopathology: a critical review of the MMPI and MMPI-2. Psychological Bulletin. 1993 May;113(3):453.
23. Crocker AG, Nicholls TL, Seto MC, Charette Y, Côté G, Caulet M. The National Trajectory Project of individuals found not criminally responsible on account of mental disorder in Canada. Part 2: the people behind the label. The Canadian Journal of Psychiatry. 2015 Mar;60(3):106–16.
24. Magnotta c. R., 2015 [cited 2018 June 28]. QCCA 340 (CanLII) [Internet]. Available from: http://canlii.ca/t/ggf08
25. Wobeser WL, Datema J, Bechard B, Ford P. Causes of death among people in custody in Ontario, 1990–1999. Canadian Medical Association Journal. 2002 Nov 12;167(10):1109–13.
26. Ross DL. Factors associated with excited delirium deaths in police custody. Modern Pathology: an official journal of the United States and Canadian Academy of Pathology. 1998 Nov;11(11):1127–37.
27. Hall C, Votova K, Heyd C, Walker M, MacDonald S, Eramian D, Vilke GM. Restraint in police use of force events: examining sudden in custody death for prone and not-prone positions. Journal of Forensic and Legal Medicine. 2015 Apr 1;31:29–35.
28. Vaughan AD, Zabkiewicz DM, Verdun-Jones SN. In custody deaths of men related to mental illness and substance use: a cross-sectional analysis of administrative records in Ontario, Canada. Journal of Forensic and Legal Medicine. 2017 May 1;48:1–8.
29. Lindon G, Roe S. Deaths in police custody: a review of the international evidence.
30. Carleton R, Afifi T, Turner S, Taillieu T, Duranceau S, Lebouthillier D, et al. Mental disorder symptoms among safety personnel in Canada. Can J Psychiatry. 2018;63(1):54–64.
31. Oehme K, Donnelly E, Martin A. Alcohol abuse, PTSD, and officer-committed domestic violence. Policing. 2012;6(4):418–30.
32. Barbato A, WHO Nations for Mental Health Initiative, World Health Organization. Schizophrenia and public health. 2012.
33. Wing JK. Schizophrenia: towards a new synthesis. Academic Press; 1978.
34. Cooper B. Epidemiology in schizophrenia: towards a new synthesis. Wing, J, editor. New York: Grune-Straton; 1978.
35. Frewen PA, Dozois DJ, Lanius RA. Neuroimaging studies of psychological interventions for mood and anxiety disorders: empirical and methodological review. Focus. 2010 Jan;8(1):92–109.
36. Boland JR, Duffy B, Myer NM. Clinical utility of pharmacogenetics-guided treatment of depression and anxiety. Personalized Medicine in Psychiatry. 2017 Dec 13.
37. Pérez-Wehbe AI, Perestelo-Pérez L, Bethencourt-Pérez JM, Cuéllar-Pompa L, Peñate-Castro W. Treatment-resistant depression: a systematic review of systematic reviews. International Journal of Clinical and Health Psychology. 2014 May 1;14(2):145–53.
38. Nieuwlaat R, Wilczynski N, Navarro T, Hobson N, Jeffery R, Keepanasseril A, Agoritsas T, Mistry N, Iorio A, Jack S, Sivaramalingam B. Interventions for enhancing medication adherence. The Cochrane Library. 2014 Jan 1.
39. Serban G, Siegel S. Response of borderline and schizotypal patients to small doses of thiothixene and haloperidol. The American Journal of Psychiatry. 1984 Nov.

40. Owusu Y. Combined psychotherapy with psychopharmacology. In: Psychotherapy for immigrant youth. Cham: Springer; 2016. p. 109–26.
41. O'Brien CP. Neuroplasticity in addictive disorders. Dialogues in clinical neuroscience [Internet]. 2009 Sep [cited 2018 Mar];11(3):350–3. Available from: https://www.ncbi.nlm.nih.gov/pmc/articles/PMC3181920/
42. Barlow, DH. Psychological treatments. American Psychologist. 2004;59(9), 869.
43. Jean-Paul S. The effectiveness of motivational interviewing with mandated clients: a review of literature. Southern Connecticut State University; 2014.
44. Hudson, CG. Socioeconomic status and mental illness: tests of the social causation and selection hypotheses. American Journal of Orthopsychiatry [Internet]. 2005 [cited 2018 Mar];75(1):3–18. Available from: http://www.apa.org/pubs/journals/releases/ort-7513.pdf
45. Maloney MP, Ward MP. Psychological assessment: a conceptual approach. New York: Oxford University Press; 1976.
46. Evans AN. Using basic statistics in the behavioral and social sciences. 5th ed. Thousand Oaks: Sage Publications; 2014. p. 16–17.
47. Hare RD. Manual for the revised psychopathy checklist. 2nd ed. Toronto: Multi-Health Systems; 2003.
48. Wechsler D. Wechsler adult intelligence scale–fourth edition (WAIS–IV). San Antonio: Psychological Corporation; 2014.
49. Sapers H. Annual report of the office of the correctional investigator 2009-2010 [Internet]. The Office of the Correctional Officers. Available from: http://www.oci-bec.gc.ca
50. Livingston JD. Contact between police and people with mental disorders: a review of rates. Psychiatric services. 2016 Apr 15;67(8):850–7.
51. William-Bates F. Lost in transition: how a lack of capacity in the mental health system is failing Vancouver's mentally ill and draining police resources. Vancouver Police Department. 2008. p. 52–54. Available from: https://www.cbc.ca/bc/news/bc-080204-VPD-mental-health-report.pdf
52. Shore K, Lavoie JA. Exploring mental health-related calls for police service: a Canadian study of police officers as 'frontline mental health workers.' Policing: A Journal of Policy and Practice. 2018 Apr 5.
53. Payne J, Gaffney A. How much crime is drug or alcohol related? self-reported attributions of police detainees. Trends and Issues in Crime and Criminal Justice. 2012 Jun(439):1.
54. *British Columbia (Information and Privacy Commissioner) v. British Columbia (Police Complaint Commissioner)*, 2015 [cited 2018 June 28]. BCSC 1538 (CanLII) [Internet]. Available from: http://canlii.ca/t/gkwx4

CHAPTER 2

Bipolar and Other Mood Disorders

Stephanie J. Laue, *Correctional Services of Canada*

John R. Reddon, *Department of Psychology, University of Alberta and Forensic Psychiatry, Alberta Hospital Edmonton*

LEARNING OBJECTIVES

1. Understand the history of mood disorders and their DSM-5 descriptions
2. Report the incidence and prevalence rates of mood disorders
3. Differentiate between primary/secondary and endogenous/exogenous mood disorders
4. Explain therapeutic and medical interventions for the different mood disorders

HISTORY OF MOOD DISORDERS

The recognition of mood disorders goes back to the time of Hippocrates, 460–370 BCE. Prolonged symptoms of sadness, anxiety, and irritability, in addition to somatic symptoms, thought to be caused by black bile build-up in the spleen, were given the name "melancholia." When melancholia included symptoms of delusions and manic rage, yellow bile was considered to be present. At this time, various solutions were advocated for melancholia: bathing, dieting, interpretation of dreams, and purgatives. Normal sadness to events or bereavement was distinguished from melancholia and was not pathologized. Mania, on the other hand, was deemed a result of excess blood; thus, bloodletting was also a treatment option. To the end of antiquity, mania was viewed and recognized as an extreme form of melancholia that could precipitate suicide.

During the Middle Ages (500–1500 CE) the biological perspective of mood disorders was replaced by religious and metaphysical interpretations. These new beliefs entailed the persecution of those experiencing mental illness (and of anyone deemed not a proper Christian) by attributing their illness to demonic possession. Largely responsible for this was the publication of the **Malleus Maleficarum** (The Hammer of Witches), published in 1487 by two Catholic monks. The book authorized the torture of witches and dominated thinking for approximately 250 years.

Lastly, during the late Middle Ages, modern medicine began to gain ground and in 1621 Robert Burton published *The Anatomy of Melancholy*. This book described mood disorders, their causes, symptoms and cures, and made reference to mixed episodes of both depression and mania. Burton attributed some causes of melancholy to astrology, the seasons, and intense love; however, biological causes such as heredity and diet were also discussed. During this period melancholia was considered a severe form of depression that could include psychotic features (mania).[1] Over time, the concept of mood disorders continued to evolve, suggesting that melancholia was a severe form of a mood disorder with "partial insanity" or depression with insanity (mania).[2] In 1845, it was established that mania and depression were linked, and the terms "la folie à double forme" (dual-form insanity) and "la folie circulaire" (circular insanity) were coined to explain this phenomenon.[1]

Prior to the mid-1800s, psychiatry advocated the "unitary hypothesis," that all psychoses were different manifestations of the same disease and not classified into discrete categories. This began to change in the 1850s, when the term *dementia praecox* (later known as schizophrenia) was coined. Morel considered dementia praecox to be the "dementia" of youth, and it was attributed to the most severely psychotic patients; due to its poor prognosis and chronic nature, dementia praecox was different from manic-depressive insanity.[1]

This laid the groundwork for "Kraepelin's dichotomy," when in the late 1800s, Emil Kraepelin (1856–1926) classified manic-depressive as a diagnosis distinct from dementia praecox (i.e., schizophrenia) based on the course and prognosis of the disease. This dichotomy of psychotic disorders dominated psychiatric thinking until the 1980s. Lastly, in 1957, Karl Leonhard proposed that the term bipolar replace manic-depressive, and suggested a distinction be made between unipolar and bipolar depression. Since the early 1900s, there has been a debate over whether psychotic mood disorders lie on a continuum or whether they are distinct identities. The DSM-5 currently classifies the disorders as distinct disorders, but the debate about whether schizophrenia is distinct from the other psychotic mood disorders continues.[1,3] Although bipolar was identified before the first century, its symptoms and sub-types were not clearly differentiated until the fourth edition of the DSM in the early 1990s.[4]

BIPOLAR DISORDER IN THE DSM-5

In the current DSM-5 manual, mood disorders are now separated into two categories: Bipolar and Related Disorders and Depressive Disorders.[5]

Bipolar Disorder

In the DSM-5 **Bipolar Disorder** (BPD) is separated into seven categories: Bipolar I (BP-I), Bipolar II (BP-II), Cyclothymic Disorder, Substance/Medication Bipolar and Related Disorder, Bipolar and Related Disorder Due to Another Medical Condition, Other Specified Bipolar and Related Disorder, and Unspecified Bipolar and Related Disorder.

The diagnosis of **Major Depressive Disorder** (MDD) requires the same A-C criteria as Major Depressive Episode (MDE) but adds in two other qualifiers: 1) The occurrence is not better explained by a schizophrenia spectrum or another psychotic disorder, and 2) There has never been a manic or hypomanic episode.

Included under the diagnostic category of Depressive Disorders are six disorders: Disruptive Mood Dysregulation Disorder; Persistent Depressive Disorder (PDD; previously known as dysthymia); Premenstrual Dysphoric Disorder; Substance/Medication Induced Depressive Disorder; Depressive Disorder due to another Medical Condition; Other Specified and Unspecified Depressive Disorder.

The diagnosis for BP-I according to the DSM-5 is presented in table 2.1 and the DSM-5 criteria for MDE in table 2.2. The diagnosis of a manic episode can be further qualified in regard to its severity, whether it contained psychotic features, a remission specifier, and any other applicable specifier, such as catatonic features, anxiety, etc. Because BPD typically includes a period of depressed mood, the criteria for an MDE is also discussed. Although a period of hypomania may occur rather than an MDE, that criterion will not be discussed here, and is not required for diagnosis of BP-I. Mood disorders comprise a wide spectrum of moods, including levels of depression (mild, moderate, severe, or severe depression with psychosis) to elation (hypomania, mania, or mania with psychosis).[6]

Table 2.1: DSM-5 Diagnosis Criteria for BP-I

For a diagnosis of BP-I disorder, criteria for a manic episode must be met, in which a hypomanic or major depressive episode can have occurred prior to or after the manic episode.

A manic episode has four criteria:

A. A distinct period of abnormally and persistently elevated, expansive, or irritable mood and goal-directed activity or energy lasting at least one week and present most of the day (if hospitalized this duration is unnecessary).

B. During this above-stated period, three or more of the following symptoms (four if mood is only irritable) are present to a significant degree and represent a noticeable change from usual behaviour.
    · Inflated self-esteem or grandiosity
    · Decreased need for sleep (rested after three hours)
    · More talkative or pressured talking
    · Flight of ideas or subjective experience of racing thoughts
    · Distractibility as reported or observed
    · Increase in goal-directed activity (work/school/sexual) or psychomotor agitation (non-goal-directed activity).
    · Excessive involvement in activities that have a high potential for painful consequences (sexual indiscretions, shopping sprees, foolish business investments, etc.).

C. The mood disturbance is sufficiently severe to cause a marked impairment in social or occupational functioning, requires hospitalization, or exhibits psychotic features.

D. The episode is not attributable to physiological effects of a substance or other medical condition.

Table 2.2: DSM-5 Diagnosis Criteria for MDE

The DSM-5 requires criteria A-C for an MDE:
A. Five or more of the following symptoms have been present for the same two-week period and at least one of the symptoms is either item 1 or 2. 　　1. Depressed mood most of the day, nearly every day, as identified by self or others (sad, empty, hopeless, tearful; children can present as irritable). 　　2. Markedly diminished interest or pleasure in all or almost all activities most of the day, or nearly every day (subjective or observed by others). 　　3. Significant weight loss/gain (when not dieting/change of > 5%) or decrease/increase in appetite nearly every day. 　　4. Insomnia or hypersomnia nearly every day. 　　5. Psychomotor agitation/retardation (subjective or observed by others) nearly every day. 　　6. Fatigue or loss of energy nearly every day. 　　7. Feelings of worthlessness or excessive/inappropriate guilt nearly every day. 　　8. Diminished ability to think and concentrate or indecisiveness nearly every day (subjective or observed by others). 　　9. Recurrent thoughts of death/suicidal ideation with or without a specific plan or suicide attempt.
B. The symptoms cause clinically significant distress or impairment in social/occupational or other important areas of functioning.
C. The episode is not attributable to the physiological effects of substance use or medical condition.
The DSM-5 criteria for MDE also allow for specifying the severity of the most recent episode (manic or depressed) and whether there is the presence of any of the following: anxious distress, mixed features, melancholic features, atypical features, psychotic features (mood congruent or incongruent), catatonia, peripartum onset, with seasonal pattern, and whether symptoms are in partial or full remission.

MOOD DISORDER PREVALENCE

Unipolar mood disorders are more common than the BPDs. In Canada the prevalence rate for unipolar MDD annually is 3.9% and 9.9% experience it for a lifetime, with women's annual rate being 4.9% and men's 2.8%.[7] Major depression has been found to be a global concern affecting 350 million people and is the second leading cause of disability worldwide.[7,8] In accordance with the DSM-5, the 12-month estimate in the United States for BP-I is 0.6%.[5] The average age of onset is 18; family history increases one's risk ten-fold, and the suicide risk is

15 times that of the general population.[5] Within the first decade of the disorder, the average person will experience four major episodes. However, if untreated, over their lifetime individuals will typically experience 10 manic-depressive episodes, with manic episodes lasting four months (median) and depressive episodes six months (median), although the episodes can last up to a year.[9]

The first bipolar episode usually occurs between late adolescence and the early thirties, with either a manic or depressive episode presenting first. Onset can occur quickly or slowly, and always presents with a major change in usual behaviour.[2] Manic episodes dominate in youth, while depressive episodes are more prevalent in later years. Men experience more manic episodes than women, and women have more depressive and mixed episodes than men.[2,9] **Hypomania** is a less severe form of **mania** and is distinguished from mania by a lack of psychotic features. BPD always includes periods of normal mood regardless of whether the depressive episodes are preceded by hypomanic or manic episodes. By far the most debilitating feature of BPDs are the depressive episodes, with most individuals experiencing them for half their life.[9]

Case Study: Domestic Violence

George is a 10-year veteran of the Regina Police Service (RPS) in Saskatchewan. During his tenure with RPS he has accumulated a wide range of experiences. On patrol one evening he and his junior partner Ed are called to what appears to be a case of domestic violence. George has learned, however, that situations are not always as simple as they first appear. When George and Ed arrive at the residence, they hear a man yelling and a woman screaming. The man is very agitated and the woman has bruises on her face. The man is so hyper-aroused that he appears to be almost in a trance-like state. It takes them nearly 30 minutes to control the situation.

Questions

1. Once the situation has been controlled, what are the next steps?
2. How might what you have learned about mental health affect the way you would relate to these individuals?
3. How would you determine if the man is in a manic state or just angry, and how would that impact the outcome?

COMORBIDITIES AND DIFFERENTIAL DIAGNOSIS

Mood disorders rarely occur in isolation but more commonly coincide with one another and can have a bi-directional influence. To accurately diagnose BP-I, the disorder must be distinguished from other BPDs, from anxiety disorders, and from whether the manic episode is due to illicit substances or medications. In children, Attention Deficit Hyperactivity Disorder (ADHD) must be ruled out. By far the most common comorbidities with any BPD are the anxiety disorders, having a lifetime comorbidity rate of 74.9% and a rate of 92.3% for any psychiatric diagnosis.[10] Personality disorders such as the Cluster B Personality Disorders (i.e., antisocial, borderline, histrionic, and narcissistic personality disorders) also create diagnostic difficulties and can be comorbid with BPD. Features distinguishing the disorders are the episodic nature and greater symptom severity of BPD, and the lack of euphoric mood and inability to maintain satisfying relationships found in the personality disorders.[2,11] Medical conditions such as metabolic syndrome, endocrinological disorders, and migraines are found at much higher rates in those with BPD than the general population, and must also be ruled out.[2,9] If an individual presents during a depressive episode, bipolar depression must be distinguished from unipolar depression.

Once unipolar depression has been differentiated from bipolar depression, it must be further demarcated from some medical diseases due to overlapping symptoms such as weight loss, poor appetite, poor sleep, and fatigue. Medical conditions that mimic depression include dementia, diabetes, hyperthyroidism, hypothyroidism, Lyme disease, multiple sclerosis, and cardiovascular disease.[12] Medications prescribed by physicians, such as beta blockers and steroids, can produce symptoms similar to that of depression. Lastly, alcohol has been found to be a causal factor in the development of MDD due to its depressant properties. Interestingly, it has been proposed that alcohol triggers genetic markers, thereby increasing the risk of developing MDD.[13]

Reactive versus Endogenous Mood Disorders

The genetic versus environmental debate, or "nature versus nurture," has a long history in the origin of mood disorders and has been used to aid in diagnosis, to differentiate between disorders, and ultimately to guide treatment. Mood disorders believed to be the result of genetics (i.e., nature) are considered **endogenous**. This type of depression is said to "come out of the blue," with no identifiable antecedents. With endogenous depression, the symptom presentation is more physical in nature (i.e., psychomotor disturbances, vegetative symptoms, psychosis, and cognitive impairment). Because of this, medication is considered a first-line treatment for endogenous depression, reportedly eliciting a better response.[14]

Conversely, **exogenous** depression (also known as reactive or neurotic depression) is considered a result of negative life stressors or adverse events.[14] This distinction has been challenged, however, as adverse childhood events, such as neglect, severe physical abuse, sexual abuse and antipathy, have been found to be significantly associated with endogenous depression.[15]

Lastly, mood disorders have further been classified as primary or secondary. A **primary mood disorder** is classified based upon the absence of this criterion. Rather, it is based upon age of onset and family history. Conversely, a **secondary mood disorder**, such as depression, develops as result of a medical disease (e.g., Parkinson's) or a non-affective psychiatric condition (e.g., schizophrenia). This distinction gets at the root cause of the mood disorder and aids in treatment decisions, as two out of five patients seen in psychiatric clinics present with secondary depression.[16]

Case Study: Postpartum Depression

I had my first serious bout with mental illness after the birth of my second child in 1973. It was textbook postpartum depression. I was told I had 'the baby blues.' I was 3,000 miles away from my support system, which had always been my family, and my husband criticized me daily. I was alone. I just thought I was going to live my life as this very desperately sad person, who wept uncontrollably. My waves of sadness were often followed by soaring highs—a condition only exaggerated by my wealth and social position. When I was manic, it was a grand mania; where someone else might have run off with the guy from the 7-Eleven, I ran off with the Rolling Stones. I would spend all my money buying Birkin bags; somebody else would have spent all the grocery money. It's paralyzing either way. You don't have the ability to have a second, sober thought. I took lithium for a time but stopped because the medication made me gain weight.

My son Michel died in an avalanche during a ski trip in 1998, which proved a tragic tipping point. I was devastated; the pain of losing a child proved too much to bear. I can remember imploring my doctor to be put into a medically

continued

induced coma, just to make it stop. I couldn't deal with it. In the months that followed, I dropped 30 pounds and refused to leave the house; my family staged an intervention, which led to my hospitalization and diagnosis. I was diagnosed with BPD in 2000. I now monitor myself closely for signs of imbalance. A big part of being healthy is making the choice not to be addicted to the mania. If I feel an episode coming on, I declare a 'lock-down' day, up my medication, and stay home. I don't make decisions. I don't get in my car. This one day for me is how a lot of mentally ill people live every day of their lives. My name is Margaret Trudeau, ex-wife of the 15th Prime Minister of Canada Pierre Elliott Trudeau and mother of the 23rd Prime Minister of Canada, Justin Trudeau.[17]

Questions
1. Identify the signs and symptoms consistent with BPD.
2. What factors likely contributed to the misdiagnosis of Margaret Trudeau over the years?

CAUSAL FACTORS

Biology of Mood Disorders

A biological basis for mood disorders has always been implicated in their development. From the musings of Hippocrates and his black bile hypothesis to the modern-day sophistication of neurotransmitters and the expanding field of epigenetics, we have grown exponentially in our understanding. The traditional neurobiological hypothesis proposes that low levels of neurotransmitters, particularly serotonin and norepinephrine, are the drivers of unipolar depression. The specific neurobiology behind bipolar depression, however, remains unclear.[2]

Bipolar Disorder

BPD has a stronger heritable component than major depressive disorder and twin studies seem to bear this out, suggesting a 79% correlation between genetic factors and the development of BPD.[9] The risk to first-degree relatives inheriting BPD ranges from 3-8%, thereby greatly increasing one's risk.[2] Nonetheless, genetic heterogeneity seems to be the case, and different genes may give rise to the varying features (depression and mania) of BPD. Temperament has also been proposed as having a causal relationship with BPD. Emil Kraepelin suggested temperaments such as depressive, manic, cyclothymic, and/or irritable predisposition expressed in adolescence may predispose an individual to a major affective mood disorder.[18]

Environmental factors such as the role of positive family support, or alternatively negative high expressed emotion in the familial milieu, can impact the course and expression of BPD. Positive family support can reduce the number of bipolar depressive episodes. Nevertheless, a causal relationship with environmental factors in the development of BPD has not been found.[2,9]

Major Depressive Disorder

One cause implicated in the development of major depressive disorder is the transporter gene 5HT (the serotonin transporter gene) on chromosome 17. This gene has polymorphic characteristics and results in two different alleles (long and short), in which the short allele has been implicated in the reduced synthesis of serotonin, resulting in depressed mood.[19]

Neurobiology versus childhood adversity has been investigated in relation to the development of depression. Harknees and Monroe found that severe levels of childhood adversity (severe physical abuse, sexual abuse, antipathy, neglect, and supervision/discipline that were high and poor, respectively) were significantly correlated with endogenous depression.[15] In fact, the risk of endogenous depression was doubled for those who experienced severe childhood adversity. Moreover, sexual abuse history was most associated with severity of depression and greater levels of suicidal ideation.[15]

Overall, the impact of a specific gene on the development of MDD is believed to be small and is supported by monozygotic (MZ) twin studies. In their research, Kendler and Aggen found that MDD symptom differences in the MZ twins were due to environmental experiences of the individual and not to genetics or familial history.[20] Findings revealed that specific symptom presentation was due to a multitude of factors, including quality of child–parent interactions, biological/genetic factors, childhood trauma, and personality.[20]

Growing in popularity is the field of epigenetics, as it is now recognized that *how* a gene is expressed can be modulated by the environment. Environmental factors such as prenatal and postnatal factors and adverse childhood events such as abuse and neglect can turn genes on or off, including those which may be responsible for the different psychiatric disorders.[12,20]

SUICIDE RISK

Suicide can result from psychiatric suffering, and individuals with MDD and BPD are at an increased risk.[5,21,22] This risk is further heightened if combined with substance abuse, an anxiety or personality disorder, and if there is a diagnosis of BP-I.[9,22] Specific to BPD, rapid cycling, mixed states, and severe depressive episodes elicit the highest suicide risk.[9] The suicide risk for those with BP-I is 15 times that of the general population, with 32.4% of those with BP-II and 36.3% of BP-I attempting suicide over their lifetime.[5] The risk factors that increase one's likelihood of suicidal behaviours in BPD include past attempt history, childhood abuse, female sex, feelings of hopelessness, cyclothymic/depressive temperament, severity of depressive symptoms, presence of psychotic/mixed/atypical characteristics, early age of onset, the evolution of the disorder (i.e., predominant depressive), and other comorbid mental disorders.[23] Interestingly, the use of lithium as treatment for BPD has been found to be an antisuicidal agent. This antisuicidal effect is limited to lithium and not found in other mood stabilizers. The mechanism of how lithium works is not fully understood, yet even if the mood disorder does not improve, the antisuicidal effect remains.[24]

Case Study: Depression and Suicidality

Later that night George and Ed are called to a residence where Samantha, a young woman in her teens with a history of depression, is threatening to cut her wrists. When the mother called 911, she reported that she was unable to calm Samantha or to have her give up the knife. George and Ed are the first responders. Samantha is crying and her mother is hysterical.

Questions
1. What steps must be taken to get control of the situation and ensure the safety of all participants?
2. Would the steps be different if it was an attempted suicide instead of a threatened suicide?
3. Are there community resources that you can recommend to the family?

PSYCHOPHARMACOLOGY TREATMENT

Winston Churchill endured a lifelong battle with recurrent depression. In fact, he described his mood nemesis as his "black dog."[25] It is argued that Churchill lived with BPD due to inheriting a "cyclothymic temperament" from his ancestors and father. However, it is more likely that he experienced bouts of depression.[25,26] To treat his "black dog" Churchill used the distractions of painting, writing, and bricklaying, but as these activities did not eradicate his depression, physicians further treated him with amphetamines and sedatives.[25,26]

In the mid-1800s, a build-up of uric acid was found in the blood of patients with gout; subsequently the theory of "brain gout" was proposed as underlying the presence of mania and depression. Because the chemical lithium was found to dissolve uric acid build-up, it was used as a treatment for gout and, ultimately, for mental illness. By the 1900s, the use of lithium was abandoned as a practice in the medical field due to the toxic effects of high levels of lithium. Nevertheless, the public consumption of lithium continued, marketed as having health benefits and used in beverages—the most notable being "Bib-Label Lithiated Lemon-Lime Soda," later relabelled as "7 Up."[2] Although known to be toxic, lithium was not removed from beverages until 1948. With the advent of the ability to monitor toxic levels of lithium in a patient's blood, lithium was approved for use in bipolar patients in France in 1961, 1970 in the United States, and as a preventative treatment for the disorder in 1974.[2]

Because lithium is potentially toxic, levels must be constantly monitored in the blood along with monitoring an individual's thyroid and kidney function. Toxic effects of lithium include hand tremor, muscle weakness, nausea, seizures, vomiting, diarrhea, hypothyroidism, and hair loss, to name a few. Since its use for treatment in 1961, it has been recognized that lithium addresses the manic symptoms in BPD, but the biochemical mechanisms of *how* this occurs remain a mystery.[2]

Bipolar depression is less responsive to pharmacological treatments than unipolar depression, making it more difficult to treat with medication.[9,27] **Antidepressants** that are commonly used for unipolar depression are contraindicated as a treatment option for bipolar depression, as they may trigger a manic episode.[9,27]

Major Depressive Disorder

Antidepressants are considered the first-line pharmacological treatment for moderate to severe unipolar depression.[28] Nonetheless, antidepressants are prescribed for mild depression when preferred by the patient, if there has been a previous antidepressant response, or if no improvement was found using non-pharmacological interventions.[28] Although antidepressants are commonly used to treat unipolar depression, there are differences in the types prescribed.

Second-generation antidepressants such as the selective serotonin reuptake inhibitors (SSRIs) and serotonin–norepinephrine reuptake inhibitors (SNRIs) are considered the first-line pharmacological treatment.[28] These antidepressants inhibit the reuptake of serotonin and/or norepinephrine, thereby increasing the levels of the transmitter within the synapse. Common SSRIs include Prozac, Celexa, Paxil, and common SNRIs include Cymbalta and Effexor. The side effects of these classes of antidepressants include nausea, dry mouth, dizziness, headache, excessive sweating, and sexual dysfunction.

Antidepressants must be tapered off slowly, as abrupt discontinuation, depending on the class and dosage, can result in symptoms such as sleep problems, headache, fatigue, feelings of electrical shock, "pins and needles" (SSRIs), and dizziness.[12]

Neurostimulation Treatments

Neurostimulation treatments involve the use of electrical or magnetic stimulation applied externally or internally to specific areas of the brain. These treatments are considered only if an individual has treatment resistant depression or BPD. Neurostimulation treatments can be invasive (internal) or non-invasive (external). **Noninvasive treatments** include transcranial direct current stimulation (tDCS), electroconvulsive therapy (ECT), magnetic seizure therapy (MST), and repetitive transcranial magnetic stimulation (rTMS). **Invasive treatments** include vagus nerve stimulation (VNS) and deep brain stimulation (DBS) and require implantation of a pulse generator or electrodes, respectively, into specific areas of the brain.

Repetitive transcranial magnetic stimulation uses electromagnetic coils placed against the scalp to deliver a magnetic pulse over several treatments. ECT, on the other hand, uses electrical currents sent through the brain either bilaterally (whole brain) or unilaterally (one hemisphere) to induce a seizure. Due to its efficacy, the first-line treatment recommended is rTMS, with ECT considered a second-line treatment.[29] Other studies have challenged this rTMS recommendation, showing ECT to have greater therapeutic benefits for both unipolar and bipolar depression. However, due to the disadvantage of potential memory impairment, the requirement of general anaesthetic, and the induction of a seizure, ECT is considered a second-line approach.[30,31]

Cognitive Behavioural Therapy

Different psychotherapies have been used for both BPD and MDD, with findings revealing little efficacy for their use with BPD (except as adjunctive treatment), but effective for mild to moderate forms of MDD.[32,33]

Recommended psychological treatments for unipolar depression include **cognitive behavioural therapy** (CBT), **interpersonal psychotherapy** (IPT), and **behavioural activation** (BA).[32] These psychological treatments were found to be effective for mild to moderate MDD but not for severe MDD.[32] The majority of the research has focused on CBT, which was established by Aaron Beck to address the faulty thinking of depressed individuals. He proposed the "cognitive triad," whereby depressed individuals tend to view themselves, the world, and the future in a negative light, thereby perpetuating their depressed mood. Generally, findings indicate CBT is effective for mild to moderate forms of depression but, when combined with an antidepressant, the positive effect is superior to either treatment alone.[12,32]

For BPD, psychotherapy has been found to be less effective, but it is often used as an adjunct with mood-stabilizing medication. The CBT techniques taught to treat bipolar depression include addressing negative thoughts, cognitive restructuring, activity scheduling, and how to resolve problems before they become distressing.[33] Unfortunately, CBT for severe BPD may not be the best treatment, as findings reveal that as the number of lifetime mood episodes increase (over 12 episodes), the less likely CBT will be effective.[33,34]

Psychoeducation, which has been found to be slightly more useful for BPD, teaches an understanding of the disorder, monitoring of symptoms and mood, how to look for prodromes for early intervention, understanding the role of medication for better adherence, and creating a relapse prevention plan.[33] Altogether, the usefulness of psychotherapy for BPD is limited and of most benefit to patients in the early stages of the disorder.[2]

Alternative Treatments

For unipolar depression, other treatments such as mindfulness, St. John's Wort (SJW), yoga, acupuncture, exercise, Omega-3 fatty acids, sleep deprivation, and tryptophan have all been investigated as to their efficacy in treatment.

The alternative treatments that have shown efficacy are light therapy for seasonal depression (10,000 lux 30 min/day), exercise (30 min moderate intensity 3 times/week for 9 weeks), and SJW (500-1800mg/day), all of which can be considered as standalone therapy for mild to moderate depression but only as an adjunct to medication for severe MDD.[12,35] A 2011 meta-analysis by Piet and Hougaard examined the effects of **mindfulness-based cognitive therapy** (MBCT) in the treatment of depression.[36] MBCT was found to reduce risk of relapse by 43% for those with three or more previous depressive episodes, yet no effect was found for those individuals with two or fewer previous depressive episodes.[36]

Mindfulness as adjunct to medication for BPD has shown no benefit for symptom reduction or relapse prevention but may be helpful in reducing anxiety symptoms.[2]

MENTAL HEALTH AND POLICING

During the commission of their duties, police officers will frequently be involved in interactions with those experiencing a mental illness. On average these interactions occur four times per month and, fortunately, injuries to police officers or offenders are rare.[37] In 2009–2011, a study was carried out by the Mental Health Commission of Canada to examine the interactions between individuals with mental illness and police. This report found that almost half the surveyed participants (42.2%) were diagnosed with BPD, with the second largest group being schizophrenia (25%).[38] The majority of mental health participants had been hospitalized at some point in their lifetime (85.2%) and had experienced multiple arrests, with 40% having been arrested at some point.[38]

The increases in police calls involving persons with mental health disorders have been blamed partially on the deinstitutionalization and the non-institutionalization of mentally ill populations. Since the 1960s, there has been a movement away from hospitalization of persons with mental health disorders towards community-based treatment facilities. Additionally, there has been a reluctance to hospitalize people experiencing mental illness, and they are often released from a psychiatric facility within a few days after admission.[39]

Canadian health legislation falls under the auspices of the provincial and territorial governments. Each province and territory has enacted mental health legislation that allows for the apprehension of individuals if they are deemed to be a risk to themselves or others or are identified as having a mental disorder. In the latest revision of the Alberta Mental Health Act (2010), section 12 indicates that a police officer, using form 10, may apprehend individuals who meet the criteria and transport them to a hospital, subsequently releasing them into a physician's care.[40]

To address this growing population and the demands on police services, many police departments across Canada have teamed up with mental health professionals to better address the needs of persons experiencing mental health concerns. These **mobile crisis response teams** can be found in large and small Canadian cities. Some include the Police and Crisis Team (PACT) in Edmonton, the Mobile Response Team (MRT) in Calgary, the Crisis Outreach and Support Team (COAST) in Hamilton, and the Integrated Mobile Crisis Response Team (IMCRT) in Victoria.

Case Study: Homelessness

James is a 26-year-old police officer new to the force. As a new recruit to the Vancouver police department in British Columbia, he has been assigned to patrol the inner city, East Hastings Street. James has come to know some of the more notorious residents and is familiar with behaviours associated with mental illness and substance abuse. Over the course of a year, James has removed residents off the streets who have overdosed on drugs, alcohol, or even Listerine.

James has built relationships with some of the residents, one being Paul, who he often sees in the neighbourhood. James knows what to expect from Paul. When they meet, Paul is often on his favourite park bench looking as if he is struggling to stay awake, or he may display a quiet demeanour. Today is different. Paul approaches James and he seems frantic. Paul is walking fast, scanning his environment, seems agitated, and blurts out to James, "Why are you following me?" James expresses confusion, identifies himself, and attempts to reassure him, but Paul interrupts and begins to rapidly yell obscenities, claiming that James is trying to stop him from completing his holy mission to heal the homeless. James is finding it difficult to understand what Paul is saying but talks calmly to him and grabs him by the arm to direct him towards a nearby bench. Paul quickly pulls out a knife from his pocket and waves it at James.

Questions
1. How would you differentiate between signs of an addiction and BPD?
2. What could James have done differently so as not to elicit a hostile reaction from Paul?
3. How could James best assist Paul without endangering himself or others?

SUMMARY

Our understanding of the development and treatment of mood disorders has evolved over centuries, with discoveries establishing both biological and environmental influences as important factors. BPD and the other mood disorders are debilitating disorders, with MDD alone being the second leading cause of disability worldwide.[7] Psychopharmacological treatments have been successful in treating mood disorders, specifically lithium for BPD and antidepressants for major depression. Although psychotherapies such as CBT are less effective for BPD, they remain a powerful tool for mild to moderate depression. Controversial alternative treatments vary in their usefulness for depression and are not indicated for use in BPD.

Policing is not immune to the problems that mental health disorders create and officers are often on the front lines addressing these problems. Police officers have the power to apprehend those who are a danger to themselves or others and to place them in a physician's care. Because of this, it is incumbent for police officers to be aware of how mental health disorders manifest, as their interventions can ultimately ensure their safety and that of the offender.

REFLECTION QUESTIONS

1. What are the implications of mental illness/mood disorders for policing?
2. Do you believe a knowledge of mental illness is advantageous for police officers? Why?
3. Has your view of a police officer's role changed after reading this chapter? If so, how?

REFERENCES

1. Lake CR. Schizophrenia is a misdiagnosis: implications for the DSM-5 and the ICD-11. New York: Springer Science + Business Media; 2012. p. 33–54. DOI: 10.1007/978-1-4614-1870-2
2. Fountoulakis K. Bipolar disorder: an evidence-based guide to manic depression. Berlin, Heidelberg: Springer; 2015. p. 1–60, 461–70. DOI: 10.1007/978-3-642-37216-2
3. Allardyce J, Gaebel W, Zielasek J, van Os J. Deconstructing psychosis conference February 2006: the validity of schizophrenia and alternative approaches to the classification of psychosis. Schizophr. Bull. 2007;33(4):863–7.
4. History of bipolar disorder. Bipolar bandit [Internet]. Cited 2017-Jul 21. Available from: https://www.pinterest.com/bipolarbandit/bipolar-bandit/

5. American Psychiatric Association. Diagnostic and statistical manual of mental disorders (DSM-5). American Psychiatric Pub; 2013 May 22.

6. Mood disorders picture [Internet]. [cited 2017 June 15]. Available from: https://www.pinterest.com/pin/407786941230561678/

7. Marcus M, Yasamy M, van Ommeren M, Chisholm D, Saxena S. Depression: a global public health concern. WHO Department of Mental Health and Substance Abuse [Internet]. 2012. Available from: www.who.int/mental_health/.../depression/who_paper_depression_wfmh_2012.pdf

8. Lam R, McIntosh D, Wang J, Enns M, Kolivakis T, Michalak E, et al. Canadian network for mood and anxiety treatments (CANMAT) 2016 clinical guidelines for the management of adults with major depressive disorder: section 1: disease burden and principles of care. Can J Psychiatry. 2016;61(9):510–23. DOI: 10.1177/0706743716659061

9. Vieta E. Managing bipolar disorder in clinical practice. 3rd ed. London: Springer Healthcare; 2013.

10. Merikangas K, Akiskal H, Angst J, Greenberg P, Hirschfeld R, Petukhova M, et al. Lifetime and 12 month prevalence of bipolar spectrum disorder in the national comorbidity survey replication. Arch Gen Psychiatry. 2007;64:543–52. DOI: 10.1001/archpsyc.64.5.543

11. Bassett D. Borderline personality disorder and bipolar effective disorder. Spectra or spectre? A review. Aust NZJ Psychiatry. 2012;46(4):327–39.

12. Friedman E, Anderson I, Arnone D, Denko T. Handbook of depression. 2nd ed. London: Springer Healthcare; 2014.

13. Fergusson D, Boden J, Horwood J. Tests of causal links between alcohol abuse or dependence and major depression. Arch Gen Psychiatry. 2009;66(3):206–66. DOI: 10.1001/archgenpsychiatry.2008.543

14. Mizushima J, Sakurai H, Mizuno Y, Shinfuku M, Tani H, Yoshida K, et al. Melancholic and reactive depression: a reappraisal of old categories. BMC Psychiatry. 2013;13:311. DOI: 10.1186/1471-244X-13-311

15. Harkness K, Monroe S. Childhood adversity and the endogenous versus nonendogenous distinction in women with major depression. Am J Psychiatry. 2002;159:387–93. DOI: 10.1176/appi.ajp.159.3.387

16. Clayton PJ, Lewis CE. The significance of secondary depression. J Affect Disord. 1981;3(1):25–35. DOI: 10.1016/0165-0327(81)90016–1

17. Kuczynski A. First lady wild child: Margret Trudeau. Harpers Bazaar [Internet]. 2016. Available from: http://www.harpersbazaar.com/culture/features/a14456/margaret-trudeau-0416/

18. Rihmer Z, Gonda X. Temperament in suicidal behavior. In: Courtet, P, editor. Understanding suicide: from diagnosis to personalized treatment. Switzerland: Springer International; 2016. p. 43–52.

19. aan het Rot M, Mathew S, Charney D. Neurobiological mechanisms in major depressive disorder. CMAJ. 2009 Feb;180(3):305–13. DOI: 10.1503/cmaj.080697

20. Kendler K, Aggen S. Symptoms of major depression: their stability, familiarity, and prediction by genetic, temperamental, and childhood environmental risk factors. Depress Anxiety. 2017;34:171–7. DOI: 10.1002/da.22591

21. Swann A, Dougherty D, Pazzaglia P, Pham M, Steinberg J, Moeller F. Increased impulsivity associated with severity of suicide attempt history in patients with bipolar disorder. Am J Psychiatry. 2005;162:1680–7. DOI: 10.1176/appi.ajp.162.9.1680

22. Bolton J, Pagura J, Enns M, Grant B, Sareen J. A population-based longitudinal study of risk factors for suicide attempts in major depressive disorder. J Psychiatr Res. 2010;44(13):817–26. DOI: 10.1016/j.jpsychires.2010.01.003

23. Olie E, Traver D, Lopez-Castroman J. Key features of suicidal behavior in mental disorders. In: Courtet, P, editor. Understanding suicide: from diagnosis to personalized treatment. Switzerland: Springer International; 2016. p. 199–210. DOI: 10.1007/978-3-319-26282-6_16

24. Bellivier F, Guillaume S. Lithium: the key antisuicide agent. Clinical evidence and potential mechanisms. In: Courtet, P, editor. Understanding suicide: from diagnosis to personalized treatment. Switzerland: Springer International; 2016. p. 303–12.

25. Storr, A. Churchill's black dog, and other phenomena of the human mind. Glasgow: Fontana/Collins; 1990. p. 1–51.

26. Attenborough, W. Churchill myths and misquotes: did Churchill have bipolar disorder? 2016. Churchill Central [Internet]. Available from: https://www.churchillcentral.com/blog/did-churchill-have-bipolar-disorder

27. Fountoulakis KN, Grunze H, Pantagiotidis P, Kaprinis G. Treatment of bipolar depression: an update. J Affect Disord. 2008;109(1–2):21–34.

28. Kennedy S, Lam R, Mcintrye R, Tourjman V, Bhat V, Blier P, et al. Canadian network for mood and anxiety treatments (CANMAT) 2016 clinical guidelines for the management of adults with major depressive disorder: section 3: pharmacological treatments. Can J Psychiatry. 2016;61(9):540–60. DOI: 10.1177/0706743716659417

29. Milev R, Giacobbe P, Kennedy S, Blumberger D, Daskalakis Z, Downar J, et al. Canadian network for mood and anxiety treatments (CANMAT) 2016 clinical guidelines for the management of adults with major depressive disorder: section 4: neurostimulation treatments. Can J Psychiatry. 2016;61(9): 561–75. DOI: 10.1177/0706743716660033

30. Minichino A, Bersani F, Capra E, Pannese R, Bonno C, Salviati M, et al. ECT, rTMS, and deepTMS in pharmocoresistant drug-free patients with unipolar depression: a comparative review. Neuropsychiatr Dis Treat. 2012;8:55–64.

31. Berlim M, Van den Eynde F, Daskalakis Z. Efficacy and acceptability of high frequency repetitive transcranial magnetic stimulation (rTMS) verses electroconvulsive therapy (ECT) for major depression: a systematic review and meta-analysis of randomized trials. Depress Anxiety (2013);30:614–23.

32. Parikh S, Quilty L, Ravitz P, Rosenbluth M, Pavlova B, Grigoriadis S, et al. Canadian network for mood and anxiety treatments (CANMAT) 2016 clinical guidelines for the management of adults with major depressive disorder: section 2: psychological treatments. Can J Psychiatry. 2016;61(9):524–39. DOI: 10.1177/0706743716659418

33. Deckersbach T, Eisner L, Sylvia L. Cognitive behavioral therapy for bipolar disorder. In Petersen T, Sprich S, Wilhelm S, editors. The Massachusetts General Hospital handbook of cognitive behavioral therapy. New York: Springer Science + Business Media; 2016. p. 87–103. DOI: 10.1007/978-1-4939-2605-3_7

34. Scott J, Paykel E, Morriss R, Bentall R, Kinderman P, Johnson T, et al. Cognitive behavioral therapy for bipolar disorder. Br J Psychiatry. 2006;188:313–20. DOI: 10.1192/bjp.188.5.488

35. Ravindran A, Balneaves L, Faulkner G, Ortiz A, MacIntosh D, Morehouse R, et al. Canadian network for mood and anxiety treatments (CANMAT) 2016 clinical guidelines for the management of adults with major depressive disorder: section 5: complementary and alternative medicine treatments. Can J Psychiatry. 2016;61(9): 576–87. DOI: 10.1177/0706743716660290

36. Piet J, Hougaard E. The effects of mindfulness-based cognitive therapy for prevention of relapse in recurrent major depressive disorder: a systematic review and meta-analysis. Clin Psychol Rev. 2011;31(6):1032–40. DOI: 10.1016/j.cpr.2011.05.002

37. Kerr A, Morabito M, Watson A. Police encounters, mental illness and injury: an exploratory investigation. J Police Crisi Negot. 2010;10:116–32. DOI: 10.1080/15332581003757198

38. Brink J, Livingston JD, Desmarais SL, Greaves C, Maxwell V, Parent R, et al. A study of how people with mental illness perceive and interact with the police [Internet]. 2011. Available from: http://www.mentalhealthcommission.ca/English/document/437/study-how-people-mental-illness-perceive-and-interactpolice?terminitial=24

39. Kara F. Police interactions with the mentally ill III: the role of procedural justice. CGJSC/RCESSC. Spring 2014;3(1):79–94.

40. Mental Health Act [Internet]. Province of Alberta: Alberta Queen's Printer; 2010. Available from: www.qp.alberta.ca/documents/Acts/M13.pdf

CHAPTER 3

Schizophrenia and Other Psychotic Disorders

Alberto Choy, *Alberta Health Services*

LEARNING OBJECTIVES

1. Define a psychotic disorder and the common signs and symptoms of psychosis
2. Describe the difference between schizophrenia and psychotic disorders
3. Explain the course of psychotic disorders and schizophrenia
4. Understand the treatment for psychotic disorders and schizophrenia, and the reasons for non-compliance with treatment
5. Understand why law enforcement personnel come in contact with persons who are psychotic or who have schizophrenia
6. Identify approaches to de-escalating persons experiencing psychosis

INTRODUCTION

It is not uncommon that law enforcement personnel are called upon to deal with a person who is acting in a bizarre or erratic manner.[1] Odd and unpredictable behaviour can be frightening to the public, and when combined with anger, verbal threats, or physical aggression, frequently culminates in a call for assistance from law enforcement. Police contacts with mentally disordered persons account for approximately 30% of all calls for service.[2] Lord found that approximately 23% of cases attended to by a mobile crisis unit that involved law enforcement dealt with persons who were experiencing psychosis.[1] It is of primary importance for first responders to be aware of the range of presentations of psychotic disorders, and to understand the wide range of possible underlying causes of psychotic presentations. As the etiology of psychosis can include acute, medically emergent, or even life-threatening conditions, it is incumbent upon first responders to manage these cases in a manner that both protects themselves and provides the best opportunity for the affected person to receive appropriate medical and/or psychological care.

FOUNDATIONAL CONCEPTS

Psychosis

Psychosis is a general term describing being grossly out of touch with reality. This abnormality does not, however, imply any underlying cause or etiology. As such, psychosis connotes a description of an experienced range of abnormal phenomena and/or an observable abnormality in a person's mental processes, rather than describing a specific mental illness. As will be discussed below, there are several medical illnesses, substances, and mental illnesses that can lead to psychosis. Psychotic symptoms can be roughly grouped into three main abnormalities: 1) disorganization of behaviour, thought, and speech, 2) **positive symptoms** (presence of symptoms that should be absent, such as delusions or hallucinations), and 3) **negative symptoms** (absence of symptoms that should be present, such as emotional affect).

Medically, the term psychosis describes an observable dysfunction in important brain processes, which may lead to abnormalities in a wide range of areas such as thinking, perceptions, emotions, behaviour, and, possibly, awareness.[3] Abnormalities of thought are frequently described as **disorganized thinking**, which generally describes the inability to logically sequence the thinking process to a logical end. Normal thinking processes can be conceptualized as a series of words that are logically sequenced to make sentences, which in turn must be logically sequenced to make paragraphs, and then logically sequenced to a specific end. Abnormalities seen in disorganized thinking are disconnections of these logical sequences. As such, disorganized thinking might lead to individuals speaking in a manner where their discussion jumps in a nonsensical fashion among a series of ideas, such that the affected person is unable to engage in a cogent discussion. This type of disorganization can also occur at the level of phrases, or even at the level of individual words, in which one word uttered has no connection to the next, graphically described as **word salad**. Other phenomena seen in psychotic thinking processes can include **circumstantiality**, where the person talks all around an issue but never gets to a logical end, or **over-inclusiveness**, where the person talks in excessive and irrelevant details, making it very difficult for them to reach a logical end.

Abnormalities of thinking in psychosis can also include problems with the specific topic of thinking, or what is medically termed abnormal "thought content." When psychotic persons cannot utilize external, objective reality to come to a logical belief, they may be described as experiencing a **delusion**. These are fixed but false beliefs, not in keeping with the person's social or cultural background, that frequently fall into various themes, such as persecutory (often called paranoia), religious, grandiose, infidelity, or even beliefs surrounding medical conditions or the person's own body (called somatic delusions). Delusional beliefs may be wildly out of the range of possible human experience, such as beliefs about being controlled by unseen external forces, or a belief that people around the person have been replaced by imposters. Other abnormalities in thought content can include the belief that external forces are placing ideas into the person's mind, that thoughts or bodily functions are being controlled by others, or that innocuous things that the person might see or hear (billboards, songs on the radio) are specifically referring to the persons themselves. Delusional content may be completely random, but unfortunately there is a greater tendency for the themes to generate fear and/or frustration because of their tendency to be persecutory in nature.[4]

Abnormalities of perception in psychosis include an experience of any sensory modality without the stimulation of that modality being present, termed a **hallucination**. The most common hallucinations are auditory, in which the person is "hearing voices." As any sensory modality can be affected, psychotic persons may also experience visual hallucinations, physical sensations without stimuli ("feeling bugs crawling on my skin"), and olfactory and gustatory hallucinations (smelling and tasting). If a hallucination is a physical sensation, olfactory, or gustatory, the underlying cause of the psychosis is more likely to be a medical illness such as a seizure or a brain tumour.[5,6]

Abnormalities of emotions in psychosis can occur in a manner similar to abnormalities in thinking. Psychosis can lead to emotions that appear to change and shift in a manner that is not organized and not in keeping with external circumstances. However, sometimes the emotions expressed can be logically connected to underlying beliefs, even if they originate from delusions. For example, psychotic individuals experiencing persecutory delusions may present illogical beliefs about their own safety, but their emotional state of fear or anger would be logically connected to their understanding of subjective reality. Their behaviour may similarly be affected; it may be disorganized and without purpose, seemingly random. Alternatively, there may in fact be a logical connection between an underlying delusional belief system that motivates the erratic behaviours, which, to an external observer, appear to make no sense. Abnormalities in thought content, perception, and emotions are frequently defined as the positive symptoms of psychosis.[7]

Lastly, it should be noted that psychosis does not always present with recognizable abnormalities in a person's mental state. In some cases, the underlying brain dysfunction leads to a depreciated mental state, or what are termed negative symptoms, described as a slowing of or significant decrease in thinking, emotions, and behaviour. Emotions may be flattened rather than disorganized or exaggerated. Thinking may be slowed, or there may be a lack of content to thought, leading to a presentation where there is a low level of spontaneous response to conversation. Individuals may become unaware of their surroundings. This deficit state can be severe enough that they remain conscious but are minimally to completely unresponsive to the environment, which is described as **catatonia**.[8]

Psychopathy versus Psychosis

Special attention should be given to the terms psychosis and psychotic being distinct from the term psychopathy. Psychopathy is a term aligned with personality traits and observable behaviour, specifically antisocial personality disorder. Persons who are described as psychopaths have shown a well-engrained pattern of violating the rules, rights, and mores of others for personal gain (see chapter 5). Psychopathic individuals can be callous, remorseless, manipulative, and deceptive.[9] Though they may be braggarts, grandiose, and aggressive, they would not be described as psychotic unless they experienced a separate underlying medical or psychiatric condition that would lead to the brain dysfunction and/or accompanying loss of objective reality which encompasses psychosis, including diagnostic criteria of psychosis (such as hallucinations).

CAUSAL FACTORS

While the symptoms and signs of psychosis can be reliably identified, the term does not connote any specific underlying causes of the brain abnormality. The causes of psychosis are wide-ranging. As such, it is often best to consider psychosis as generally one of the many ways that any type of significant brain dysfunction may manifest itself.

Substance Use

Illicit substances are well-known to increase the risk of psychosis. Most obviously, acute intoxication with hallucinogens and stimulants can lead to auditory and visual hallucinations and in turn can lead to paranoia. These symptoms attenuate as the illicit substance(s) wear off. In some cases, persons can become psychotic when they go into withdrawal after habitual use of a substance. The "pink elephants" and confusion in alcohol withdrawal is described in non-medical depictions of alcoholism. Chronic use of illicit substances and alcohol may lead to syndromes where the psychosis may take months to resolve. In some cases, the psychotic symptoms may never completely resolve, leading to residual and ongoing psychotic symptoms.[10] Legitimately prescribed medications may also cause psychosis. In this case, misuse of medication or unexpected reactions to medication may lead to psychosis either due to a toxic effect of the improper dosage of medication, or to an unforeseeable adverse reaction to a new medication.[11]

Medical Conditions

Any significant medical condition that may lead to brain dysfunction can cause psychosis. Physical abuse of the brain, whether acute trauma leading to a concussion, or repeated, long-term injuries, can lead to a psychotic presentation just as serious as that of chemical abuse.[12] Among middle-aged and older adults, cerebral vascular accidents (strokes), seizure disorders, cardiac events such as myocardial infarctions or arrhythmias, endocrinological diseases such as diabetes, tumours in the body or the brain, and serious infections of the lung, blood, or brain tissues may lead to psychosis. In fact, any significant medical condition that may compromise oxygenation or circulation of the brain may lead to psychosis. For persons who are psychotic due to general medical causes, the underlying medical illness may be obviously fulminant. However, since most medical illnesses among older adults are chronic, that is, long-standing in nature, the psychosis can sometimes be the first obvious sign of an acute deterioration in the individual. In these cases, medical examination and investigations may uncover the medical cause of the psychosis.

Psychological Factors

The second most common mental disorder cause of psychoses are mood disorders, whether depressive disorders or bipolar disorders. Though these mental illnesses primarily affect mood/emotions and biologically modulated bodily rhythms (sleep, energy, and appetite), psychotic symptoms are not diagnostic features.

However, in very severe cases of any type of mood disorder, psychotic symptoms can develop as a part of the entire clinical syndrome. Two other general mental disorder presentations may lead to development of psychotic symptoms. In any physical brain insult where there is a rapid onset of confusion, typically about time, place, or memory, an acute change in awareness of the environment, or a change in level of consciousness, the presentation is termed **delirium**. If these same signs and symptoms are present but occur with gradual onset and/or are chronic, it is described as **dementia**. While the hallmark of both delirium and dementia is confusion and difficulties with memory and awareness, in some cases these features can be accompanied by the classic symptoms commonly seen in any psychotic person.

SCHIZOPHRENIA

Among the mental illnesses that can lead to psychosis, the most commonly encountered by front-line providers is schizophrenia. **Schizophrenia** describes a mental illness whose hallmark is chronic psychosis. Most commonly, the symptoms of schizophrenia include what are termed positive symptoms, such as auditory hallucinations and delusions, negative symptoms, such as a lack of energy, motivation, and emotional expression, and signs of disorganization, typically in the form of disorganized thinking, as noted above.[13]

SCHIZOPHRENIA IN THE DSM-5

The cause of schizophrenia is not known, but there is some component that can be genetic, with studies showing that the risk of developing schizophrenia

---

Table 3.1: The DSM-5 Diagnosis Criteria for Schizophrenia

A.	Delusions: False fixed beliefs
B.	Hallucinations: Perception of visual, tactile, or auditory stimuli that is actually not present
C.	Disorganized Speech: Non-sense or poor speech or thought
D.	Disorganized Behaviour or Catatonia: Non-goal-directed behaviour as well as abnormal motor movements
E.	Negative Symptoms: Absence of emotional affect, lack of pleasure and interest in activities, lack of motivation

among affected family members is between 10-25% compared to the general population of approximately 1%.[14] Studies have also demonstrated abnormalities in the brains of persons with schizophrenia that suggest pathological development and processing functions of the brain, but a clear etiology of the illness has not yet been discovered.[15] The onset of symptoms of schizophrenia is typically between the ages of 16 to 25 for males and approximately five to 10 years later for females.[16] However, it is not uncommon that personality and behavioural changes are seen in the years prior to the onset of classic psychotic symptoms, referred to as the prodromal phase of schizophrenia.[17] At any point in time, it is estimated that approximately 1% of the population will be diagnosable with schizophrenia,[18] which is approximately the same percentage for illnesses such as rheumatoid arthritis and congestive heart failure.

Symptoms and Course of Schizophrenia

The hallmark of this disease is life-long, chronic psychosis unless the illness is successfully treated. The abnormalities in thinking, perception, and motivation may be relatively unobtrusive, but may also lead to significant functional disturbances and long-term disability. Longitudinal studies indicate that 20% of individuals will function well and that approximately two-thirds of individuals with schizophrenia will suffer only a moderate degree of impairment, being able to lead lives in the community with some form of productive employment and interpersonal relationships. These individuals may do well enough that they are never hospitalized, or at the very least may only have a few exacerbations of symptoms serious enough over their lifespan that necessitate in-patient admission. The latter third of afflicted individuals suffers severe dysfunction, whereby they may be unemployable and unable to live independently.[19] These individuals may have a treatment-resistant form of illness where positive symptoms and disorganization do not respond well to medication, or they may have severe or progressive negative symptoms. Given the fact that this illness usually starts in early adulthood and is life-long, it is recognized that schizophrenia causes a significant personal and societal burden, with estimates suggesting a heavy cost to society due to health care costs, lost productivity/employment, and reliance on many social supports due to one's inability to work or care for oneself. A 2016 study in Norway, which is economically similar to Canada in the availability of social supports and welfare but has seven times less population, determined the economic costs of schizophrenia. It was estimated that the average societal cost per person with schizophrenia was US$ 106,000 per year, which totalled US$ 890 million per year for the entire country.[20]

To the untrained observer, a diagnosis of schizophrenia may be difficult to understand, in part because the constellation of symptoms is extensive, such that afflicted individuals may have distinctive symptoms. In the past, diagnostic schemes had identified specific sub-types of schizophrenia, depending on the most predominant symptoms and signs, whereby afflicted persons would have been diagnosed as having "paranoid schizophrenia," "disorganized schizophrenia," or "catatonic schizophrenia." Though the diagnostic sub-types are not a part of the current nomenclature, the practical relevance is to remain mindful that the diagnosis of schizophrenia may present differently from person to person.

Table 3.2: Sub-types of Schizophrenia

Paranoid: Symptoms characterized by thoughts and feelings of persecution that someone (or an entity) is out to harm the person.
Disorganized (hebephrenic): Impoverished or abnormal response of emotion, behaviour, and speech. Pronounced thought disorder with poor contact with reality and dishevelled appearance. This includes an inability to engage in goal-directed behaviour or produce spoken syntax. Some examples of disorganized speech include • loose associations between topics • derailment of thought • word salad (putting random words together) • preservation (repetition of words and phrases) • use of rhyming • making up words (neologism)

Catatonic: Inability to control psychomotor abnormalities characterized by
• motor immobility or excessive motor activity such as rigidness, agitation, fidgeting (hyper movement), or stupor (physical unresponsiveness)
• negativism (resistance to directions such as shaking hands often or doing the opposite of what is asked)
  • echolalia (mimicking the posture or movements of others)
  • echopraxia (mimicking the words of others)
  • posturing (production of bizarre or peculiar postures such as grimacing)
  • waxy flexibility (maintaining a position when body or limbs are moved by others)

Undifferentiated: A significant interference of schizophrenia symptoms that cannot be neatly or predominantly organized in other schizophrenia sub-types. A combination of abnormality in feelings/emotion and mood, physical motors such as tardive dyskinesia (involuntary motor movements, awkward walking, awkward eye movement), mood, **anhedonia** (inability to feel pleasure or interest in activities), perception, cognition, social syntax and cues, presence of hallucination, presence of delusions.

TREATMENT OF SCHIZOPHRENIA

The foundational treatment for schizophrenia is **antipsychotic medications**, which can be taken by mouth or administered by injections. Oral medications are typically dosed one to three times a day, but the injectable forms can include long-acting preparations that are administered weekly to monthly. All available antipsychotic medications can decrease the positive psychotic symptoms, such as auditory hallucinations and delusions, and can assist with disorganization of thinking. Unfortunately, these medications are less successful in helping deficit symptoms of schizophrenia such as low energy and low motivation.[21] Overall, about 70% of individuals have a meaningful decrease in their symptoms with appropriate antipsychotic treatment. As helpful as antipsychotics are for schizophrenia, people who are treated with them may experience a multitude of adverse effects, some of which may be intolerable. The most common side effects of antipsychotics include sedation, weight gain, and blood sugar and blood cholesterol abnormalities, while some patients may also experience an unpleasant dampening of their emotions or thinking, which may be confused with the "negative" symptoms of the schizophrenia itself. Other patients may experience a physical restlessness, motor tics, or muscle spasms and stiffness. Sometimes, additional medications are prescribed to manage these side effects of antipsychotic treatment. In rare cases, there can be very serious side effects, including blood cell abnormalities or cardiac problems.[22] It is necessary to continue treatment life-long, as the medications do not cure the disorder; rather, medications are effective for at least the significant attenuation of most of the overt symptoms, which in turn allows the afflicted person to engage in other modalities of treatment.

Psychological and social supports can be just as important in the treatment of schizophrenia. Frequently, afflicted individuals lack insight into or awareness of their own illness and symptoms. Psychological treatments can include counselling and education so that individuals gain a better understanding of their illness. While medications are useful for symptom control, social and rehabilitative interventions are often necessary for improvement in functioning. For those patients who struggle with unemployment or homelessness, social supports provide a stable environment in the community. As the onset of illness is typically in early adulthood, the affected person may not have a well-developed history of independent living or employment. As such, rehabilitation, including occupational rehabilitation, may improve work skills and play a key role in maintaining independence in the community.

The Phenomenon of Non-Compliance

Non-adherence to treatment (non-compliance) is common for many medical treatments. For chronic illnesses, it is estimated that the rate of medication non-compliance may be as high as 57%.[23] In schizophrenia, rates of medication non-compliance are estimated to reach 75%.[24] The reasons for medication non-compliance may include unpleasant side effects, lack of insight into the benefits of treatment, an unstable social environment such as being in a state of homelessness, the symptoms of the illness itself such as disorganization or negative symptoms, and lack of funds to purchase medication.[25] First responders should always consider the possibility of non-compliance with medication when called for assistance due to an exacerbation of symptoms in a person with schizophrenia.

SCHIZOPHRENIA AND SUBSTANCE ABUSE AS COMORBID DISORDERS

It is estimated that up to 50% of individuals with schizophrenia will also be diagnosable with a substance use disorder,[26] which is much greater than the general population. The relationship between a substance use disorder and a diagnosis of schizophrenia is complex. It is unlikely that one simple explanation, such as substance use leads to schizophrenia, or, conversely, someone with schizophrenia just uses substances to cope with their illness, explains the entire phenomenon of increased substance use rates among those with schizophrenia. Furthermore, confirming a diagnosis of schizophrenia as the cause of psychosis is complicated when there has been concomitant substance abuse. In some cases, clinicians are simply not able to confirm any diagnosis of schizophrenia until months or years after the person has been substance free, due to long-lasting effects of chronic substance abuse. For the first responder, the relevant issue is simply to be aware of the significant likelihood that substance use may be a part of the person's history or current presentation.

Case Study: Robbie's Downward Spiral

A call for service came in from the parents of Robbie on Wednesday at midnight. Robbie is 22 years old and his parents are worried about him because he has become belligerent and broke a window when they asked him yet again

continued

to come out of his bedroom in the basement and clean up. He locked himself in the bedroom, yelling at them not to come in "or else!" He barricaded the door with a clothes hamper, and when his father tried to push it open Robbie yelled out threats. When officers arrived on scene, they could hear him smashing the mirror in the bathroom. He yelled at them, warning them to stay away.

Robbie's parents related that Robbie had become lazy and described him as a "freeloader." For the past two years, he had socialized less with the family, and he also seemed to have dropped his friends from high school. He stopped playing recreational hockey at about the same time. He had a steady job for a few years with a company as a drywaller but was let go about 11 months ago. His parents complained that his room became a mess, as he seemed to not be doing much, spending most evenings alone downstairs on his computer, which was in his bedroom. His father was frustrated because he was not paying rent, did few chores, and would stay up all night, sleeping most of the day away. His mother tearfully related that she suspected he was using drugs. The parents indicated that he was behaving similarly about 5 months ago. They convinced him to go to the emergency room because they thought he was depressed. He reluctantly agreed to be admitted to the psychiatry ward, but after a week he called home and said he was signing himself out of hospital because he "was allowed to be free." His family called the hospital, but they indicated that they were not allowed to keep him or treat him against his will because he was not a threat to anyone. They suggested the family refer him to his family doctor or a local mental health clinic for treatment, but advised that there was no way that the hospital or the family could really force him to attend.

When the officers tried to speak to Robbie again, he yelled back, warning them to stay away. He seemed to be agitated and very nervous. When officers reassured him that they did not want to arrest him or harm him, he yelled out that he knew they would shoot him, because "that is what cops do!" He told them that he knew they were part of Zion and the Iberian–Illuminati Connection. The officers stayed outside his room but resumed communication. The lead officer continued to reassure Robbie that they did not want anyone to be hurt. He asked Robbie to tell him about the Illuminati Connection, telling him that he did not know about this but was interested in what Robbie was saying. Robbie scoffed and swore at the officer, indicating that the officer was trying to trick him. The officer again reassured Robbie, observing that Robbie was obviously angry, and possibly worried, and then asked Robbie to help him understand why Robbie might be so upset. In a distraught manner, Robbie then began to explain how he had been hearing the radio transmissions in his head and in his teeth, and he began to figure out that this was the work of Zion. The officer continued to ask about Robbie's safety—if he was in danger in any way and if he needed to protect himself. Robbie continued to explain what was happening to him and to society. Eventually, the officer relayed to Robbie that they did not want to arrest him, that they just wanted to get him help because he was understandably upset by all of this. When Robbie asked if the doctors would "lock me up again and force medications on me?" the officer responded that he did not know what the doctor would do, but he was sure that the doctor was not going to be a part of any conspiracy and was not going to try and hurt him. The officer also urged Robbie to allow the doctors to help him out, as being arrested and charged would do nothing to keep him safe. They asked Robbie if he needed a few minutes to collect himself before coming out, and when Robbie seemed calmer, he voluntarily came out of the bedroom.

Commentary

Robbie is showing symptoms of a psychotic disorder, with possible evidence of persecutory delusions and auditory hallucinations. Though he was eventually diagnosed with schizophrenia, this is much less important for first responders than immediately recognizing the psychosis. The officers in this scenario did well by keeping in mind possible mental health issues despite Robbie's disrespect towards them and his verbally abusive and belligerent behaviour.

In this case, the officers succeeded because they maintained their position to Robbie as wanting to assist him rather than being an authority in control. Their continued reassurance was helpful. Though the officers could not make sense of the "Iberian Connection," they recognized very quickly that Robbie was both angry and very afraid, and they earned some of his trust by relating to him that they could see he was very upset, and they wanted to understand why he was feeling this way. Though they obviously could not agree with his view of reality, they continued to simply identify that he was very worried, and they reassured him that they wanted everyone to be safe.

The officers were challenged by Robbie when he asked for reassurance that he would not be "locked up" and forcibly medicated, and they managed

continued

this well by avoiding deception, which might set up a distrust of police in the future. They were honest in indicating that they did not know what the doctors would do, but they reassured him about the doctor's intent. Lastly, the officers did not pressure Robbie, even though the whole interaction took some time to resolve. They wisely gave Robbie time to collect himself before coming out, which provided him with some degree of control.

Questions
1. What might be the cause of Robbie's situation?
2. Why might Robbie have become more socially isolated in the last few years?
3. What are the most prominent risks in this scenario?

MISCONCEPTIONS ABOUT SCHIZOPHRENIA

As a first responder, it is important to remember that assistance is called for when there is a need or when members of the public are not able to resolve situations on their own. As such, it is highly likely that first responders will deal with individuals with schizophrenia when they are in crisis, behaving bizarrely, or causing difficulties for others. First responders will not typically have experience with persons with schizophrenia who are functioning well in the community. First responders' repeated experience of only dealing with illness when it is fulminant may lead to erroneous conclusions called the observer-expectancy effect, which develops a belief that those with schizophrenia are more often violent or in crisis than is the case. Fictional depictions of schizophrenia and even news reports involving schizophrenia have a tendency to over-report the connection between schizophrenia and violence.[27,28] In fact, persons with severe mental illnesses are two-and-a-half times more likely to be victims of violence than those without a mental illness.[29] While having any mental disorder increases the likelihood of self-reported violence as compared to persons without a mental disorder, it is clear that the relationship between schizophrenia and violence is actually small, especially compared to other factors, such as substance abuse. The combination of a mental disorder diagnosis and substance abuse further elevates the risk of violence.[29] One other factor that may lead to an over-emphasis of the connection between schizophrenia and violence is the fact that, on occasion, there may be very high-profile, relatively inexplicable criminal events that garner a great amount of media attention.[30] It is important to remember that these are extremely rare events, especially compared to other tragic events that are much more easily explained and understood by the public because they are related to drugs and/or criminal violence.[31]

A diagnosis of schizophrenia increases the risk of social marginalization, unemployment, and homelessness.[32] Along with this comes an increase in the likelihood of substance abuse. The rate of any substance abuse among persons with schizophrenia in their lifetime is estimated to be up to 80%.[33] Social stressors such as homelessness and substance abuse undoubtedly worsen symptoms and may lead to more severe presentations. Again, first responders must be aware that these issues also increase the likelihood of contact with law enforcement and may not be the typical course of the illness for the majority of diagnosed persons. It is important to balance this experience of persons ill with schizophrenia with those many persons who are living well in the community or even recognized as excelling in their personal and professional lives despite the diagnosis. Austin Mardon was diagnosed with schizophrenia but went on to complete his PhD and was appointed a Member of the Order of Canada in 2007.[34]

OTHER PSYCHOTIC DISORDERS

Though it is outside the first responder's purview to officially diagnose disorders, there are other identified disorders that share similar features to schizophrenia.

Brief Psychotic Disorder can include the prototypical symptoms of schizophrenia, but this diagnosis is applied if there is no external or medical cause for the psychosis, and if the symptoms have not been present for more than one month. If the symptoms are present longer than one month but no more than six months, a diagnosis of schizophreniform disorder is made.

If an individual's psychosis solely involves delusions, that is, does not involve significant disorganization or negative symptoms, the diagnosis of Delusional Disorder is applicable. Delusional disorders can come in various types, such as grandiose, jealous, persecutory, or religious. When a delusional disorder is based on an erroneous belief about the body, it is termed a somatic delusional disorder. When the delusional theme is that someone else is in love with the delusional person, the delusion is termed erotomanic. Interestingly, sometimes persons experiencing erotomanic delusions paradoxically harass or stalk the person they are delusional about, often with accompanying delusional justifications, such as they are "divinely meant to be together."

Table 3.3: Overview of Psychotic Disorders

Schizophrenia: Presence of delusions, hallucinations, disorganized speech and thought, disorganized behaviour or catatonic behaviour, and negative symptoms lasting longer than six months.
Schizophreniform: Diagnostic criteria similar to schizophrenia but with a shorter duration of less than six months but more than one month.
Brief Psychosis: Diagnostic criteria similar to schizophrenia but with a shorter duration of less than one month.
Schizoaffective: A combination of psychosis and a mood disorder, with slightly more emphasis on psychosis.
Psychotic Disorder Due to a Medical Condition: Psychosis caused by medical conditions.
Substance-Induced Psychotic Disorder: Psychosis caused by the use of substances.
Delusional Disorder: Non-bizarre delusions lasting longer than one month without the diagnosis of schizophrenia or impairment of functioning. Sub-Types include • Erotomanic: Having a special relationship with someone such as being in love with a higher-status person. • Grandiose: Believing in a strong, exaggerated sense of self-importance and superiority deserving of special attention and admiration. Reflective of cult leaders and some politicians who present narcissistic tendencies. • Jealous: A strong pattern of belief that one's partner is unfaithful. • Persecutory: A strong belief that one is being conspired against or spied on, typically by authority or government officials. • Somatic: A belief in a physical defect. • Mixed: Two or more existing delusions.

If the psychosis is caused by an external substance, whether illicit or not, the diagnoses are termed substance- or medication-induced psychotic disorders. Lastly, medical causes for psychosis are described simply as psychotic disorder due to a medical condition, accompanied by a description of the medical condition.

THE LIVED EXPERIENCES OF PSYCHOSIS AND SUICIDE RISK

Symptoms such as auditory hallucinations and thought form disorganization can be disabling because they directly interfere with independent living skills or social functioning. The experience of these symptoms can also be distressing to the affected person, thereby causing other forms of illness. The risk for depression and suicide is elevated among persons with schizophrenia.[35] Illicit substances can be a way for afflicted persons to cope with their illness.[33] Persons with schizophrenia may feel a loss of control, perhaps directly due to symptoms such as feeling as if someone can read their thoughts, outside forces can force them to experience auditory hallucinations, or someone is persecuting them. In addition, they may have had real-life prior experiences of being involuntarily hospitalized or even involuntarily medicated when they were acutely ill. Some individuals will have great difficulty in accepting that they are diagnosed with a chronic mental illness that may make it difficult for them to reach previously held career or life goals.

It is these kinds of experiences of persons with schizophrenia that first responders must deal with. As such, it is not uncommon for persons with psychosis to be hostile or angry when confronted with authority. However, it is important to understand the anger may be secondary to a more primary underlying emotion, specifically fear, likely due to the sense of a loss of control. Along with the acute exacerbation of symptoms such as paranoia and delusional beliefs that may include law-enforcement personnel, people with schizophrenia often do not have memory problems and may be acutely aware that first responders are involved with forcible conveyance and detainment at an emergency department. Lastly, some individuals may also be aware of tragic encounters between first responders and persons with mental illness,[36] and may themselves have misconceptions about the approach that law-enforcement personnel take in crisis situations.

Spotlight: Lauren

My name is Lauren and I was diagnosed with schizoaffective disorder in 2016 at the age of 25. My childhood was fairly normal, but something shifted however during high school and I began to struggle with my mood. I started to experience some negative symptoms, which led to an increased apathy in participating in school and generally withdrawing. This is also when I started to experience thought broadcasting—where I thought people could hear my thoughts, which was another early indicator. I skipped a lot of classes, which led to lower grades, but I was still able to scrounge together decent enough grades to not raise too many red flags.

continued

I began university shortly after high school, and I was struggling quite a bit and so with a little encouragement from my boyfriend at the time, I decided to visit a family doctor. She diagnosed me with depression during this visit, when I was 19 years old. I continued to struggle with what I thought was depression for several years. There were a couple of periods scattered throughout this, though, where I would feel really great. During these periods, I would be really productive, and would go off on adventures travelling or running in the mountains. But the depression always returned and almost felt worse each time. During this time, I realized that I wanted to pursue a career in social work and so decided to transfer to the University of Waterloo in Ontario to complete my studies there. I got through my first Bachelor of Arts degree okay, and did quite well academically, earning several scholarships and awards. It was the year I started my Bachelor of Social Work degree at 22, though, that things really started to go sideways.

My depression came to a really severe place that fall, where I was constantly thinking about ending my own life. It was at this point that I decided something needed to be done and so I sought out counselling. I was then connected with a family doctor and a psychiatrist at the university who diagnosed me with bipolar disorder II due to my severe depression and history of periods that sounded like hypomania. Despite this, however, the depression came to a point where I decided to take my own life that winter. I overdosed but was taken to the hospital in time for them to treat me. This was unfortunately my first hospitalization of many to come.

I was so afraid of what people would think if they found out what I had been going through, so I mostly kept things quiet and to myself, which really didn't help things. I struggled a great deal with my mood, and it was around this time that I started to hallucinate regularly. It began with just hearing my name spoken every now and then, even when I was completely alone. I kind of brushed this off, however, thinking my imagination was just running amuck, and so never mentioned this to my doctors or counsellor. I then began to have olfactory hallucinations where I would smell awful smells whose source I couldn't identify or locate.

I struggled silently with these symptoms and a year after my first suicide attempt, I tried again—this time it was more serious. For whatever reason, my counsellor decided to send the police to do a wellness check on me the morning I overdosed again, and they arrived just in time to see what had happened and to

rush me to the hospital. I was put into a medically induced coma and was on life support for several days.

After being released from the hospital, I had my first episode of psychosis at the age of 24. During this time, the hallucinations intensified, and I became delusional as well. I was hearing and seeing helicopters circling overhead all the time and hearing voices. I became obsessed with retrieving my medical files as I was convinced that the doctors were conspiring to kill me and poisoning me using medications for mind control. I hardly slept at all and was flying off the walls with this paranoid energy. I was sleeping outside the medical clinic in my car waiting for the clinic to open so I could go in and again try to obtain access to my files. I remember one particular night of doing this where I hallucinated an elderly man trying to break into my car and reaching in to take some of my files. It was a really terrifying time. My boyfriend at the time was witnessing this drastic deterioration and finally got me to go to the hospital with him. I don't remember a lot of details about how exactly he managed this but upon talking with him afterwards, I think what was helpful was focusing on the emotions I was feeling. I was very scared, and he talked to me about that rather than the hallucinations and delusions I was experiencing. He convinced me they would be able to help me at the hospital. I was admitted immediately, and my diagnosis was changed to bipolar disorder I with psychotic features.

They were able to stabilize me with medications, and I was able to graduate that spring. I landed a dream job doing research for Cancer Care Ontario and made the move to Toronto to begin my professional career. On paper I was doing really well—I had just graduated from my second degree

continued

program and had started a fantastic new job, I had a lot of friends and a long-term boyfriend, and I was living on my own and supporting myself. The hallucinations did not ever fully go away, however, and that summer I was struggling so much with these symptoms that I had to make the really difficult decision to resign from my new position and to move back home to Alberta to be closer to family and friend supports. Even after this move closer to supports, I could tell things were getting worse and the delusions were starting to come back. It was because of this that I decided to stop taking my medications again, as I thought again that they were using them for mind control or poisoning me with them. I had my second psychotic episode that fall at the age of 25 when I was diagnosed with schizoaffective disorder, as the psychotic symptoms continued without a mood episode present. It was scary to get what seemed like an even more severe label. But at the same time, it also almost came as a relief. There was finally an explanation for the things that I was experiencing. All of a sudden, the things I was experiencing seemed a little less scary and a little more understandable. I still went through a grieving period, though, when I received this diagnosis. There are not a lot of success stories for people experiencing schizophrenia or schizoaffective disorder in broad circulation. I was no longer sure where my life was going to end up and this added an additional element of fear.

I ended up in the Alberta Hospital for a month this time, and it was a really difficult experience. I refused medication and food for fear of being poisoned. I was being commanded by the voices to kill myself and would continuously try to appease these voices by any means possible. Finally, at the threat of being forced into electroconvulsive therapy, I agreed to eat and to take the medications. I eventually stabilized and was discharged from the hospital.

It was then that I really started to grapple with the internalized stigma of my mental illness. I was so scared of what people in my life would think if they found out, and worse, that I would never be able to hold the stable job I had always dreamed of having. I also continued to struggle with the idea of taking medications, which is something I still struggle with to this day. But I have come to learn the importance of doing so and have come to identify my own pattern of stopping medication leading to hospitalization or worse.

The hallucinations can be difficult to manage at times and I still deal with them even while on medications. Also, the negative symptom of blunted affect is a really hard one for me to bear. I identify as a fairly empathic person and so when I am cut off from my emotions and the emotions of others, it can be very difficult to handle. I am very happy and proud to say, though, that I have not been in the hospital since this last time in October 2016. I have been working as a social worker at a couple of different jobs, and I have started my Master of Science in Public Health in order to continue with my career in health care research.

It has been a real fight to get to this point and to overcome not only my symptoms but also the stigma I had internalized. I've learned a lot about myself, though, through this process and I learned just how resilient I can be. I lost a lot of hope for a period of time when I was first diagnosed, but I am learning that it is possible to still lead a meaningful and productive life even with the diagnosis of schizoaffective disorder. I live with a mental illness, but I am not defined by my mental illness.

DEINSTITUTIONALIZATION

It is believed that there has been an increase in contact between persons with mental illness and the criminal justice system over the last few decades.[1] The reasons for this may be related to the process of deinstitutionalization, which began in the 1950s, when large psychiatric facilities were appropriately downsized in favour of promoting supported functions of persons with mental health disorders within the community. Unfortunately, as housing supplies and community supports did not keep up with the need, homelessness rates among persons with mental illness have increased. While the move away from "warehousing" persons with mental illness and promoting integration and functioning in the community remains very valid, lowered lengths of hospital stays may also contribute to greater first responder contacts. It has been suggested that these increased contacts and decreased health and social supports have led to the phenomenon called "criminalization of the mentally ill," in which behaviours that may have previously led to hospitalization are now streamed into the criminal justice system, leading to a significant increase of persons with mental illness in remand and correctional facilities.[37] This period becomes critical to assessing mental illness among those who are incarcerated. An interdisciplinary approach between police and mental health professionals is critical to provide care to identifying inmates with serious mental health concerns.

SUMMARY

Psychosis describes alterations in mental state in which the affected person loses contact with objective reality. The changes in mental state include abnormalities in awareness, thinking process or beliefs, perceptions, and possibly emotions. The causes of psychosis may include mental illnesses, substance use, and medical illnesses, but there may be more than an individual cause that leads to psychotic symptoms. Schizophrenia is a mental illness in which there is chronic psychosis that is not caused by external factors such as substance use. Most symptoms of schizophrenia are treatable by medications, and this, in conjunction with social, psychological, and rehabilitation services, can help affected individuals function independently in the community.

REFLECTION QUESTIONS

The Experience of Psychosis

Consider what it might be like one day to start hearing two strangers speaking about you every moment of the day. You hear this as if you had headphones on and the volume is low, so that you can still hear conversations with others, but the two strangers are continuously commenting in your ears. They seem to be critical of everything you are saying or doing. You have cleaned your ears and checked your room, and you still cannot stop the strangers from talking. The logical part of your brain is intact, so you think that this might be a figment of your imagination. However, you hear them despite the fact you tell yourself that there is no way that you have a mental illness.

1. How would you start explaining the presence of these two voices to yourself?
2. As you come up with explanations for this experience of hearing the strangers' voices (maybe it is a hidden radio, or a Wi-Fi signal), do you notice that you may now be coming up with delusional beliefs to try and make sense of this perceptual disturbance?

Non-Compliance with Treatment

We all know that we should not overeat or eat "junk food." We all know that we should get at least eight hours of sleep at night. We all know that we should exercise at least three times a week. And yet, almost no one adheres to all of this even though we know that this will help to keep us healthy.

1. Why do we not follow these simple, logical directions to keep ourselves healthy?
2. Can this help you understand why those diagnosed with schizophrenia might not follow up on treatment or take their medications?

REFERENCES

1. Lord VB, Bjerregaard B. Helping persons with mental illness: partnerships between police and mobile crisis units. Vict Offender. 2014;9:455–74.
2. Boyce J, Rotenberg C, Karam M. Mental health and contact with police in Canada, 2012. Juristat: Canadian Centre for Justice Statistics; 2015. p. 1.
3. American Psychiatric Association. Diagnostic and statistical manual of mental disorders (DSM-5). American Psychiatric Pub; 2013 May 22. p. 87–8.
4. Bentall RP, Rowse G, Shryane N, Kinderman P, Howard R, Blackwood N, et al. The cognitive and affective structure of paranoid delusions. Arch Gen Psychiatry. 2009 Mar;66(3):236–47.
5. Chen C, Shih YH, Yen DJ, Lirng JF, Guo YC, Yu HY, et al. Olfactory auras in patients with temporal lobe epilepsy. Epilepsia. 2003 Feb;44(2):257–60.
6. Morrison DP. Abnormal perceptual experiences in migraine. Cephalagia. 1990 Dec;10(6):273–7.
7. Crow TJ. Molecular pathology of schizophrenia: more than one disease process? Br Med J. 1980 Jan 12;280:66–8.
8. American Psychiatric Association. Diagnostic and statistical manual of mental disorders (DSM-5). American Psychiatric Pub; 2013 May 22. p. 119.
9. Hare RD. Psychopathy: a clinical construct whose time has come. Crim Justice Behav. 1996 Mar;23(1):25–54.
10. Jordaan GP, Emsley R. Alcohol-induced psychotic disorder: a review. Metab Brain Dis. 2014 Jun;29(2):231–43.
11. Soutullo CA, Cottingham EM, Keck Jr. PE. Psychosis associated with pseudoephedrine and dextromethorphan. J Am Acad Child Adolesc Psychiatry. 1999 Dec;39(12):1471–2.
12. Zgaljardic DJ, Seale GS, Schaefer LA, Temple RO, Foreman J, Elliot TR. Psychiatric disease and post-acute traumatic brain injury. J Neurotrauma. 2015 Dec;32:1911–25.
13. American Psychiatric Association. Diagnostic and statistical manual of mental disorders (DSM-5). American Psychiatric Pub; 2013 May 22. p. 99–105.
14. Erlenmyer-Kimling L, Cornblatt B. The New York High-Risk Project: a followup report. Schizophr Bull. 1987;13(3):451–61.
15. Opler MGA, Perrin MC, Kleinhaus K, Malaspina D. Factors in the etiology of schizophrenia: genes, parental age, and environment. Prim Psychiatry. 2008;15(6):37–45.
16. Castle D, Sham P, Murray R. Differences in distribution of ages of onset in males and females with schizophrenia. Schizophr Res. 1998 Oct;33(3):179–83.
17. Yung A, McGorry PD. The initial prodrome in psychosis: descriptive and qualitative aspects. Aust J Z J Psychiatry. 1996 Oct;30(5):587–99.
18. Regier DA, Narrow WE, Rae DS, Manderscheid RW, Locke BZ, Goodwin FK. The de facto US mental and addictive disorders service system. Arch Gen Psychiatry. 1993 Feb;50(2):85–94.

19. American Psychiatric Association. Diagnostic and statistical manual of mental disorders (DSM-5). American Psychiatric Pub; 2013 May 22. p. 102–3.
20. Evensen S, Wisløff T, Lystad JU, Bull H, Ueland T, Falkum E. Prevalence, employment rate, and cost of schizophrenia in a high-income welfare society: a population-based study using comprehensive health and welfare registers. Schizophr Bull. 2016 Mar;42(2):476–83.
21. Remington G, Foussias G, Fervaha G, Agid O, Takeuchi H, Lee J, et al. Treating negative symptoms in schizophrenia: an update. Curr Treat Options Pysch. 2016;3:133–50.
22. Lally J, MacCabe JH. Antipsychotic medication in schizophrenia: a review. Br Med Bull. 2015 Jun;114(1):169–79.
23. Osterberg L, Blashke T. Adherence to medication. N Engl J Med. 2005 Aug 4;353(5):487–97.
24. Young JL, Zonana HV, Shepler L. Medication noncompliance in schizophrenia: codification and update. Bull Am Acad Psychiatry Law. 1986;14(2):105–22.
25. Fenton WS, Blyler CR, Heinssen RK. Determinants of medication compliance in schizophrenia: empirical and clinical findings. Schizophr Bull. 1997;23(4):637–51.
26. Blanchard JJ, Brown SA, Horan WP, Sherwood AR. Substance use disorders in schizophrenia: review, integration, and a proposed model. Clin Psychol Rev. 2000 Mar;20(2):207–34.
27. Huang B, Priebe S. Media coverage of mental health care in the UK, USA, and Australia. Psychiatr Bull. 2003;27:331–3.
28. Owen PR. Portrayals of schizophrenia by entertainment media: a content analysis of contemporary movies. Psychiatr Serv. 2012 Jul;63(7):655–9.
29. Hiday VA, Swartz MS, Swanson JW, Borum R, Wagner HR. Criminal victimization of persons with severe mental illness. Psychiatr Serv. 1999 Jan;50(1):62–8.
30. Swanson JW, Holzer CE. Violence and ECA data. Hosp Community Psychiatry. 1991 Sep;42(9):954–5.
31. CBC News. Greyhound killer believed man he beheaded was an alien [Internet]. CBC News; 2012 May 22. Available from: http://cbc.ca/news/canada/Manitoba/greyhound-killer-believed-man-he-beheaded-was-an-alien-1.1131575
32. Bolan K. REAL SCOOP: 21 murders so far in 2017, few arrests. Vancouver Sun [Internet]; 2017 [2017 Apr 7; updated 2017 Apr 8]. Available from: http://vancouversun.com/news/staff-blogs/real-scoop-21-murders-so-far-in-2017
33. Foster A, Gable J, Buckley J. Homelessness in schizophrenia. Psychiatr Clin North Am. 2012 Sep;35(3):717–34.
34. Westermeyer J. Comorbid schizophrenia and substance abuse: a review of epidemiology and course. Am J Addict. 2006 Sep-Oct;15(5):345–55.
35. Mardon A, Throckmorton V. Opinion: acceptance and early treatment key to coping with mental illness [Internet]. Edmonton Journal [Internet]; 2017 [2017 Jul 4; updated 2017 Jul 4]. Available from: http://edmontonjounal.com/opinion/columnists/opinion-acceptance-and-early-treatment-key-to-coping-with-mental-illness
36. American Psychiatric Association. Diagnostic and statistical manual of mental disorders (DSM-5). American Psychiatric Pub; 2013 May 22. p. 104.
37. Kennedy B. Why did mentally ill man have to die? Toronto Star [Internet]; 2010 Sep 19. Available from: https://thestar.com/news/crime/2010/09/19/why_did_mentally_ill_man_have_to_die.html

CHAPTER 4

Substance Use Disorders

Adam Howorko, *Concordia University of Edmonton*

Rick Csiernik, *King's University College*

LEARNING OBJECTIVES

1. Distinguish between drug misuse, drug abuse, physical dependence, and psychological dependence
2. Differentiate the distinct components of the DSM-5 definition of substance use disorder
3. Define addiction in a holistic manner
4. Describe the different groupings of psychoactive substances

INTRODUCTION

Psychoactive drug use is intertwined with law enforcement, for, in Canada, formal legislation is the primary drug enforcement—which is the direct responsibility of police officers. Federal legislation has historically controlled who may use psychoactive substances and under what circumstances. This, in turn, has led drugs to being among the leading reasons citizens interact with police officers; however, there is far more to the intersection of drugs and the police than criminalization. Substance use disorders truly do not discriminate: they affect everyone.

Case Study: Adric's Path

Adric was a typical adolescent growing up in Western society. He started sneaking beers from his parents' refrigerator first to satisfy his curiosity and then to fit in with his friends. Into young adulthood he would classify himself as a responsible "social drinker"; that is, he would not drink and drive. During his college years, he maintained his responsible approach to drinking. In college, he drew the attention of a classmate in his criminology course, and eventually the two of them married and wanted a family. His wife became pregnant and life seemed ideal until one life-changing episode: Adric's wife was killed by a drunk driver at mid-day. Soon afterwards, Adric left his undergraduate degree and joined a security company. Adric's drive was noble, but he found his days off too painful and his drinking was no longer "sociable," as it was done alone. The supervisor of his division was concerned for Adric and recommended counselling. Adric downplayed his drinking to the counsellor and poured his energy into working. What Adric did not recognize was that he was developing a powerful tolerance to alcohol, and he was at risk for driving under the influence. While working extra shifts to combat loneliness was challenging, Adric tried to give up drinking, knowing it was depleting his energy and having an immense impact on his health and well-being.

At the urging of his supervisor, Adric engaged in a more balanced approach to his lifestyle. He worked fewer shifts, but having more free time brought up feelings of longing for his wife, so at the prompting of some fellow co-workers he revisited the social scene. His co-workers liked him and Adric started to loosen up for the first time since the loss of his wife. At first it was only non-alcoholic drinks, but the empty apartment became too much, and drinking became the only way he could manage his loneliness after watching fellow co-workers go back to their respective partners. Alcohol was back in his life, but he rationalized to himself that he was not harming anyone, as he was all alone.

Questions

1. What can Adric do for himself to begin the healing journey?
2. What obstacles is he going to encounter and how can these be mitigated?
3. What advice and support can you provide to someone dealing with addiction?

FOUNDATIONAL CONCEPTS

Prior to defining Substance Use Disorders (SUDs) in a police context, definitions of some key and often-misused terms are required to fully understand substance use in the context of addiction. A **psychoactive drug** is either a chemical not naturally found in the body (e.g., synthetic marijuana), or a normal body chemical (e.g., nicotine, as it has a similar structure to acetylcholine) administered in a larger dose than is normal to the body.[1] The substance's function is to change the nervous system, influencing one's perception of the environment. The ground-breaking Le Dain Commission[2] defined a psychoactive drug as any substance, either natural or synthesized, that by its chemical nature alters the structure or function of the body or mind of a living organism.

Associated with consuming psychoactive drugs are the ideas of **drug misuse** and **drug abuse**. Drug misuse refers to the periodic or occasional improper or inappropriate use of either a social or prescription psychoactive drug. The term drug abuse has been used in a broader social context to define any instance of drug administration that is disapproved of by society and is often legally prohibited or restricted. A more consumer-oriented definition of drug abuse limits its use to a description of drug administration that causes an adverse effect on the individual user rather than on society. According to the medical model, the term drug abuser is limited to individuals who persistently consume a substance to such an extent that they impair their quality of life in a substantive way.[3] Adverse effects can include medical complications,[4] behavioural alterations,[5] difficulties with interpersonal relationships,[6] financial concerns,[7] and legal problems.[8]

SUBSTANCE USE IN THE DSM-5

The DSM formerly used the terms substance abuse and substance dependence, but now it refers to SUDs, which better captures substance use on a spectrum rather than by separate disorders. SUDs can be mild, moderate, or severe, which is determined by the number of diagnostic criteria met by an individual. SUDs occur when the recurrent use of alcohol and/or drugs causes clinically and functionally significant impairment, such as health problems, disability, and failure to meet major responsibilities at work, school, or home. According to the DSM-5, a diagnosis of SUD is based on evidence of impaired control, social impairment, risky use, and pharmacological criteria.[9] The DSM-5 lists nine types of Substance-Related Disorders but does not classify caffeine as an SUD.

Regardless of the substance, the diagnosis of an SUD is based upon a pathological set of behaviours related to the use of that substance.[10]

SUBSTANCE DEPENDENCE

Drug dependency is the stage following drug abuse. Dependency is what is meant by most people when they use the term addiction, more specifically, the compulsion to engage in behaviours to a problematic or socially maladaptive degree. Meaning that an individual spends a lot of time seeking out the substance, and their day-to-day activities revolve around searching for and using that substance. Relationships, work, and all other activities are secondary to using the substance. This dependency assumes an increasingly central role in the person's life.

Physical dependence is a physiological state of cellular adaptation occurring when the body becomes so accustomed to a psychoactive drug that it can only function normally when the drug is present. Without the drug, the user experiences physical disturbances or illnesses, known as **withdrawal**. Withdrawal symptoms can be prevented or promptly relieved by the administration of a sufficient quantity of the original drug or, often, by one with a similar pharmacological activity. The latter case, in which different drugs are used interchangeably in preventing withdrawal symptoms, is called **cross-dependence**. For example, methadone can be used to suppress withdrawal in persons physically dependent on heroin.[11]

The development of physical dependence is important in the maintenance of drugs because administration, either to alleviate or to prevent withdrawal, results in reinforcement of behaviour. Instead of returning to a neutral state, homeostasis, there may be an overshooting effect resulting in further satisfaction. Physical dependency is typically preceded by serious personal, psychological, social, and physiological complications.

The complement to physical dependence is **psychological dependence**, also referred to as behavioural or emotional dependence. Psychological dependence occurs when a drug becomes so important to people's thoughts or activities that they believe they cannot manage without it. Psychological dependence can range from mild yearning to compelling emotional need and may include feelings of loss or even desperation if the drug is unavailable. In the case of psychological dependence, individuals begin to believe they need the drug effect to cope with life situations. In most cases, the psychological aspects are considerably more important than physical dependence in maintaining chronic drug use. The major problem with chronic dependence is not the physical aspect, as withdrawal can usually be overcome within days, but the psychological reasons.

INCIDENCE AND PREVALENCE

Canadians purchased $22.1 billion worth of alcoholic beverages during the fiscal year ending March 31, 2016, up 3.5% from the previous year, with Canadians consuming 264.4 million litres of absolute alcohol.[12] Just under 23 million Canadians, over 77% of the population 15 years or older, reported consuming alcohol, with more men (81%) than women (73%) using the substance. The rate among young adults ranged from 83% for those aged 20-24 to 59% for those between 15-19, which of course is primarily underage drinkers. Quebec saw the greatest percentage of consumers of alcohol (82%), while Prince Edward Island, the last province to repeal prohibition, continued to have the lowest percentage (73%).[13]

The prevalence of cigarette smoking among Canadians was 13% in 2015, down from 15% in 2013. This was the lowest national smoking rate in the history of the country, with youth smoking at an even lower national rate of 10%. Only 10% of British Columbians 15 years and older reported smoking, compared to 18% in Nova Scotia and Newfoundland and Labrador. The lowest average number of cigarettes consumed by daily smokers was in Manitoba, at 10.9 per day, while those in New Brunswick had the greatest daily use, at 15.5.[13]

Rates of cannabis use are nearly equal with that of tobacco, with 12% of Canadians surveyed indicating they used this substance, although this study was conducted while cannabis was still an illicit drug. Interestingly, while those in British Colombia have the lowest rate of tobacco use, they had the highest rate of cannabis use at 17% of the population, while again Prince Edward Island had the lowest rate of use at 8%. Overall use of illicit drugs other than cannabis remains low, with only 2% of respondents indicating use of cocaine, amphetamines, hallucinogens, or heroin. However, there is the risk of selection bias because these numbers are dependent on who is sampled in this Health Canada study. Interestingly, Canadians were found to be 6.5 times more likely to use a prescription opioid and five times more likely to use a benzodiazepine than an illicit drug.

In 2015 there were 96,000 reported offences under the Controlled Drugs and Substances Act, resulting in a rate of 269 per 100,000 of the population—although just over half were for possession of cannabis, and 9% were related to the trafficking, production, or distribution of cannabis. While there was a decrease in cocaine-related crimes by 14%, increases were reported between 2014 and 2015 for possession, trafficking, production, and distribution of methamphetamine (25%), heroin (18%), and ecstasy (7%). In comparison, there were 201 incidents per 100,000 of the population of impaired driving due to alcohol, along with another 3,000 drug-impaired driving charges. While drinking and driving rates have steadily fallen in Canada, drug-impaired driving charges doubled in number between 2009 and 2015.[14] Lastly, it is estimated that the value of contraband tobacco smuggled into Canada exceeds $1 billion a year.[15]

DEVELOPING A HOLISTIC UNDERSTANDING OF ADDICTION

This brings us to the term **addiction** and a holistic understanding of this complex phenomenon. Physical dependency is relatively easy to accomplish. Non-medical withdrawal management and detoxification centres assist thousands of individuals every year in Canada, while severe alcohol or barbiturate withdrawal requiring more specialized medical attention is rare. In fact, most people can be physically withdrawn from almost any psychoactive drug in a few days to two weeks (typically with strenuous physical and emotional strain). There are even medications (Narcan (naloxone)) available that can quickly reverse the effects of an opioid (heroin, fentanyl) overdose without requiring hospitalization. Psychological dependency is more complicated and intricate, and often requires specialized counselling. There is, however, a third dimension to addiction, one that has historically been ignored by counselling professionals specifically and society generally: the social dimension. The lack of societal addressment of SUDs in a holistic manner explains, in part, why one in six counsellors treating addiction have their clients leave treatment with negative outcomes.[16]

The term addiction itself has been used so loosely that it has become ineffective vernacular. The term has been misused and overused not only for medical, political, criminal justice, and economic purposes, but also for entertainment and amusement. Addiction derives from the Latin word *addicto*, meaning bound or devoted, or bondage to a practice. Compulsive drug users are typically labelled addicted, either to their substance or, more frequently, substances of choice, without appreciating the entire latitude of the term. The DSM-5 uses neither the term physical nor psychological dependency, but rather, more generally, substance use disorders. The focus of the DSM-5 is on cognitive, behavioural, and physiological symptoms that indicate continued substance use despite problems arising due to the use of psychoactive drugs.[17]

Sussman and Sussman,[18] in a review of the literature, found five primary themes repeated in discussing the idea of addiction:

- feeling different from others who were using the drug
- preoccupation with drug use

- only temporary satiation before using more
- loss of control
- negative consequences of using

However, it was psychologist Stanton Peele[19-21] who in the twentieth century was the first to openly challenge a purely bio-psycho conceptualization of addiction. He claimed that addiction was not merely a chemical reaction. Addiction, for him, was a social experience that in and of itself could bring about dependency to a substance in an otherwise well person. He claimed that individuals could become dependent on a particular state of body and mind. For Peele, no substance was inherently addictive, nor was substance addiction a single phenomenon. Rather, he claimed that addiction occurs along a continuum, and even those at the extremes of addictiveness showed the capacity to act in other than an addicted way under appropriate circumstances. Social context was found by Peele to be a substantial determinant of substance use.

The incorporation of the social context of addiction draws from systems and ecological theory and takes into consideration the person-in-environment. By examining addiction as a biopsychosocial phenomenon, we not only consider the pharmacological characteristics of the psychoactive drug and the characteristics of the individual user, but also the environment in which the individual is using. What are the key environmental factors that contribute to the development and maintenance of drug-using behaviour? In a policing context, this would mean the individuals' community, if they feel marginalized as individuals or because of the group they belong to, be it based on race, culture, religion, sex, or sexual orientation. Thus, relapse—the return to drug use once individuals have stopped—is not merely a personal failing, or an indication of denial, or the fault of unmotivated users; it is also an effect of their situation. Addiction is not viewed merely as a neurobiological phenomenon dependent upon improper brain chemistry or a disease process.[22] In a longitudinal study of babies born during the crack epidemic of the late twentieth century in the United States, it was realized that it was not the mothers' drug use that led to developmental issues throughout childhood and adolescence, but rather issues of poverty. Children from lower socioeconomic communities whose mothers had and had not used crack experienced the same cognitive and academic delays compared to national averages.[23,24] Buchanan,[25] in his work in Liverpool, England, illustrated how stigmatization and social exclusion are components that are regularly excluded from the discussion of addiction, yet they are of significance to those who struggle daily with the reality of their psychoactive drug use.

Stigma serves as a substantive barrier to help-seeking for those with addiction issues, and the way the individual is described and self-identifies can either perpetuate or diminish stigmatizing attitudes, and as such increase or decrease the likelihood of persons seeking to change their situation. This is critical, given that those with drug-use issues are more stigmatized than individuals with other mental health issues, due in part to the pervasive belief that drug users are responsible for their behaviour. This stigma is perceived not only by the public but by health care providers and those misusing substances themselves.[26-29] Looking beyond blame and stigmatization, a more proactive approach is required.[30]

A holistic understanding of addiction also necessitates examining language. Historically in the addiction field, those abusing substances have been called addicts as opposed to a person with addiction, and this is where feeling labelled first takes hold. An addict is an object that is described by contributing factors, whereas when the expression person with an addiction is used, individuals misusing substances are placed first, rather than one of their attributes. While the addiction may be the central organizing principle of the person's life, it is still only one of many characteristics and behaviours: addiction is not the entire person. The dominant societal and media portrayals of addicts rather than people with an addiction further damage and dehumanize those misusing and abusing drugs, acting as a further barrier to accessing treatment.[31] The individual misusing drugs has many additional qualities and attributes, many of which are strengths that are often ignored rather than acknowledged and built upon in the addiction counselling relationship. While the expression a person with an addiction is much longer to both type and speak, it is much less oppressing. To use the label **addict** implies a judgement, has a negative connotation, and further contributes to making a person feel less a member of the community and thus less bound to societal rules.[32] This is further witnessed by the language employed when a drug user becomes abstinent; the person is now labelled clean, which of course means those who are not abstinent are dirty. The dominant perspective through which addiction is still viewed in Canada, and more so globally, is a moralistic one leading addiction to be primarily considered a criminal issue. Some have moved cautiously forward to claim addiction is a brain disease, though this too makes the phenomenon an individual's responsibility (e.g., an individual's failing). These views are inadequate, incomplete, and fail to offer holistic responses to the oppression of addiction. These paradigms not only minimize the individual and blame the victim, but also divert our attention away from the social context of use and the environments wherein addiction can exist. Figure 4.1 illustrates the intersection of the three distinct but interconnected components of addiction.

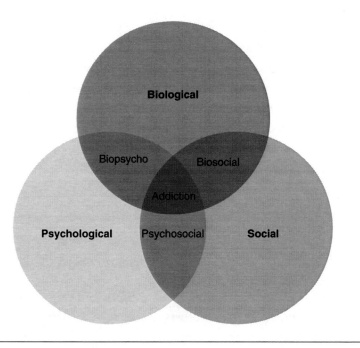

Figure 4.1: Holistic View of Addiction

Source: Authors' original work—Rick Csiernik.

AN OVERVIEW OF PSYCHOACTIVE DRUGS

Psychoactive drugs are categorized depending upon how they alter the central nervous system and thus in turn alter the autonomic nervous system (see table 4.1):

1. Slowed down, depressed
2. Sped up, stimulated
3. Disrupted so that the brain does not perceive what is occurring in the physical world, thus producing hallucinations

Depressants

Psychoactive drugs that are placed into the depressant family produce a reduction of arousal and activity in the **central nervous system** primarily through altering the neurotransmitter Gamma-Aminobutyric Acid (GABA). These drugs have a range of therapeutic uses that revolve around sedation and the reduction of anxiety—while used to enhance sleep, doing so also typically negatively impacts the dream cycle, which in turn has a negative impact upon mental health.

Depressants slow the body's metabolism and the functioning of the autonomic and central nervous systems. Mood enhancement occurs because of the disinhibiting properties of this drug group. While central nervous system depressants slow brain activity, they do not necessarily depress a person's mood. The members of this group are barbiturates, non-barbiturate sedative-hypnotics (NBSH), benzodiazepines, inhalants, including solvents, aerosols and anaesthetics, antihistamines, and alcohol.

Opioids

Opioids are a specific sub-group of central nervous system (CNS) depressants. However, rather than affecting GABA, they replace endorphins in the brain, the body's natural pain masker. **Opioids** are primarily used to treat pain, though they are also able to suppress coughs and resolve issues with diarrhea. As do other CNS depressants, opioids slow brain and central nervous system activity. Although Opioid Antagonists are not psychoactive drugs, they are important to be aware of because they reverse the respiratory depressant effects of opioids, which can be fatal, and have been used as pharmacological therapies for treating physical dependency.

Stimulants

Stimulants enhance the activity of the central nervous system, producing enhanced mood and increased vigilance, and postponing fatigue. Stimulants also suppress appetite, are used as decongestants, and can treat attention deficit disorder with hyperactivity (ADHD) in children.

Hallucinogens

Hallucinogens affect the central nervous system in a distinct manner when compared to both CNS depressants and stimulants. Rather than decreasing or increasing CNS activity to produce euphoria, **hallucinogens** disrupt the way in which the brain perceives stimuli, which creates a disconnect between the physical world and the user's perception. There are four distinct families of hallucinogens: three alter serotonin in producing their primary effects, while cannabis alters endocannabinoids in the brain. Thus, cannabis is the only hallucinogen that creates a physical dependency and thus is a fully addicting substance.

Table 4.1: Psychoactive Drugs by Family

Depressants
• Barbiturates (amobarbital, Nembutal, phenobarbital, Seconal)
• Non-Barbiturate Sedative Hypnotics (Mandrax, Placidyl, Quaalude)
• Benzodiazepines (Ativan, clonazepam, Rohypnol, Valium, Xanax)
• Antihistamines (Benadryl, Claratin, Gravol, Rohist, Sinutab)
• Solvents (benzene, gasoline, glue, nitrous oxide, toluene)
• Alcohol (beer, wine, spirits)
Opioids
• Codeine, Fentanyl, Methadone, Morphine, OxyContin
Opioid Antagonists
• Narcan, Naltrexone
Stimulants
• Amphetamines, bath salts, caffeine, cocaine, decongestants, khat, methamphetamine, nicotine, Ritalin
Hallucinogens
• Indolylalkylamines (Psilocybin, LSD)
No secondary psychoactive effects, only hallucinogenic effects
• Phenylethylamines (ecstasy, jimson weed, mescaline)
Hallucinogenic effects plus secondary stimulant effects
• Dissociative anaesthetics (ketamine and phencyclidine (PCP))
Depressant properties along with their hallucinatory effects
• Cannabis

Case Study: Mik's Agitation

You are called out to a residence following a phone call by a distraught woman who reports that her 19-year-old, Mik, is acting erratically. Ms. Sovary indicates that Mik had been to see the family doctor earlier in the day due to Mik telling her about feeling increasingly anxious, uncertain, and paranoid that others were watching everything that he was doing. Ms. Sovary also reported that Mik was having trouble sleeping, difficulty concentrating, is irritable and

continued

restless, always feels tense, and that she could not get Mik to stop pacing tonight. This distressed her and she called 911.

The difficulty a police officer faces when called out to a situation such as Mik presents is that there is no way of knowing what substance(s) a person has taken or if there is an ongoing interaction with prescription medicine and illicit or recreational drugs, or even if there has been no psychoactive drug use and it is a mental health issue that is manifesting itself. The effects of depressants and opioids can look similar to the withdrawal from some stimulants, while the effects of stimulants can look like severe withdrawal from alcohol or other potent CNS depressants. To further complicate matters, even if you ask what drugs Mik has taken and you are given an honest response, Mik may think it was ecstasy when in fact what he consumed was ketamine.

Commentary

The appropriate response to Mik is the same as with any other crisis: ensure the safety of individuals and those around them. All psychoactive drugs alter the central nervous system and thus alter who the person is. They affect executive brain functioning to varying degrees, which means that engaging in a logical and rational conversation is not always possible, and Mik might not respond in an appropriate manner when asked simple questions. Communication skills and comprehension are impaired with the use of psychoactive drugs. Since you cannot tell what drug a person has consumed by simply observing behaviour, your response in each case must take into consideration all the situational factors you face when entering Mik's house. What is vital to keep in mind is that when you enter the Sovary home, this is a health emergency and not a criminal situation, and your goal is to keep it that way.

Questions

1. What questions can you ask the person or family members to determine if prescription, recreational, or illicit drugs were used?
2. What sorts of behaviours can you observe if someone is under the influence of drugs?

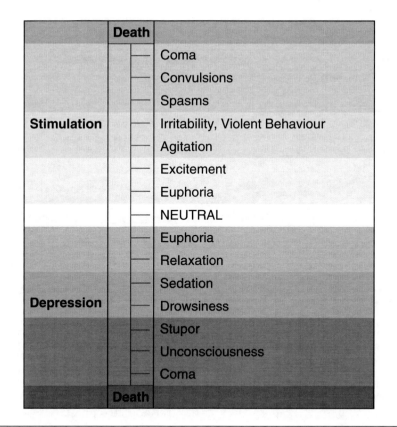

Figure 4.2: Effects of Central Nervous System Depressants and Stimulants

Source: Authors' original work—Rick Csiernik.

THE PROCESS OF DRUG USE

The process from initial contact with a drug to addiction, while not complex, is typically a lengthy progression (figure 4.3). Among adult first-time treatment admissions in the United States, an average of 15.6 years elapses between the first use of the primary substance of abuse and treatment entry.[9] Regardless of why a person first tries a drug, initial contact is the entry phase. Some users stop after an initial experimentation phase or at the integrated use level. Integrated use is the casual and/or occasional drink, smoke, or toke, and drug use remains at a controlled level. Integrated or experimental use can both, however, lead to excessive use. When individuals begin using a drug at a level that is excessive to their physical, psychological, or social well-being, one of four outcomes is possible: 1) individuals seek assistance to stop on their own; 2) a return to the integrated phase

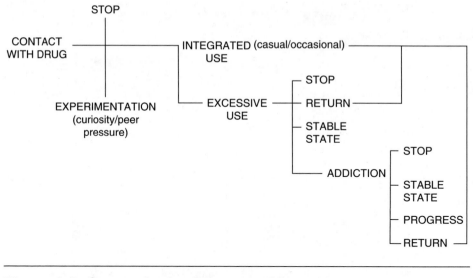

Figure 4.3: Stages in the Process of Drug Use

Source: Authors' original work—Rick Csiernik.

may occur; 3) individuals might remain at the excessive level of drug use, with its associated problems; 4) individuals can move on to the addicted phase. As in the excessive use phase, four alternatives exist in the addicted phase:

1. Stop: Successfully ending drug use typically entails seeking external assistance, which can be professional, through self-help groups, or a combination of the two. The model of the **continuum of care** presented in figure 4.4 introduces the various resources available to assist individuals in stopping their use of psychoactive drugs;

2. Stable State: This involves drug substitution, where an individual switches from smoking tobacco to wearing a nicotine patch but never weans off the patch, or a person moving from using OxyContin to methadone or Suboxone. In these instances, the person is still physically dependent on the drug and psychologically dependent on using the substance; it is just a different drug.

3. Progress: Progression in one's addiction means increasing the disorganization in the person's life affecting all facets, as well as having negative implications for families, workplaces, the health care system, and often the criminal justice system—and ultimately ending in premature death.

4. Return to a Stable State: This is the most controversial component of the entire model and states that once individuals have developed a physical and psychological dependency to a psychoactive agent, they can now

use at a lower risk level. There are substantive ethical issues that come with counselling an addicted person to use less. While engaging in a harm-reduction process can address some of the concerns, using less alone is not equivalent to using in an integrated manner.

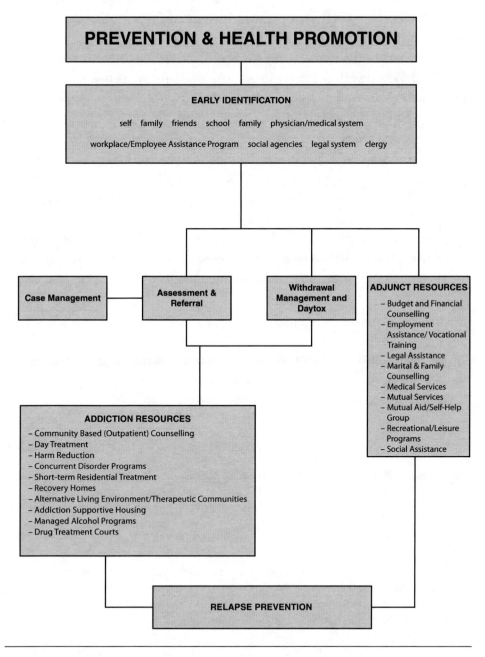

Figure 4.4: Substance Abuse Continuum of Care

Source: Authors' original work—Rick Csiernik.

SUMMARY

There is no facet of life that addiction does not touch. It is rare to meet anyone who does not know of someone whose life has been negatively affected by psychoactive substances. Police officers will face issues of drug use not only in their professional lives but in the lives of their co-workers and sometimes in their own lives. This is acknowledged, as nearly every police service has Employee and Family Assistance Programs (EFAP) in place as a paid benefit to deal not only with drug use but with the stress that policing entails. Addiction can enter your own space just as easily as it enters those that you will encounter in your careers.

This chapter has attempted to provide facts and information to assist you in moving beyond the stereotypes that accompany this area of practice, including the shame and guilt of being "an addict." No one you will encounter in your role as a police officer set out to become addicted to a substance. Even though their actions led individuals to societally unacceptable behaviour, as police officers you can still understand how something seemingly innocuous can become the central principle of the individual's life. Becoming familiar with the treatment options for individuals with SUDs can help you become a more effective officer, one with the empathy and competence to manage situations like Mik's during your career.

REFLECTION QUESTIONS

1.   Define SUD and identify when substance use becomes a clinical issue.
2.   Describe the holistic view of addiction.
3.   What are some resources to obtain help with addiction?

REFERENCES

1.   Julien RM. A primer of drug action: a concise nontechnical guide to the actions, uses, and side effects of psychoactive drugs. Revised and updated. Holt Paperbacks; 2013.
2.   Le Dain Commission. Final report of the commission of inquiry into the non-medical use of drugs. Ottawa; 1973.
3.   Csiernik R. Substance use and abuse: everything matters. Toronto: Canadian Scholars Press; 2016.
4.   Pittenger C. Disorders of memory and plasticity in psychiatric disease. Dialogues in clinical neuroscience [Internet]. 2013;15(4):455–63. Available from: PMCID: PMC3898683
5.   Nyberg F. Cognitive impairments in drug addicts. INTECH Open Access Publisher; 2012.
6.   Miller-Day MA, Alberts J, Hecht ML, Trost MR, Krizek RL. Adolescent relationships and drug use. Psychology Press; 2014.
7.   International Narcotics Control Board. Economic consequences of drug abuse. Annual Report. United Nations; 2013.

8. Kellen A, Powers L, Birnbaum R. Drug use, addiction and the criminal justice system. In: Csiernik R, Rowe WS, editors. Responding to the oppression of addiction. 3rd ed. Toronto: Canadian Scholars Press; 2017.

9. Substance Abuse and Mental Health Administration. Treatment episode data set report: length of time from first use to adult treatment admission. Rockville, MD: SAMSHA; 2011.

10. Hovarth T, Misra K, Epner AK, Cooper M. Developmental model of addiction and recovery implications [Internet]. March 24, 2016. Available from: https://www.mentalhelp.net/articles/developmental-model-of-addiction-and-recovery-implications/

11. Balster RL, Walsh S. Cross-Tolerance. Encyclopedia of psychopharmacology. Berlin: Springer; 2010. p. 362.

12. Statistics Canada. Sales of alcohol beverages by volume, value and per capita 15 years and over, fiscal years ended March 31. Stats Can [Internet]; 2017. Available from: http://www.statcan.gc.ca/daily-quotidien/170502/dq170502a-eng.htm

13. Health Canada. Canadian tobacco, alcohol and drugs survey: 2015 summary [Internet]. 2017. Available from: https://www.canada.ca/en/health-canada/services/canadian-tobacco-alcohol-drugs-survey/2015-summary.html

14. Perrault S. Impaired driving in Canada, 2015. Statistics Canada catalogue number 85-002-x. Ottawa: Statistics Canada; 2016.

15. Morissette C. The underground economy in Canada, 1992–2011; 13-604-M, number 73. Ottawa: Statistics Canada; 2015.

16. Kraus D, Castonguay L, Boswell J, Nordberg S, Hayes J. Therapist effectiveness: implications for accountability and patient care. Psychotherapy Research. 2011;21(3):267–76.

17. American Psychiatric Association. Diagnostic and statistical manual of mental disorders (DSM-5). American Psychiatric Pub; 2013 May 22.

18. Sussman S, Sussman A. Considering the definition of addiction. Environmental Research and Public Health. 2011;8(10):4025–38.

19. Peele S. The science of experience. Toronto: Lexington Books; 1983.

20. Peele S. What treatment for addiction can do and what it can't; what treatment for addiction should do and what it shouldn't. Journal of Substance Abuse Treatment. 1985;2(4):225–8. Available from: PMID: 3834103

21. Peele S. Ain't misbehavin' – addiction has become an all purpose excuse. The Sciences. 1989;29(4):14–21. Available from: DOI: 10.1002/j.2326-1951.1989.tb02166.x

22. Graham D, Young R, Vlach L, Wood A. Addiction as a complex social process: an action theoretical perspective. Addiction Research and Theory [Internet]. 2008;16(2):121–33. Available from: http://dx.doi.org/10.1080/16066350701794543

23. Hurt H, Brodsky N, Roth H, Malmud E, Giannetta J. School performance of children with gestational cocaine exposure. Neurotoxiology and Teratology. 2005;27(2):203–11. Available from: DOI: 10.1016/j.ntt.2004.10.006

24. Hurt H, Giannetta J, Korczkowski M, Hoang A, Tang K, Beancourt L, Detre J, et al. Functional magnetic resonance imaging and working memory in adolescents with gestational cocaine exposure. Journal of Pediatrics. 2008;152(3):371–7.

25. Buchanan J. Tackling problem drug use: a new conceptual framework. Social Work in Mental Health [Internet]. 2004;2(2/3):117–38. Available from https://julianbuchanan.wordpress.com/2011/11/17/tackling-problem-drug-use-a-new-conceptual-framework-by-julian-buchanan/

26. Hamilton H, Mann R, Noh S. Adolescent immigrant generation and stigmatizing attitudes toward drug addiction. Addiction Research and Theory [Internet]. 2011;19(4):344–51. Available from: http://dx.doi.org/10.3109/16066359.2010.530713

27. Hunte H, Finlayson T. The relationship between perceived discrimination and psychotherapeutic and illicit drug misuse in Chicago, IL, USA. Journal of Urban Health. 2013;90(6):1112–29. Available from: DOI: 10.1007/s11524-013-9822-y

28. Keyes KM, Hatzenbuehler ML, McLaughlin KA, Link B, Olfson M, Grant BF, et al. Stigma and treatment for alcohol disorders in the United States. American Journal of Epidemiology. 2010 Dec 15;172(12):1364–72. Available from: DOI: 10.1093/aje/kwq304

29. van Boekel L, Brouwers E, van Weeghel J, Garretsen H. Comparing stigmatising attitudes towards people with substance use disorders between the general public, GPs, mental health and addiction specialists and clients. Social Psychiatry. 2015;61(6):539–49.

30. Livingston JD, Milne T, Fang ML, Amari E. The effectiveness of interventions for reducing stigma related to substance use disorders: a systematic review. Addiction. 2012;107: 39-50. Available from: DOI:10.1111/j.1360-0443.2011.03601.x

31. Cortina S. Stigmatizing harm reduction through language: a case study into the use of "addict" and opposition to supervised injection sites in Canada. Addictions Nursing. 2013;24(2):102–7. DOI: 10.1097/JAN.0b013e3182929466

32. Pearson M. Stigma and substance use: a methodological review [Internet]. 2015. Available from: http://sites.nationalacademies.org/cs/groups/dbassesite/documents/webpage/dbasse_170044.pdf

CHAPTER 5

Antisocial and Other Personality Disorders

Andrew M. Haag, *Alberta Health Services, University of Alberta Psychiatry Department*

LEARNING OBJECTIVES

1. Describe antisocial personality disorder in the context of other personality disorders noted in the Diagnostic and Statistical Manual
2. Demonstrate an understanding that antisocial personality is both similar and distinct from psychopathy
3. Recognize that antisocial personality disorder is found in numerous populations
4. Interpret current research in terms of prevention and treatment for antisocial personality disorder

INTRODUCTION

The term **personality** typically refers to consistent patterns of thinking, feeling, and behaving,[1] and personality is typically thought of as being relatively stable over time.[2,3] Within this context, personality theory has traditionally aimed at developing an inclusive description of a particular person within the context of individual-differences.[4]

Modern ideas of Personality Disorders (PDs) first appeared with the publication of the Diagnostic and Statistical Manual III in 1980.[5] The DSM-III described personality disorders as constellations of personality traits that were inflexible and maladaptive. The most recent version of the Diagnostic and Statistical Manual, the 5th edition (DSM-5), defines a **personality disorder** as "an enduring pattern of inner experience and behaviour that deviates markedly from the expectations of the individual's culture, is pervasive and inflexible, has an onset in adolescence or early adulthood, is stable over time, and leads to distress or impairment."[6] Table 5.1 comes directly from the DSM descriptions of 10 different personality disorders organized into three clusters.

It is noted that persons with a personality disorder will often be comorbid for other personality disorders.[7] In other words, persons with one personality disorder will also often meet the diagnostic criteria for other personality disorders.

ARE PERSONALITY DISORDERS DIMENSIONAL OR CATEGORICAL?

For years, there has been a debate in the literature about whether a personality disorder is best understood as being categorical (the current DSM method for

Table 5.1: DSM-5 Personality Disorders

Cluster A	Paranoid	a pattern of distrust and suspiciousness such that others' motives are interpreted as malevolent.
	Schizoid	a pattern of detachment from social relationships and a restricted range of emotional expression.
	Schizotypal	a pattern of acute discomfort in close relationships, cognitive or perceptual distortions, and eccentricities of behaviour.
Cluster B	Antisocial	a pattern of disregard for, and violation of, the rights of others.
	Borderline	a pattern of instability in interpersonal relationships, self-image, and affects, and marked impulsivity.
	Histrionic	a pattern of excessive emotionality and attention seeking.
	Narcissistic	a pattern of grandiosity, need for admiration, and lack of empathy.
Cluster C	Avoidant	a pattern of social inhibition, feelings of inadequacy, and hypersensitivity to negative evaluation.
	Dependent	a pattern of submissive and clinging behaviour related to an excessive need to be taken care of.
	Obsessive-compulsive	a pattern of preoccupation with orderliness, perfectionism, and control.

diagnosing personality disorders) or dimensional.[5] Stated differently, there has been a debate in the literature about whether the distinction between different personality disorders are matters of *degree* (dimension) or *kind* (categorical). Are personality disorders an extreme variant of *normal* personality or are they *unique* disorders? It should be noted that there is no consensus in the literature on this matter. Under a categorical model, a personality disorder is coded as being present or absent.[6] However, in any one personality disorder, a person must satisfy a subset of the criteria in order to meet the diagnostic threshold for the respective personality disorder.[5] In other words, for a personality disorder to be diagnosed, one must meet an adequate cut score of symptoms. The consequence of having cut scores is that there is great heterogeneity within any one personality disorder. For instance, there are 126 ways to meet diagnostic criteria for borderline personality disorder.[5] Furthermore, the DSM does not rate how fully a person meets a diagnosis. One is simply identified as having or not having the diagnosis. However, the latest version of the DSM does acknowledge that seeing personality disorders on a continuum (dimensional) is an alternative perspective to viewing personality disorders.[6]

An advantage of the categorical system is that it helps to clarify who needs treatment and who does not. From this perspective, persons who meet a diagnosis require treatment and persons who do not would be less inclined to be referred for treatment.[5] Another advantage in providing a diagnosis is greater efficiency and ease of communication among professionals. However, both of the above points can also be problematic. For instance, if a person fell short of a personality disorder diagnosis because they were lacking a single potential criterion, would this somehow imply that this person would not benefit from treatment? Moreover, given the heterogeneity of personality disorders, it could be argued that efficiency of communication may fall short of the goal of optimal communication.

ANTISOCIAL PERSONALITY DISORDER (ASPD)

Within the context of health, people with **Antisocial Personality Disorder** (ASPD) are among the most dramatic individuals that mental health professionals may encounter in their practice.[8] ASPD was first identified as a medical problem at the start of the nineteenth century.[8,9] However, descriptions of persons with antisocial tendencies can be found in much of recorded history.[10] Descriptions consistent with ASPD have had several names over the years. Philippe Pinel[11] discussed a condition he labelled *manie sans délire* (mania without delirium). Persons with this condition were said to have unusual emotional responses and impulsive rages; however, they did not have deficits in reasoning ability.[8,11] Other labels have included *moral insanity, egopathy, psychopathy, sociopathy,* or *dyssocial personality disorder*; however, it should be clarified that although these terms overlap, they have distinct constructs.[6,12,13]

ASPD IN THE DSM-5

The cardinal feature of ASPD is contained in Criterion A of the DSM-5 criteria: the pervasive pattern of disregard for (violation of) the rights of others that is consistent over the life course.[6] In order to receive a diagnosis of ASPD, one must be at least 18 years of age at the time of assessment and have a history of conduct disorder prior to the age of 15 years.[6] To meet the criteria for **conduct disorder**, one must have had a consistent pattern of behaviour that involved the violation of the basic rights of others or the violation of age-appropriate societal norms/rules. In ASPD, the rule/societal violations observed in childhood/adolescence continue to be displayed in adulthood. Some of these individuals repeatedly involve themselves in behaviours/activities that are grounds for arrest and/or demonstrate a reckless disregard for the safety of themselves or others. Such individuals can be oblivious of the well-being or desires of other people; additionally, persons

Table 5.2: DSM-5 Diagnostic Criteria of ASPD

A. A pervasive pattern of disregard for and violation of the rights of others, occurring since age 15 years, as indicated by three (or more) of the following:
1. Failure to conform to social norms with respect to lawful behaviours, as indicated by repeatedly performing acts that are grounds for arrest.
2. Deceitfulness, as indicated by repeated lying, use of aliases, or conning others for personal profit or pleasure.
3. Impulsivity or failure to plan ahead.
4. Irritability and aggressiveness, as indicated by repeated physical fights or assaults.
5. Reckless disregard for safety of self or others.
6. Consistent irresponsibility, as indicated by repeated failure to sustain consistent work behaviour or honour financial obligations.
7. Lack of remorse, as indicated by being indifferent to or rationalizing having hurt, mistreated, or stolen from another.

B. The individual is at least age 18 years

C. There is evidence of conduct disorder with onset before age 15 years

D. The occurrence of antisocial behaviour is not exclusively during the course of schizophrenia or bipolar disorder

with ASPD are often deceitful and manipulative.[8,14] The goal of the deceit is typically personal profit or pleasure (e.g., to obtain money, sex, or power). Such persons may repeatedly lie, use an alias, con others, or malinger. There is often a pattern of **impulsivity** (non-informed decisions characterized by recklessness and risk-taking behaviours with no consideration of consequences); consequently, it may be the case that this person has difficulty in planning ahead or fails to plan altogether. Exceptionally expeditious decisions are often normative and without meaningful forethought or a consideration of the consequences of one's actions. Individuals with ASPD will make frequent employment, residential, or relationship changes, and are noted as irritable and aggressive; physically assaultive behaviour is common (see section below on criminality). Such persons will often fail to maintain long-term commitments. When others are harmed, typically there will be little remorse demonstrated for the consequences of their actions; indeed, apathy towards other persons is common.

ASPD AND PSYCHOPATHY

One condition that is sometimes incorrectly assumed to be synonymous with ASPD is psychopathy. The concept of **psychopathy** was first articulated by Cleckley (1941) in his classic work, *The Mask of Sanity*.[15] From Cleckley's perspective, psychopaths were intelligent but lacked affect and shame, were superficially charming and irresponsible, and had inadequate motivation.[5] Psychologist Robert Hare has been involved in systemic research pertaining to the assessment and diagnosis of psychopathy. Hare constructed a measure of psychopathy entitled the *Psychopathy Checklist*,[16,17] a widely used 20-item rating form for the assessment of psychopathy. The measure is currently in the second edition, the Psychopathy Checklist – Revised (PCL-R).

Psychopathy Checklist – Revised (PCL-R).

The PCL-R has been found to have a two-factor structure.[16] These factors can then be further sub-divided into four additional facets. The first factor contains items highlighting emotional and interpersonal symptoms noted on the PCL-R. The second factor consists of items pertaining to social deviance and antisocial behaviour. One should note that the diagnosis of ASPD does have some overlap with the construct of psychopathy.[5] However, ASPD emphasizes antisocial/criminal behaviours and places less emphasis on personality traits than psychopathy. Given this reality, antisocial personality has a greater prevalence than psychopathy.

It should be noted that there is an ongoing debate about whether psychopathy and ASPD are really two distinct disorders.[18,19] Moreover, the scant literature concerning ASPD is completely independent of the psychopathy literature.[20] In other words, there is little published research examining persons with ASPD while excluding those who meet diagnostic criteria for psychopathy.[20] This dearth of research pertaining to ASPD is surprising, considering the majority of incarcerated offenders have this disorder.[21] In addition, persons with ASPD can be a significant burden to society. For instance, they have high absenteeism in the workforce and cause harm/distress to others. Moreover, many demonstrate, from early adolescence onwards, serious patterns of substance abuse and dependence.[22,23] In addition, males and females with ASPD often exhibit inadequate parenting practices.[24]

PREVALENCE

The DSM notes that the 12-month prevalence rate of ASPD is between 0.2% and 3.3%.[6,7,25,26] Data acquired from individuals in Edmonton, Alberta, reveal that about 3% of adults meet the criteria for ASPD.[27] When considering gender, the prevalence rates are typically higher for males than females (3% in males and less than 1% in females).[28] There is a disproportionately high prevalence of ASPD (greater than 70%) in substance abuse clinics, prisons, and other forensic settings.[29,30] There is also a higher prevalence among persons who are disadvantaged by adverse socioeconomic or sociocultural factors.

When comparing ASPD to psychopathy, the prevalence of psychopathy in males, according to the Cleckley/Hare criteria, is noted to be about 1%.[31] When considering forensic settings, ASPD is observed in 50% to 80% of cases and psychopathy at a rate of about 15% to 25%.[16] About one-third of individuals who meet the criteria of ASPD exceed the PCL-R cut-off for psychopathy.

As noted earlier, in incarcerated samples, a diagnosis of ASPD is common. Data from an international review study considered the prevalence of mental disorders among representative samples of convicted offenders.[21] It was noted that 47% of males and 21% of females obtained a diagnosis of ASPD in convicted samples.[21] However, prisoner studies have not consistently found that ASPD is associated with crimes of violence. Data involving federally sentenced persons from Quebec (i.e., two years or longer) compared persons with ASPD to those without the diagnosis and found that those with ASPD had more convictions in general but equivalent quantities of violent offences.[32] It should be noted that this study did not exclude persons who met the diagnosis of psychopathy.

DEVELOPMENT AND COURSE

ASPD has a chronic course over an individual's lifetime; however, it may become less manifest or possibly remit with age.[6] The decreased manifestation of ASPD is often observable by the fourth decade of life, particularly in terms of criminal behaviour and substance use. In general, longitudinal and cross-sectional investigations of population cohorts provide evidence that ASPD has its onset in childhood and persists across the lifespan.[33-35] Moreover, younger age of onset and greater number of symptoms are related to an increased likelihood that a conduct disorder will develop into ASPD in adulthood.[34] Prospectively (that is, in foresight), approximately half of children with conduct disorder will develop ASPD.[36]

INFLUENTIAL FACTORS OF ASPD

Biological Considerations with ASPD

ASPD is observed at higher rates among first-degree biological relatives when compared to the general population.[6] There is a higher concordance rate with female relatives when compared to male relatives. The DSM reports that adoption data suggest that both genetic and environmental factors contribute to the development of ASPD. In other words, "both adopted and biological children of parents with ASPD have an increased risk of developing ASPD, somatic symptom disorder, and substance use disorders."[6] When offspring are adopted, they resemble their biological parents more than their adoptive parents; however, the adoptive family environment does influence the risk of developing ASPD. Parenting practices are noted to impact genetic vulnerability.[37,38] Moreover, genetic vulnerability is also impacted during pregnancy by factors such as maternal smoking[39] and/or malnutrition.[40]

Social Influences of ASPD

The DSM reports that ASPD is likely associated with low socioeconomic status and residing in urban environments.[6] However, given that antisocial behaviour may actually be protective behaviour in some settings, an assessor should be mindful of the context in which antisocial behaviour is occurring. Examining the correlates of antisocial behaviour, Gendreau et al.[41] found that among six groups of risk factors, antisocial attitudes/associates had the strongest correlation with criminal conduct ($r = 0.22$). Similar findings were obtained in a subsequent meta-analysis, including 133 studies to determine the best predictor domains of recidivism in the community.[41] Indeed, of the variables considered, one's companions was the variable with the second highest predictive strength. Antisocial attitudes and antisocial associates have theoretical and empirical ties.[42]

It is noted that the modelling/learning of antisocial behaviour is more likely to occur in environments with higher noted frequencies of these types of behaviour or in environments that support anti-sociality and violence.[43] **Shared environmental factors** such as poor supervision from parents, single-parent households, antisocial parents, siblings who are delinquent, parental conflict, harsh discipline, neglect, large family size, and having a young and/or depressed mother are risk factors for antisocial behaviour.[44] Non-shared environmental influences can also contribute to anti-sociality. **Non-shared environmental factors** include delinquent peers, an individual's social and academic experiences, sexual abuse, or sustaining an injury (e.g., a head injury) can all potentially contribute to antisocial behaviour.[45]

Psychological Influences of ASPD

Psychological studies have proposed that persons with ASPD have a deficiency in internalizing the standards of the society.[46,47] Beck and Freeman suggested that there are developmental delays in the moral maturity and cognitive functioning of antisocial individuals.[48] Antisocial persons have been found to struggle with empathic ability, i.e., perceiving from another person's point of view. Antisocial persons will often perceive themselves as loners, autonomous, and strong.[47] It is also fairly common for antisocial persons to express the view that they have been abused and mistreated by society.[47] Other persons may be perceived as worthy of exploitation or weak/vulnerable.[48] Those with ASPD will often rely on themselves and distrust others, as they fear being exploited or humiliated.[47]

In terms of global intellectual findings, many antisocial individuals are intact in most areas of intelligence, memory, and executive ability.[45] Indeed, we find a positive correlation between violence and intelligence scores in psychopathic adults.[49] Similar findings are noted in terms of positive relationships with verbal, analytic, creative, and practical abilities in children.[50] That being said, the characteristics of lack of successful planning and frequent impulsive behaviour are suggestive of subtle cognitive deficits.[45] For instance, antisocial persons may experience deficits in sustained attention, response modulation, and preservation.[51-52] In particular, psychopaths will continue behaviours even when doing so is maladaptive; moreover, they will often fail to consider appropriate contextual information useful for choosing alternate responses.[53]

CRIMINALITY

The most difficult issue regarding ASPD from the perspective of clinical management is the disproportionate rate of violent behaviour within this population. This concern is particularly salient for those people assessed as being psychopathic.[54] Psychopathic criminals are typically three to five times more violent than non-psychopathic criminals;[16] however, to be clear, even the most violent persons are not violent most of the time. Measurement of violence risk in both psychiatric and offender populations has found that psychopathy typically accounts for the largest proportion of explainable variance when it comes to violent behaviour.

A Danish birth cohort studied over 320,000 individuals up to the age of 43 years.[55] Persons with a diagnosis of ASPD relative to those with no psychiatric admission had a relative risk of conviction for a violent crime of 7.2 (95% CI 6.5-8.0) for males and 12.1 (95% CI 8.8-16.9) for females. It is thought that these numbers likely underestimated actual offending rates, as the persons in this study were receiving a *hospital* diagnosis of ASPD.

When dealing with violent behaviour, it is important to consider different pathways to violence/aggression; Reis[56] distinguished between "affective" and "predatory" aggression.[57-62] Affective (emotional, reactive) aggression is violence that is accompanied by high levels of arousal (i.e., elevations in the sympathetic nervous system) and emotion. Such aggression is typically a reaction to an imminent threat. **Predatory aggression** (otherwise known as instrumental aggression) is violence that is accompanied by little arousal. The violence is emotionless, planned, and purposeful. Research has shown that psychopathic criminals are more likely than other criminals to engage in both affective and predatory violence.[63-67]

TREATMENT

People with a diagnosis of ASPD rarely seek medical assistance for their personality disorder.[68] More specifically, about one in seven will be open enough to discuss their symptoms with a doctor.[69] Concurrent problems will often bring someone with ASPD to the attention of health care providers; moreover, antisocial behaviour, even in one's early years, is predictive of poor prognosis in treatment and treatment attrition.[70,71] In a study of Canadian offenders that examined the relationship between psychopathy, therapeutic change, and violent recidivism, 152 high-risk violent offenders were treated in a high-intensity violence reduction program.[72] Positive therapeutic change was found to have a negative correlation with the PCL-R. In other words, the higher one's PCL-R score (which is related to psychopathy), the less successful one would be in refraining from violence following treatment. However, to be fair, observed therapeutic change was significantly associated with reductions in violent recidivism after controlling for psychopathy.[72]

Even if one is optimistic that treating those with ASPD is possible/effective, treatment efforts with ASPD are notoriously difficult. Many psychiatrists/psychologists are reluctant to treat patients with ASPD because of the widespread belief that such patients are untreatable.[73] There is some evidence, however, that ASPD may, in certain cases, be treatable. To date, the primary treatment for ASPD has been psychological therapy.[74-76] However, there have been only a small number of high-quality treatment trials pertaining to persons with ASPD; hence, it is reasonable to state that the evidence base to draw upon regarding effective treatments is limited.[74-76] In general, the programs that have the largest effect sizes adhere to the risk-need-responsivity model.[77,78] Such programs will focus on (1) risk, by targeting persons at greatest risk of reoffending, (2) need, by addressing empirically established dynamic criminogenic risk factors, and (3) responsivity, by delivering interventions in a such a way that the person with ASPD can be maximally engaged in the treatment process.[68] A review of the literature on rehabilitating general, psychopathic, and high-risk offenders[79] provides some optimism that intensive, targeted, and appropriate psychosocial interventions based on risk-need-responsivity principles have the potential to reduce recidivism risk in psychopathic individuals. Lower recidivism rates are said to be more likely when cognitive-behavioural techniques are applied to address risk for recidivism.[68] Moreover, in terms of therapeutic alliance, the treatment relationship between offender and provider must be characterized by caring, fair, trustworthy, and authoritative styles.[79] Interventions that were primarily punitive or focused on control/surveillance had the potential to increase the risk of recidivism in the absence of other rehabilitative efforts. Moreover, it should be noted that the more rigorous the study design, the less likely it is that treatment will be shown to be effective. Indeed, relatively recent review studies found no high-quality evidence for ASPD treatment.[76,80-82]

A review of the treatment research pertaining to those diagnosed with psychopathy (arguably the most severe form of ASPD) has challenged the view that psychopathy per se is always untreatable.[13,81] D'Silva et al.[83] reviewed ten studies of the treatment of psychopaths, four of which concluded that psychopaths respond poorly to treatment; however, another four studies suggested the opposite. Salekin et al. reported three out of eight studies with positive treatment outcomes.[82] Moreover, there is evidence that the treatment of psychopathic youths is more promising than that of those being treated later in life, with six out of eight studies showing treatment benefits.[68] Globally, although there is some evidence that psychopathy may be somewhat treatable, the evidence for any given treatment is minimal.[18]

PREVENTION

Given that (1) the diagnostic criteria for ASPD stipulates that for a diagnosis to be made there must be evidence that the person being assessed had conduct disorder in childhood,[6] (2) there is evidence to suggest that ASPD impacts people over most of their life-course trajectory,[33-35] and (3) the presence of pessimism regarding treatment of ASPD in adults,[73] there has been an emphasis in the literature on interventions for children/families designed to prevent conduct disorder and, subsequently, ASPD. Globally, the literature supports the following variables as risk factors for developing ASPD: (1) child behaviour problems at preschool, middle school, and adolescence, (2) the presence of Attention Deficit Hyperactivity Disorder (ADHD), (3) parenting styles, parents' antisocial behaviour, and parental disharmony/separation, and (4) social deprivation.[73] Thus it would seem reasonable that prevention efforts targeting the above factors and/or other factors related to conduct disorders in children could have the potential to reduce ASPD occurrence and/or severity.[84]

Globally, prevention programs adopt one of three prevention strategies. Each strategy is defined by the group targeted: (1) universal, (2) selected, and (3) indicated. **Universal strategies,** or primary prevention strategies, are directed at the general population.[73] **Selected prevention strategies** (an idea similar to secondary prevention) are applied to people who are at risk of developing the disorder or who may show early signs. Such strategies attempt to address risk factors and maximize the potential for resilience. **Indicated intervention strategies** (similar to tertiary prevention) are aimed at persons in whom prodromal symptoms of the disorder are already present but do not yet have the disorder fully developed. When these prevention strategies are subject to research evaluation, quasi-experimental investigations tend to produce promising findings; however, once more rigorous research methodology designs are employed, the positive results do not tend to stand up.[85] Moreover, there is also the issue of follow-up time, in that few universal/primary prevention studies check in with persons long enough to know if ASPD is actually prevented by their strategies.[73,85] It is generally thought to be too early to assess the success of prevention programs addressing ASPD.[8] Nonetheless, given the major issues regarding effective treatment for adults, it is suggested that prevention may be one of the most effective approaches to this problem.

Although there are many issues in diagnosing and treating persons with ASPD, this is an area that is fertile ground for future research. Indeed, to date, there have been few high-quality studies of persons with ASPD. With an increased emphasis on approaches based on established theory and informed by the risk-need-responsivity model, it is hoped that (1) empirically validated means of ASPD prevention can be established and (2) research will be able to inform better means of treating/managing ASPD in the future.

Case Study: Tyson

Tyson is a 35-year-old with an extensive criminal record dating back to the age of 13 years. He has a criminal record that includes sexual assault, robbery, drug offences, escaping lawful custody, and assault with a weapon. Tyson has received multiple sentences involving probation or other forms of conditional release. He has often been required to attend various types of therapy as a condition of his being in the community. He has attended therapy but stated explicitly that he was there because the courts required him to be there. Tyson has worked in various labour positions over the years, with the longest single period of employment lasting six months at a pulp and paper mill. Tyson has been fired from three jobs: twice because he failed to show up for work after becoming intoxicated and once because he was stealing tools from his job site. Tyson sold these tools to "make an extra buck." When asked about his theft, he stated, "the business was insured; what's the big deal? No one was hurt." Tyson does not have anyone he would consider a real friend; however, he has many acquaintances. He lived with one female for about six months but left after "she was cheating on me with all my friends." Tyson thinks that his common-law partner might have become pregnant, but has no interest in knowing if the child was his, as she was a "whore." Tyson stated that he has one-night stands about once a week with females and that he gets drunk and high with them.

Questions

1. Let's say Tyson is being seen after he was just convicted for a robbery and will be in an institution for the next few years; what could be done with Tyson to minimize his odds of future violence upon returning to the community?
2. You are seeing Tyson while he is on parole/probation; what would you want to monitor? What would you recommend in terms of treatment? Where should he live?
3. What would need to be done for treatment/supervision to have the best chance of success with Tyson?

CRIMINAL BEHAVIOURS AND OTHER PERSONALITY DISORDERS

Impulsivity is tied to criminal behaviours due to recklessness and risk-taking. It is present in personality disorders other than ASPD.[86,87] Impulsivity is often present in borderline, histrionic, and narcissistic personality disorder,[6,86,87] with a higher association to substance use among borderline, narcissistic, and ASPD, making these PDs more of a risk in terms of violent and eruptive aggression.[6,88] Often the intersection of a personality disorder and criminal behaviour is difficult to decipher (even with ASPD, due to manipulative and cunning behaviours).[6] Other times, there is a clear connection between criminal behaviour and personality disorders in terms of entitlement and aggression, especially with narcissistic, antisocial, and borderline PD.[88,89] Because personality disorders are a life-long and rigid behaviour pattern, identifying impulsive behaviours helps us understand recklessness, recidivism, and potential for crime.

SUMMARY

This chapter sought to provide a brief overview of the personality disorders noted in the Diagnostic and Statistical Manual, with a special emphasis on ASPD. Various taxonomical approaches to the diagnosis of personality disorders were discussed, the diagnostic criteria for ASPD were reviewed, and ASPD was differentiated from psychopathy. It was noted that there are biological, environmental, social, and psychological correlates to ASPD. Criminal behaviour is often a complicating factor in dealing with ASPD. Moreover, it was shown that there is a dearth of quality data on the treatment of ASPD. Given the current state of the literature, it might be wise to work at preventing the development of ASPD. When one considers the impact of ASPD, not only on the directly impacted individual(s) but on society as a whole, it is axiomatic that this is an area that must be given serious and long-term research attention in terms of management/treatment.

REFLECTION QUESTIONS

1. Describe the core features of each of the personality disorders.
2. List the DSM-5 criteria for ASPD.
3. Discuss possible treatments and treatment outlooks for individuals with ASPD.

REFERENCES

1. Jones SE, Miller JD, Lynam DR. Personality, antisocial behavior, and aggression: a meta-analytic review. J Crim Justice [Internet]. Elsevier B. V.; 2011;39(4):329–37. Available from: http://dx.doi.org/10.1016/j.jcrimjus.2011.03.004
2. Roberts BW, DelVecchio WF. The rank-order consistency of personality traits from childhood to old age: A quantitative review of longitudinal studies. Psychol Bull. 2000;126:3–25.
3. West SG, Graziano WG. Long-term stability and change in personality: an introduction. J Pers. 1989;57(2):175–93.
4. Barratt ES. History of personality and intelligence theory and research. In: Saklofske DH, Zeidner M, editors. International handbook of personality and intelligence [Internet]. Boston: Springer US; 1995. p. 3–13. Available from: https://doi.org/10.1007/978-1-4757-5571-8_1
5. Trull TJ, Durrett CA. Categorical and dimensional models of personality disorder. Annu Rev Clin Psychol. 2005;1:355–80.
6. American Psychiatric Association. Diagnostic and statistical manual of mental disorders (DSM-5). American Psychiatric Pub; 2013 May 22.
7. Lenzenweger MF, Lane MC, Loranger AW, Kessler RC. DSM-IV personality disorders in the National Comorbidity Survey Replication. Biol Psychiatry. Elsevier; 2007;62(6):553–64.
8. Barlow DH, Durand VM, Stewart SH, Lalumière ML. Abnormal psychology: an integrative approach. 4th Can. ed. Toronto: Nelson; 2015.
9. Pinel P. A treatise on insanity. New York: Hafner; 1962.
10. Abdul-Hamid WK, Stein G. The Surpu: exorcism of antisocial personality disorder in ancient Mesopotamia. Ment Health Relig Cult. Taylor & Francis; 2013;16(7):671–85.
11. Charland LC. Science and morals in the affective psychopathology of Philippe Pinel. Hist Psychiatry. London: Sage Publications; 2010;21(1):38–53.
12. Kosson DS, Lorenz AR, Newman JP. Effects of comorbid psychopathy on criminal offending and emotion processing in male offenders with antisocial personality disorder. J Abnorm Psychol. American Psychological Association; 2006;115(4):798–806.
13. Hare RD, Hart SD, Harpur TJ. Psychopathy and the DSM-IV criteria for antisocial personality disorder. J Abnorm Psychol. American Psychological Association; 1991;100(3):391.

14. Widiger TA, Corbitt FM. Antisocial Personality Disorder. In: Livesley W, editor. The DSM-IV personality disorders. New York: Guilford Press; 1995. p. 103–26.
15. Cleckley H. The mask of sanity. St Louis: C. V. Mosby Co; 1955.
16. Hare RD. Manual for the revised psychopathy checklist. 2nd ed. Toronto: Multi-Health Systems; 2003.
17. Vien A, Beech AR. Psychopathy: theory, measurement, and treatment. Trauma Violence Abuse [Internet]. Sage Publications; 2006 Jul [cited 2012 Mar 25];7(3):155–74. Available from: http://www.ncbi.nlm.nih.gov/pubmed/16785285
18. Hare RD, Neumann CS, Widiger TA. Psychopathy. In: Widiger TA, editor. The Oxford handbook of personality disorders. New York: Oxford University Press; 2012. p. 478–504.
19. Lynam DR, Vachon DD. Antisocial personality disorder in DSM-5: Missteps and missed opportunities. Personal Disord Theory, Res Treat. Educational Publishing Foundation; 2012;3(4):483.
20. De Brito SA, Hodgins S. Antisocial personality disorder. Personality, personality disorder and violence. In: McMurran M, Howard R, editors. Personality, personality disorder, and risk of violence. 2009. p. 133–53.
21. Fazel S, Danesh J. Serious mental disorder in 23000 prisoners: a systematic review of 62 surveys. Lancet. 2002;359(9306):545–50.
22. Kessler RC, Nelson CB, McGonagle KA, Edlund MJ, Frank RG, Leaf PJ. The epidemiology of co-occurring addictive and mental disorders: implications for prevention and service utilization. Am J Orthopsychiatry. 1996;66(1):17–31.
23. Robins LN, McEvoy L. Conduct problems as predictors of substance abuse. In: Robins LN, Rutter M, editors. Straight and devious pathways from childhood to adulthood. Cambridge: Cambridge University Press; 1990. p. 182–204.
24. Jaffee SR, Caspi A, Moffitt TE, Taylor A. Physical maltreatment victim to antisocial child: evidence of an environmentally mediated process. J Abnorm Psychol. 2004;113(1):44–55.
25. Goldstein RB, Dawson DA, Saha TD, Ruan W, Compton WM, Grant BF. Antisocial behavioral syndromes and DSM-IV alcohol use disorders: results from the National Epidemiologic Survey on Alcohol and Related Conditions. Alcohol Clin Exp Res. 2007;31(5):814–28.
26. Torgersen S, Kringlen E, Cramer V. The prevalence of personality disorders in a community sample. Arch Gen Psychiatry. 2001;58(6):590–6.
27. Swanson MC, Bland RC, Newman SC. Antisocial personality disorders. Acta Psychiatr Scand. 1994;376:63–70.
28. Sutker PB, Bugg F, West JA. Antisocial personality disorder. In: Sutker PB, Adams HF, editors. Comprehensive handbook of psychopathology. 2nd ed. New York: Plenum Press; 1993. p. 337–69.
29. Bucholz KK, Hesselbrock VM, Heath AC, Kramer JR, Schuckit MA. A latent class analysis of antisocial personality disorder symptom data from a multi-centre family study of alcoholism. Addiction. 2000;95(4):553–67.
30. Moran P. The epidemiology of antisocial personality disorder. Soc Psychiatry Psychiatr Epidemiol. 1999;34(5):231–42.
31. Hare RD, Cooke DJ, Hart SD. Psychopathy and sadistic personality disorder. In: Millon T, Blaney PH, Davis RD, editors. Oxford Textbook of Psychopathology. 1999. p. 555–84.
32. Hodgins S, Cote G. The criminality of mentally disordered offenders. Crim Justice Behav. 1993;20(2):115–29.
33. Goldstein RB, Grant BF, Ruan W, Smith SM, Saha TD. Antisocial Personality Disorder with childhood- vs adolescence-onset Conduct Disorder: results from the national epidemiologic survey on alcohol and related conditions. J Nerv Ment Dis. 2006;194(9):667–75.

34. Lahey BB, Loeber R, Burke JD, Applegate B. Predicting future antisocial personality disorder in males from a clinical assessment in childhood. J Consult Clin Psychol. 2005;73(3):389–99.
35. Moffitt TE, Caspi A, Rutter M, Silva PA. Sex differences in antisocial behaviour: conduct disorder, delinquency, and violence in the Dunedin Longitudinal Study. New York: Cambridge University Press; 2001.
36. Simonoff E, Elander J, Holmshaw J, Pickles A, Murray R, Rutter M. Predictors of antisocial personality. Continuities from childhood to adult life. Br J Psychiatry. 2004;184:118–27.
37. Hodgins S, Kratzer L, McNeil TF. Obstetric complications, parenting, and risk of criminal behavior. Arch Gen Psychiatry. 2001;58(8):746–52.
38. Caspi A, McClay J, Moffitt T, Mill J, Martin J, Craig IW, et al. Role of genotype in the cycle of violence in maltreated children. Science. 2002;297(5582):851–4.
39. Maughan B, Taylor A, Caspi A, Moffitt TE. Prenatal smoking and early childhood conduct problems: Testing genetic and environmental explanations of the association. Arch Gen Psychiatry. 2004;61(8):836–43.
40. Neugebauer R, Hoek HW, Susser E. Prenatal exposure to wartime famine and development of antisocial personality disorder in early adulthood. JAMA. 1999;282(5):455–62.
41. Gendreau P, Little T, Goggin C. A meta-analysis of the predictors of adult offender recidivism: what works! Criminology [Internet]. 1996;34(4):575–608. Available from: http://doi.wiley.com/10.1111/j.1745-9125.1996.tb01220.x
42. Mills JF, Anderson DY, Kroner DG. The antisocial attitudes and associates of sex offenders. Crim Behav Ment Heal. 2004;14:134–45.
43. Eron L. The development of antisocial behavior from a learning perspective. In: Stoff DM, Brieling J, Maser J, editors. Handbook of antisocial behavior. New York: Wiley; 1997. p. 140–7.
44. Farrington DP. Family background and psychopathy. Handbook of psychopathy. New York: Guilford; 2006. p. 229–50.
45. Derefinko KJ, Widiger TA. Antisocial Personality Disorder. In: Fatemi SH, Clayton PJ, editors. The medical basis of psychiatry. New York: Springer; 2016. p. 229–45.
46. Freeman A, Pretzer J, Fleming B, Simon KM. Clinical applications of cognitive therapy. New York: Plenum Press; 1990.
47. Sargın AE, Özdel K, Türkçapar MH. Cognitive-behavioral theory and treatment of Antisocial Personality Disorder. Psychopathy – new updates on an old phenomenon [Internet]. 2017. p. 99–116. Available from: http://www.intechopen.com/books/psychopathy-new-updates-on-an-old-phenomenon/cognitive-behavioral-theory-and-treatment-of-antisocial-personality-disorder
48. Beck AT, Freeman A. Cognitive theory of personality disorders. New York: Guilford Press; 1990.
49. Harris G, Rice M, Lalumière M. Criminal violence: the roles of psychopathy, neurodevelopmental insults and antisocial parenting. Crim Justice Behav. 2001;28:402–26.
50. Loney B, Frick P, Ellis M, McCoy M. Intelligence, psychopathy, and antisocial behavior. J Psychopathol Behav Assess. 1998;20:231–47.
51. Jutai JW, Hare RD. Psychopathy and selective attention during performance of a complex perceptual-motor task. Psychophysiology. Oxford: Blackwell Publishing; 1983. p. 146–51.
52. Newman JP, Patterson CM, Kosson DS. Response perseveration in psychopaths. Journal of Abnormal Psychology. American Psychological Association; 1987. p. 145–8.
53. Newman J, Lorenz AR. Response modulation and emotion processing: Implications for psychopathy and other dysregulatory psychopathology. In: Davidson R, Scherer K,

Goldsmith H, editors. Handbook of affective sciences. New York: Oxford University Press; 2003. p. 1043–67.

54. Hare RD, McPherson LM. Violent and aggressive behavior by criminal psychopaths. Int J Law Psychiatry and Psychiatry. Elsevier Science; 1984;7(1):35–50.

55. Hodgins S, Mednick SA, Brennan PA, Schulsinger F, Engberg M. Mental disorder and crime: evidence from a Danish birth cohort. Arch Gen Psychiatry. 1996;536(6):489–96.

56. Reis DJ. Central neurotransmitters in aggression. Res Publ Res Nerv Ment Dis. Raven Press; 1974;52:119–48.

57. Eichelman B. Aggressive behavior: from laboratory to clinic: quo vadis? Arch Gen Psychiatry. American Medical Association; 1992;49(6):488–92.

58. Meloy JR. Predatory violence during mass murder. J Forensic Sci. ASTM International; 1997;42(2):326–9.

59. Meloy JR. Empirical basis and forensic application of affective and predatory violence. Aust New Zeal J Psychiatry. London: Sage Publications; 2006;40(6–7):539–47.

60. McEllistrem JE. Affective and predatory violence: a bimodal classification system of human aggression and violence. Aggress Violent Behav. Elsevier; 2004;10(1):1–30.

61. Siegel A, Victoroff J. Understanding human aggression: new insights from neuroscience. Int J Law Psychiatry. Elsevier; 2009;32(4):209–15.

62. Siever LJ. Neurobiology of aggression and violence. Am J Psychiatry. Am Psychiatric Assoc; 2008;165(4):429–42.

63. Cornell DG, Warren J, Hawk G, Stafford E, Oram G, Pine D. Psychopathy in instrumental and reactive violent offenders. J Consult Clin Psychol. American Psychological Association; 1996;64(4):783.

64. Serin RC. Psychopathy and violence in criminals. J Interpers Violence. Sage Publications; 1991;6(4):423–31.

65. Walsh TC. Psychopathic and nonpsychopathic violence among alcoholic offenders. Int J Offender Ther Comp Criminol. Sage Publications; 1999;43(1):34–48.

66. Williamson S, Hare RD, Wong S. Violence: criminal psychopaths and their victims. Can J Behav Sci Can des Sci du Comport. Canadian Psychological Association; 1987;19(4):454.

67. Woodworth M, Porter S. In cold blood: characteristics of criminal homicides as a function of psychopathy. J Abnorm Psychol. American Psychological Association; 2002;111(3):436.

68. Meloy JR, Yakeley J. Antisocial Personality Disorder. In: Gabbard GO, editor. Gabbard's treatments of psychiatric disorders. 5th ed. American Psychiatric Pub; 2014.

69. Robins LN, Tipp J, Przybeck T. Antisocial personality. In: Robins LN, Regier DA, editors. Psychiatric disorders in America: the epidemiological catchment area study. New York: Free Press; 1991. p. 258–90.

70. Kazdin AE, Mazurick JL. Dropping out of child psychotherapy: distinguishing early and late dropouts over the course of treatment. J Consult Clin Psychol. American Psychological Association; 1994;62(5):1069–74.

71. Olver ME, Stockdale KC, Wormith JS. A meta-analysis of predictors of offender treatment attrition and its relationship to recidivism. J Consult Clin Psychol [Internet]. 2011 Mar [cited 2014 Oct 30];79(1):6–21. Available from: http://www.ncbi.nlm.nih.gov/pubmed/21261430

72. Olver ME, Lewis K, Wong SCP. Risk reduction treatment of high-risk psychopathic offenders: the relationship of psychopathy and treatment change to violent recidivism. Personal Disord Theory, Res Treat. 2013;4:160–7.

73. National Institute for Health and Clinical Excellence. Antisocial personality disorder [Internet]. 2013. Available from: https://www.nice.org.uk/guidance/cg77/evidence/full-guideline-242104429

74. Duggan C, Huband N, Smailagic N, Ferriter M, Adams C. The use of psychological treatments for people with personality disorder: a systematic review of randomized controlled trials. Personal Ment Health. Wiley Online Library; 2007;1(2):95–125.

75. Gibbon S, Duggan C, Stoffers J, Huband N, Völlm BA, Ferriter M, et al. Psychological interventions for antisocial personality disorder. Cochrane Database Syst Rev [Internet]. John Wiley & Sons; 2010 Jun 16 [cited 2018 Apr 2]; Available from: http://doi.wiley.com/10.1002/14651858.CD007668.pub2

76. Warren F, Preedy-Fayers K, McGauley G, Pickering A, Kingsley N, Geddes J, et al. Review of treatments for severe personality disorder. Home Office Online Report 30/03. London; 2003.

77. Andrews D, Bonta J. The level of service inventory – revised. Toronto: Multi-Health Systems; 1995.

78. Andrews D. The psychology of criminal conduct and effective treatment. In: McGuire J, editor. What works: reducing reoffending: guidelines from research and practice. Oxford: John Wiley & Sons; 1995. p. 35–62.

79. Skeem JL, Polaschek DLL, Manchak S. Appropriate treatment works, but how?: rehabilitating general, psychopathic, and high-risk offenders. In: Skeem JL, Douglas KS, Lilienfeld S, editors. Psychological science in the courtroom: consensus and controversy. New York: Guilford Press; 2009. p. 358–84.

80. Salekin RT. Psychopathy and therapeutic pessimism: clinical lore or clinical reality? Clin Psychol Rev. 2002;22(1):79–112.

81. Hecht L, Latzman R, Lilienfeld S. The psychological treatment of psychopathy. In: Hecht LK, Latzman RD, Lilienfeld SO, David D, Jay Lynn S, H Montgomery G, editors. Evidence-based psychotherapy: the state of the science and practice. 2018. p. 271–98.

82. Salekin RT, Worley C, Grimes RD. Treatment of psychopathy: a review and brief introduction to the mental model approach for psychopathy. Behav Sci Law. Wiley Online Library; 2010;28(2):235–66.

83. D'Silva K, Duggan C, McCarthy L. Does treatment really make psychopaths worse? A review of the evidence. J Pers Disord. Guilford Press; 2004;18(2):163–77.

84. Gordon R. An operational classification of disease prevention. Public Health Rep. 1983;98:107–9.

85. Olds DL, Sadler L, Kitzman H. Programs for parents of infants and toddlers: recent evidence from randomized trials. J Child Psychol Psychiatry Allied Discip. 2007;48:355–91.

86. Hollander E, Evers M. New developments in impulsivity. The Lancet. 2001 Sep 22;358(9286):949–50.

87. Hollander E, Rosen J. Impulsivity. Journal of Psychopharmacology. 2000 Mar;14(2_suppl1):S39–44.

88. James LM, Taylor J. Impulsivity and negative emotionality associated with substance use problems and Cluster B personality in college students. Addictive Behaviors. 2007 Apr 1;32(4):714–27.

89. Vazire S, Funder DC. Impulsivity and the self-defeating behavior of narcissists. Personality and Social Psychology Review. 2006 May;10(2):154–65.

CHAPTER 6

Childhood Conduct and Other Childhood Disorders

Nicol Patricny, *Forensic Psychiatry, Alberta Hospital Edmonton*

Erin Newman, *Institute of Child Psychology*

John R. Reddon, *Department of Psychology, University of Alberta and Forensic Psychiatry, Alberta Hospital Edmonton*

Salvatore B. Durante, *Alberta Hospital Edmonton*

LEARNING OBJECTIVES

1. Understand the history and development of Conduct Disorder (CD)
2. Discuss the incidence rates and normal trajectory of rule-violating behaviour among children and adolescents in the general population
3. Interpret diagnostic criteria of CD and how it relates to criminal behaviour
4. Explain other childhood disorders commonly found within the Youth Criminal Justice System (YCJS) and their comorbidity with CD
5. Reflect upon specific challenges faced by many Indigenous adolescents involved in the YCJS
6. Explore the etiology of CD in terms of neurobiological, genetic, and social factors
7. Review current practice recommendations for the treatment and management of CD within the YCJS

INTRODUCTION

The roots of criminality can often be traced back to childhood and adolescence. Youth aged 12 to 17 years old comprise only 7% of the Canadian population, yet they represent 13% of individuals accused of crimes and, excluding traffic crimes, are currently overrepresented within the Canadian criminal population.[1] The above data are believed to underrepresent the prevalence of youth antisocial behaviour because youth are charged less frequently (48%) than accused adults (63%),[1] as it is often assumed that there is a greater chance for remediation with youth.

The single most common mental health diagnosis of youth within the Youth Criminal Justice System (YCJS) is Conduct Disorder (CD). CD is characterized by violating the basic rights of others and violating age-appropriate societal norms or rules. Over half of all male and female young offenders in correctional facilities meet the diagnostic criteria of CD.[2] CD is also one of the most highly represented diagnoses in child and adolescent mental health treatment settings.[3] Frequently, CD is comorbid (i.e., coexisting) with other mental health disorders. Individuals with careers relating to the YCJS (e.g., police officers, correctional officers, and mental health professionals) are bound to encounter CD and will benefit from an understanding of the complex issues underlying CD.

HISTORY OF CONDUCT DISORDER

There is historical evidence of societal concerns with childhood conduct long before the modern era. For example, during a House of Commons Speech in 1843, a British earl ranted, "[Boys] with dogs at their heels and other evidence of dissolute habits ... [girls who] drive coal-carts, ride astride upon horses, drink, swear, fight, smoke, whistle, and care for nobody ... the morals of children are tenfold worse than formerly."[4] In 1968, conduct problems appeared formally as an established medical diagnosis in the second edition of the Diagnostic and Statistical Manual of Mental Disorders (DSM-II). By 1980, CD and Oppositional Defiant Disorder (ODD) emerged as distinct diagnoses in the DSM-III, with both disorders being characterized by symptoms that cause conflict with adults and authority figures.[5]

Estimates of the prevalence of CD range from 2% to more than 10% in youth populations.[5] CD is more common in males than females and presents differently between genders. Specifically, females demonstrate mostly relational aggression (e.g., damaging a friend's social status) and males demonstrate physical aggression and relational aggression.[5] Of those diagnosed with CD, less than half will develop Antisocial Personality Disorder (ASPD),[6] which is a personality disorder associated with adult criminality.

ADOLESCENCE-LIMITED VERSUS LIFE-COURSE-PERSISTENT ANTISOCIAL BEHAVIOUR

Delinquent adolescents fall into one of two categories: adolescence-limited versus life-course-persistent antisocial behaviour.[7] The onset, severity, and consistency of antisocial behaviour are helpful indicators of which category adolescents fall into. Those whose antisocial behaviour persists across the lifespan tend to show emerging conduct issues early in childhood (e.g., suspensions or fighting during elementary school) and are generally arrested at a younger age.[7] In contrast, those whose antisocial behaviour is limited to adolescence typically show no significant conduct issues during childhood and have an abrupt onset of antisocial behaviour during their teenage years.[7] Adolescence-limited individuals tend to have less severe antisocial behaviour and show lower consistency in antisocial behaviour across settings (e.g., communities, home, school).

The adolescence-limited category comprises 95% of delinquent adolescents and is, therefore, considered normative rather than pathological.[7] Involvement in crime is temporary and limited to their adolescent developmental period.[7] It is hypothesized that their antisocial behaviour is motivated by a gap between their biological and social maturity.[7] For example, a 16-year-old male who desires more independence may decide to start missing classes at school so he can spend more time with his friends who routinely miss class. Gradually, such non-delinquent adolescents may become increasingly involved with and influenced by delinquent peer groups.[7]

By age 17, nearly all adolescents have some association with delinquent peers and many will have engaged in at least minor crime.[8] At age 17, antisocial behaviour often decreases rapidly.[7] By their mid-20s, over three-quarters of once-delinquent adolescents will no longer engage in antisocial behaviours and/or criminality.[9]

Adolescents who persist with offending are represented by the **life-course-persistent category**. These adolescents will continue to engage in antisocial behaviour throughout adulthood and across different circumstances,[7] with many receiving a diagnosis of ASPD as adults. Life-course-persistent represents only 5% of males[10] and is marked by significant impairment across different life domains. Life-course-persistent antisocial behaviour is generally viewed as having a biological basis[11] predisposing individuals to a maladaptive temperament (e.g., poor emotion regulation) and environments that could exacerbate their predispositions to antisocial behaviour. Children with a genetic predisposition for poor self-control and aggression are likely to be rejected by peers and adults.[12] Rejection by peers and relatives could offer fewer opportunities for practice and development of social skills.[7] Moreover, poor self-control and impulsivity often lead to academic and vocational difficulties, substance abuse, and a criminal record that could impede future academic and career opportunities.[7] Over time, these individuals cumulatively become ill-equipped to live a prosocial lifestyle and increasingly gravitate towards a criminal lifestyle.

CONDUCT DISORDER IN THE DSM-5

The DSM-5 lists CD in the Disruptive, Impulse-Control, and Conduct Disorders chapter, which describes disorders characterized by difficulties with emotional and behavioural self-control. Because CD and ODD are not exclusive diagnoses, an adolescent could have both. The DSM-5 includes subtypes based upon the age of onset of the disorder:

1. Childhood-onset type (at least one symptom prior to age 10 years)
2. Adolescent-onset type (no symptoms prior to age 10 years)
3. Unspecified onset (inadequate information available to determine the onset of the first symptom)[5]

The DSM-5 has also added the specifier "With Limited Prosocial Emotions" based upon an individual displaying at least two of the following characteristics over one year in multiple relationships and settings: lack of remorse or guilt, callousness (lack of empathy), unconcern with performance, and shallow or deficient affect.

Table 6.1: DSM-5 Diagnostic Criteria for Conduct Disorder

CD requires at least three of the following 15 criteria in the past 12 months and one present in the past six months:[5]

A.   A repetitive and persistent pattern of behaviour in which the basic rights of others or major age-appropriate societal norms or rules are violated.

Aggression to People and Animals

1. Often bullies, threatens, or intimidates others.
2. Often initiates physical fights.
3. Has used a weapon that can cause serious physical harm to others (e.g., a bat, brick, broken bottle, knife, gun).
4. Has been physically cruel to people.
5. Has been physically cruel to animals.
6. Has stolen while confronting a victim (e.g., mugging, purse snatching, extortion, armed robbery).
7. Has forced someone into sexual activity.

Destruction of Property

1. Has deliberately engaged in fire setting with the intention of causing serious damage.
2. Has deliberately destroyed others' property (other than by fire setting).

Deceitfulness or Theft

1. Has broken into someone else's house, building, or car.
2. Often lies to obtain goods or favours or to avoid obligations (i.e., "cons" others).
3. Has stolen items of nontrivial value without confronting a victim (e.g., shoplifting but without breaking and entering; forgery).

Serious Violations of Rules

1. Often stays out at night despite parental prohibitions, beginning before age 13 years.
2. Has run away from home overnight at least twice while living in the parental or parental surrogate home, or once without returning for a lengthy period.
3. Is often truant from school, beginning before age 13 years.

B.   The disturbance in behaviour causes clinically significant impairment in social, academic, or occupational functioning.

C.   If the individual is age 18 years or older, criteria are not met for antisocial personality disorder.

It is important to note that category B is necessary for clinical diagnosis because of the significant impairment feature. The category B specification is common among DSM disorders. With respect to Category C, CD occurs below the age of 18 and is needed for clinicians to differentiate and to examine if the individual is developing an antisocial personality disorder.

OTHER CHILDHOOD DISORDERS

In general, youth with behaviour disorders are at risk for other mental health diagnoses.[13] Common comorbid disorders with CD include ODD, Attention Deficit Hyperactivity Disorder (ADHD), depression, anxiety, substance use, Post-Traumatic Stress Disorder (PTSD), Fetal Alcohol Syndrome Disorder (FASD), and Traumatic Brain Injury (TBI). There are several implications for assessment, treatment, and rehabilitation when other disorders accompany CD. For example, treating trauma can alleviate some of the symptoms of CD. Thus, it is important for treatment providers and the judicial system to acknowledge any comorbid disorders.

ODD

ODD is characterized by mood issues, defiant behaviour, and vindictiveness.[5] ODD is considered by some to be a progression towards CD in many youth because of its less severe symptoms and similar risk factors.[14] Around 75% of young children diagnosed with CD meet the criteria for ODD earlier on.[14] Youth may be diagnosed with both disorders, as there is clear differentiation between the two. ODD involves intense emotional experiences (e.g., rage) while CD is often marked by an absence of emotion and more severe behaviours.[5]

ADHD

ADHD is a neurodevelopmental disorder marked by an inability to focus or concentrate, hyperactivity, and impulsive behaviour.[5] It is often viewed as a precursor to ODD and possibly CD.[13] Research has found comorbidity rates as high as 80% for either CD or ODD with ADHD.[15] Impulsive decision-making, which is a characteristic of ADHD, could enable youth with CD to engage in crime without forethought of the consequences of their offending behaviour.

Mood and Anxiety Disorders

Depression is a disorder marked by intense feelings of sadness, which can present as irritability in adolescents and is often comorbid with CD.[5] Prevalence rates of comorbid depression found in youth diagnosed with CD or ODD are estimated at 20%.[16-18] It may be that depression arises in relation to the consequences (e.g., school expulsion or incarceration) of delinquent behaviour. Bipolar disorder (a related mood disorder) is another common comorbid diagnosis with CD.[17] It is marked by a cycling of depression and mania (elated mood) and may present as anger or rage in youth.[5] The prevalence of incarcerated youth with mania is estimated to be around 20%;[18] however, only 1% of those meet the diagnostic criteria for bipolar disorder. Anxiety is also often comorbid with CD at rates of 20-40% in clinical samples.[19,20] Anxiety is a debilitating fear that can be general or a reaction to a specific situation, item, or animal.[5] The presence of CD with an anxiety disorder may exacerbate CD symptoms. For example, in a study of 11-year-olds, those with comorbid anxiety disorder and CD were rated as more aggressive than youth with no comorbid anxiety.[21]

Stress-Related Disorders

Post-Traumatic Stress Disorder (PTSD) is a reaction to an adverse event that exceeds one's available coping mechanisms.[5] It is suggested that some of the symptoms seen in PTSD (e.g., anger, acting out, lack of feeling, and concentration issues) may be misdiagnosed as CD.[22] Furthermore, research has shown a relationship between abuse and its impact on delinquent behaviour. One such study examined rates of sexual abuse in those diagnosed with CD and found a comorbidity rate of 27%.[23] Youth may "act out" significantly as a result of past trauma. Therefore, knowledge of a youth's stress and trauma history is imperative.

Substance Use Disorders

Substance use disorders are characterized by drug, alcohol, or other substance use that interferes with an individual's functioning.[5] Numerous studies have examined the genetic basis for CD and antisocial behaviours and the association with substance use disorder.[24] One theory suggests that an inability to delay gratification is a predisposition for both substance use disorders and CD.[25] It has been found that 38% of youth receiving treatment for substance abuse meet the criteria for CD.[26] This is not surprising, considering substance use can increase the risk of offending by impairing impulse-control, inhibition, and judgement.

FASD and TBI

The effects of prenatal alcohol exposure, formally diagnosed in the DSM-5 as an "Other Specified Neurodevelopmental Disorder," are described as a wide range of disabilities.[5] Symptoms of **FASD** are similar to CD[27] and are caused by brain dysfunction.[28] The effects of prenatal alcohol exposure should be considered at all stages within the legal process for young offenders with a fetal-alcohol-related diagnosis for their treatment and rehabilitation.[27]

The delinquent behaviours seen in CD are also associated with **TBI**, due to significant trauma to the brain.[29] An examination of research on young offenders within a correctional setting found that at least 16.5% of incarcerated youth have sustained a brain injury[29] that can in some instances greatly alter behaviour and cognitive functioning.

INDIGENOUS CONSIDERATIONS IN CANADA

Indigenous individuals comprise a large number of Canada's offender population. Despite representing only 4% of the total population in Canada,[30] Indigenous people make up 23% of the population in Canada's federal prisons.[31] Indigenous youth are also overrepresented in the prison system, accounting for 33% of the total youth admissions in federal institutions.[32] What accounts for the high rates of Indigenous people in Canadian prison populations? The answer to this question is complex and requires knowledge of historical factors and an understanding of intergenerational trauma.

Treaties and Residential Schools

After the Dominion of Canada was formed in 1867, land titles were purchased by the federal government and 11 treaties were created between the government and Indigenous Peoples.[33] These treaties effectively moved the Indigenous population to small pieces of land while promising provisions, education, and sustainability.[34] To fulfil the education promises outlined in the treaties, residential schools were created by the Canadian government and in coalition with various religious groups.[35] Under the guise of education, **residential schools** were used as a tool to further assimilate the Indigenous cultures into European culture. Children were often taken from their parents (i.e., a period referred to as "The Sixties Scoop," which occurred during the 1960s and saw numerous Indigenous children taken from their homes) and placed into residential schools. Only English and European cultural values were taught, which resulted in a generational loss of Indigenous languages and cultural practices. Harsh punishments (e.g., corporal punishment) for not assimilating and sexual assaults occurred in several residential schools across Canada.[36] The last residential school closed in 1996.

Intergenerational Trauma

The phenomenon of intergenerational trauma[37] is believed to play a large part in many aspects of Indigenous life (e.g., mental health, socioeconomic status, and criminal behaviour). **Intergenerational trauma** is described as a collective trauma that crosses generations.[37] As a result, both the individuals that directly experience the trauma and their offspring suffer socially, mentally, and physically. Trauma is "inherited," as the effects of the collective trauma continue to cycle down to each new generation. Intergenerational trauma is associated with ineffective or maladaptive child-rearing practices, low socioeconomic status, and criminal behaviour (e.g., violence and gang activity).

The historical events and associated intergenerational trauma could accelerate the development of CD and increase the risk of criminal offence in the Indigenous population. Many Indigenous parents whose children were placed in residential schools experienced trauma from having their children removed from their care.[38] The lack of modelled parenting coupled with the effects of trauma and substance use may have resulted in maladaptive parenting skills, which are a risk factor for the development of CD.[38]

Socioeconomic Status

Socioeconomic status (SES) is a combined measure of education, occupation, and income. Many Indigenous people in Canada have low SES[39] due to unequal access to resources (e.g., education), employment opportunities, nutritious food, and social support. Low SES is one of the biggest risk factors for gang involvement, violence, and mental health concerns. In addition, low SES is linked to both crime and poor mental health[40] and can create the necessary environmental conditions for the development of CD.

Exposure to Violence

Violence occurs in Canadian Indigenous populations at a rate much higher than the national average.[41] In particular, violence against Indigenous women is extremely high, with 24% of Indigenous women experiencing domestic violence.[42] According to the Royal Canadian Mounted Police (RCMP), there have been 1,181 cases of murdered or missing Indigenous women in Canada.[43] Indigenous youth and young adults (age 15-34) are 2.5 times more likely than other youth to be victims of crime.[42] With this in mind, adverse childhood events may increase the likelihood of Indigenous youth engaging in criminal or antisocial behaviour.[44]

Organized Gang Involvement

Risk factors that predict gang involvement include the following: gang activity in the immediate community; maladaptive or ineffective parenting; peer pressure; low level of commitment to one's education due to intellectual delay, learning disability, or other social factors; level of delinquent behaviour a youth is already engaging in; motivation for social status; negative attitude towards authority; and external attribution of blame.[45] Indigenous youth who are exposed to these risk factors could become involved in gang activity at higher rates.[46]

ETIOLOGY OF CONDUCT DISORDER

The etiology of CD is complex and conceptualized as the by-product of incompatibility between child and environment.[47] This translates into conduct problems being expressed when the individual characteristics of the child (e.g., temperament or impulsivity) do not fit well with external environmental factors (e.g., caregivers, neighbourhood, or schools).[47] There are multiple, reciprocal factors of neurobiological (reduced serotonin and cortisol), genetic (biological inheritance), environmental (maternal alcohol use in utero), psychological (diminished fear), and social (such as parenting, peers, and the neighbourhood) influences implicated in CD.[48]

Research on environmental and genetic risk factors suggest that both can impact neurocognitive function.[6] Antisocial development begins to emerge in childhood among highly aggressive and mainly male youth who show verbal deficits and ADHD symptoms.[49] Without intervention, youth are at risk of developing CD and antisocial behaviour into adulthood. Nearly all the individual risk factors for offending among youth (e.g., negative attitudes, risk-taking/impulsivity, substance use difficulties, anger management problems, low empathy/remorse, attention deficit/hyperactivity problems, poor compliance, poor school achievement and low interest/commitment to school)[50] are either characteristic of or associated with CD.

Neurobiological Influences

It is believed that CD involves neurobiological impairment (e.g., deficits in executive and cognitive functioning and/or verbal skills).[49] These deficits make it difficult for youth to self-regulate and achieve goals and can lead to the development of oppositional and defiant behaviour.[49] **Emotion dysregulation theory** proposes that antisocial behaviour and aggression arises in CD through abnormalities in neurobiological circuits involved in regulating negative emotions and processing environmental cues.[48,51] Neurocognitive dysfunctions associated with CD include

1. Deficient empathy,
2. Low physiological arousal,
3. Heightened threat sensitivity, and
4. Deficient decision-making.[6]

Deficient Empathy

Youth with CD and callous-unemotional traits show reduced activation in their amygdala (a brain structure responsible for emotional perception). Response to fearful faces is an approach used to measure deficient empathy[6] and impairment in processing emotional cues.[48] Specifically, reduction in amygdala activity and a lack of empathy are believed to be related to displays of aggression in youth with CD.[48] In addition, studies have also shown that youth with CD have reduced right temporal lobe and right temporal grey matter volume, which are structures associated with empathy.[48] Lastly, the anterior cingulate cortex (involved in decision-making and impulse control) is deactivated in youth with CD during a conflict. This finding may provide one reason youth with CD display decreased emotional control and increased risk of impulsive aggression.[52]

Low Physiological Arousal

Research suggests that youth with CD who display aggressive behaviour have decreased physiological arousal (e.g., lower heart rate).[48] Children with CD who show significantly high conduct issues also show decreased **cortisol**[48] (a stress hormone) and a lack of sensitivity to punishment.[53] This aligns with fearlessness theory, which proposes that individuals with CD have little fear of punishment or negative repercussions and do not learn to inhibit their antisocial behaviours in childhood.[48] Youth with CD also prefer dangerous activities and fail to experience many prosocial emotions.[53] Stimulation-seeking theory suggests that low physiological arousal (often found in youth with CD) results in the display of aggressive behaviours as a means to obtain and maintain stimulation.[48]

Heightened Threat Sensitivity

Youth with CD without callous-unemotional traits show elevated amygdala responses to threats, eliciting their "fight, flight, or freeze" responses, thereby, heightening their risk of reactive aggression.[6] They often show verbal deficits and temperamental vulnerabilities towards emotional dysregulation.[53] Youth with CD also display reduced serotonin levels,[48] which is linked to emotional dysregulation and aggression.[51]

Deficient Decision-Making

Poor decision-making is common in youth with CD (both with and without callous-unemotional traits) and occurs because of a failure to learn how to make choices that generate rewards rather than punishments.[6] This is believed to be related to deficiencies in the use of their striatum (involved in the brain's reward system) and ventromedial prefrontal cortex (involved in processing risk and fear, and implicated in decision-making and self-control).[54]

Genetic Influences

Twin studies, such as the Virginia Twin Study of Adolescent Behavioural Development,[55] have found strong genetic influences on externalizing behaviours (specifically aggression) commonly associated with CD.[48] Several genetic sex differences may explain why males show more aggression beginning early in childhood and exhibit more severe antisocial behaviour than females during adolescence and adulthood. Both animal and human research provides some evidence that males have a psychological disposition for aggressive behaviour (e.g., physical rough play among preschool-age boys)[49] and fearlessness.[56] By puberty, males have much higher levels of testosterone than females, which may increase their likelihood of aggression in stressful situations.[49] In contrast, females have more estrogen than males, which may reduce their likelihood of aggression. Additionally, females are more likely to seek social support in stressful situations[49] than males, but it is unclear if estrogen is a factor in this approach to alleviating stress.

Social and Environmental Influences

Postnatal environmental risk factors for conduct issues include low parental monitoring, exposure to violence, harsh and inconsistent discipline, and poverty.[6] Social factors associated with risk of offending in youth include exposure to violence in the home, history of abuse, peer delinquency, peer rejection, stress and poor coping, poor parental management, lack of personal or social support, and community disorganization.[50] Compared to adolescents attending school, incarcerated adolescents have a history of greater traumatization, with delinquent males showing an association between physical/emotional trauma and psychopathic characteristics.[57] In contrast, delinquent females show an association between family-related variables (e.g., non-parental living arrangements in foster homes) and psychopathic characteristics.[57] This provides some credence to the notion that early traumatization acts as an environmental and biological stressor that influences affective deficits (e.g., lack of empathy) and anger control.

Case Study: Aiden's Struggle

Aiden is a 16-year-old Indigenous male who was raised by his maternal grandparents on a reserve rife with gang-related violence and crime. Aiden's mother was unable to care for him due to her Alcohol Use Disorder, while Aiden's biological father has been incarcerated for most of Aiden's life. Aiden has always been a challenge to care for at home because of his difficult temperament and impulse control deficits. At school, he struggled academically and was often suspended for swearing at the teachers, fighting with his peers, and truancy. Aiden was assessed by a school psychologist at age 10 and was diagnosed with Conduct Disorder, Childhood Onset. When Aiden was 12, he dropped out of school and began running away from home for extended periods of time, during which he would stay with older friends and experiment with drugs. When he was 13, he was recruited by an organized gang and became involved in drug trafficking. Aiden was arrested for the first time when he was 14 in relation to his drug trafficking.

Questions
1.   Identify some of the behaviours that suggest a diagnosis of CD for Aiden.
2.   Which environmental factors may have contributed to the development of CD in Aiden?
3.   Outline some potential challenges Aiden may face in attempting to refrain from further criminal behaviour. Identify some of his specific risk factors for offending.
4.   What supports would you recommend for Aiden to prevent him from reoffending?

ASSESSMENT AND TREATMENT

Risk-Need-Responsivity Model

Within the criminal justice system, the Risk-Need-Responsivity (RNR) model[58] is a widely used model for both adult and young offender assessment and rehabilitation. According to the RNR model for young offenders,

1.   The level of service should match the youth's risk of reoffending;
2.   The criminogenic needs of youth should be assessed to determine the specific risk factors for offending to target in treatment; and
3.   The rehabilitative interventions youth receive should be tailored to their individual learning style, motivation, abilities, and strengths.[58]

For example, intensive treatment would be recommended for a young offender with a high risk of reoffending. Treatment would focus specifically on addressing the young offender's specific risk factors for offending (e.g., substance dependence, antisocial attitudes, and involvement in an organized gang) and would utilize an evidence-based approach that matches the young offender's cognitive abilities.

Youth's risk level and criminogenic needs should be assessed using structured professional judgement tools designed for youth (e.g., The Structured Assessment of Violence Risk in Youth[50] or the Youth Level of Service/Case Management Inventory 2.0).[59] Results of risk assessment are typically introduced during sentencing or transfer proceedings and are referred to in 76% of cases.[60] Risk assessment can be supplemented with additional measures, such as the Hare Psychopathy Checklist: Youth Version[61] (identifies antisocial traits) or The Estimate of Risk of Adolescent Sexual Offence Recidivism[62] (specific to sexual offending). In addition, psychological assessment of cognition, academic abilities, and personality profile is recommended to understand adolescents' strengths and weaknesses. The assessments can further develop individualized treatment plans for young offenders.

Early treatment intervention for conduct issues is crucial because behavioural issues can be targeted, and clinicians can capitalize on the **plasticity** (i.e., changing) of a youth's developing brain. CD with callous-unemotional traits is difficult to treat[6] because youth with these traits show more severe, stable, and aggressive patterns of antisocial behaviour.[53] Early intervention for youth with CD and callous-unemotional traits could prevent or minimize the development of antisocial traits into adulthood. Studies have found that youth with CD use disproportionate mental health, juvenile justice, and special education resources.[63] Although there are many effective research-based interventions for antisocial behaviour in youth, many service systems (including mental health and juvenile justice) do not meet the complex needs of youth with CD.[63]

Presently, treatment is focused on alleviating the symptoms of CD rather than the less understood underlying mechanisms.[6] Because there are various developmental pathways to antisocial behaviour and because of the neuropsychological differences between those with or without callous-unemotional traits, proper assessment is critical to determining appropriate treatment targets[53] (i.e., identification of comorbid disorders)[64] and treatment format. For example, peer interventions appear to be more effective when used preventatively with younger children, rather than for older youth with more risk factors.[65] Promoting the development of protective factors (e.g., prosocial involvement, strong social support, strong attachment and bonds, positive attitude towards intervention and authority, strong commitment to school, and resilient personality) may help reduce the likelihood of offending.[50] For example, incorporating fitness and sports into young male offenders' routines could help them develop a prosocial identity during community reintegration.[66] Regardless of the type of modality used, effective treatment of CD should be multi-modal and involve a family social systems-based approach.[64]

Cognitive-Behavioural Therapy (CBT)

Symptoms of CD, such as reactive aggression, can be targeted through the use of CBT by decreasing threat hypersensitivity and modifying negative cognitive patterns[6] that perpetuate antisocial behaviours. Interventions can also focus on anger management for those youth who do not exhibit callous-unemotional traits.[53] A related form of therapy, dialectical behaviour therapy (a therapy that combines CBT and mindfulness interventions to target emotion dysregulation), has shown some effectiveness in reducing externalizing behaviours in youth with ODD[67] and managing aggression for incarcerated male adolescents.[68]

Parenting/Family

Other effective psychosocial interventions for youth conduct problems are family-based and focus on parenting skills; for example, teaching parents ways to reduce stress in the home, to use supportive limit-setting practices, to monitor children's activities, and to seek other support services.[6] The Parent Training and Behaviour Family Therapy models that focus on changing problematic parental discipline patterns and improving parent-child interactions[69] have proven effective.[15] Interventions involving families have been found to benefit girls and ethnic minority youth in particular[65]—although comprehensive approaches that involve parents are also recommended for preventative interventions for antisocial behaviour among boys.[65] Another psychosocial treatment model is **Collaborative Problem Solving**, which focuses on improving the fit of the child with the demands of the environment.[70] Vulnerability to incompatibility with the environment is influenced by environmental demands as well as skill deficits in areas such as flexibility/adaptability, frustration tolerance, and problem solving. Caregivers must understand problematic behaviours as a form of skill deficiency rather than as a character flaw; they should work with the child collaboratively rather than unilaterally to achieve improved functioning in situations that have been difficult or problematic.

Early intervention in the parent-child relationship allows parents to foster empathy and perspective-taking abilities in their children.[53] Developing empathy and perspective-taking at a young age could be effective for parents with children with CD (especially children with callous-unemotional traits). Children ages four to nine[71] with and without callous-unemotional traits were found to respond equally well to treatment interventions focused on teaching parents' positive reinforcement methods to encourage prosocial behaviour.[53] Later in development, it is hypothesized that interventions should be focused on appealing to the youth's self-interest to be effective.[72]

Pharmacological

Pharmacotherapy can be implemented when youth have not responded well to other interventions or display increased aggression and/or violence.[64] Pharmacotherapy is often used in combination with psychosocial therapies.[73] Antipsychotic medications have shown some effectiveness in reducing irritability and aggression in children.[74,75] Conversely, antipsychotic medications can have adverse side effects (e.g., sedation, disrupted metabolic and neurological function).[6] Psychostimulants also reduce aggression for youth with CD (with or without ADHD)[75] and have fewer adverse side effects than antipsychotic medication.

Interventions within the YCJS

The YCJS is experiencing increases in the number of youth with mental health concerns and other environmental risk factors.[76] Fortunately, early adolescence offers opportunities for risk reduction that could be coordinated with the juvenile justice system and other social organizations.[77] Developmental processes should be considered for treatment of all juvenile offenders.[77] Intervening early and using a multifaceted approach could help promote coping abilities for youth in the system prior to their encountering challenges in adulthood.[77]

Counselling services have the largest effect on recidivism with young offenders, followed by skill building, restorative programs, surveillance, deterrence, and discipline.[78] Therapeutic interventions (e.g., counselling and skills training) are often more effective than interventions that rely on control or coercion (e.g., deterrence, discipline, and surveillance).[78] Higher-quality implementation (i.e., low drop-out rates, consistent staff, well-trained personnel) also decreases recidivism rates.[78] Programs show some effectiveness regardless of where they were implemented (i.e., diverted, on probation, versus a custodial institution). Counselling has reduced effectiveness within young offender facilities, while skill-building approaches show increased effectiveness as prevention programs in the community.[78] Continually assessing individual treatment/service plans to meet youths' changing needs shows the most efficacy.

SUMMARY

Youth conduct issues have a significant impact on Canadian society. They lead to crime and ultimately substantial financial resource allocation. Some antisocial behaviour is considered normative for adolescents (particularly males in mid-to-late adolescence). Those with a persistent pattern of significant antisocial behaviour during childhood and/or adolescence meet DSM-5 diagnostic criteria for CD. Youth with early onset of CD and callous-unemotional traits have more severe behaviour and are more likely to continue with antisocial behaviour and offending into adulthood. Generally, CD coexists with other mental health disorders (most commonly ADHD). The etiology of CD can be understood from a developmental perspective that considers genetic, neurobiological, and environmental/social factors that interact with one another to increase the likelihood of psychopathology and antisocial behaviour. The impact of intergenerational trauma and exposure to contextual risk factors help us understand why Indigenous youth are highly overrepresented within the YCJS. Best practices for treatment of CD and management of risk include early identification of behavioural issues, comprehensive psychological/psychiatric assessment, and a multifaceted evidence-based treatment approach to address criminogenic needs and community reintegration.

REFLECTION QUESTIONS

1. What differentiates normative antisocial behaviour in adolescents from pathological antisocial behaviour that warrants a diagnosis of CD?
2. What are some other childhood disorders that commonly coexist with CD?
3. How does CD with callous-unemotional traits differ from CD without callous-unemotional traits?
4. What are some risk factors for offending commonly found among adolescents with CD?
5. When is treatment for CD most highly recommended and why?

REFERENCES

1. Allen MK, Superle TS. Youth crime in Canada. Statistics Canada. 2014.
2. Fazel S, Doll H, Phil D, Langstrom N. Mental disorders among adolescents in juvenile detention and correctional facilities: a systematic review and metaregression analysis of 25 surveys. Journal of the American Academy of Child & Adolescent Psychiatry. 2008;47:1010–19. DOI: 10.1097/CHI.0b013e31817eecf3
3. Klahr AM, Burt SA. Practitioner review: evaluation of the known behavioural heterogeneity in conduct disorder to improve its assessment and treatment. Journal of Child Psychology and Psychiatry. 2014;55:1300–10. DOI: 10.1111/jcpp.12268
4. Seder J. 15 historical complaints about young people ruining everything [Internet]. Available from: http://mentalfloss.com/article/52209/15-historical-complaints-about-young-people-ruining-everything
5. American Psychiatric Association. Diagnostic and statistical manual of mental disorders (DSM-5). American Psychiatric Pub; 2013 May 22.

6. Blair RJ, Leibenluft E, Pine DS. Conduct disorder and callous–unemotional traits in youth. N Engl J Med. 2014;371:2207–16.

7. Moffitt TE. Adolescence-limited and life-course-persistent antisocial behavior: a developmental taxonomy. Psychological Review. 1993;100(4):674–701. DOI: 10.1037/0033-295X.100.4.674

8. Elliot DS, Huizinga D. Social class and delinquent behavior in a national youth panel: 1976-1980. Criminology. 1983;21:149–77. DOI: 10.1111/j.1745-9125.1983.tb00256.x

9. Farrington DP. Age and crime. In: Tonry M, Morris N, editors. Crime and justice: an annual review of research, volume 7. Chicago: University of Chicago Press; 1986. p. 189–250.

10. Robbins LN. Epidemiology of antisocial personality. In: Cavenar JO, editor. Psychiatry, volume 3. Philadelphia: Lippincott; 1985. p. 1–14.

11. Moffitt TE. The neuropsychology of delinquency: a critical review of theory and research. In Morris N, Tonry M, editors. Crime and justice, volume 12. Chicago: University of Chicago Press; 1990. p. 99–169.

12. Coie JD, Belding M, Underwood M. Aggression and peer rejection in childhood. In Lahey B, Kaxdin A, editors. Advances in clinical child psychology, volume 2. New York: Plenum Press; 1988. p. 125–58. DOI: 10.1007/978-1-4613-9829-5_3

13. Biederman J, Faraone SV, Milberger S, Jetton JG, Chen L, Mick E, et al. Is childhood oppositional defiant disorder a precursor to adolescent conduct disorder? Findings from a four-year follow-up study of children with ADHD. J Am Acad Child Adolesc Psychiatry. 1996 Sep;35:1193–204. DOI: 10.1097/00004583-199609000-00017

14. Boden JM, Fergusson DM, Horwood LJ. Risk factors for conduct disorder and oppositional/defiant disorder: evidence from a New Zealand birth cohort. J Am Acad Child Adolesc Psychiatry. 2010;49:1125–33. DOI: 10.1016/j.jaac.2010.08.005

15. Greene R, Biederman J, Zerwas S, Monuteaux M, Goring JC, Faraone S. Psychiatric comorbidity, family dysfunction, and social impairment in referred youth with oppositional defiant disorder. American Journal of Psychiatry. 2002;159:1214–24. DOI: 10.1176/appi.ajp.159.7.1214

16. Ollendick TH, Jarrett MA, Grills-Taquechel AE, Hovey LD, Wolff JC. Comorbidity as predictor and moderator of treatment outcome in youth with anxiety, affective, attention deficit/hyperactivity disorder, and oppositional/conduct disorders. Clinical Psychology Review. 2008;28:1447–71. DOI: 10.1016/j.cpr.2008.09.003

17. Olvera RL, Semrud-Clikeman M, Pliszka SR, O'Donnell L. Neuropsychological deficits in adolescents with conduct disorder and comorbid bipolar disorder: a pilot study. Bipolar Disorder. 2003;7:57–67. DOI: 10.1111/j.1399-5618.2004.00167.x

18. Pliszka SR, Sherman JO, Barrow MV, Irick S. Affective disorder in juvenile offenders: a preliminary study. American Journal of Psychiatry. 2000;157:130–2. DOI: 10.1176/ajp.157.1.130

19. Garland JE, Garland OM. Correlation between anxiety and oppositionality in a children's mood and anxiety disorders clinic. Canadian Journal of Psychiatry. 2001;46:953–8.

20. Angold A, Costello EJ, Erkanli A. Comorbidity. Journal of Child Psychology and Psychiatry. 1999;40:57–87. DOI: 10.1111/1469-7610.00424

21. Anderson JC, Williams S, McGee R, Silva PA. DSM-III disorders in preadolescent children: prevalence in a large sample from the general population. Archives of General Psychiatry. 1987;44:69–76. DOI: 10.1001/archpsyc.1987.01800130081010

22. Terr LC. Childhood traumas: an outline and overview. American Journal of Psychiatry. 1991;148:10–20. DOI: 10.1176/foc.1.3.322

23. Maniglio R. Prevalence of sexual abuse among children with conduct disorder: a systematic review. Clin Child Fam Psychol Rev. 2014;17:268–82. DOI: 10.1007/s10567-013-0161-z

24. Beaver KM, Wright JP, Delisi M, Walsh A, Vaughn MG, Boisvert D, et al. A gene x gene interaction between the DrD2 and DrD4 is associated with conduct disorder and antisocial behavior in males. Behavioral and Brain Functions. 2007 Jun;3(30). DOI: 10.1186/1744-9081-3-30

25. Grant S, Contoreggi C, London ED. Drug abusers show impaired performance in a laboratory test of decision making. Neuropsychologia. 2000;38:1180–7. DOI: 10.1016/S0028-3932(99)00158-X

26. Castel S, Rush B, Urbanoski K, Toneatto T. Overlap of clusters of psychiatric symptoms among clients of a comprehensive addiction treatment service. Psychology of Addictive Behaviors. 2006;20:28–35. DOI: 10.1037/0893-164X.20.1.28

27. Fast DK, Conry J. Fetal alcohol spectrum disorders and the criminal justice system. Developmental Disabilities Research Reviews. 2009;15:250–7. DOI: 10.1002/ddrr.66

28. Astley SJ. Diagnostic guide for fetal alcohol spectrum disorders: the 4-digit diagnostic code. 3rd ed. Washington, DC: FAS Diagnostic and Prevention Network; 2004. p. 59–81.

29. Hughes N, Williams WH, Chitasbesan P, Walesby RC, Mounce LTA, Clasby B. The prevalence of traumatic brain injury among young offenders in custody: a systematic review. J Head Trauma Rehabil. 2015;30:94–105. DOI: 10.1097/HTR.0000000000000124

30. Statistics Canada. Aboriginal people in Canada: First Nations people, Metis, and Inuit: national household survey, 2011. Minister of Industry [Internet]. 2013. Available from: http://www12.statcan.gc.ca/nhs-enm/2011/as-sa/99-011-x/99-011-x2011001-eng.cfm

31. Reitano K. Adult correctional statistics in Canada [Internet]. 2014/2015. 2016. Available from: http://www.statcan.gc.ca/pub/85-002-x/2016001/article/14318-eng.htm

32. Correctional Services Canada. Youth correctional statistics [Internet]. 2014/2015. 2016. Available from: http://www.statcan.gc.ca/pub/85-002-x/2016001/article/14317-eng.htm

33. Indigenous and Northern Affairs Canada. The numbered treaties (1871–1921) [Internet]. 2013. Available from: https://www.aadncaandc.gc.ca/eng/1360948213124/1360948312708

34. Ray AJ. An illustrated history of Canada's Native people. Toronto: Lester Publishing; 2010.

35. Truth and Reconciliation Commission of Canada. Residential schools [Internet]. Available from: http://www.trc.ca/websites/trcinstitution/index.php?p=4

36. Indigenous and Northern Affairs Canada. Residential schools [Internet]. 2016. Available from: http://www.aadnc-aandc.gc.ca/eng/1100100015576/1100100015577

37. Urban Society for Aboriginal Youth, YMCA Calgary and University of Calgary. Intervention to address intergenerational trauma. Overcoming, resisting and preventing structural violence [Internet]. 2012. Available from: https://www.ucalgary.ca/wethurston/files/wethurston/Report_InterventionToAddressIntergenerationalTrauma.pdf

38. Hotton T. Childhood aggression and exposure to violence in the home. Statistics Canada Crime and Justice Research Paper Series. Ottawa: Statistics Canada; 2003.

39. Totten M. Preventing Aboriginal youth gang involvement in Canada: a gendered approach paper prepared for Aboriginal policy research conference [Internet]. 2009 Feb. Available from: https://www.nwac.ca/wp-content/uploads/2015/05/2011-Aboriginal-Youth-Gang-Involvement-APRC.pdf

40. Galabuzi G. Social exclusion. In Raphael D, editor. Social determinants of health: Canadian perspectives. Toronto: Canadian Scholars Press; 2016. p. 235–52.

41. Brzozowski J, Taylor-Butts A, Johnson S. Victimization and offending among the Aboriginal population in Canada. Ottawa: Canadian Centre for Justice Statistics; 2006.

42. Scrim K. Aboriginal victimization in Canada: a summary of the literature. Victims of Crime Digest [Internet]. 2017(3). Available from: http://www.justice.gc.ca/eng/rp-pr/cj-jp/victim/rd3-rr3/p3.html

43. The Royal Canadian Mounted Police. Working together to end violence against Indigenous women and girls. National scan of RCMP initiatives [Internet]. 2017. Available from: http://www.rcmp-grc.gc.ca/en/working-together-end-violence-indigenous-women-and-girls-national-scan-rcmp-initiatives-may-2017

44. O'Brien K, Daffern M, Chu CM, Thomas SDM. Youth gang affiliation, violence, and criminal activities: a review of motivational, risk, and protective factors. Aggression and Violent Behavior. 2013;18:417–425. DOI: 10.1016/j.avb.2013.05.001

45. Augustyn MB, Thornberry TP, Krohn MD. Gang Membership and pathways to maladaptive parenting. Journal of Research on Adolescence. 2014;24:252–67. DOI: 10.1111/jora.12110

46. Herrenkohl TI, Maguin E, Hill KG, Hawkins JD, Abbott RD, Catalano RF. Developmental risk factors for youth violence. Journal of Adolescent Health. 2000;26:176–86. DOI: 10.1016/S1054-139X(99)00065-8

47. Greene RW. Conduct disorder and ODD. In: Thomas JC, Hersen M, editors. Handbook of clinical psychology competencies. New York: Springer; 2010. p. 1329–50.

48. Cappadocia MC, Desrocher M, Pepler D, Schroeder JH. Contextualizing the neurobiology of conduct disorder in an emotion dysregulation framework. Clinical Psychology Review. 2009;29:506–18. DOI: 10.1016/j.cpr.2009.06.001

49. Eme RF. Sex differences in child-onset, life-course-persistent conduct disorder. A review of biological influences. Clin Psychol Rev. 2006;27:607–27. DOI: 10.1016/j.cpr.2007.02.001

50. Borum R, Bartel P, Forth A. Manual for the structured assessment of violence risk in youth (SAVRY). Odessa, FL: Psychological Assessment Resources; 2006.

51. Davidson RJ, Putnam KM, Larson CL. Dysfunction in the neural circuitry of emotion regulation: a possible prelude to violence. Science. 2000;289:591–4. DOI: 10.1126/science.289.5479.591

52. Sterzer P, Stadler C, Krebs A, Kleinschmidt A, Poustka F. Abnormal neural responses to emotional visual stimuli in adolescents with conduct disorder. Biological Psychiatry. 2005;57:7–15. DOI: 10.1016/j.biopsych.2004.10.008

53. Frick PJ. Extending the construct of psychopathy to youth: implications for understanding, diagnosing, and treating antisocial children and adolescents. Canadian Journal of Psychiatry. 2009;54:803–12. DOI: 10.1177/070674370905401203

54. O'Doherty JP. Beyond simple reinforcement learning: the computational neurobiology of reward-learning and valuation. Eur J Neurosci. 2012;35:987–90. DOI: 10.1111/j.1460-9568.2012.08074.x

55. Eaves LJ, Silberg JL, Meyer JM, Maes HH, Simonoff E, Pickles A, et al. Genetics and developmental psychopathology, 2: the main effects of genes and environment on behavioral problems in the Virginia twin study of adolescent behavioral development. J Child Psychol Psychiatry. 1997;38:965–80. DOI: 10.1111/j.1469-7610.1997.tb01614.x

56. Maccoby E. The two sexes growing up apart, coming together. Cambridge, MA: The Belknap Press of Harvard University Press; 1998.

57. Krischer MK, Sevecke K. Early traumatization and psychopathy in female and male juvenile offenders. Int J Law Psychiatry. 2008;31:253–62. DOI: 10.1016/j.ijlp.2008.04.008

58. Bonta J, Andrews DA. Risk-need-responsivity model for offender assessment and rehabilitation. Public Safety Canada; 2007.

59. Hoge RD, Andrews DA. Youth level of service/case management inventory 2.0 (YLS/CMI 2.0): user's manual. Toronto: Multi-Health Systems; 2011.

60. Urquhart TA, Viljoen JL. The use of the SAVRY and YLS/CMI in adolescent court proceedings: a case law review. International Journal of Forensic Mental Health. 2014; 13:47–61. DOI: 10.1080/14999013.2014.885470

61. Forth A, Kosson D, Hare R. The Hare psychopathy checklist: youth version, technical manual. New York: Multi-Health Systems; 2003.

62. Worling JR, Curwen TC. The "ERASOR" estimate of risk of adolescent sexual offense recidivism version 2.0. Sexual Abuse: Family Education & Treatment (SAFE-T) Program, Thistletown Regional Centre for Children & Adolescents, Ontario Ministry of Community & Social Services. Toronto; 2001.

63. Shufelt JS, Cocozza JC. Youth with mental health disorders in the juvenile justice system: results from a multi-state, multi-system prevalence study. Delmar, NY: National Center for Mental Health and Juvenile Justice; 2006.

64. Buitelaar JK, Smeets KC, Herpers P, Scheepers F, Glennon J, Rommelse NN. Conduct disorders. Eur Child Adolesc Psychiatry. 2013;22:49–54. DOI: 10.1007/s00787-012-0361-y

65. Sawyer AM, Borduin CM, Dopp AR. Long-term effects of prevention and treatment on youth antisocial behavior: a meta-analysis. Clinical Psychology Review. 2015;42:130–44. DOI: 10.1016/j.cpr.2015.06.009

66. Hout MC, Phelan D. A grounded theory of fitness training and sports participation in young adult male offenders. Journal of Sports and Social Issues. 2014;38:124–47.

67. Nelson-Gray RO, Keane SP, Hurst RM, Mitchell JT, Warburton JB, Chok JT, et al. A modified DBT skills training program for oppositional defiant adolescents: promising preliminary findings. Behaviour Research and Therapy. 2006;44:1811–20.

68. Shelton D, Kesten K, Zhang W, Trestman R. Impact of a dialectic behavior therapy – corrections modified (DBT-CM) upon behaviorally challenged incarcerated male adolescents. Journal of Child and Adolescent Psychiatric Nursing. 2011;24:105–13.

69. McMahon RJ, Wells KC. Conduct problems. In: Mash EJ, Barkley RA, editors. Treatment of childhood disorders. 2nd ed. New York: Guilford; 1998. p. 111–210.

70. Greene RW. Collaborative problem solving. In Murrihy RC, Kidman, AD, Ollendick, TH, editors. Clinical handbook of assessing and treating conduct problems in youth. New York: Springer; 2010. p. 193–220.

71. Hawes DJ, Dadds MR. The treatment of conduct problems in children with callous unemotional traits. J Consult Clin Psychology 2005;73(4);737–41. DOI: 10.1037/0022-006X.73.4.737

72. Moffitt TE. Life course persistent and adolescence limited antisocial behaviour: a 10 year research review and research agenda. In: Lahey BB, Moffitt TE, Caspi A, editors. Causes of conduct disorder and juvenile delinquency. New York: Guilford Press; 2003. p. 49–75.

73. Hambly JL, Khan S, McDermott B, Bor W, Haywood A. Pharmacotherapy of conduct disorder: challenges, options and future directions. Journal of Psychopharmacology. 2016;30(1):967–75. DOI: 10.1177/0269881116658985

74. Findling RL. Atypical antipsychotic treatment of disruptive behavior disorders in children and adolescents. J Clin Psychiatry [Internet]. 2008;69(4):9–14. Available from: http://europepmc.org/abstract/med/18533763

75. Connor DF, Glatt SJ, Lopez ID, Jackson D, Melloni RH. Psychopharmacology and aggression. I: a meta-analysis of stimulant effects on overt/covert aggression-related behaviours

in ADHD. J Am Acad Child Adolesc Psychiatry. 2002;41(3):253–61. DOI: 10.1097/00004583-200203000-00004

76. Underwood LA, Warren KM, Talbott L, Jackson L, Dailey FLL. Mental health treatment in juvenile justice secure care facilities: Practice and policy recommendations. Journal of Forensic Psychology Practice. 2014;14(1):55–85. DOI: 10.1080/15228932.2014.865398

77. Skeem JL, Scott E, Mulvey EP. Justice policy reform for high-risk juveniles: using science to achieve large-scale crime reduction. Annu Rev Clin Psychol. 2014;10:709–39. DOI: 10.1146/annurev-clinpsy-032813-153707

78. Lipsey MW. The primary factors that characterize effective interventions with juvenile offenders: a meta-analytic overview. Victims and Offenders. 2009;4:124–47. DOI: 10.1080/15564880802612573T

CHAPTER 7

Paraphilic and Other Sexual Disorders

Debra Jellicoe, *Forensic Assessment and Community Services, Alberta Health Services*

LEARNING OBJECTIVES

1. Discuss normative and non-normative behaviours of human sexuality
2. Demonstrate an understanding of the diagnostic criteria and the prevalence of paraphilic disorders
3. Implement assessment and treatment of sexual offenders
4. Discuss some of the myths and facts associated with sexual offenders

INTRODUCTION

Human sexuality encompasses not only anatomy and physiology, but also culture and personal perception of gender and attraction. Attitudes and behaviours towards sex shift throughout one's lifespan and with society's changing norms. In Canada, 13% of youth have engaged in sexual intercourse by the age of 14 or 15 years, with minimal differences based on gender.[1] However, different factors were related to early sexual intercourse for girls and boys. Girls were more likely to engage in early sexual intercourse if they had an early onset of puberty, were not overweight, held a weak self-concept, and had tried smoking or drinking. Boys were more likely to engage in early sexual intercourse if they had a poor parent-child relationship, low family income, and had tried smoking.[1] What was viewed as risqué to talk about or see on television in the 1950s is dramatically different from today's norm. For example, pornography is by no means a new domain within sexuality. However, with the advent and availability of the Internet, pornography has found a new medium in which to flourish. Ninety-five percent of teenagers have access to the Internet, with 74% having mobile access. Internet pornography allows for not only ease in access but also increased affordability and anonymity. Individuals are free to explore and expand their sexual interests, and to find allies amid the vast Internet community for the less accepted sexual peculiarities. Approximately 87% of men view pornography, and sex is the most searched topic on the Internet.[2] Frequent viewing of pornography is related to potentially risky sexual behaviour, including casual sexual encounters.[3] Delinquent behaviour, however, such as rape or bestiality is typically viewed as loathsome across all cultures. Nonetheless, many topics remain discussable, such as transvestism, fetishes, and promiscuity—especially if these behaviours violate the rights of others.

PARAPHILIC DISORDERS

Of all the sexual disorders, police officers are most likely to encounter individuals with paraphilic disorders, for most of the associated behaviours are deemed criminal. The DSM-5 defines **paraphilia** as "any intense and persistent sexual interest"[4] other than that involving genital stimulation and associated behaviours with consenting partners. Paraphilias may involve erotic targets or activities.

Encompass sexual stimuli or acts that are deviant from typical sexual behaviours but are integral to one's sexual pleasure while causing distress or impairment to others. These include pedophilia, frotteurism, voyeurism, exhibitionism, sexual sadism, sexual masochism, and fetishism. Many other paraphilias have been identified, but as they are more rare or lawful in nature, they are only briefly described in table 7.1.

Table 7.1: List of Paraphilias

Paraphilia	Target of sexual arousal
Coprophilia	Feces
Hebephilia	Pubescent children
Hypoxyphilia	Altered state of consciousness
Necrophilia	Deceased individuals
Scatologia	Making obscene phone calls
Urophilia	Urine
Zoophilia	Animals

According to the DSM-5, there are two components to each diagnosis of paraphilic disorder:

- Criterion A specifies the qualitative nature of the sexual arousal (e.g., attraction to prepubescent children) and noted timeframe: "Over a period of at least six months, recurrent and intense sexual arousal."
- Criterion B specifies the impact of the sexual arousal: "The individual has acted on these sexual urges with a nonconsenting person, or the sexual urges or fantasies cause clinically significant distress or impairment in social, occupational, or other important areas of functioning."[4]

The "recurrent"[4] aspect of the diagnosis is generally interpreted as three or more victims on separate occasions. While a paraphilia is necessary for the disorder, it is not sufficient. More precisely, an individual can have a paraphilia without distress or negative impairment, thereby not meeting the criteria for the clinical disorder. Subjective distress may include shame, guilt, embarrassment, frustration, and/or loneliness. Impairment may also consist of legal involvement.

For each disorder, the diagnosis can be made even if the individual does not admit to the attraction, so long as there is sufficient objective evidence that supports the behaviour. For example, a large collection of bondage materials and participation in Dominance/Submission, and Sadism/Masochism (BDSM) is a strong suggestion of the presence of a sexual attraction for sadism and/or masochism. The diagnosis for paraphilic disorder can also be made if the individual admits to the sexual arousal, but has never acted on the attraction, so long as there is reported distress. In such cases it may be that the sexual arousal is ego-dystonic, that is, inconsistent with the individual's self-image. For example, a man may experience a sexual attraction towards children and fantasize about sexual contact but has never acted on such urges and makes attempts to avoid arousing stimuli.

CAUSAL FACTORS

There is no clear etiology for paraphilic disorders.[5] Biologically, some differences have been noted, but overall, the research remains mixed and inconclusive.[6,7] Unfortunately, given the multitude of possibilities, there have been no agreed upon predisposing factors, except for gender. Men are more likely to report fantasies involving fetishism, sadism, and exhibitionism, as well as be diagnosed with paraphilic disorders. Women are more likely to report fantasies involving masochism.[8] It may be that since men have typically higher sex drives than women, it is the sex drive that represents the distinguishing factor for paraphilic interests. One theory is that individuals with higher sex drives habituate more quickly to stimuli and have more energy to pursue continued sexual interests, including novel ones.[8] Individuals who show greater paraphilic interests have also shown greater degrees of impulsivity and sensation-seeking,[8] which may contribute to engaging in sexual behaviours related to their interests.

Most of the paraphilic disorders are only diagnosed for adults, given that adolescent sexuality is more fluid and experimental;[9] however, individuals generally start to become aware of their sexual interests in adolescence. The prevalence and incidence for most paraphilic disorders is generally unknown. Common comorbid disorders may include anxiety, mood, or personality disorders,[7] as well as meeting criteria for other paraphilias.[4]

VOYEURISTIC DISORDER

In the vernacular, voyeuristic individuals have been referred to as Peeping Toms: individuals who watch others (usually women) naked or undressing through windows from afar. According to the DSM-5, **Voyeuristic Disorder** involves "observing an unsuspecting person who is naked, in the process of disrobing, or engaging in sexual activity, as manifested by fantasies, urges, or behaviours."[7] With the advancement of technology, voyeuristic acts have evolved from watching individuals through windows or bathroom stalls to more sophisticated means. Acts such as upskirting have emerged; this involves recording the undergarments of unsuspecting women typically wearing skirts or dresses. An estimated lifetime prevalence for voyeuristic acts, in non-clinical samples, is 12% for males and 4% for females, and they are noted as the more common paraphilias that cross over into the legal world.[10]

EXHIBITIONISTIC DISORDER

In contrast to the Peeping Toms are the Flashers, those who expose themselves to others. **Exhibitionism** involves sexual arousal related to "exposure of one's genitals to an unsuspecting person, as manifested by fantasies, urges, or behaviours."[7] The prevalence of the disorder has been estimated to be 2-4% for males. The prevalence for females is uncertain but assumed to be much lower than males.[10] In contrast, lifetime victimization rates for women have ranged from 33% to 52%.[11] Exhibitionism as related to criminal behaviour is typically associated with the criminal offence of Indecent Act. This may consist of individuals exposing themselves in cars, alleyways, or through windows visibly accessible to others. Exhibitionists may expose themselves to random targets or may select certain individuals (e.g., adult women with blond hair). When diagnosing someone with the disorder, the assessor must specify the subtype, that is, if the nonconsenting party is prepubescent children, physically mature individuals, or both.

FROTTEURISTIC DISORDER

Frotteuristic Disorder is a paraphilia related to "recurrent and intense sexual arousal from touching or rubbing against a nonconsenting person, as manifested by fantasies, urges, or behaviours."[10] This disorder is often exhibited by individuals rubbing up against individuals in crowded places, such as a public transit system. While the prevalence for the disorder is unknown, it has been estimated that frotteuristic acts are committed by up to 30% of adult males in the general population.[10]

PEDOPHILIC DISORDER

Pedophilic Disorder involves sexual arousal to prepubescent children and is one of the more common of all the paraphilias.[8] The DSM-5 criteria are as follows:

1. Over a period of at least six months, recurrent, intense sexually arousing fantasies, sexual urges, or behaviours involving sexual activity with a prepubescent child or children (generally age 13 years or younger)
2. The individual has acted on these sexual urges, or the sexual urges and fantasies cause marked distress or interpersonal difficulty
3. The individual is at least age 16 years and at least five years older than the child or children in Criterion A
   Note: Does not include an individual in late adolescence involved in an ongoing sexual relationship with a 12- or 13-year-old.[7]

Diagnosis involves specifying exclusive type (only attracted to children) or non-exclusive type (attraction to children and adults). A diagnosis also specifies if the individual is sexually attracted to males, females, or both. The DSM-5 estimates that the highest estimate of prevalence for pedophilic disorder is approximately 3% to 5% for males. The prevalence for females is unknown.

An interesting subset of this population comprises individuals with sexual attraction to children, but who have not offended. Currently in Canada, the stigma against such an attraction can inhibit the individual acknowledging such thoughts or seeking help. Campaigns such as the Dunkelfeld Project in Germany aim to provide treatment services to those experiencing pedophilic thoughts or urges prior to them offending.[10]

Spotlight: Zebra Child Protection Centre (Zebra Centre)

When danger appears, zebras form a protective circle around their young. The Zebra Child Protection Centre (Zebra Centre) works the same way, bringing together a community of professionals to provide support to children and youth, who are victims of sexual and physical abuse. The Zebra Centre was the first Child Advocacy Centre (CAC) in Canada and has been supporting children, youth, and their non-offending caregivers through the Criminal Justice System (CJS) since 2002. Prior to that, when children or youth came forward to disclose their story of abuse, they found themselves navigating an adult world: repeating their story to many different agencies, being interviewed in the same room their suspect would be in just hours later, and unable to access therapeutic services until the conclusion of the criminal case. A group of professionals and some passionate community members knew they had to do better for the country's most vulnerable. Now, when an allegation of child abuse is made, the child, youth, and family are supported throughout the disclosure, investigative, healing, and prosecution journeys. Today, there are over 25 established and emerging CACs in Canada making significant strides to ensure children are supported, regardless of where they live.

As a community response model, the Zebra Centre brings together child advocacy staff, community volunteers (child advocates), and professional partners, including health services, police services, government services, and crown prosecutors. Together they provide a collaborative response to child abuse through intervention, advocacy, and a continuum of support in a child-friendly environment.

Anyone who has "reasonable and probable grounds" to believe that a child or youth is being harmed or is at risk has an obligation to report their concerns to the local policing agency or Children's Services. These reports are referred to the Zebra Centre's daily multi-disciplinary intake meeting, where on- and off-site partners review all files and determine the next steps for the investigations. By meeting the families where they are, individualized support plans are established and may include the following:

- Forensic interview: A recorded conversation where children or youth can tell their story in a safe and comfortable environment.
- Very Important Paws: Accredited facility dogs are here to provide comfort within the Zebra Centre and at the courthouse.
- Care Calls: Child advocates provide regular check-ins to offer file updates, referrals, and emotional support to caregivers.
- Crisis Response: The Zebra Centre provides 24-hour crisis response and advocacy to children and youth who are in immediate need of intervention.
- Mental Health Program: The Zebra Centre connects children and youth to counselling and trauma support professionals, helping them continue their healing journey.
- Court Preparation: When a case proceeds to court, court preparation is offered, a key step in addressing some of the questions and concerns that children, youth, and their families may have about the court process.
- Court Accompaniment: Child advocates stay with children, youth, and families throughout proceedings, liaising with those involved and guiding them through the process.
- Child Advocacy: The Zebra Centre ensures a child's or youth's needs remain everyone's top priority.
- Community Education and Awareness: Through presentations, events, donors, and corporate supporters, the Zebra Centre engages the community in the fight against child abuse.

In the years since the Zebra Centre has opened its doors, we have been fortunate to witness the successes of children, youth, and families through their act of bravery in telling their story, their engagement in the investigation, and their strength in testifying at court. The collaborative CAC model has become leading practice in fostering resilience in children and youth who have experienced abuse. As the professional and community partnerships continue to strengthen and expand, the Zebra Centre advances its vision of a community where child abuse is not tolerated.

To find the closest CAC resource, visit http://cac-cae.ca/.

For more information on the Zebra Child Protection Centre, visit www.zebracentre.ca.

SEXUAL OFFENCES

Not all paraphilias constitute criminal behaviour. The significant factor involved in distinguishing criminal from non-criminal sexual behaviour is the issue of consent. As outlined previously, many of the paraphilias can be practised in a safe and consensual manner. However, when the sexual behaviours disregard others' needs and rights, they become criminal. According to the Canadian Criminal Code (CCC), consent is defined as "the voluntary agreement of the complainant to engage in the sexual activity in question."[12] All sexual activity committed without consent is considered a criminal act. There are additional circumstances that void the consent. The most obvious is the individual's age. In Canada, the legal age to provide consent to sexual activity is 16 years. However, there are many exceptions and constraints applied. A close-in-age exception specifies that 12-and 13-year-olds can consent to sexual activity if their partner is not more than two years older. Therefore, a 12-year-old can consent to sexual activity with a 14-year-old. For 14- and 15-year-olds, they can consent to sexual activity with those who are less than five years older. Thus, a 14-year-old can consent to sexual activity with a 19-year-old,[13] but there are still conditions that remain attached to the consent. A child under the age of 12 years cannot consent to sexual activity under any circumstance. In Section 273.1(2) of the CCC, consent is not obtained under the following circumstances, regardless of age:

(a) the agreement is expressed by the words or conduct of a person other than the complainant;

(b) the complainant is incapable of consenting to the activity;

(c) the accused induces the complainant to engage in the activity by abusing a position of trust, power or authority;

(d) the complainant expresses, by words or conduct, a lack of agreement to engage in the activity; or

(e) the complainant, having consented to engage in sexual activity, expresses, by words or conduct, a lack of agreement to continue to engage in the activity.

These conditions include individuals who are intoxicated or do not have the cognitive capacity to consent. Furthermore, the CCC specifies that the belief that the partner consented is not a sufficient defence. While the CCC is specific in its definitions, there remains much confusion and ignorance regarding consent to sexual activity in both victims and perpetrators. It is estimated that only 5% of sexual crimes are reported to police.[14] Social efforts, such as the #IBelieveYou campaign, work to support and build awareness for victims of sexual assault.

Once individuals have engaged in harmful behaviour, and the behaviour is reported, the police will become involved. The CCC has numerous designations for sexual offences, including Sexual Assault, Sexual Interference, Indecent Act, Sexual Exploitation, Incest, and Voyeurism.[15]

In Canada, individuals convicted of certain designated sexual offences may be required to be placed on the National Sex Offender Registry as part of the Sexual Offender Information Registries Act (SOIRA). This involves re-registering annually and any time they change their address, legal name, employment, or volunteer activity.

PRECIPITATING AND PERPETUATING FACTORS

Sexual offenders are a highly heterogenous population, resulting in an unclear etiology with diverse, complex, and interconnected factors. Sifting through these variables is difficult with respect to methodological implications. Further, much of the research combines sexual offenders into one category even though examining specific sub-types may provide more fruitful information. For example, access to individuals with pedophilia largely comes from those who have interacted with the criminal justice system. Unfortunately, this group generally comprises sexual offenders with child victims, not specifically presented as being diagnosed with pedophilia. Also missing from the research are individuals who possess a sexual attraction to children but have not offended.

Biological Factors

Examination of possible neurological or neurodevelopmental factors associated with sexual offending has been more closely researched in the past couple of decades. While no causal factors have been determined, some interesting correlational findings are emerging. Research has outlined an association between pedophilia and poor brain functioning.[10] Sexual offenders with child victims have shown correlations with low intelligence quotient (IQ),[15] especially in comparison to sexual offenders with adult victims.[16] Individuals with pedophilia have shown deficits in memory and decreased rates of right-handedness.[10] The latter finding suggests a connection of pedophilia to early brain development. However, what is not clear is whether there are specific differences among sexual offenders with child victims (e.g., individuals with pedophilic disorder versus child molesters).[12]

Sexual offenders against adults tend to score similarly to non-sexual offenders on many neuropsychological measures.

Psychosocial Factors

Historically, sexual offenders have been explained by psychodynamic theories involving unresolved anxiety stemming from childhood: repressed infantile sexuality.[17] Cognitive theories focus on distorted thinking and attitudes that support sexual offending.[5] Learning and behavioural theories underscore the pairing of a particular target (fetishized object) with sexual arousal, conditioning the individual to then become aroused by that target.[6]

Developmental factors linked with sexual offending include childhood victimization,[7,21] problematic early sexual development, delinquent tendencies,[18] parenting experiences, community violence, self-regulation, and behaviour problems.[7] However, the problem is that not one factor alone can explain sexual offending or even be determined to have a causal relationship. For example, sexual offenders tend to have higher incidence rates of childhood victimization[5] and yet there is minimal to no empirical support for the abused/abuser theory of offending.[19]

ASSESSMENT AND TREATMENT OF SEXUAL OFFENDERS

Individuals who have committed a sexual offence may receive a forensic mental health assessment. These assessments include a clinical evaluation and usually a risk assessment. The clinical evaluation is helpful in assessing the presence of the paraphilia as well as any comorbid mental health problems, such as depression, anxiety, substance use, or personality disorders. Forensic mental health assessments rely on an in-person clinical interview and collateral information. Collateral information is important to corroborate the individual's information and examine any differences that arise.[20] Documentation can include legal documentation (e.g., criminal record, probation order, court transcripts, police reports), medical documentation (e.g., emergency room visits, psychiatric hospitalizations, prior mental health assessments), and other information as available or necessary (e.g., school records, Child and Family Service reports). Assessors are also encouraged to speak with collateral contacts such as family members, personal supports, professionals, and probation officers.

The clinical interview outlines a psychosocial history that covers the domains of family history (e.g., presence of any mental health or substance disorders), early developmental history (e.g., physical or emotional complications, developmental delays), education/employment history, social and intimate relationship history, sexual history, criminal history, and medical and psychiatric history. A current mental health assessment is typically completed to ascertain the presence of any acute or chronic psychiatric conditions, including paraphilic disorders.

The risk assessment is important for determining the individual's likelihood to reoffend, the intensity level of treatment programming, and specific treatment targets. Common risk assessment tools utilized by forensic clinicians include Static-99R,[21] STABLE-2007,[22] Risk for Sexual Violence Protocol (RSVP),[23] and the Violence Risk Scale—Sexual Offender Version (VRS-SO).[24] These tools require specialized training to ensure they are being administered in a reliable and valid manner. A risk assessment involves multiple steps, but it starts with identifying the risk factors for each individual.

While causal factors for sexual offenders are unknown, research has demonstrated more success in outlining predictive risk factors. Risk factors are those that can increase the risk for an individual to reoffend. They are often separated into static and dynamic risk factors. **Static risk factors** are historic in nature and rarely change. Examples include the number of prior criminal offences, age at release, and having unrelated victims.[19] **Dynamic risk factors** are changeable and generally the targets of treatment.[21] Examples include attitudes that support sexual offending, social rejection, negative emotionality, emotional congruence with children, and sexual deviancy.[25] Some of the risk tools only consider static factors (e.g., Static-99R), while others examine a blend of static and dynamic factors (e.g., STABLE-2007, RSVP). Once the risk factors have been identified, an overall risk rating is generated, often labelled as low, moderate, or high risk to sexually reoffend.

Another aspect of a risk assessment is providing a contextual framework for risk management. An individual who has been identified as a moderate risk for sexual **recidivism** (i.e., reoffending) provides minimal information about how to proceed. Therefore, it is important for the assessor to define what future offence behaviour may look like, who probable victims may be, situations in which the individual is more likely to reoffend, and circumstances that may facilitate risk management. Lastly, recommendations are made to assist with supervision and treatment planning.[19,25]

Most individuals who are in treatment for paraphilic disorders or associated behaviours are mandated to attend as a result of criminal behaviour. However, there are some individuals who have not offended and voluntarily seek out treatment, often due to internal distress or family pressure. In Canada, treatment is most readily available in a federal correctional institution setting or a forensic mental health clinic.

Treatment for sexual offenders has evolved from focus on shaming and denial to understanding and addressing the underlying factors that contribute to sexual offence. A more positive, strength-based approach has been more recently adopted.[26] These treatments incorporate a self-regulation model and/or good lives theory that may focus on engaging the client, developing a future-oriented pro-social life plan, and skills that enhance self-management of thoughts, emotions, and behaviours.[24] Treatment is often delivered in group settings, although it can also be completed on an individual basis. Some forensic mental health clinics offer multiple treatment groups based on the individual's risk level or developmental needs. Healthy sexuality, healthy relationships, emotional regulation, sexual deviance, and risk management planning are some of the issues addressed.

MYTHS AND FACTS

There are many unfortunate myths and stereotypes regarding individuals who have committed sexual offences that contribute to the population being highly stigmatized. Some of the more common ones are discussed below.

Myth: All sexual offenders will reoffend.

Fact: The sexual recidivism rate is estimated to be approximately 7-15% for all sexual offenders, regardless of treatment, after an average follow-up time of 68 months.[27] Not all sexual offenders recidivate at the same rate. Incest offenders have the lowest rate of recidivism at 5% over five years. Offenders with adult victims sexually reoffended at a rate of 14% over five years. The highest type of recidivists comprises individuals who offend against male children. They reoffended at a rate of 23% over five years.[28]

Myth: Sexual offenders cannot be treated.

Fact: Treatment for sexual offenders has been a controversial topic. This is due in part to the inherent challenges when attempting to study such a construct, especially given the different approaches to treatment. One meta-analysis showed modest support for treatment, outlining that recidivism rates for treated offenders were 11% compared to 17.5% for untreated sexual offenders.[29]

Myth: Sexual assault is perpetrated by predatory psychopaths; practice "stranger danger."

Fact: Women and children are much more likely to be sexually assaulted by someone who is known to them. In Canada in 2011, women reported that they knew the sexual perpetrator in 75% of the cases, with 45% identified as a casual acquaintance or friend, 17% as an intimate partner, and 13% as a non-spousal family member.[30]

Case Study: Frank

Frank is a 24-year-old male who was convicted of Theft and Indecent Act. The victim, an adult woman, awoke in the middle of the night to find Frank in her laundry room masturbating with her underwear. She immediately called the police. Frank fled the scene and was later tracked down by the K-9 unit and arrested. During his interview, Frank admitted his actions and was tearful. Further investigation ties him to multiple break and enters in the nearby vicinity. He pleaded guilty to four counts of break and enter to commit and one count of indecent act. He was sentenced to one year of custody and three years of probation. Frank was assessed by a forensic psychologist post-sentencing to determine his treatment needs. It was established that while growing up Frank was physically abused by his father. He did not have many friends and presented as socially awkward. He struggled in school and, when tested, was found to have some minor cognitive deficits. Frank reported no history of intimate relationships. He has no other criminal history. He endorsed symptoms consistent with anxiety and obsessive-compulsive disorder. He was assessed to be at a moderate risk to reoffend sexually and was recommended for treatment.

Questions
1.   Does Frank seem to meet the criteria for any paraphilic disorders?
2.   Are there any comorbid mental health disorders that may be notable?
3.   Which risk factors seem significant for Frank?
4.   What treatment targets seem to be most relevant for Frank?

OTHER PARAPHILIC DISORDERS

Fetishistic Disorder

According to the DSM-5, **fetishism** involves "recurrent and intense sexual arousal from the use of non-living objects or a highly specific focus on nongenital body part(s), as manifested by fantasies, urges, or behaviours."[7] While a wide range of stimuli can become a fetish, stimuli can be grouped as either a non-living object or a body part(s). More frequent inanimate objects can include shoes or undergarments. Tactile sources may include leather, rubber, or lace. Individuals with this disorder may require that the object be rubbed against them (e.g., masturbating to women's underwear) or that their partner be wearing the object (e.g., high-heeled shoes) to achieve sexual gratification. There are also cases in which the individual is sexually aroused by inserting objects, such as pencils, into his urethra. When the fetish involves nongenital body parts, this can be referred to as partialism.[7,31] Frequent body parts that become sexualized are feet, toes, or hair. More rare fetishes may include **urophilia** (sexual arousal to urine) or **coprophilia** (sexual arousal to feces), both of which may involve the individual performing the act on the partner or having the partner urinate or defecate on the individual.

Individuals with fetishistic disorders can come into contact with law enforcement for engaging in behaviours that support their paraphilia. A common example is an individual with a fetish for women's underwear and who steals the underwear to meet his need. Other rare paraphilias, necrophilia (sexual arousal and desire to engage in sexual activity with dead bodies) and zoophilia (sexual arousal to non-human animals), would be considered illegal acts based on the inability of the persons to consent to sexual activity.

Transvestic Disorder

Transvestic disorder involves sexual arousal paired with cross-dressing, that is, dressing in clothing opposite to one's sex. The cross-dressing can vary from one article of clothing to an entire wardrobe. It should be noted that there can be individuals who cross-dress but do not meet the disorder, as the clothing is not part of their sexual excitement. This disorder is almost exclusively male, and the men are generally heterosexual. The DSM-5 outlines two subtypes: fetishism (sexual arousal by fabrics, materials, or garments) and autogynephilia (sexual arousal to thoughts or images of self as female). While the prevalence of the disorder is unknown, estimates suggest that fewer than 3% have identified sexual arousal to dressing in women's clothing.[10] Unlike most other paraphilias, transvestism does not easily intersect with the criminal justice system.

Sexual Masochism and Sexual Sadism Disorders

Both disorders involve intense sexual arousal from the acts of aggression, binding, humiliation, or suffering. **Masochism** involves suffering or pain being inflicted upon the self, whereas **sadism** involves sexual pleasure from inflicting/seeing the physical or psychological suffering of another person. Sexual masochism disorder has a subtype that involves asphyxiophilia, or sexual arousal related to the restriction of breathing. Approximately 30% of individuals who enjoy masochism have concurrent fantasies involving sadism.[7] With both masochism and sadism there may be overlapping paraphilias in which sexual arousal is tied to objects, such as whips, chains, or collars. As with the other paraphilias, sadomasochism can be practised in a consensual manner that does not cause distress requiring clinical diagnosis or intervention. A 2008 study from Australia estimated that 2.2% of men and 1.3% of women who were sexually active engaged in some form of BDSM activities in the previous year.[32] Therefore, it is important to separate BDSM from the clinical diagnoses of masochism and sadism. Such practices become concerning to clinicians and police when they escalate to imposing the behaviours upon non-consenting partners, such as in the context of sexual assault. The disorder is estimated at fewer than 10% among civilly committed sexual offenders in the United States, although rates are higher for individuals who have committed sexually motivated homicides (37-75%).[10]

SEXUALITY AND GENDER

In general, sexuality comprises four factors: sexual identity, gender identity, sexual orientation, and sexual behaviour. Sexual behaviour involves the physical responses and activities associated with sex. These include the sexual response cycle, masturbation, and intercourse. Sexual behaviour may also include sexual expression.

Stigma and shame have been socially imposed on individuals expressing anything other than a cisgender-heterosexual experience. As these beliefs and attitudes are challenged, more individuals are expressing their genuine identities. However, it is not always done without fear and trepidation. Underlying anxieties regarding interacting with traditional systems (e.g., police, education, health care) may still be present. Police officers have an opportunity to demonstrate fairness, acceptance, and tolerance. It is understandable that with so many labels and social customs, it can be confusing for police officers to act considerately. When interacting with individuals from a sexual minority, a simple solution is to ask them how they wish to be addressed or which pronouns to use.

Sexual identity refers to the biological aspects of a person's sexual characteristics. An individual's sex includes chromosomes, hormones, and sexual genitalia. For most individuals, their sex is cohesive and determined in utero.[33] Gender, on the other hand, refers to the social construct of maleness or femaleness, or some combination thereof.

Gender identity is the self-perception of one's gender. Kohlberg's 1966 theory posits that gender identity is established gradually throughout early childhood and becomes constant during the late preschool and early school years.[34] Gender identity can be influenced by parental, cultural, and personal experiences. For example, many men in Canadian culture learn that aggression, power, and success are esteemed masculine characteristics, while crying and sensitivity may be portrayed as signs of weakness. Children and youth measure themselves against such standards in developing their own identities. Cisgender refers to consistency with one's biological sex. **Transgender** is an umbrella term encompassing all individuals who have a discrepancy between their gender and their biological sex. Those whose physical body is opposite from their gender can be referred to as transsexual. Some individuals may feel that they are between genders or questioning their orientation, and may refer to themselves as queer or genderqueer.[35]

Sexual orientation involves the object of one's physical and sexual attraction. Sexual orientation is typically noticed during childhood.[8] Heterosexual, homosexual, bisexual, **pansexual** (attracted to all genders), and **asexual** (without sexuality) are the most frequent descriptions of orientation. Sexual orientation can also be viewed as a continuum. A woman may feel comfortable engaging in certain sexual acts (e.g., kissing) with either gender and other acts (sexual intercourse) with only one gender. Approximately 2-4% of the population identify as homosexual.[8] An acronym for all the sexual minorities can be GLBTT2IQA, which refers to Gay, Lesbian, Bisexual, Transgender, Transsexual, 2-spirited, Intersexed, Queer/Questioning, and Allies. It is more commonly shortened to GLBT/LGBT. An average age for youth to "come out," or disclose their sexual or gender identities to others, is 14 years.[36]

Although they will not be explained in detail in this textbook, there is a set of psychiatric disorders outlined in the DSM-5 that addresses sexual dysfunctions and gender dysphoria. Sexual dysfunction disorders focus on the impact of an individual's ability to respond to sexual stimulation, arousal, and ejaculation, or to experience pain associated with sexual activity. This may include Male Erectile Disorder or Orgasmic Disorders. Treatment may consist of pharmacology and/or therapy.[8] Individuals with gender dysphoria are distinguished from transgender individuals because transgendered individuals will not experience distress and therefore do not meet the criteria for the disorder. Often, struggles arise for individuals with gender dysphoria who are not able to receive interventions to match the physical and hormonal characteristics to their identified gender.

SUMMARY

Sexual disorders represent a widely diverse set of difficulties ranging from individuals struggling with their own identity, unable to achieve orgasm, and having sexual arousal to deviant stimuli, to engaging in harmful sexual behaviours. Sexuality and sexual behaviours are complex, with multiple individual and societal factors intersecting. Police officers may interact with individuals as both victims and perpetrators. In either case, it is helpful to have an understanding, based on facts, that will more accurately influence thoughts and perceptions. At times in the police world, an effort is required to see the humanity in offenders, and yet, when achieved, this is more likely to reflect safety and justice.

REFLECTION QUESTIONS

1. How can you determine if someone has a paraphilic disorder?
2. What are some of the common risk factors for sexual offending?

3. What is some information about treatment that you could provide to an individual who has been arrested for a sexual offence?

4. What can you do to continue to learn about the research related to sexual offending?

REFERENCES

1. Garriguet, D. Early sexual intercourse. Health Reports, Statistics Canada. 2005 May;16(3):9–18. Catalogue 82–003.

2. Tlyka, TL. No harm in looking, right? Men's pornography consumption, body image, and well-being. Psychology of Men and Masculinity. 2014 Jan:1–11.

3. Braithwaite SR, Coulson G, Keddington K, Fincham FD. The Influence of pornography on sexual scripts and hooking up among emerging adults in college. Archives of Sexual Behavior. 2015;44:111–23.

4. American Psychiatric Association. Diagnostic and statistical manual of mental disorders (DSM-5). American Psychiatric Pub; 2013 May 22.

5. Miller, DL. An application of the theory of planned behavior to the proximal and distal etiology of sexual offending. Trauma, Violence & Abuse. 2010;11(3):113–28.

6. Sadock BJ, Sadock VA, Ruiz, P. Kaplan and Sadock's synopsis of psychiatry. Philadelphia: Wolters Kluwer.

7. Rodriguez M, Ellis A. The neuropsychological function of older, first-time child exploitation material offenders: a pilot study. International Journal of Offender Therapy and Comparative Criminology [Internet]. 2017. Available from: https://doi.org/10.1177/0306624X17703406

8. Dawson, SJ, Bannerman BA, Lalumière ML. Paraphilic interests: An examination of sex difference in a nonclinical sample. Sexual Abuse: A Journal of Research and Treatment. 2016;28(1):20–45.

9. Seto MC, Kingston DA, Bourget D. Assessment of the paraphilias. Psychiatric Clinics of North America [Internet]. 2014 June [cited 2017 Sep 15]. Available from: http://dx.doi.org/10.1016/j.psc.2014.03.001

10. Beier KM, Grundmann D, Kuhle LF, Scherner G, Konrad A, Amelung T. The German dunkelfeld project: a pilot study to prevent child sexual abuse and the use of child abusive images. The Journal of Sexual Medicine. 2014. Available from: DOI: 10.1111/jsm.12785

11. Clark SK, Jeglic EL, Calkins C, Tatar JR. More than a nuisance: the prevalence and consequences of frotteurism and exhibitionism. Sexual Abuse: A Journal of Research and Treatment. 2016;28(1):3–19.

12. Consolidation Criminal Code, R. S. C. [Internet]. 1985, c. C-46. 2017 Aug 27 [cited 2017 Sep 11]. Available from: http://laws-lois.justice.gc.ca

13. Department of Justice. Age of consent to sexual activity. Government of Canada [Internet]. 2008 [cited 2017 Sep 11]. Available from: http://www.justice.gc.ca/eng/rp-pr/other-autre/clp/faq.html

14. Allen M. Police reported crime statistics in Canada, 2015. Juristat [Internet]. 2016 July [cited 2017 Sep 11]. Catalogue no. 85-002-X. Available from: http://www.statcan .gc.ca/pub/85-002-x/2016001/article/14642-eng.pdf

15. Cantor JM, Blanchard R, Christensen BK, Dickey R, Klassen PE, Beckstead AL, et al. Intelligence, memory, and handedness in pedophilia. Neuropsychology. 2004;18(1):3–14.

16. Joyal CC, Plante-Beaulieu J, de Chanterac A. The neuropsychology of sex offenders: a meta-analysis. Sexual Abuse: A Journal of Research and Treatment. 2014;26(2):149–77.

17. Brenner C. An Elementary Textbook of Psychoanalysis. Revised ed. 1973. New York: Anchor Books.

18. Brouillette-Alarie S, Proulx J. The etiology of risk in sexual offenders: a preliminary model. Sexual Abuse. 2018. Available from: DOI: 10.1177/1079063218759325

19. Furnham A, Haraldsen E. Lay theories of etiology and "cure" for four types of paraphilia: fetishism; pedophilia; sexual sadism; and voyeurism. Journal of Clinical Psychology. 1998;54(5):689–700.

20. Heilbrun K, NeMoyer A, King C, Galloway M. Using third-party information in forensic mental-health assessment: a critical review. Court Review. 2015 Feb; 51:16–35.

21. Hanson RK, Thornton D. Static 99: Improving actuarial risk assessments for sex offenders. Ottawa, Ontario: Solicitor General Canada; 1999 Sep.

22. Fernandez Y, Harris AJR, Hanson KR, Sparks J. STABLE-2007: Coding manual. Public Safety Canada. 2014.

23. Hart SD, Kropp PR, Laws RD, Klaver J, Logan C, Watt KA. Risk for sexual violence protocol (RSVP): structured professional guidelines for assessing risk of sexual violence. Burnaby: Mental Health, Law, and Policy Institute, Simon Fraser University. 2003.

24. Wong S, Olver ME, Nicholaichuk TP, Gordon A. The violence risk scale – Sexual offender version (VRS–SO). Saskatoon: Regional Psychiatric Centre and University of Saskatchewan. 2003.

25. Beech AR, Fisher DD, Thorton D. Risk assessment of sex offenders. Professional Psychology: Research and Practice. 2003;34(4):339–52.

26. Marshall WL, Marshal LE. Psychological treatment of sex offenders. Psychiatric Clinics of North America. 2014;37:163–71.

27. Hanson KR, Harris AJR, Helmus M, Thorton D. High risk offenders may not be high risk forever. Journal of Interpersonal Violence. 2014 Mar.

28. Assessment and Treatment of Sexual Abusers (ATSA). Eight things everyone should know about sexual abuse and sexual offending [Internet]. 2014 June [cited 2017 Sep 15]. Available from: http://www.atsa.com/pdfs/Policy/8ThingsEveryoneShouldKnow.pdf

29. Hanson KR, Yates PM. Psychological treatment of sex offenders. Current Psychiatry Reports [Internet]. 2013;15(348) [cited 2017 Sep 15]. Available from: DOI: 10.1007/s11920-012-0348-x

30. Sinha M, editor. Measuring violence against women: statistical trends. Juristat [Internet]. 2013 [cited 2017 Sep 15]. Available from: http://www.statcan.gc.ca/pub/85-002-x/2013001/article/11766-eng.pdf

31. Kafka MP. The DSM diagnostic criteria for fetishism. The Archives of Sexual Behavior. 2009 [cited 2017 Sep 11]. Available from: DOI: 10.1007/s10508-009-9558-7

32. Richters J, De Visser RO, Rissel CE, Grulich AE, Smith AMA. Demographic and psychosocial features of participants in bondage and discipline, "sadomasochism" or dominance and submission (BDSM): data from a national survey. The Journal of Sexual Medicine. 2008;July 5(7):1660–8.

33. Sadock BJ, Sadock VA, Ruiz P. Kaplan and Sadock's synopsis of psychiatry. Philadelphia: Wolters Kluwer.

34. Berk L. Child Development. 6th ed. Boston: Allyn and Beacon; 2003.

35. Kinsey Confidential. The Trustees of Indiana University [Internet]. 2017 [cited 2017 Sep 10]. Available from: https://kinseyconfidential.org/resources/gender-sexual-orientation/

36. Russell ST, Fish JN. Mental health in lesbian, gay, bisexual, and transgender (LGBT) youth. The Annual Review of Clinical Psychology. 2016;12:465–87.

CHAPTER 8

Acute and Post-Traumatic Stress Disorders

Stephanie J. Laue, *Correctional Services of Canada*

John R. Reddon, *Department of Psychology, University of Alberta and Forensic Psychiatry, Alberta Hospital Edmonton*

LEARNING OBJECTIVES

1. Understand the origins and evolution of Post-Traumatic Stress Disorder (PTSD)
2. Demonstrate a knowledge of incidence and prevalence rates of PTSD in civilians and first responders
3. Interpret symptoms and signs of PTSD
4. Differentiate between Acute Stress Disorder and PTSD
5. Understand the differences between pretraumatic, peritraumatic, and post-traumatic factors
6. Describe the best treatment practices for PTSD

INTRODUCTION

Policing is a career that is likely to expose individuals to many traumatic events while they perform their duties. Police officers are required to attend to situations that are outside the range of typical human experience. Police are often called out to violent assaults and deadly motor vehicle accidents, and are witnesses to death, injury, domestic violence, and child abuse. They must deal with perpetrators as well as their victims. It is not surprising, then, that first responders (police officers, paramedics, corrections officers, firefighters) are at increased risk for Post-Traumatic Stress Disorder (PTSD) and/or **Acute Stress Disorder** (ASD). In 2016, Victoria News reported that the number of first responders in Canada

Case Study: A Common Disorder in Policing

I started my career in law enforcement as a correctional officer in provincial facilities and then moved to the federal system. After three years I became a police officer in a large Canadian city. I grew up in a family of police officers; my father, uncle, and brother were all members of the same police service. The concept of PTSD was not talked about in my family as I grew up; however, through our discussions it is apparent that we all suffer from the disorder and that the exposure to traumatic events has affected our lives in several different ways.

I spent the first several years of my career in a front-line patrol function, mostly in the inner city. I saw the effects of addiction first-hand and witnessing the aftermath of violence was a daily occurrence. The area I was assigned to had significant gang issues as well as a large amount of street prostitution. The youngest sex trade worker that I dealt with was 10 years old and had been turned out on the street by her own mother. Witnessing this level of betrayal was something I did not realize had such a profound effect on me until much later in life. The level of violence in this area was exceptional, but one gang home invasion always stands out to me because a young teenage girl was babysitting at the house where the attack happened, and she was stabbed multiple times; she survived, but the trauma she experienced was incredible.

I later moved into investigative roles and found myself investigating homicides. This was definitely a career goal for me, as I was always interested in death investigations. In this role I attended numerous crime scenes, all with varying levels of trauma. To this day I can close my eyes and see each of the victims, what they were wearing, and how they were positioned. Several of these investigations profoundly affected me.

These events culminated in my behaviour changing. I focused on one thing: work. I started neglecting my family; I also started to withdraw from the people who cared about me. I couldn't drive anywhere in the city without a flashback of a crime scene. Certain items would cause a visceral reaction. Things like purple potatoes remind me of deceased bodies in stages of decomposition, specific cartoon characters flash as they appeared on the pyjamas of tender-aged victims; to this day these images provoke an immediate and intense emotional reaction.

It wasn't until my life really started to spiral that I eventually reached out for help. The odd thing is, I had been told numerous times that I should, yet I had refused, believing it would make me look weak. I was a homicide detective; why would this impact my life? what is wrong with me? Once I received help, I started to understand flashbacks, trauma, and vicarious trauma. I started to function again as a family member and friend; I was again myself. I still have flashbacks, nightmares, and reactions to things that trigger my memories. However, I also understand what has caused my mental injury and how to manage it. One of my greatest learnings has been on how to share my pain in a healthy way, how to talk to the people in my life about what was bothering me rather than holding it in. The knowledge that PTSD is a mental injury, which, like any injury, can be properly managed, allows me to function.

There is still an uphill battle in police culture to ensure that police officers take care of their mental health. This has been on a steady increase since I started my career, and I believe that awareness and understanding of PTSD and many other mental health issues will allow police officers to reach out for help before it is too late.

Questions

1. Identity some of the behaviours associated with PTSD.
2. What are some of the stigmas and barriers associated with pursuing help for a mental illness?
3. What can you do to diminish mental health stigmas?

---

who committed suicide that year was 19, seven of them police officers.[1] Suicide is just one outcome, sadly fatal, which can result from chronic or acute exposure to traumatic events. Although the reasons for suicide are multifaceted, a diagnosis of PTSD has been correlated with an increased risk for taking one's life.[2,3]

The diagnosis of PTSD is unique among psychiatric illness in that an identifiable event is required for diagnosis. For the individual presenting with PTSD, the traumatic event does not only take place once but over and over in the mind, as if it were happening presently. Bessel van der Kolk, one of the leading researchers in trauma, describes the effects of trauma on the human body: "Being traumatized means continuing to organize your life as if the trauma were still going on—unchanged and immutable—as if every new encounter or event is contaminated by the past."[4]

HISTORY OF TRAUMATIC STRESS

Although the term PTSD is relatively new in our lexicon, the symptoms and signs of PTSD were identified and recorded as early as the 1600s. Johannes Hofer, a military physician, championed the term "nostalgia" in 1688 to label and categorize the physical and mental symptoms he was seeing in soldiers. These included sadness, weeping, anorexia, and suicide attempts, which Hofer believed were the result of soldiers' longing to return home.[5] In 1874, Jacob Mendes Da Costa coined the diagnosis "soldier's heart," and, finally, during the First World War these symptoms were given the name "shell shock" or "war hysterics."[6,7] These terms implied more than that injuries were a result of the war; the term **hysteria** (used only for women at the time) implied a male weakness, a faking of symptoms, thereby challenging the notion of the brave, tough, victorious solider.[7] This thinking influenced the treatment of war hysterics by medical professionals. Treatments included persuasive psychotherapy, hypnosis, electric shock treatments, physical exercises, military re-education, and a retraining of the moral will.[7]

Although different names have been used over the centuries, physicians were attempting to classify and understand the psychological and physical symptoms they witnessed as a result of warfare. Over time, common symptoms identified included vivid images in the mind, missing home, bodily dysfunctions, feeling sad, sleep problems, physical disabilities, and anxiety.

HISTORY OF TRAUMATIC STRESS SYNDROMES

Significant strides in understanding the effects of wartime traumatic experiences as being psychological in nature were made during the First and Second World Wars. These lessons were applied to subsequent wars such as the Korean War, where combat tours were shortened to nine months as a way to attenuate the effects of wartime trauma, and the Vietnam War, where psychological casualties were reduced by the implementation of rest and relaxation breaks for the soldiers, fixed duty tours, and the provision of mental health services.[8] Despite these efforts to control for psychological damage, Vietnam veterans were arriving home displaying behaviours that included suicide attempts, substance abuse, and antisocial behaviours.[6] Due to these psychological casualties, Lifton and Shatan in 1975 approached the head of the Diagnostic and Statistical Manual—Third Revision (DSM-III) task force to request the inclusion of the term "post-Vietnam syndrome" into the DSM-III.[6] As a result of their efforts,

Table 8.1: Historical Identification of Post-Traumatic Stress Disorder

1678	Nostalgia—Hoffer
1865	Irritable Heart/Soldier's Heart—Da Costa
1882	Railway spine—Erichson
1887	Hysteria—Charcot
1890	Sensory Overload—Oppenheim
1895	Nervous Shock—Page
1918	Shell Shock—First World War
1920	Traumatic fixation—Freud
1945	Battle fatigue—Second World War
1951	Brainwashing—Korean War
1980	Post-Traumatic Stress Disorder—Vietnam War
1991	Gulf War Syndrome—First Gulf War
1990–Present	Increasing recognition of civilian PTSD syndromes
2003–Present	Resurgence of PTSD and Traumatic Brain Injury (TBI) as the "signature injuries" of the Second Gulf War

the American Psychiatric Association (APA) in 1980 accepted what was to become known as PTSD—an anxiety disorder defined by a past event that creates dysfunction in the present.[6] Over time clinicians found that this diagnosis was no longer attributable only to those who had served in the military; survivors of other traumatic events, such as sexual assault, natural disasters, abuse, torture, accidents, etc., were also included because they exhibited similar symptoms, thereby warranting a diagnosis of PTSD.[8-10]

PTSD IN THE DSM-5

Currently, the DSM-5 describes PTSD as a combination of eight criteria, all of which are required for a diagnosis.[11]

PREVALENCE

According to the DSM-5, the lifetime projected risk in the United States for PTSD (at age 75) is 8.7%, with the 12-month prevalence rate of adults at 3.5%. Lower estimates are seen in most European, Asian, African, and Latin

Table 8.2: DSM-5 Diagnostic Criteria for Post-Traumatic Stress Disorder

Criterion A: Exposure to actual or threatened death, serious injury, or sexual violence which can occur in one or more ways:
- directly to the individual
- being a witness to an event happening to others
- learning that a violent or accidental death occurred to a close family member or friend
- experiencing repeated/extreme exposure to aversive details of the traumatic event (e.g., first responders)

Criterion B: Recurrent intrusive distressing symptoms associated with the traumatic event, occurring in one or more ways after the event:
- distressing memories
- recurring distressing dreams
- dissociative reactions (flashbacks)
- intense or prolonged psychological distress at exposure to internal or external cues that symbolize or resemble an aspect of the event
- marked physiological reactions to internal or external cues that symbolize or resemble an aspect of the event

Criterion C: Persistent avoidance of stimuli associated with a traumatic event beginning after the event such as one or both of
- avoidance or efforts to avoid distressing memories, thoughts, or feelings about or closely related to the traumatic event
- and/or avoidance or efforts to avoid external reminders (people, places, etc.) that arouse distressing memories, thoughts, or feelings about or closely related to the traumatic event

Criterion D: Negative alterations in cognitions and mood associated with the traumatic events beginning or worsening after the event as evidenced by two or more of the following:
- inability to remember an important aspect of the trauma
- negative beliefs or expectations about oneself, others, or the world
- persistent blame of self or others for the causes or consequences of the trauma
- persistent negative affect
- marked disinterest/participation in activities
- feelings of detachment/estrangement from others
- persistent inability to experience positive affect

Criterion E: Marked arousal and reactivity that began or worsened after the trauma, in two or more of the following way(s):
- irritable behaviour and aggression, expressed verbally or physically
- reckless or self-destructive behaviour
- hypervigilance
- exaggerated startle reaction
- problems concentrating
- sleep disturbances

Criterion F: Criteria B, C, D, & E must last for more than one month.
Criterion G: Symptoms cause significant distress or functional impairment (e.g., social, occupational, etc.)
Criterion H: Symptoms are not due to substance use, medication, or other medical condition.
The criteria for Acute Stress Disorder (ASD) and PTSD are similar, with the differences being largely temporal, that is, the duration of symptoms in addition to a different number of symptoms required. A diagnosis of PTSD requires more than one month of active symptoms, whereas ASD is three days up to one month after the traumatic event. The disorder of PTSD can occur at any age, with symptoms beginning typically within three months of the trauma but that may be delayed by months or years.

American countries, with rates around 0.5-1.0%. Rates are higher in veterans and first responders, with the highest rates occurring in rape survivors, military combat and captivity, ethnic or politically motivated internment, and genocide.

These higher rates in veterans are illustrated in a 2013 Canadian Armed Forces Report.[12] This report indicates that for regular force members the lifetime percentage of being diagnosed with PTSD is 11.1% and the 12-month rate is 5.3%. In addition, the report found that PTSD was higher in female members than males, with almost double the rates (8.8% versus 4.7% respectively). However, male members had a much higher rate of alcohol abuse or dependence than their female counterparts (4.8% versus 2.3%). Much of the focus has been on military personnel, with little focus on the Canadian general population. However, in 2002 a nationwide study undertaken by researchers Van Amerigen, Mancini, Patterson, and Boyle surveyed 2,991 Canadians over the age of 18.[13] They found that the lifetime prevalence rate of PTSD for Canadians was 9.2%, which is comparable to rates in the United States.

The literature on PTSD in first responders, who due to the nature of their work attend traumatic events, has discovered that these groups are at greater risk for developing PTSD.[14] Among these occupational groups, however, police officers had the lowest rates.[14,15] In a large Canadian study, police officers were found to have a lifetime rate of developing PTSD of 8%, which is a lower rate than for other first responders, military personnel, and the general Canadian population.[16] Possible reasons for this difference will be described later in this chapter.

COMORBIDITIES AND DIFFERENTIAL DIAGNOSIS

It is not uncommon for mental health disorders to co-occur, and PTSD is no exception. PTSD has been shown to have a comorbidity rate of 65%-98% and co-occurs with other mental health disorders such as anxiety and adjustment disorders, major depressive disorders, personality disorders, psychotic disorders, eating disorders, substance abuse, dementia, conduct disorder, and with physical injuries such as Traumatic Brain Injury (TBI).[11] As the focus of PTSD research has primarily been on military populations, the problem of TBI has been front and centre and creates a diagnostic challenge. The symptoms of each diagnosis overlap and can both co-occur, which complicates the course of PTSD and adds challenges for treatment.[17] In addition to discerning an appropriate diagnosis for treatment, it is also important for the clinician to be aware of patient malingering.

Malingering is the purposeful and false presentation of symptoms motivated by some external reward. These external rewards or incentives include financial gain, such as insurance settlements or disability payments, and evading military duty and/or criminal prosecution.[18] Those who attempt to evade criminal conviction will often claim diminished capacity (such as being Not Criminally Responsible (NCR)) or use a diagnosis of PTSD as a mitigating factor to receive a lighter sentence.[8,18]

BIOLOGY OF TRAUMA

In order to better understand how the disorder of PTSD develops, we need a basic understanding of our body's physiological response to stress and traumatic events, and in particular how this interaction creates a response of flight or fight.[19]

The limbic system is often referred to as our "lizard brain" due to its role in primitive animal functioning. It regulates the basic functions of the five Fs: fight, flight, feed, freeze, and fornication. When an extreme threat is encountered, the limbic system activates our body's two main stress response systems: the sympathetic nervous system (SNS) and the hypothalamic pituitary adrenal (HPA) axis. The SNS activates the fight-flight-freeze response, which quickly discharges adrenaline from the adrenal medulla to prepare the body to respond to the threat.

The HPA (a neuroendocrine system) activates a series of reactions in which several hormones are released, including the "stress hormone" cortisol, from the cortex of the adrenal glands. Normally, when the traumatic event is over, the systems are turned off and return to a state of balance (i.e., homeostasis). However, in PTSD the HPA feedback system becomes disrupted and cannot return to homeostasis. The effort expended in attempting to achieve homeostasis is termed allostatic load. Studies have shown higher levels of the hormone cortisol in persons with PTSD, suggesting that cortisol is unable to shut down the SNS response, thereby remaining in a hyperaroused state.[18]

Another system implicated in the stress response and the development of PTSD is the cortical-limbic system, which contains three large brain structures: the amygdala, the medial pre-frontal cortex, and the hippocampus. The amygdala is the brain's emotion centre and controls anger, sadness, fear, and aggression; it plays a key role in our body's response to a threat by activating the SNS fight-flight-freeze response. In traumatic events, the amygdala is activated to mobilize the individual into action. However, in the development of PTSD the amygdala's response remains heightened and does not turn off.[18,20]

The medial pre-frontal cortex is responsible for the executive functioning of the brain. Executive functioning regulates problem solving, planning, reasoning, regulating social behaviours, attentional control, and cognitive flexibility. The medial frontal cortex is thought to exert restraint over the amygdala and helps return the amygdala to baseline functioning. In PTSD this inhibitory control is dysfunctional.[18,20]

Lastly, the hippocampus is the centre of episodic and declarative memory retrieval and formation.[21] Low hippocampal volumes have been seen in patients with PTSD, and it is hypothesized that this atrophy impacts memory, learning, and makes it difficult for an individual to distinguish safe from unsafe environments.[22,23] Currently, it is unclear if smaller hippocampal volumes, low cortisol levels, and increased amygdala activity create a vulnerability for PTSD or are a result of PTSD.[23]

CAUSAL FACTORS IN PTSD

Most people who have experienced a stressful or traumatic event continue to function well during and after the event. But for those who do not, causal factors that contribute to their response and whether they will develop PTSD can be broken down into a sequential timeline. The timeline is divided into three parts: (1) factors that pre-exist the traumatic event are considered **pre-traumatic**, (2) factors that arise during the event are **peritraumatic**, and (3) factors that contribute to the development of PTSD following the event are categorized as **post-traumatic**.

Pre-traumatic Factors

An individual's reaction to a traumatic event has been shown to be mitigated or exacerbated by several pre-traumatic factors. **Pre-traumatic factors** can include an individual's personality (such as hardiness and trait anger), prior trauma exposure such as childhood abuse and neglect, psychiatric disorders such as depression, and genetics.[13,14,18,20,24] Demographics can also play a role; factors such as gender, age, and ethnicity can contribute to and/or protect against the development of PTSD.[17,21] For the sake of brevity, only gender, psychiatric history, and pre-traumatic variables specific to policing will be discussed here.

Gender

There is a strong relationship between gender and the development of PTSD, with women having almost double the rates of men.[25] A 2008 study showed that this trend also holds true for Canadians, with a current rate of 1.3% for men and 3.4% for women.[13] It has been hypothesized that women are more susceptible to the HPA axis dysregulation than men, with women showing lower levels of basal cortisol than men.[9] However, this argument does not seem to hold true for women in policing, as prevalence rates for PTSD are not higher for females than their male counterparts. In fact, no gender differences are found.[9,26] This trend is further solidified when comparing the rates of female police officers to female civilians, where female police officers still report fewer PTSD symptoms.[27]

Psychiatric History

As discussed earlier, PTSD is comorbid with many other psychiatric diagnoses. Depression has been commonly cited as a factor in the development of PTSD for both civilian and police populations.[25] It is estimated that during their careers 35% of police officers will experience irritability, depressive symptoms, anxiety, loss of interest in life, difficulty with sleep, headaches, and other mental health symptoms that create a vulnerability for developing PTSD. In contrast, good mental health has been found to be a protective factor.[28-30]

Police-Specific Factors

Activities related to job duties were found to contribute to the higher rates of PTSD in firefighters, ambulance personnel, and policing. These activities include the level of risk to the responder's life, the hours worked (erratic and shift work), and past military experience.[15] Nevertheless, police officers are seemingly more resilient to PTSD than other first responders, and this has been attributed to how officers are selected and the rigorous training involved.[14,16,31] The training of police officers involves preparation for violent attacks, measures to take when being assaulted, and strategies to employ in threatening situations. These preparations have been found to be protective factors in the development of PTSD.[26]

Peritraumatic Factors

Peritraumatic factors are those that occur during or immediately after the trauma. These risk factors include the severity and duration of the trauma, interpersonal violence (such as being attacked), dissociation during the event, feelings of helplessness, and being a perpetrator of or witness to atrocities.[9,13,20]

In a recent article, protective and risk factors were retrospectively examined in a sample of 132 Canadian police officers.[16] The results from this research indicate that the major predictor of whether PTSD develops was peritraumatic factors (i.e., dissociation and positive social support from colleagues). Factors of dissociation, emotional reactions, and other physical reactions were found to be significantly intercorrelated; this suggests that emotional arousal leads to physical arousal, which may induce dissociative states. In the case of female police officers, it may be that less intensity of emotion experienced during the trauma (than in civilian populations) protected them from developing PTSD.[27] Lastly, social support from colleagues during or immediately after a traumatic event was found to be a protective factor.[16]

Post-Traumatic Factors

Factors that occur right after the event or further into the future are considered post-traumatic. **Post-traumatic factors** include social support following trauma exposure, development of ASD, access to clinical intervention, physical injuries, subsequent negative events, substance use, litigation, and feelings of guilt and shame.[13,20]

Approximately 60-80% of individuals who met the criteria for ASD after the traumatic event will qualify for a diagnosis of PTSD two years later.[32] Substance use, particularly alcohol abuse, has been found to co-exist with persons diagnosed with PTSD, with 25% of police officers reporting problematic drinking.[33] Many studies have shown a positive correlation with self-medicating and hyperarousal, as those experiencing PTSD symptoms use substances to manage those symptoms.[33] This complicates recovery, as the individual is less likely to access services, and alcohol use has been implicated in reduced resiliency.[30,33] Clinical interventions developed for police officers have been shown to be protective for female officers but not male officers. It may be that female officers are more likely to utilize these services than their male counterparts.[28,33]

Within police agencies, the camaraderie/social support of fellow officers and the belief that the organization supports officers creates a buffer for stress. But when a police officer is diagnosed with PTSD and subsequently medically discharged from the police organization, this community of support disappears and members are left feeling a sense of shame and failure, often perceiving themselves as weak.[34] A further sense of betrayal is reported when officers state feeling little or no support from the policing organization "family" when engaged in litigation with insurance companies to receive treatment, or during legal proceedings or disciplinary action.[27,34] These negative post-traumatic experiences exacerbate, prolong, and complicate the recovery process and increase one's risk for suicide.[2]

Case Study: Dave, Policing, and PTSD

Dave is 40 years old, married, the father of two young children, and a model police officer working in a large Canadian city. He has been a member of a police agency for 20 years, and over the course of his duties has been exposed to numerous traumatic events. He has been the first on scene at deadly motor vehicle accidents and suicides, walked into homes where domestic violence was occurring, and has been involved in the exchange of gunfire. Recently, Dave was offered a promotion to work on the newly created Alberta Integrated Child Exploitation (ICE) Unit. This unit was developed to investigate offences involving child pornography and any other computer-related child sexual abuse, such as child luring and the child sex trade.

Initially, Dave attacked his new position with gusto and spent countless hours searching the Internet for individuals seeking to exploit children. Dave sought out chat rooms, child pornography sites, and other social media sites that were known to be used for child exploitation. After a few months of working in the ICE unit, Dave began using alcohol after work, either with his colleagues or when he arrived home from his shift. He began to experience feelings of depression, had difficulty sleeping, began isolating himself from his wife and children, and became fearful and hypervigilant about the safety of his children. Dave began to notice that during his off hours he would experience intrusive images of the child victims he was charged with protecting. Dave began to think that all his efforts at work were futile and that he would never be able to make a difference, as there were just too many child victims. A feeling of hopelessness set in.

Questions

1. Does Dave qualify for a diagnosis of PTSD?
2. If not, what missing information is needed for that diagnosis?
3. Identify the pre-traumatic and post-traumatic factors involved in Dave's case.
4. What could have mitigated Dave's reaction to his traumatic exposure?

TREATMENT

According to Bessel van der Kolk, "the challenge of recovery is to re-establish ownership of your body and your mind—of yourself."[35] In order to re-establish ownership for those experiencing PTSD, different therapies have been developed to address the overwhelming symptoms of depression, anxiety, flashbacks, etc. Talk therapies, medication, art therapies, yoga, Emotional Freedom Techniques (EFT), mantra-based meditation, animal therapy, and others have all been used, each with different results.[36] Depending upon the sources reviewed, the efficacy of treatment greatly varies.

A report commissioned by the United States Department of Veterans Affairs in 2008 tasked the Institute of Medicine (IOM) committee to review the evidence for the efficacy of both psychological and pharmacological treatments of PTSD.[37] In their exhaustive review, all classes of medications (SSRIs, MAOIs, antipsychotics, benzodiazepines, etc.) showed inadequate evidence to determine efficacy of treatment for PTSD patients. For all approaches (such as Eye Movement Desensitization and Reprocessing (EMDR), cognitive restructuring, coping skills, etc.), evidence of efficacy was not found, with the exception of exposure therapies that established moderate to high evidence of clinical benefit.[37] The authors of this study did note that most exposure therapies often had an element of and/or included different CBT approaches.[37,38]

CBT-Based Therapies

Cognitive behavioural therapy (CBT) is a structured treatment approach that addresses the faulty beliefs/thoughts that impact an individual's feelings/emotions and ultimately one's behaviour. One CBT-based therapy for PTSD, originally developed for female sexual trauma victims, is **cognitive processing therapy** (CPT).

CPT is designed as a 12-session manualized treatment that can be delivered in a group setting or individually.[20,39] The focus of this therapy is to address the "stuck points" of negative/faulty thoughts about the experience of trauma and the individual. Treatments involve individuals challenging these thoughts, often of guilt and shame, and changing them to more realistic, balanced interpretations. Beliefs in five domains are addressed: safety, power/control, intimacy, esteem, and trust. Ultimately, the goal of CPT therapy is to incorporate a balanced view of the trauma, of the individuals themselves, and the world around them. The efficacy of CBT approaches has been widely cited in the literature; however, as with most interventions, the reviews of CPT are mixed. One critique is that CPT is not exclusively CBT-based due to its narrative component, which is considered an element of exposure therapy.[20]

Exposure Therapy

Exposure therapies can be done in vivo (real world setting), in the imagination, or using new technologies such as virtual reality systems. **Exposure therapies** reintroduce the individual to the traumatic event that precipitated their PTSD. The participant is often gradually reintroduced to the most intense event or stimulus; this contrasts with "flooding," in which the individual is only exposed to the most strongly feared stimuli. It is theorized that prolonged exposure to the fearful stimuli disconfirms the expectations of harm, thereby reducing the individual's fear response. Although exposure therapy has been validated as a primary treatment for PTSD, researchers expressed concerns over high dropout rates. Recent research, however, has indicated that the dropout rates for prolonged exposure protocols do not differ from other CBT or person-centred therapies.[39]

Group Intervention

A therapeutic approach adopted by many organizations is crisis intervention strategies. These interventions provide emotional support to participants and encourage them to discuss their traumatic experiences. These approaches have been used by police agencies and other first responder agencies following natural and/or manmade disasters such as the September 11 attacks and Hurricane Katrina. Although these examples are large-scale disasters, using the approaches for smaller incidents where individuals are involved in traumatic events is also appropriate. One of the most commonly used strategies of this kind is Critical Incident Stress Debriefing (CISD). **CISD** group debriefing should be conducted within two to seven days after traumatic event exposure and provides participants with social support, a sense of meaning, and a mastery of the event, thus helping to facilitate symptom relief.[39]

Like CISD, **Critical Incident Stress Management** (CISM) allows the individual to process and defuse the emotions tied to a traumatic event in a group setting. CISM was developed for first responder agencies but since then has been applied to other organizations and settings.[40] CISM differs from CISD, as it is more tailored to an individual's needs. Moreover, CISD is only one component of CISM. CISM provides interventions from the pre-crisis to the post-crisis phases of the traumatic event.[41]

The effectiveness of all these approaches has come into question, and other services such as individual counselling are now also offered.[31] Regardless, services must be utilized and the willingness of police officers to use them is often reduced by the fear of being stigmatized, of having advancement opportunities negatively affected, of participating in ineffective treatment, or that utilization of mental health services will not be confidential.[34] Willingness to accept treatment appears to be tied to the organizational culture and whether it fosters education and support of positive mental health for its members. The willingness to use mental health services varies by country, with officers from Canada and New Zealand being more willing to do so than those in the United States, the United Kingdom, and Australia.[37]

As previously discussed, support of colleagues is a protective factor and beneficial to first responders. In 1988, after witnessing a horrific homicide, Vince Savoia, a Toronto paramedic, created TEMA in memory of Tema Lisa Conter (see tema.ca). TEMA is a Canadian peer support network for dealing with the effects of PTSD.[42] This group works with and for first responders who often suffer from the effects of chronic traumatic exposure. Although it began as a peer support community, TEMA has grown into advocating for increased awareness of PTSD, research, and social and psychological support for first responders and their families.

Medication

Although the efficacy of psychiatric mediation for PTSD has been questioned, the use of medication for PTSD symptoms is a widely accepted practice.

Antidepressants are considered the first-line approach for medication treatment and are used to treat the core symptoms of PTSD, such as avoidance/numbing, re-experiencing, and hyperarousal.[43] Antidepressant medication is also used for those whose PTSD is comorbid with depressive and/or anxiety disorders. Atypical antipsychotics are used for insomnia and paranoia, severe impulsivity, and mood fluctuations.[43] The most controversial medications are the benzodiazepines. These medications are most often used for anxiety disorders such as panic, generalized anxiety, and social anxiety disorders. However, even with these disorders, fierce debate over their use is ongoing due to their addictive properties. Regarding PTSD, there is further concern that the use of benzodiazepines will prevent consolidation of memories and interfere with exposure therapy treatment.[43]

SUMMARY

The evolution of our understanding of PTSD goes back centuries and, until recently, research has focused on military personnel. Traumatic experiences can affect and touch anyone, as can their debilitating consequences. Many factors influence an individual's response to stressful experiences, including those that exist prior to the traumatic event, how we respond during the event, and, ultimately, how the event is managed after a traumatic situation is over.

Police officers are not immune to the physical and psychological consequences of their dangerous and stressful policing duties, yet current research indicates they are at lower risk than other first responders and the general public. Our understanding of vulnerabilities and protective factors that contribute to and protect against the development of PTSD in the general population, and specifically in policing, can help in the development of supportive strategies and treatments to mitigate the negative effects of trauma and a traumatic work environment.

REFLECTION QUESTIONS

1. Prior to experiencing a traumatic event, what can you do to reduce the future risk of developing PTSD?
2. If you have just experienced a traumatic event, what might you do to deal with symptoms?
3. What pre-existing conditions are relevant to developing PTSD?
4. What treatments might be appropriate for PTSD?
5. What factors might reduce treatment effectiveness?

REFERENCES

1. Roth, P. 2016 sees rise in first responder suicides. Victoria News [Internet]; 2017 [cited 2017 Jan 11]. Available from: http://www.vicnews.com/news/410404025.html
2. Violanti JM, Andrew ME, Mnatsakanova A, Hartley TA, Fekedulegn D, Burchfiel CM. Correlates of hopelessness in the high suicide risk police occupation. Police Pract Res. 2016;17(5):408–19. DOI: 10.1080/15614263.2015.1015125
3. Stanley IH, Horn MA, Joiner TE. A systematic review of suicidal thoughts and behaviours among police officers, firefighters, and paramedics. Clin Psychol Rev. 2016;44:25–44. DOI: 10.1016/j.cpr.2015.12.002
4. van der Kolk BA. The body keeps the score. Brain, mind and body in the healing of trauma. New York: Viking; 2014. p. 53.
5. Sedikides C, Wildschut T, Baden D. Nostalgia. In: Greenberg J, editor. Handbook of experimental existential psychology. New York: Guilford Press; 2004. p. 200–14.
6. Jones JA. Military 1 [Internet]. American military university. A brief history of PTSD: the evolution of our understanding. 2013 [cited 2017 Mar 25]. Available from: https://www.military1.com/army/article/405058-a-brief-history-of-ptsd-the-evolution-of-our-understanding/
7. Kohne JB. Screening silent resistance: male hysteria in first world war medical cinematography. In: Crouthamel J, Leese P, editors. Psychological trauma and the legacies of the first world war. Switzerland: Springer International; 2017. p. 49–79. DOI: 10.1007/978-3-319-33476-9_3
8. Miller L. PTSD and forensic psychology: applications to civil and criminal law. New York: Springer; 2015. p. 1–82. DOI: 10.1007/978-3-319-09081-8
9. Echterling LG, Field TA, Stewart AL. Evolution of PTSD diagnosis in the DSM. In: Safir MP, Wallach AR, editors. Future directions in post-traumatic stress disorder: prevention, diagnosis and treatment. New York: Springer; 2015. p. 189–212. DOI: 10.1007/978-1-4899-7522-5_9
10. van der Kolk BA. The history of trauma in psychiatry. In: Friedman MJ, Keane TM, Resick PM, editors. Handbook of PTSD: science and practice. New York: Guilford; 2007. p. 19–36.
11. American Psychiatric Association. Diagnostic and statistical manual of mental disorders (DSM-5). American Psychiatric Pub; 2013 May 22.
12. Pearson C, Zamorski M, Janz T. Health at a glance: mental health of the Canadian armed forces. Cat. no. 82-624-X. Ottawa: Statistics Canada. 2014. p. 1–10.
13. Van Ameringen M, Mancini, Patterson B, Boyle MH. Post-traumatic stress disorder in Canada. CNS Neurosci Ther. 2008 Aug;14(3):171–81. DOI: 10.1111/j.1755-5949.2008.00049.x
14. Berger W, Coutinho ESF, Figueira I, Marques-Portella C, Luz MP, Neylan TC, et al. Rescuers at risk: a systematic review and meta-regression analysis of the worldwide current prevalence and correlates of PTSD in rescue workers. Soc Psych Psych Epid. 2012 Jun;47(6):1001–11. DOI: 10.1007/s00127-011-0408-2
15. Wilson LC. A systematic review of probable posttraumatic stress disorder in first responders following man-made mass violence. Psychiat Res. 2015;229:21–6. DOI: 10.1016/j.psychres.2015.06.015

16. Martin M, Marchand A, Boyer R, Martin N. Predictors of the development of posttraumatic stress disorder among police officers. J Trauma Dissociation. 2009;10:451–68. DOI: 10.1080/15299730903143626

17. Committee on the Assessment of Ongoing Efforts in the Treatment of Posttraumatic Stress Disorder. Treatment for posttraumatic stress disorder in military and veteran populations: initial assessment. Washington, DC: The National Academies Press; 2012.

18. Taylor S, Asmundson, GJG. Posttraumatic stress disorder: current concepts and controversies. Psychol Inj Law. 2008;1:59-74. DOI: 10.1007/s12207-008-9009-0

19. Kim M. Rolfing NYC. Anatomy of fear [image on Internet]. Oct 2014. Available from: http://rolfing.nyc/anatomy-of-fear/

20. Friedman M. Posttraumatic and acute stress disorders. 6th ed. Switzerland: Springer International; 2015. p. 93–114. DOI: 10.1007/978-3-319-15066-6

21. Bar-Shai M, Klien E. Neurobiological risk factors and predictors of vulnerability and resilience to PTSD. In: Safir MP, Wallach AR, editors. Future directions in post-traumatic stress disorder: prevention, diagnosis and treatment. New York: Springer; 2015. p. 31–64. DOI: 10.1007/978-1-4899-7522-5_2

22. Kolassa IT, Illek S, Wilker S, Karabatsiakis A, Elbert T. Neurobiological findings in post-traumatic stress disorder. In: Ulrich S, Cloitre M, editors. Evidence-based treatments for trauma-related psychological disorders: a practical guide for clinicians. Switzerland: Springer. 2015. p. 479–95.

23. Sherin JE, Nemeroff CB. Post-traumatic stress disorder: the neurobiological impact of psychological trauma. Dialogues Clin Neurosci. 2011;13(3):263–78.

24. Meffert SM, Metzler TJ, Henn-Haase C, McCaslin S, Chemtob C, Neylan T, et al. A prospective study of trait anger and PTSD symptoms in police. J Trauma Stress. 2008 Aug;21(4):410–16. DOI: 10.1002/jts.20350

25. Breslau N. The epidemiology of posttraumatic stress disorder: what is the extent of the problem? J Clin Psychiat. 2001;6(17):16–22.

26. Hartley TA, Sarkisian K, Violanti JM, Andrew ME, Burchfiel CM. PTSD symptoms among police officers: associations with frequency, recency, and types of traumatic events. Int J Emerg Ment Health. 2013;15(4):241–53.

27. Lilly MM, Pole N, Best SR, Metzler T, Marmar CR. Gender and PTSD: what can we learn from female police officers? J Anxiety Disord. 2009 Feb;23:767–74. DOI: 10.1016/j.janxdis.2009.02.015

28. Ellrich K, Baier D. Post-traumatic stress symptoms in police officers following violent assaults: a study on general and police-specific risk and protective factors. J Interpers Violence. 2017;32(3):331–56. DOI: 10.1177/0886260515586358

29. Andersen JP, Papazoglou K, Koskelainen M, Nyman M. Knowledge and training regarding the link between trauma and health: a national survey of Finnish police officers. J Pol Emerg Res. 2015:1–12. DOI: 10.1177/2158244015580380
    McCanlies EC, Mnatsakanova A, Andrew ME, Burchfiel CM, Violanti JM. Positive psychological factors are associated with lower PTSD symptoms among police officers: post hurricane Katrina. Stress and Health. 2014;30:405–15. DOI: 10.1002/smi.2615

30. Marchand A, Boyer R, Nadeau C, Beaulieu-Prévost D, Martin M. Predictors of post-traumatic stress disorder among police officers: a prospective study. Psychol Trauma. 2015;7(3):212-22. DOI: 10.1037/a0038780

31. Koch WJ, Douglas KS, Nicholls TL, O'Neill ML. Psychological injuries: forensic assessment, treatment and the law. New York: Oxford University Press; 2006. DOI: 10.1093/acprof:oso/9780195188288.001.0001

32. Menard KS, Arter ML, Khan C. Critical incidents, alcohol and trauma problems, and service utilization among police officers from five countries. Int J Comp Appl Crim Justice. 2016;40(1):25–42. DOI: 10.1080/01924036.2015.1028950

33. McCormack L, Riley L. Medical discharge from the "family," moral injury, and a diagnosis of PTSD: is psychological growth possible in the aftermath of policing trauma? Traumatology. 2016;22(1):19–28. DOI: 10.1037/trm0000059

34. van der Kolk BA. The body keeps the score. Brain, mind and body in the healing of trauma. New York: Viking; 2014. p. 203.

35. Metcalf O, Varker T, Forbes D, Phelps A, Dell L, Dibattista A. Efficacy of fifteen emerging interventions for the treatment of posttraumatic stress disorder: a systematic review. J Trauma Stress. 2016 Feb;29:88–92.

36. Institute of Medicine of the National Academies. Treatment of posttraumatic stress disorder: an assessment of the evidence. Washington, DC: The National Academies Press; 2008.

37. Haugen PT, Evces M, Weiss DS. Treating posttraumatic stress disorder in first responders: a systematic review. Clin Psychol Rev. 2012;32:370–80. DOI: 10.1016/j.cpr.2012.04.001

38. Mott JM, Teng EJ. Evidence-based cognitive behavioral treatments for PTSD in adults. In: Martin CR, Preedy VR, Patel VB, editors. Comprehensive guide to post-traumatic stress disorders. Switzerland: Springer; 2016. p. 1871–85. DOI: 10.1007/978-3-319-08613-2_17-2

39. CISM International. Critical Incident Stress Management [Internet]. 2015. Available from: http://criticalincidentstress.com/what_is_cism_

40. Everly GSJ, Flannery RBJ, Mitchell JT. Critical incident stress management (CISM): a review of the literature. Aggress Violent Behave. 2000;5(1):23–40. DOI: 10.1016/S1359-1789(98)00026-3

41. Tema.ca: because heroes are human [Internet]. 2017. Available from: https://www.tema.ca/home

42. Davis LL, Van Deventer LJ, Jackson CW. Pharmacologic treatment for trauma-related psychological disorders. In: Ulrich S, Cloitre M, editors. Evidence-based treatments for trauma-related psychological disorders: a practical guide for clinicians. Switzerland: Springer; 2015. p. 63–86. DOI: 10.1007/978-3-319-07109-1_26

PART II

Responding to Mental Health

Use of force frameworks provide guidelines to law enforcement professionals regarding the amount of force that is adequate and appropriate in various situations. Each police agency has slightly different regulations on the use of force. However, most use of force frameworks indicate that the amount of force used should correspond to the person's behaviours. Use of force typically begins with police presence and escalates to communication, soft control, hard control, and then to intermediate weapons such as conducted energy weapons, and finally lethal force. The National Use of Force framework, which is used by many Canadian policing agencies, is currently being re-examined, with many recommendations being made for change, especially in Ontario. The recommended changes are being propelled by the major incidents that have occurred in policing nationally. Based on the examination of some of these specific incidents, best practice recommendations to assist police officers to de-escalate crisis situations are being made to police and governmental bodies,[1,2] which include the following:

- Enhancing mental health services and reducing mental health stigma
- Increasing police education on mental health services
- Enhancing coordination of services and communication between police and mental health professionals, and increasing shared information so police have background history information on the mental health of persons

- Enhancing police culture in terms of mental health, hiring qualified police officers with a good decision-making capability
- Increased use of pepper spray and other non-lethal force options as well as use of body-worn and in-car cameras
- Decreased use of weapons
- Re-assessing the use of force framework, which is considered out-dated and inflexible
- Supervising police in all stages when engaged in a crisis situations as well as using crisis intervention teams
- Assessing the mental health of police officers on an ongoing basis

Reviews of multiple cases found current use of force practices to be unresponsive to the needs of police and individuals involved in a crisis.[1,2] Based on these cases, the chapters in this section address techniques and strategies to respond to situations involving persons with mental health symptoms and episodes.

REFERENCES

1. Dubé PA. Matter of life and death. Ombudsman Ontario Report; June 2016.
2. McNeilly G. Police interactions with people in crisis and use of force: OIPRD systematic review interim report. Ontario: Office of the Independent Police Review; March 2017.

CHAPTER 9

Police Legitimacy, Interpersonal Response, and Community Trust

Daniel J. Jones, *University of Huddersfield*

Shea-Lyn Boychuk, *Concordia University of Edmonton*

Abigail Smith, *Concordia University of Edmonton*

Uzma Williams, *MacEwan University*

LEARNING OBJECTIVES

1. Understand the importance of police legitimacy and how it impacts the interactions between police and community
2. Learn techniques to foster police legitimacy and community trust
3. Enhance communication techniques to become an effective officer and determine the effects of police officers' communication on police legitimacy
4. Describe the core values of the human service fields
5. Develop and demonstrate skills for interacting with persons with mental illness to effectively communicate during crisis situations
6. Identify characteristics of effective and highly functioning police officers

INTRODUCTION

Between January 1, 1996, and December 31, 2010, there were 113 local police custody deaths (for example, police cell, station, car, ambulance, home, hospitals, etc.) in Ontario.[1] Fifty-three of the 113 (46.9%) had a reported history of mental illness, and 64 of the individuals (56.6%) had a reported history of substance use.[1] Familiar and recent names from some of these Canadian tragedies include Sammy Yatim, Edmond Yu, and Michael MacIsaac. These cases garnered significant media attention and are notable examples of excessive use of force by police. Retrospectively, the public believed certain actions could have been used rather than fatal force. These three individuals were unfortunately not the only victims to have reported mental health struggles and to meet a fatal end at the hands of police.[2] Police and law enforcement will continue to come into contact with individuals with mental health struggles, and the number of deaths will drop only once the necessary procedures are taken to properly resolve calls involving mental health crises.

POLICE LEGITIMACY AND COMMUNITY TRUST

The public's view of police can be fragile in that the words and actions of police have a quicker and more direct impact on civilians' perception of the police organization's competence and trust. **Police legitimacy** pertains to the public's perception of police ethics and professional conduct that impacts a person's likelihood to obey law enforcement.[3] The concept of police legitimacy is the representation of justice that the community feels will be provided when they report something to the police (or, conversely, a lack of police legitimacy is the belief that nothing will be accomplished).[4] Sampson found that the marginalized communities of African-Americans and Latinos had a lower tolerance for crime and disorder than the Caucasian community but reported crime at lower levels due to dissatisfaction with the police and legal system.[4]

Physical force, whether implemented appropriately or inappropriately, threatens police legitimacy. Civilian mistreatment is detrimental to how law enforcement personnel are viewed, causing a disconnect between police personnel and the public and fostering distrust. The negative publicity surrounding the use of lethal force on individuals in a mental health crisis sparks a nationwide uproar, causing reactions that lead to questions about the officers' suitability for police work and ability to act competently in such incidents.[2]

Community trust is affected by the size of the organization, geographical region, and police operating model. For larger metropolitan Canadian cities such as Toronto and Vancouver, police are more likely to be viewed as a singular, impersonal 'other' because of shorter amounts of contact between police officers and community members.[5] These cities have a high population density and require more personnel to control civilian needs, whereas smaller communities have fewer personnel who become known and acquainted with community members.[5] Rapport is built within these smaller communities, and the police is not known as a singular "other," but instead as recognizable individuals. Civilians, particularly adolescents and young adults, view police in a more optimistic light when contact is made outside critical situations.[6] Informal interactions between civilians and the police should be encouraged and fostered to promote the formation of bonds and understanding, both outside and within mental health communities. Many policing organizations host events such as "coffee with the police" or "lunch with the school constable" in which police and community members intermingle and learn more about each other. These interactions foster higher perceptions of police legitimacy—especially in communities where police trust is lacking.

Police in major centres have faced scrutiny due to poor communication with, and use of force on, individuals with a history of mental health. These interactions not only affect the police agency where the incident occurs but can also be detrimental to policing for an entire country. A clear example of poor police communications in times of crisis is the arrest of Rodney King on March 3, 1991. This arrest resulted in significant questions regarding police communications and use of **excessive force** (an unproportionate, excessive police response to the behaviour and actions of the person). The issue climaxed on April 29, 1992, when the four officers in question were acquitted and outrage from the verdict resulted in riots that killed 63 people and injured over 2,000. This incident arguably affected police legitimacy on a global scale.

More recently, the role of technological globalization is impacting change in the perception of police legitimacy and community trust during police interactions.[7] Social media platforms such as Twitter or Facebook allow the public to play a more active role in police interactions, and the platforms provide an opportunity for police to demonstrate legitimate interactions through the use of body cameras, for example.[7] These social media platforms also provide a new bridge between police and the community by fostering connections and relationships.[8]

Legal Cynicism

Discussing the concept of police legitimacy must go hand in hand with the topic of legal cynicism. **Legal cynicism** refers to a community's perception that the police are corrupt, unjust, and unresponsive; in short, that there is a lack of police legitimacy. A society that sees the police as legitimate will offend less, reoffend less, and abide by the rule of law, whereas societies with high levels of legal cynicism have higher crime rates and less respect for law enforcers.[9] One factor that can reduce (or increase) legal cynicism is the concept of **teachable moments**, whereby the police have an opportunity with every interaction to build (or erode) legitimacy—and every effort should be taken to increase legitimacy.[10] In terms of policing deployments, the police are deployed to and interact with marginalized communities on a more regular basis than with non-marginalized areas. How police communicate with individuals experiencing a mental health crisis or dealing with a mental health diagnosis can either build or erode legitimacy. The concepts of legal cynicism and police legitimacy may be ones that lead communities to not report police victimization—which in turn results in increased victimization. Communities with high levels of legal cynicism are more likely to believe that reporting crimes and police failures will result in nothing at best and harm at worst; therefore, legal cynicism causes these communities to disregard the law and its enforcers. If the police are legitimate, or seen as a legitimate power holder, there is more compliance, cooperation, and satisfaction with police actions, and less reoffending, resistance, and support for vigilante violence.[11] As we build on Tyler's[10] concept that every interaction with police is an opportunity to erode or build legitimacy, it is imperative that policing professionals have good communication skills and enact ethical behaviours. If police are dealing with an individual in an obvious state of mental health crisis in a public space, that interaction can weaken or strengthen the concept of the police as a legitimate power holder, depending on the perceived legitimacy of that interaction.

COMPASSION

Compassion is showing kindness to others when they are experiencing hardship. Compassion is an essential component in building trust between police and the communities they serve; however, it can be difficult to have compassion for others when interacting with people from diverse cultures, upbringings, and ways of life. To put this in the present context, compassion for those who struggle with mental health may be stunted as a result of the negative stigma, myths, and lack of knowledge regarding mental illness. Poor judgements are often made due to a lack of necessary training, education, and experience with vulnerable populations. A variety of strategies to constantly keep up with education on mental illness may assist an officer in effectively handling mental health scenarios. Given the cases of Sammy Yatim, Edmond Yu, and Michael MacIsaac, it is obvious that a clearer distinction must be made between appropriate and excessive force, which elicits a discussion of what should be happening to promote safe and effective strategies to reduce harm during calls involving mental illness.

Strategies to Enhance an Understanding of Mental Health

There are a few ways police and law enforcement can become more proficient in their dealings with people with mental health or substance use struggles. Below are three proven strategies.

1. **Keep learning and remain up to date on training resources.**
    One necessary step to equip police and law enforcement for situations involving people with mental health issues is to constantly maintain and refresh one's knowledge about mental health and how to approach different scenarios related to mental health. The Mental Health Commission of Canada (MHCC) offers training programs that can benefit police and law enforcement personnel and also the general public. A plethora of programs exist through the MHCC,[12] including the following:

    -   Mental Health First Aid (MHFA) is recommended for everyone, whether through a personal or a professional connection. Its goal is "to improve mental health literacy and provide the skills and knowledge to help people better manage potential or developing mental health problems in themselves, a family member, a friend or a colleague."
    -   Training and Education about Mental Illness for Police Organizations (TEMPO) focuses on communication and interpersonal skills, and on methods to de-escalate high-stress situations. The purpose of TEMPO is to "address the learning necessary to prepare police personnel for encounters with persons with a mental illness."[13]
    -   Road to Mental Readiness (R2MR) opens the conversation about mental health within the workplace, addressing the mental health of employees to ensure they are aware of their own mental health, and how to obtain help when they need it.

2. **Be aware of community resources.**
    Another step that can be taken is remaining up to date on and aware of the resources the community offers for those in need. For example, police calls involving individuals who abuse substances or who are struggling with addiction happen quite frequently, and if officers are unsure of the community support designed for these individuals,

continued

they'll be missing the opportunity to help people in the long run. With a knowledge of these resources or with a pocked-sized pamphlet, officers can be proactive rather than reactive in their exchanges.

3. **Know yourself and your limitations.**

A third step that can be taken to ensure positive contact between police and civilians involves officers maintaining their good characteristics and being aware of who they are, as well as sustaining their motivations for being involved in policing. Officers should frequently reflect on their goals in the field and analyze their behaviours to determine whether or not there is harmony between them.

It is much more difficult to help others in a crisis situation when struggling with one's own mental health. Therefore, it's important for all officers to be cognizant of their own mental health. **Introspection**, a reflection into one's own thoughts and feelings, is an important aspect of self-awareness. Introspection is a valuable tool for officers and other law enforcement personnel to grow into competent handlers of crisis situations. Being self-aware lends itself to personal and professional growth, enhancing the way we behave with others. In knowing ourselves, we can become more effective communicators and supporters for those in need.

ENHANCING INTERPERSONAL SKILLS AND COMMUNICATION IN POLICING

What makes a good police officer? The answer is an intricate, complex relationship between personality traits, attitude, age, organization style (community policing versus large metropolis policing), leadership style, occupational culture, and experience that differ from officer to officer. For this reason, defining what makes a good officer is difficult. Much research has tried to narrow down the "perfect" officer profile, with mixed results, and the stereotypical "police personality"—authoritarian, aggressive, cynical—is not scientifically supported.[14] Instead of asking ourselves what traits a good police officer has, we should be asking what aspects make a police officer competent. With a consensus from policing science research, we can begin to formulate an answer.

In the majority of situations, a police officer can be professional, kind, humane, and respectful. There are other situations where difficult persons do not

cooperate—even when the officer is kind, respectful, and assertive. Often, individuals experiencing active mental health symptoms are uncooperative because
of their own internal struggle rather than frustrations with police, and showing
compassion for these individuals is an important aspect of not reverting to excessive force.[15] A key to assisting individuals during a mental health episode is
to be respectful, patient, and professional by enhancing interpersonal responses
with both colleagues and persons during calls.[16] Interpersonal response involves
reacting to a situation in a way that effectively relates to and communicates with
another person or persons. By relating to another person's situation, trust is built
and effective communication occurs. In order to build interpersonal sensitivity,
we must first understand which skills and values must be targeted. More than
merely ideals, **values** are a set of practical criteria for making decisions in human
service professions. The skills listed below, as well as interpersonal skills in general, are intuitive—a person either has social skills or lacks them; however, with
attention, thoughtfulness, and daily practice, these interpersonal skills can be
obtained and strengthened if they are weak or lacking.[17]

Values of Human Service Professionals

- Respect and Dignity
- Care
- Trust
- Genuineness
- Empathy
- Active Listening
- Patience, Reasonable Flexibility, and Dependability
- Non-Judgement
- Proper Attitude, Social Modelling, and Avoiding Hostility
- Confidentiality, Privacy, and Privilege
- Self-Awareness

Respect and Dignity

Respect and dignity are important concepts in every relationship and interaction
we have.[18] Without them, communication—both verbal and nonverbal—is ineffective and bonds cannot be created or maintained. **Respect** is the due regard
for the feelings, wishes, rights, and traditions of another individual.[18] When we

respect people, we are letting them know that we are taking them and their perspectives seriously and are considering them. We want to ensure we are always striving to do things correctly, with as little damage and risk as possible, and this is done through consideration of others. From a psychological point of view, respect is the foundational concept and value from which helping interventions are built. It is more than a way of viewing someone, but rather a way of acknowledging the **dignity** (worth) of a person. Egan[18] highlights three key components that flow between a belief in the dignity of persons and respect as a value:

1. **Do no harm**: an ethical principle emphasizing a non-manipulative and non-exploitive approach
2. Become competent and committed: ensure that you continue to update your training and knowledge throughout your career to keep up with current practices and trends
3. **Be "for" the individual**: respect can be tough-minded, and being "for" individuals does not mean you agree with them, just that you are taking their perspective seriously

Care

Care is serious attention or consideration applied to doing something correctly to avoid damage or risk.[18] Caring is an ever-reaching concept that should be implemented in everything we do, from paperwork and patrolling to interacting with individuals. By caring about the outcomes of our actions, we are better equipped to make thoughtful decisions that often result in effective conclusions.

Trust

The belief in the reliability, truth, ability, or strength of someone or something is known as **trust**. Trust is a two-way street—individuals must be able to trust that what we are saying and doing is in the best interests of everyone, and that we are reliable in our actions and our words, just as we must trust citizens and their reports. Without trust there is no effective means to mediate a situation. Most situations don't innately have trust; it is something that must be built and maintained, and is often easily lost.[18] For this reason, it is important to be consistent and dependable in every interaction.

Genuineness

Genuineness allows one to be authentic, honest, and sincere. Being genuine means not overemphasizing the role you are in, avoiding defensiveness, and being open.[18] In order to be genuine, you must be aware of your strengths and deficits.

Empathy

Empathy is a rich concept. Simply stated, it involves relating to others and understanding their perspectives as fully as possible. In other words, it is "the individual's social radar through which he or she senses others' feelings and perspectives and takes an active interest in their concerns."[18]

Active Listening

Listening probably seems like an incredibly simple concept; however, many of us are not taught how to fully listen. **Active listening** requires listening fully and accurately to effectively hear what is being said, especially during crisis negotiation.[19] Active listening plays a key role in all human service professions. For example, in a doctor-patient relationship, a main patient concern is that the doctor lacks the ability to relate and communicate; therefore, when doctors fully listen to patients and treat them based on what they've heard, the patients feel that the doctors are more effective at their job. A key feature of active listening is **empathetic listening**, which centres on the kind of attending, observing, and listening needed to develop an understanding of individuals and their world, and which is highly effective for interviewing.[19] It is particularly important to respond empathetically when dealing with people experiencing mental illness because a failure to do so—either based on an invalid or superficial understanding, or on a misunderstanding—results in missing the central issue and harming rather than helping.

Patience, Reasonable Flexibility, and Dependability[20]

Patience refers to our capacity to tolerate difficult situations without getting upset or angry. It is waiting, watching, and knowing when to act. As the old adage goes: a person who angers you, captures you. If we do not learn to be patient, we tend to lose control of the situation and often end up amplifying the damage. Being patient allows us to make better decisions. Frustration is a natural emotion we all feel from time to time, but it is a stress response that often clouds our judgement and makes us act hastily. By practicing patience, we strengthen this asset, dissipate stress, and remain in control of ourselves and the situation. **Reasonable flexibility** is changing or persisting in behaviour based on what the situation affords, to a reasonable degree. In other words, when we remain rigid in every situation, we are unable to respond properly to the situation, and this often limits our outcome possibilities. By being reasonably flexible we can match our attitudes and behaviours to the situation. **Dependability** refers to being reliable—following through with promises is a key part of working in law enforcement.

Non-Judgement

When we are interviewing or questioning someone, the single most important skill is being accepting and non-judgemental. When you are **non-judgemental**, you are accepting the person and not passing moral judgement. This establishes a mutual understanding between you and the individual, resulting in more effective assessments of the situation and better solutions.[18] Accepting the individuals and their views helps to build rapport and creates a more open dialogue. They will understand you are seeking to help them in the situation and are being non-judgemental, and this allows more time to find the right solution. As mentioned above, we can accept individuals or what they are saying without agreeing with them.

Proper Attitude, Social Modelling, and Avoiding Hostility

Approaching each situation with the **proper attitude** is fundamental to the outcome. We are far more effective when we are engaged, empathetic, patient, and non-judgemental. If we enter a situation uncaring, judgemental, and annoyed, we have the potential to miss cues and assess the situation incorrectly,[18] with the very real possibility of costing someone's life.

The notion of **social modelling** refers to one person presenting certain behaviours that elicit a similar response from the person.[21] For example, if a police officer presents a hostile mood, the person will also demonstrate hostile traits and behaviours. So, if the officer wants to create conditions of calmness and openness, then the officer must exhibit these qualities. However, a similar notion of social attention describes that compliance to a police officer's requests depends on the person's perception of reputation, peer pressure, and having an audience.[22] It is obvious that the goal in every situation is to de-escalate, reduce lethality, and avoid hostility, but there are many moving pieces that contribute to the escalation of situations. Some of these factors are out of our control, but we must ensure that as the helper we remain in control of what we can, including our own reactions to triggers, stressors, and cues. For example, you get a domestic violence call in which you are told the individual has a weapon, but unbeknownst to you this person is suicidal and hoping to be killed by police. This individual will say nearly anything to get you to react poorly, including that there is a weapon present (when there may not be), to achieve a lethal outcome. If you match their stress, hostility, and fear, then the outcome will most likely be lethal; however, if you remain calm and use your assessment and communication skills, you may be able to de-escalate the situation enough to find the true nature of the situation and obtain treatment for the individual. Remaining in control and thus avoiding hostility is one of the main ways to reduce lethality.

Confidentiality, Privacy, and Privilege

Every level of helping professions has some ethical principle to maintain confidentiality. **Confidentiality** is the professional expectation that information about an individual will be treated with respect, and accessing or disclosing it will only occur in the proper course of your duties.[23] Police-held information should only be accessed for legitimate or authorized policing purposes, and we should not disclose information, on or off duty, needlessly or to unauthorized recipients. **Privacy** is the right to choose the time, circumstance, and extent of one's personal information being shared with or withheld from others.[23] Privacy is a basic human right in the Charter and an essential part of human dignity and freedom of self-determination. **Privilege** is a legal concept that addresses an individual's right to withhold information from you or any other legal proceedings.[23] The difference between these three concepts rests in the freedom of the information.

Self-Awareness

Self-awareness has been defined as "an accurate appraisal of a given aspect of one's situation, functioning, performance, or of the resulting implications."[24] Accurate self-awareness helps prevent risky behaviour[25] and allows us to "understand our own biases, values, stereotypical beliefs, and assumptions in order to serve diverse people."[26] In other words, self-awareness allows us to know what our limitations are and to make choices based on our capabilities. Some of the key aspects of self-awareness are self-reflection, insight, and mindfulness. We are all capable of being self-aware, but we must consistently practice these aspects in order to strengthen them.

TACTICAL SKILLS AND THE USE OF VERBAL LANGUAGE

Bayley and Bittner[27] describe officer competency in terms of goals, tactics, and self-presentation. Experienced officers understand the importance of focusing on long-term solutions; however, officers must often settle for short-term solutions to meet organizational challenges, such as a shortage of officers and high demand. Having a wide array of tactical skills and a flexible, adaptive decision-making process is essential to serving as an effective officer. **Tactical skills** include the use of language to instruct, inspire, and openly communicate rather than constrain situations. **Language aptitude** requires understanding and relating to others (empathy), a capacity to listen (active listening), and non-judgement. Each officer must have tactical approaches to establish immediate control, accurately diagnose the nature of the problem, and execute appropriate solutions. Of these three aspects, accurate diagnostic skills are arguably the most essential skill set for effective officers, which allows for appropriate responses. Diagnosis of a problem prior to attempting to treat it is highly valued. **Accurate diagnostic skills** include investigating further by gathering information from enough sources and taking enough time to deliberate before acting.[27] These practical reasoning skills are valued because every situation is different, and officers must be engaged while assessing each situation.

Negative, self-defeating thoughts are not unusual among people struggling with mental health.[28] Ensure that you are positive and avoid adding to any of the antagonistic thoughts the individual is experiencing. When a person does not respond, do not assume that the person cannot hear you; getting angry and believing you have been ignored will only exacerbate the situation.[29] Under no circumstance should you use inflammatory language, such as psycho or crazy.[29] Making jokes and using ridiculing words completely changes the dynamics of the situation.[29] This type of response is harmful not only to the relationship between yourself and the person, but also to the one between police officers and the community as a whole—which puts police legitimacy and community trust at risk. In order to enhance legitimacy, always provide a response worthy of an effective working officer. By normalizing the situation, we reduce stigma and can offer realistic visions of hope.[30]

With all this information on how to listen, understand, and respond, it is important not to forget that the end goal is to provide a structure for the person in crisis. The information given only provides ideal scenarios. Life is complex and best-case scenarios don't always play out in reality. Nonetheless, this information will help you form the basic skills required to begin practicing with individuals in the field, colleagues, and even people in your personal life. Once you have incorporated verbal tactics into your repertoire, they will soon become operational and second nature.

Table 9.1: Dos and Don'ts of Verbal Communication

VERBAL LANGUAGE	
DOS	**DON'TS**
Take turns speaking: dialogue is interactive and turn taking provides the possibility for mutual learning, communicates that you respect what the individual is saying, and may help defuse a situation.	Don't talk over the individual: if we are not listening to what people are saying, we are neither respecting them, nor are we being empathetic to their perspective and situation, which could result in an escalation or ineffective outcomes.
Engage and connect: ensure you are responding to what the individual is saying and guide the interaction, connecting your remarks with the individual's results in a more productive conversation.	Don't fixate on using the "right" words: there is a use for silence when we are at a loss for words, and by turning up our non-verbal behaviours while maintaining brief verbal silence, we can encourage the individual to think and often reach some insight.
Control your voice-related behaviour—this means being cognizant of your tone of voice, pitch, volume, intensity, emphases, silences, and using these aspects to navigate interactions rather than exacerbate them.	Don't give orders rapidly, shout, or argue.
Be cognizant of your choice of words.	Don't assume that a person who doesn't respond cannot hear you, use inflammatory language such as wacko or psycho, or use jokes and ridiculing words.
Initiate conversation.	Don't force discussion.
Give reassurance.	Don't lie about outcomes, argue with delusional or hallucinatory statements, or mislead the person to think that you feel or think the same way.
Ask if the person has suicidal intent.	Don't expect a rational discussion when someone is in a state of crisis.

IMPORTANT ELEMENTS OF INFORMATION

Rapport is established in a harmonious interaction and built on respect, mutual interest, and a demonstration of competency.[18] There are elements of dialogue that assist in establishing an alliance with individuals.[31]

The following demographics can help one understand an individual's mental state: age, gender, ethnicity, religion, marital or parental status, and occupational status.

While the role of the police officer is to help, not to diagnose, it is incredibly important to listen to the **chief complaint** of the individual and understand what the person is experiencing. One must consider the severity of the symptoms and the stressors in a situation to alleviate the issue as much as possible. Individuals experiencing a mental health crisis usually have no insight into their own mental health, so if they are experiencing misperceptions of reality, it is better to consult a family member. In addition to inquiring about medical history, personal history plays a role in assessing a situation; the more information we know about individuals, the better we can understand them and build a rapport, resulting in more effective solutions.

EFFECTIVE DIALOGUE TECHNIQUES

When interviewing an individual, it is important to implement helpful interviewing techniques, including clarification, summarizing, validation, verbatim playback, paraphrasing and probing, and interpretation.[32]

Clarification ensures that aspects of information have been communicated clearly and accurately by using open-ended and close-ended questions properly. Using **closed-ended questions** occurs when a person can answer with a simple yes or no, and this can often seem like an interrogation that the interviewer is leading, rather than a dialogue. Closed-ended questions are used to clarify contradictions and obtain specific information. **Open-ended questions** are questions that prompt a thoughtful response from the individual, providing rich, detailed responses such as, "tell me about... ."

During **summarizing**, large chunks of information are aggregated into a concise statement. Similarly, **paraphrasing** involves expressing the meaning of what the individual is saying using different words to achieve greater clarity. **Verbatim playback** involves restating what the individual has stated using their exact words.

Validation establishes that the individual's feelings are reasonable. For example, when individuals tell you they are upset, you can validate their feelings by saying, "I think anyone in your situation would feel that way," which encourages them to keep talking to you, providing you with more information.

Probing often involves asking thoughtful questions about what the individual is saying, without sounding like an interrogation. By doing this, we are getting at deeper information. For example, if individuals state they believe the government is out to get them, asking how they know this to be true can open you up to obtaining more information about how this belief came to be, rather than responding with, "that's not true."

Lastly, **interpretation** helps to clarify and build rapport by verifying that our understanding is correct and encouraging correction when it is not. Our interpretations are only hypotheses, not facts. We also want to ensure we are communicating an acknowledgement of understanding, which can be done verbally and nonverbally, as with nodding.

Social Skills of High-Performing Police Officers

- **Speaking skills**: Being able to use words and elements of language to instruct, inspire, and open dialogue while maintaining respectful eye contact.
- **Active listening and awareness in situation**: Attending, observing, and listening needed to develop an understanding of individuals and their world as well as avoiding distractions and being attuned to the situation through maintaining eye contact.
- **Extroverted, charismatic personality**: A likeable sociable trait that also involves being open to diversity and being responsive to the needs of others.
- **Maturity and credible professional conduct**: All professions have their own code of ethics and their members commit to adhering to that code upon assuming their role. The credibility of their profession relies on the honest, discrete, and everyday commitment to this code of ethics.
- **Practical reasoning skills**: Accurate diagnosis of a problem by gathering information and taking the time to deliberate before acting.
- **Self-presentation**: Appearing self-assured, genuinely confident (both in posture and voice), genuine, self-controlled, and assertive (rather than aggressive).
- **Good judgement**: Ability to make good decisions that are accurate and appropriate for the situation.

A PROFILE OF HIGHLY FUNCTIONING POLICE OFFICERS

Moral Reasoning—The World of Grey

It has been shown that moral reasoning is a valuable and key characteristic of police officers.[33] **Moral reasoning** is a thinking process with the objective of determining whether an idea is right or wrong, based on what one intends to accomplish rather than on decisions from personal bias. From the viewpoint of active officers, an officer's moral compass impacts every decision in a situation and is the decision-maker when it comes to solution creation. Very rarely is any situation cut and dried; the law, protocols, and norms help guide officer intervention, but they allow enough freedom for officers to make important, sometimes life-altering, decisions. In these moments of ambiguity, moral reasoning becomes the guiding principle when making discretionary decisions. Deciding what to do is largely a matter of identifying the most valuable option in a given circumstance.[2]

When dealing with people with mental health struggles, our moral reasoning plays a major role. These are the moments where our freedom to make important decisions is not guided by protocols and norms. There is no handbook on how to manage every person who is struggling, and there is no comprehensive list of what is right and what is wrong in these situations because each one is unique. However, if we consider what we know about people with mental illness and use this knowledge to navigate what we think is right and wrong, we often make impactful decisions that reach preventative conclusions. Obviously, some situations are fast-paced and require a quick observation of the individual before making a decision, but it is always important to verify the outcome we are trying to achieve and to ask ourselves if what we are doing, or how we are communicating, is the right way to achieve that outcome. For example, if there is a call to manage a situation with a homeless person who is threatening someone, the initial reaction might be to respond by arresting and processing this individual. However, knowing that mental illness is rampant in the homeless population, and that often what is perceived as threatening outbursts are a result of addiction or symptoms of mental illness, what would our moral reasoning suggest we do? What outcome are we looking for in this situation? Is the most effective method to achieve it to arrest and process this individual? Your moral reasoning is what will guide your answers to such questions.

Professional Traits

In creating a personality profile for what makes a good officer, many turn to the idea that such officers possess specific traits that make them above-average. However, Sanders[34] suggests that traits are not adequate indicators for good officers because there was little variation in traits among the officers in the study. This is not to suggest that there is no variety in officers, but rather that people with adverse traits have already been weeded out through not being accepted, being fired, quitting, etc. In terms of potential and new recruits, it is key to adopt and practice the positive traits of police officers. Sanders' findings suggest that age and attitude were better predictors of what makes a good officer than personality traits. The literature also supports that traits such as intelligence, dependability, leadership, confidence, assertiveness, and common sense are needed.[14,27,34] While personality traits alone may not determine what makes a good officer, it should be noted that these traits—sociable, open to experience, dependable, motivated, and organized[34]—can be good predictors of job performance overall.

The Role of Experience

Research has found that young officers learn their values and police traits from veteran officers, making it even more important to display values congruent with those of other helping professions. In their research, Laguna, Linn, Ward, and Rupslauky[14] compared the personalities of experienced and inexperienced officers on the psychopathology measure called the Multiphasic Minnesota Personality Inventory. Experienced officers had significantly higher hysteria scores—indicating emotionally-displayed reactions to stressful events—than newly recruited officers. Evidently, there is a relationship between experience level and hysteria reactions. Laguna et al.[14] speculate that this is because experienced officers are more aware of their limitations and the demands of situations; in addition, repeated exposure to stressful events can cause certain memories from previous situations to resurface, resulting in a more volatile reaction. Higher hysteria scores are not entirely negative, as a little more anxiety and command (hysteria) may elicit a more effective action because the experienced officer has learned the proper way to respond to difficult situations: with more caution. A nonchalant officer in a serious, demanding situation can be incredibly dangerous, as the individuals may not take the officer seriously and misread the situation. Inexperienced officers scored higher on the antisocial personality disorder scale, speaking to either a lack of maturity or the officers being less accustomed to proper comportment for the job. This can be particularly detrimental, as inexperienced officers may be more apt to engage in rule-breaking or risky behaviour—knowingly or unconsciously. This also suggests that inexperienced officers may assume an air of arrogance or invincibility, placing themselves in more unsafe situations. Experienced officers did not have more authoritarian personalities than inexperienced officers, suggesting that the job did not increase the level of authoritarian traits, as is commonly believed. Laguna's research suggests that time on the job does not harden police officers or lead to negative attitudes or traits. Age and education both assist with developing maturity and better work quality.[14]

SUMMARY

Trust that extends from this proficiency between police officers and persons is invaluable in law enforcement and can be fostered by connecting officers to community members through informal positive interactions. The importance of education and training surrounding mental health is invaluable and is crucial when attempting to bridge the divide between law enforcement and persons experiencing mental health symptoms. Traits of good police officers include empathy and compassion, effective communication skills to defuse crisis situations, attentive listening, and being assertive (yet not demanding) in communicating. To determine what makes a good cop, we must survey the intricate and complex relationship among traits, experience, attitude, skills, and occupational culture. Effective officers have a wide array of tactical skills at their disposal to mediate and create good solutions to any situation they face. Of these tactical skills, effective communication—which includes empathy and active listening—is the most valuable. Traits are a good indicator of general job performance but not useful in differentiating good officers from average ones.

Mental health and substance use concerns represent a large portion of police calls, and for officers to handle crisis situations appropriately, a few factors must be considered. Police legitimacy and a trusting community are of extreme importance in policing, and the way in which officers and civilians interact significantly impacts how people view police as competent and trustworthy. Connecting with the community, showing compassion, and demonstrating appropriate control fosters trust for police within the community and helps police to do their job effectively.

A lack of understanding surrounding mental health inhibits police and law enforcement from being completely effective in dealing with people with a mental illness. Three ways to help overcome this problem are to keep learning and maintain training (e.g., through training programs offered through MHCC), to be aware of community resources (to know who to reach out to and when), and to be self-aware (to know your limitations and improve). There are always ways to expand our knowledge and, hence, our capacity to communicate properly with those in crisis situations.

Being able to connect with others and communicate effectively is necessary when working with individuals experiencing mental health concerns. Being respectful, treating people with dignity and respect, and being empathetic, patient, and accepting can make an immense difference in helping those in need—potentially de-escalating a situation that could turn bad very quickly. Body language also plays a major role during interactions with people with mental health concerns or substance use issues. Being open, rather than forceful or demanding, with a person experiencing mental health concerns can potentially result in a much more favourable outcome and demonstrates that the officer is trustworthy and competent. Active listening is another component that enhances an officer's effectiveness; the concerns of individuals experiencing a mental illness are extremely significant to them, and to better understand what's happening, officers must actively listen.

Experience in the field, a good sense of morality, and professionalism are invaluable to the field of policing. Policing requires many quick judgements during crisis situations and those judgements are not always clear. Similar past situations, as well as a strong sense of right and wrong, guide these judgements, impacting how future situations are handled.

REFLECTION QUESTIONS

1. Determine which of your strengths would make you a good police officer. What are some of the qualities you might have to spend some time developing?

2. If you were called to a scene involving a person showing symptoms of a mental illness or substance use, what would your action plan look like? What steps could you take to ensure the safety of everyone involved?

3. What small steps can be taken within your community to connect police and citizens outside crisis situations to promote understanding and trust between the two?

REFERENCES

1. Vaughan AD, Zabkiewicz DM, Verdun-Jones SN. In custody deaths of men related to mental illness and substance use: a cross-sectional analysis of administrative records in Ontario, Canada. Journal of Forensic and Legal Medicine. 2017 May 1;48:1–8.

2. McNeilly G. Police interactions with people in crisis and use of force: OIPRD systematic review interim report. Ontario: Office of the Independent Police Review; March 2017.

3. Adorjan M, Ricciardelli R, Spencer DC. Youth perceptions of police in rural Atlantic Canada. Police Practice and Research. 2007;18(6):556–69. DOI: 10.1080/15614263.2017.1363961

4. Sampson RJ, Bartusch DJ. Legal cynicism and (subcultural?) tolerance of deviance: The neighbourhood context of racial differences. Law and Society Review. 1998 Jan;1:777–804.

5. Cotton D, Coleman TG. Canadian police agencies and their interactions with persons with a mental illness: a systems approach. Police Practice & Research: An International Journal. 2010;11(4):301–14. DOI: 10.1080/15614261003701665

6. Hinds L. Youth, police legitimacy and informal contact. Journal of Policy and Criminal Psychology. 2009;24:10–21. DOI: 10.1007/s11896-008-9031-x

7. Sampson F, Lyle A. Legal considerations relating to the police use of social media. In: Application of Social Media in Crisis Management. Cham: Springer; 2017. p. 171–90.

8. Sampson F. The ATHENA equation – balancing the efficacy of citizens' response with the reality of citizens' rights around data protection. The Police Journal. 2017 Apr. DOI: 25:0032258X17701321

9. Bottoms A, Tankebe J. Beyond procedural justice: a dialogic approach to legitimacy in criminal justice. The Journal of Criminal Law and Criminology. 2012 Jan;1:119–70.

10. Tyler TR, Fagan J, Geller A. Street stops and police legitimacy: teachable moments in young urban men's legal socialization. Journal of Empirical Legal Studies. 2014 Dec;11(4):751–85.

11. Mazerolle L, Bennett S, Davis J, Sargeant E, Manning M. Procedural justice and police legitimacy: a systematic review of the research evidence. Journal of Experimental Criminology. 2013 Sep 1;9(3):245–74.

12. Mental Health Commission of Canada. Training and Resources. Mental Health Commission of Canada [Internet]. 2018. Available from: https://www.mentalhealthcommission.ca/English

13. Coleman T, Cotton D. TEMPO: Police Interactions; a report towards improving interactions between police and people living with mental health problems. Mental Health Commission of Canada. 2014.

14. Laguna L, Linn A, Ward K, Rupslaukyte R. An examination of authoritarian personality traits among police officers: the role of experience. J Police Crime Psych. 2009;25:99–104.

15. Seed T, Fox JR, Berry K. The experience of involuntary detention in acute psychiatric care. A review and synthesis of qualitative studies. International Journal of Nursing Studies. 2016 Sep 1;61:82–94.

16. Oxburgh L, Gabbert F, Milne R, Cherryman J. Police officers' perceptions and experiences with mentally disordered suspects. International Journal of Law and Psychiatry. 2016 Nov 1;49:138–46.

17. Prince KM. Strengthening interpersonal communication skills in our changing world. Georgia Association for Positive Behavior Support Conference. 2014. Available from: https://digitalcommons.georgiasouthern.edu/gapbs/2014/2014/18

18. Egan G. The skilled helper: a problem-management and opportunity-development approach to helping. Toronto: Nelson Education; 2018.

19. Johnson KE, Thompson J, Hall JA, Meyer C. Crisis (hostage) negotiators weigh in: the skills, behaviors, and qualities that characterize an expert crisis negotiator. Police Practice and Research. 2017 Dec;24:1–8.

20. Schwartz AE, Kramer JM. "I just had to be flexible and show good patience": management of interactional approaches to enact mentoring roles by peer mentors with developmental disabilities. Disability and Rehabilitation. 2017 Jun;7:1–8.

21. Bandura A. Social learning theory. General Learning Corporation; 1971. 2016.

22. Steinmetz J, Pfattheicher S. Beyond social facilitation: a review of the far-reaching effects of social attention. Social Cognition. 2017 Oct;35(5):585–99.

23. Inwinkelried EJ. The applicability of privileges to employees' personal e-mails: the errors caused by the confusion between privilege, confidentiality and other notions of privacy. Mich. St. L. Rev. 2014;1.

24. Clare L, Rowlands J, Bruce E, Surr C, Downs M. "I don't do like I used to do": A grounded theory approach to conceptualising awareness in people with moderate to severe dementia living in long-term care. Social Science & Medicine. 2008 Jun 1;66(11):2366–77.

25. Chavoix C, Insausti R. Self-awareness and the medial temporal lobe in neurodegenerative diseases. Neuroscience & Biobehavioral Reviews. 2017 Jul 1;78:1–2.

26. Oden KA, Miner-Holden J, Balkin RS. Required counseling for mental health professional trainees: its perceived effect on self-awareness and other potential benefits. Journal of Mental Health. 2009 Oct 1;18(5):441–8.

27. Bayley DH, Bittner E. Learning the skills of policing. Critical issues in policing: contemporary issues. 2001 Dec:82–106.

28. Barlow DH, Durand VM, Hofmann SG, Lalumière ML. Abnormal Psychology: an integrative approach. In: Hunter D, editor. 5th ed. Toronto: Nelson Education; 2018.

29. Canadian Mental Health Association, BC Division. Police and mental illness: increased interactions. 2005 Mar.

30. Sartorius N. Iatrogenic stigma of mental illness: begins with behaviour and attitudes of medical professionals, especially psychiatrists. British Medical Journal. 2002 Jun 22; 324(7352):1470–1.

31. Kaplan RM, Saccuzzo DP. Psychological testing: principles, applications, and issues. Toronto: Nelson Education; 2017 Jan 27.

32. Young M. Learning the art of helping: building blocks and techniques. 6th ed. Upper Saddle River, NJ: Pearson; 2017.

33. Willis JJ, Mastrofski SD. Improving policing by integrating craft and science: what can patrol officers teach us about good police work? Policing and Society. 2018 Jan 2;28(1):27–44.

34. Sanders BA. Using personality traits to predict police officer performance. Policing: An International Journal of Police Strategies & Management. 2008 Mar 7;31(1):129–47.

CHAPTER 10

Police Behavioural Response to Critical Intervention and Emergency Situations

Daniel J. Jones, *University of Huddersfield*
Lydia Fleming, *MacEwan University*
Jaqueline Brodbin, *Concordia University of Edmonton*
April Langille, *Concordia University of Edmonton*
Uzma Williams, *MacEwan University*

LEARNING OBJECTIVES

1. Understand best behaviours to interact with individuals experiencing a mental health crisis
2. Demonstrate knowledge of intervention and best practices
3. Identify the verbal, non-verbal, behavioural, and environmental cues when someone is struggling with mental health
4. Demonstrate an ability to determine when individuals are at risk of harming themselves or others
5. Learn to approach people in crisis with safety and a consideration of the individuals' treatment

INTRODUCTION

Academic textbooks provide the public and professionals with extensive amounts of information, especially about human behaviour. However, textbooks only teach information in a theoretical sense. The reality is that in critical situations your innate responses will emerge and your knowledge learned from textbooks and training will assist you only insofar as it has been firmly ingrained. The purpose of learning this material is to build your knowledge and credibility to give you the confidence to respond appropriately during difficult encounters with persons having a mental health breakdown or episode.[1]

There are many different types of mental disorders that officers come across, as discussed in the first part of this book. An understanding of multiple disorders is necessary to help an individual through a mental health episode, for police are often one of the first points of contact to access mental health services.[2] Thus, police training in and education about mental illness allows an officer to address a situation with no misconceptions about those who suffer from a mental illness.[1] Often in calls involving mental health, what is required is the opposite of physical force. This chapter will discuss external signs and cues that signal the mental health concerns of persons, the physical and non-verbal responses to mental health, and will address when the use of force is appropriate.

A significant function of policing is to take charge of situations and people. However, when arriving at the scene of a crime involving a person with mental health concerns, the presence of the police uniform and the use of loud, sharp, and aggressive verbal commands may cause the person to become even more agitated—potentially escalating the situation towards the use of physical force;[3] the situation may further escalate rather than de-escalate.[3]

Situations involving persons in mental health distress require strong decision-making skills to choose the appropriate amount of force. It is always a challenge for police to go into a situation and immediately determine if the person is experiencing a mental health episode, and decisions must often be made in the blink of an eye. To complicate matters further, it is nearly impossible to isolate and identify the mental health symptoms of a person who is generally abrasive,[2] mainly because first responders are usually responding to extreme, abnormal behaviours where there is a strong interconnection between crime and mental health concerns.[4-5] For these reasons, there is a need to develop guidelines for good decision-making. Any perception of dangerousness prior to arriving on the scene involving persons with mental illness could set up a self-fulfilling prophesy.[1] In other words, if police anticipate a hostile situation, they more often rush to find a resolution rather than taking the time necessary to de-escalate and bring the situation to a peaceful conclusion. Thus, police officers' beliefs can influence the way they respond to the person and ultimately put themselves, the person, and others at risk. By understanding behavioural cues and practicing non-judgemental approaches, officers can react with the confidence that calm and respectful behaviour can lead to a more satisfactory and safer outcome, thus lessening the need to use force.

CONTACT WITH PERSONS EXPERIENCING A MENTAL HEALTH EPISODE

Reasons for police contact with persons experiencing mental health concerns can be complex—often resulting from social and systemic factors such as homelessness and poverty, weak social ties, or a lack of community-based health services.[4] The police are typically the first and sole community resource called to respond to urgent situations involving persons with mental illness, requiring a close liaison between police and mental health practitioners.[5] The reasons police are contacted in situations involving persons with mental illness can vary, as they respond to everything from minor offences to extreme crisis situations. A significant proportion of these interactions involve people threatening to harm or kill themselves.[6] It is important to understand the behavioural differences between a person with a mental health disorder and someone presenting behaviour more criminal in nature. Recognizing whether a person is experiencing mental illness is one of the first steps. The typical police response to suspected criminal activity (containment, interrogation, detention) is usually not appropriate when dealing with mental illness.[7] Employing traditional response measures with someone experiencing mental health symptoms may potentially escalate the situation to a point where there is a risk of injury or death for the police officer, the public, or, more often, the person in crisis.[7] When someone with a mental illness is in crisis, their perceptions may or may not be disturbed—they may be delusional or paranoid, often terrified, or simply not in touch with reality.[7] This may lead the person experiencing active mental health symptoms to act aggressively or bizarrely, potentially cueing an untrained officer to immediately use force. The complexity of incidents means that officers must exercise considerable informed judgement, and more than anything else, on-the-spot assessment and analysis.[8]

COMMON DISORDERS

Approximately one in five contacts with police involve someone with a diagnosed mental health issue or substance use disorder,[9] so it is crucial to be aware of the different types of mental disorders and abnormal behavioural cues—which signal distress or irrationality rather than criminal intent. Evidence suggests that most people with mental health problems are not violent, but they are, in fact, more likely to be victims of violence than perpetrators, including victims of homicide.[10] People with serious mental illnesses such as schizophrenia, major depression, and bipolar disorder are shunned by large segments of society due in part to often-false stereotypes.[11]

It has been found that those who live with mental illness are no more likely to act violently than a stranger walking on the street.[12] However, family members, police, and health professionals are the ones most likely to be harmed by an individual experiencing critical mental health symptoms.[12] In the extreme, there can be associated risks that contribute to the likelihood of a person with mental illness committing a violent act. For example, people experiencing feelings of persecution, paranoid schizophrenia, or bipolar disorder with psychotic features— coupled with substance abuse—have been found to be more violent than people with other diagnoses.[13-17] Furthermore, people with comorbid mental illness and substance use disorders are more likely to be reported for violent acts than people with substance use disorders alone.[17] Policies and interventions must recognize that comorbid psychiatric and substance use disorders can be a volatile mix.[11,17]

With psychosis, there are many reasons a person might exhibit psychotic symptoms in addition to a mental disorder, including brain injury, substance abuse, medical conditions, response to trauma, and victimization.[7] Positive symptoms such as persecutory or paranoid delusions may lead to an increased risk for violent crime by making the patients believe they either are in some kind of danger or possess powers to save the world from evil.[13] Much of the relationship between violence and mental illness is due to substance misuse or lack of treatment.[10] Severe mental illness alone can be very distressing for an individual, and it is important to take into consideration that there are multiple factors to consider when a person with mental illness commits a violent act. Contextual (e.g., unemployment), clinical (e.g., perceived threats), and historical (e.g., past violence) factors can also increase the risk of violence.[17]

Cues and Responses to Hallucinations and Delusions[7]

Behavioural cues of auditory hallucinations:

1. Appears preoccupied and unaware of surroundings
2. Talking to self
3. Difficulty understanding or following conversations
4. Misinterprets words and actions of others

continued

Behavioural cues of visual/tactile hallucinations:

1. Interaction with something or someone that is not there
2. Touching, scratching, or brushing things off self
3. Sniffing or holding nose
4. Spitting out food for no apparent reason

Responding to hallucinations:

1. The immediate goal of your response should be to help the person focus on the current interaction.
2. Do not pretend you also experience the hallucination, but do not try to convince the person that the hallucination does not exist; it does exist to them.
3. Ask questions about what they are hearing or seeing.
4. Get them to focus on you and your voice rather than whatever they are hearing or seeing.
5. Reassure them that you want to help them, and explain who you are, what you are doing, and why.

Responding to delusions:

1. Do not touch the person without permission.
2. Position yourself at the person's level if it is safe to do so.
3. Do not whisper or laugh, as this may be misunderstood and may increase paranoia.
4. Remember that those experiencing delusions may not always be honest about what they think or believe; they may not trust you enough to be honest, especially if their delusions consist of paranoia.
5. It is important to keep yourself safe from potentially violent reactions and to provide a comfort zone for the person experiencing delusions until you know the content and context of the delusion. Keep a safe distance from or some barrier (e.g., a piece of furniture) between the two of you.

CRISIS INTERVENTION PROGRAMS AND BEHAVIOUR

An in-depth knowledge of and education about mental health intervention training can contribute to a reduced stigma and stereotyping of individuals with mental illnesses who have been criminalized throughout society.[18] People experiencing an episode of mental illness can be criminalized because their abnormal behaviour is seen as foreign and unknown to the untrained officer. Police officers unequipped with the appropriate knowledge of psychological impairment may have trouble ascertaining the nature of a person's behaviour when confronting them, evoking a reaction of fear.[19] With limited training in mental health issues and scant service options, police officers can find calls related to mental illness challenging and often find the individuals and disposition options difficult to manage.[19] Currently, individuals with complex needs, disabilities, and disadvantages utilize an enormous amount of police and emergency resources.[1] As a result, intervention programs have been implemented and tested in many policing professions and organizations to change the nature of police response incidents involving individuals in mental health situations.[3]

Crisis intervention training allows officers to learn about mental illness, substance abuse, psychiatric medication, and techniques for responding to a mental health crisis.[19] The training provides tools that can be used in calls to improve officer assessments of danger, help respond more appropriately to a person who is potentially symptomatic, and determine the appropriate action for the individual.[19] The training includes role-play, education, visits to mental health facilities, and open discussions between the officers and individuals with a mental health illness.[19] The critical goal of crisis intervention training is to increase the likelihood that people in crisis, especially those with serious mental illnesses, will receive treatment rather than incarceration if the crime was committed due to their mental state at the time.[18] The results of these programs clearly show that the outcomes of behavioural crisis situations are greatly improved upon from previous outcomes and by following the proper training. The entire nature of encounters between police officers and those with mental health issues is drastically changed due to the presence of someone with the knowledge of how to handle these cases. Police serve as gatekeepers to the mental health and the criminal justice system, and their adequate response depends on the available training resources as well as a non-judgemental attitude to ensure an effective response.[19] The next three sections of this chapter—Initial Assessment, Signs of Mental Health Concerns, and Behavioural Response—provide a foundation for understanding and responding to mental health situations, supplemental to the training provided by a police organization.[1-2,4,7,9,13,19-28]

INITIAL ASSESSMENT

Environmental Scan

- Safety
- Know the location and surroundings
- Obtain background information

Safety

Your safety is your first priority, followed by the safety of everyone else. Safety should constantly be assessed throughout the situation for the officer, the person, and others nearby. Identify and manage any potential hazards that could put your safety at risk. Ensure that any hazards seen in the environment are under control or eliminated. Constantly check the environment for any additional hazards to ensure that you and those around you remain safe.

Know Your Location and Surroundings

There are varying levels of safety in public spaces, single-family homes, group homes, hotels, and any other setting. Recognize the different levels of safety in your area. Notice any possible exit routes or emergency resources that may be nearby. Be aware of any construction, traffic, or loud noises that could pose as a potential hazard.

Obtain Background Information That Initiated the Required Response

Officers are generally provided with a brief description over the radio and with a priority code as to the type of response generally required. Information from the dispatcher allows immediate access to important information provided during the emergency call (Is there any threat to the people involved on scene? Are there any weapons? Does the person have a way of escaping the scene? etc.), and you can and should ask as many questions over dispatch as time permits.

Officers will receive additional information via the mobile digital computers in their vehicle. This information can be very detailed, including previous call history and a detailed account of what is going on and who the reporting party is. When arriving on scene with this information, officers must work in the moment when making an analysis of any threats or hazards. The officers must determine if there is any crime or violence in progress and if their own safety and that of the person or the public is in jeopardy. As this process usually happens very quickly, there might be important information obtained from the radio that could help a police officer in making an analysis and attending to the situation as quickly as possible.

SIGNS OF MENTAL HEALTH CONCERNS

Verbal Cues of the Person

- Illogical thoughts
- Unusual speech patterns
- Extreme and inappropriate verbal excitement or hostility

Illogical Thoughts
A major indicator of mental illness is the individual's thought process. Illogical thinking is used to describe faults in logic that lead to conclusions that will interfere with everyday functioning. This may include **loose association**, the combination of unrelated or abstract topics. It may also include **grandiose ideas**, which include the individual expressing an unrealistic sense of superiority. In these situations, individuals often believe that they are a higher authority or a greater power (e.g., claiming they are Jesus). Illogical thinking could also be expressed through **ideas of persecution**. This means that individuals believe they are being harassed or threatened without any reasonable rationale; e.g., individuals who believe that the government is monitoring their thoughts through a television set. **Obsessive thoughts** are also a sign of illogical thinking. This means that individuals are preoccupied with their obsessions—whether death, germs, guilt, or a person—and are unable to properly function due to these obsessive thoughts.

Unusual Speech Patterns
Individuals may express themselves in unusual speech patterns, and this could be a sign of mental illness. They may use **nonsensical speech or chatter**, be unclear when they speak, or be unable to communicate an idea. They may also have a rapid flow of unrelated ideas or use **incoherent speech** and words that do not fit together. Individuals may also use **pressured speech**, expressing urgency when they speak, or extremely slow speech. They may fail to respond to simple questions at all, answering with a blank stare. Unusual speech patterns often also include **word repetition**, i.e., frequently stating the same words and phrases, or using rhyming words and phrases.

Extreme and Inappropriate Verbal Excitement or Hostility

Persons experiencing a mental health crisis may use extreme expressions, may speak with extreme excitement and/or volume, and be unreasonably hostile, argumentative, or belligerent. They may threaten to harm themselves or others.

Non-Verbal Cues of the Person

- Body language/movements
- Tone of voice
- Facial expression

Body Language/Movements

Ninety percent of communication is non-verbal, predominantly body language and tone. Being attentive to body language provides insight into the severity of the situation, the mental stability of individuals, and the genuineness of their words. Their body language is a good way to read intention. Consider what emotion is being conveyed through their posture and gestures, and if their body language corresponds with their verbal content. It is important to consider what signs in their body language may suggest violent behaviour before it occurs. Things such as clenched fists, a red face, or a broadened upright chest are all signs of anger.

Tone of Voice

It is important to pay attention to individuals' tone of voice, what emotions they are expressing, and whether or not their tone of voice corresponds with what they are saying. Whether it corresponds with the content or not evinces their stability and current perception. Their tone also provides insight into the level of threat they perceive.

Facial Expressions

Emotion is conveyed by facial expressions (fear, anger, sadness) and helps others interpret whether the person's facial expression corresponds with what they are saying. This will tell us how emotionally stable and aware that person is in that instance. At times we may be speaking with someone who is emotionally over-stimulated or who is extremely emotionally confused.

Behavioural Cues of the Person

- Physical appearance
- Responding to voices or objects that are not there

- Extreme paranoia or suspiciousness
- Confusion or unawareness of surroundings, loss of time
- Causing injury to self (e.g., cutting self with sharp object, cigarette burns on body)
- Inappropriate (lack of or extreme) emotional reactions

Physical Appearance

Individuals' physical appearance may suggest something about their mental state. If they are not appropriately dressed for the environment (e.g., wearing a heavy coat on a hot summer day), this may suggest mental health concerns. Another physical attribute that may suggest mental concern is bizarre or eccentric clothing or makeup.

Responding to Voices or Objects That Are Not There

When individuals experience psychosis, they are out of touch with reality because they are experiencing delusions and/or hallucinations. A delusion is a false, fixed belief or an exaggerated belief and can occur with or without hallucinations. A hallucination is when a person senses (sees, hears, feels, smells, or tastes) things that do not exist, and these can be tactile, visual, or auditory—the most common being auditory; for example, persons who smell smoke (hallucination) and believe that someone is trying to kill them (delusion). Both hallucinations and delusions can be symptoms of several different mental illnesses as well as medical illnesses.

Extreme Paranoia or Suspiciousness

Paranoia can be a symptom of several different mental disorders. Some of the common attributes of a person with paranoia are impulsive and erratic behaviours, pacing and agitation, and/or sluggish movements. Paranoid individuals can have a repetitive ritual that they do in the belief that this ritual will keep them safe. This could be just about anything, such as standing in a certain position for an hour between 3:00 and 4:00 p.m. every day, or checking the door 87 times before bed. Persons experiencing paranoia may also exhibit strange postures or mannerisms, such as continuously looking over their shoulder to check if they are being followed. People with paranoia may believe things that seem realistic (e.g., their spouse is cheating on them); therefore, paranoia can be difficult to recognize at first. However, the paranoia will manifest in an extreme and consistent pattern.

Confusion or Unawareness of Surroundings and Time

In some mental health disorders, individuals experience a complete unawareness of time and their surroundings. They may be confused as to where they are or how they got there, or unaware of the current time and what they have been doing during that lost time. This could last anywhere from a few hours or weeks to even months.

Causing Injury to Self

Recognizing individuals who have injured or are injuring themselves can be done by looking for scars and marks on sensitive and often hidden places on the body. Common methods for self-injury include cutting with sharp objects, rubbing the skin until it breaks, burning with cigarette butts or other hot objects, or pulling one's hair. The body parts that are often abused are the wrists/arms, ankles, or stomach.

Inappropriate Emotional Reactions

Inappropriate emotional reactions could mean several different things: overreacting with anger or fear, reacting with the opposite expected emotion (e.g., laughing at an auto accident), or not expressing emotional reactions at all. A rapid switch to other extremes of emotion could also indicate impulsivity or instability.

Four Behaviours That Provide Insight into a Person's Mental Health

- Eating
- Sleeping
- Grooming/bathing/hygiene
- Relationships

Eating

Although everyone responds differently, some common behaviours to look out for are found in a person's eating, sleeping, hygiene, and relationships. Changes in eating patterns—eating far less than a healthy portion, eating far more than usual, or no longer being interested in previously enjoyed meals—can be indicators that someone is mentally distressed.

Sleeping

Changes in sleep patterns also provide insight into a person's mental health. These can include insomnia (prolonged inability to sleep), hypersomnia (sleepiness throughout the day and extensive night-time sleeping), or an unnecessary noc-turnal schedule (sleeping during the day and being awake at night), among other changes to someone's regular, healthy sleeping arrangements.

Grooming/Bathing/Hygiene

If individuals are failing to groom themselves, such as forgetting to shower, wash their clothes, brush their teeth, or anything else that differs from their usual hygienic behaviours, they could be in mental distress. Changes to the opposite effect (compulsive hair brushing, showering three to four times a day, washing their clothes/bedding multiple times, etc.) are also signs of mental health concerns.

Relationships

Making changes in relationships is another typical indicator of mental health distress. If individuals are detaching themselves, pushing previously close relationships away, are isolated, or have difficulty maintaining relationships, they are likely experiencing mental health stress.

Environmental Cues

- Decorations
- Waste matter/trash
- Child-like collections

Environmental cues that are irregular or seemingly unusual can often express that individuals are having issues with mental health. Decorating choices that seem eccentric—using tinfoil to cover a window, lining the window trim with salt, having photos and artwork upside down, or having an immense number of decorations with religious or political undertones—can indicate that someone is in mental health distress. Another sign that an individual is experiencing poor mental health is excessive waste matter and trash lying around the house. Pack ratting, or hoarding, is when the person accumulates trash but is unwilling to get rid of it, often to the point of exorbitant storing of string, old newspapers, plastic bags, and other clutter. Lack of cleaning—dirty dishes piled about, thick layers of dust, or sometimes to the point of bodily fluids found on walls or floors—signals mental health concerns. Individuals facing problems with their mental health may also display child-like actions and have collections of objects that are predominantly for children. Adults with unreasonable amounts of dolls, toys, or collectibles for children, often treated as if they are sentient and emotional creatures, provide insight into the person's mental health well-being.

Totality of Cues[22]

In order to better understand the behavioural, environmental, verbal, and non-verbal cues of a person experiencing mental health problems, one must consider multiple systems, such as individual, family, and cultural factors, to create a complete picture; hence one's judgement of the situation will be far more valid. Related to situational context are the socioeconomic, cultural, and environmental contexts. Be sensitive whenever assessing seemingly bizarre or inappropriate behaviour and/or speech. What may seem abnormal to you because of how you were raised may be completely the norm for someone with a different background. Being open and understanding of other perspectives is important when engaging with anyone, whether mental health issues are present or not. For example, some homeless persons wear many layers of clothing, no matter the weather. This is because they always carry all their possessions with them, and so wearing a heavy coat in summer shouldn't be misconstrued as erratic behaviour that needs an intervention. Be aware that many Western concepts of mental illness do not exist in other cultures, and that people's illnesses may be heavily influenced by their social understanding.

Questions to Ask in Times of Distress

Family Members and Witnesses
1. Has the individual threatened or attempted to use violence or acted dangerously towards themselves or others?
2. Has the individual threatened or attempted suicide?
3. Has the individual been neglecting personal care or bodily functions?
4. Has the individual recently suffered a traumatic experience?
5. Does the individual have a history of mental illness?
6. Does the individual take medication or have any physically handicapping conditions?

Individual
1. What is your name?
2. How can I help you?

3. Where do you live?
4. Where are you right now?
5. What date/day/time is it?
6. When did you last eat?
7. When did you last sleep? For how long?
8. Why do you want to hurt yourself?
9. Tell me: what is going on?
10. What kind of problems are you having?
11. What medications are you supposed to take? When was the last time you took your medication?
12. When was the last time you saw a doctor? What is your treatment for?
13. What types of fears do you have? What is causing those fears?
14. What are your plans? What are you going to do now?

Open-ended questions elicit a more thorough explanation of the individual's experience, whereas closed-ended questions elicit specific, concise information. The person should be allowed to explain and expand on the problem or situation. Only one person or officer should talk at a time because the person may be feeling overwhelmed. Be sure to ask only one question at a time, and wait for a response before asking the next, related question. Asking multiple questions at a time can be confusing or cause the individual to answer only one. Keep in mind that the person may not be capable of understanding and responding to the directions given by police, depending on their mental state.[10]

BEHAVIOURAL RESPONSE TO ABNORMAL BEHAVIOURS

Important Tasks

- Gather information from family, friends, and bystanders
- Be aware of your equipment and presence
- Remove distractions, upsetting influences, and disruptive people from the scene

- Safeguard your own life and protect others
- Assess whether the person may have a mental illness
- Continually assess the scene for danger

Gather Information from Family, Friends, and Bystanders

Locate and ask any witnesses about what they have seen, warning signs they may have come across, possible triggers, and events that may have led to the response. Details about what has happened can help you identify any cues that are a sign of distress and danger. If family or friends of the individual are nearby, ask professionally about the their background history, including signs of mental illness, violence, or any previous suicide attempts, as well as medical illnesses and any past or recent significant negative events. Asking about psychosocial stressors and incidents that may have influenced the response can help you understand the context of the patient and how you may approach the individual. Obtaining as much background information as possible will allow you to have better judgement and plan your next steps.

Be Aware That Your Equipment (uniform, handcuffs, baton) and/or Presence Might Frighten or Intimidate the Person

Individuals might feel you are a threat and that you might use standard police response to arrest or hurt them. Being aware of this can allow you to think more carefully about the way you come across and act towards the person in distress. Remind the person that you are not there to hurt them. Expressing empathic reassurance can allow the person to feel calmer in the situation and when communicating with you. This in turn can build trust between you and the individual.

Remove Distractions, Upsetting Influences, and Disruptive People from the Scene

Removing distractions can allow the person to not feel overwhelmed by other objects or noises in the situation. This can allow you to clearly communicate and have the focused attention of the person. Upsetting influences can threaten the person's safety and may escalate the situation. Removing nuisances and threatening stimuli will allow the person to feel more comfortable. It is important to remove disruptive people from the scene who are intimidating, making loud noises, shouting, or trying to get between you and the person with whom you're communicating. Disruptive people can influence persons negatively by making them believe someone is going to harm them. This may cause them to act out or to place themselves in a dangerous position and weaken the trust that you are trying to build with them.

Protect the Public and Safeguard Your Own Life

When approaching an individual exhibiting abnormal behaviour, the most important thing is to ensure that they do not pose a threat to you or others. Survey the situation to ensure your immediate safety and the safety of others and take the necessary precautions. Throughout the incident, it is important to continuously remain aware of the safety of the situation, as the threat may escalate (e.g., persons who are suicidal may attempt suicide).

Assess Whether the Person May Have a Mental Illness

There are different reasons for abnormal behaviour, such as drugs, alcohol, or mental instability, and there are different levels of severity to consider. In order to understand the situation, it is important to identify the primary symptoms indicating mental illness, and to gather as much information as possible about the person and situation prior to arriving at the scene. As all the information passed on to you may not be completely accurate, it is important to make your own observations.

Continually Assess the Scene for Danger

Continuously scanning your environment can allow you to prevent any hazards from harming yourself, the individual, and everyone else on scene. Analyzing any cues that may signify harm to oneself or others is important. Take note of your surroundings and be on constant alert for your personal safety first, then of others on the scene.

Assessing Probability of Violence to Others

Evidence of Violence
- *Determine if there is ongoing violence.* The situation may be dangerous even if the violence is not directed at people (property destruction, hurting animals, etc.).
- *Assess if there is a specific direction of violence.* Violence that is clearly directed at a specific person is a more serious situation than "random" violence.
- *Ascertain if anyone involved in the situation is already injured.*

continued

Potential for Violence

- *Establish if there is a weapon at the scene.* This includes any potential weapons, including household items, not only items actively present.
- *Determine where the person is; bathrooms and kitchens are the most dangerous.* See if there are pills, possible weapons, or other dangerous items in the room.
- *Determine if the person is barricaded in a room or in the house,* and if the room has windows.
- *Determine if other persons are present.*
- *Determine if there is a history of violent behaviour.* Spousal or child abuse and any self-reported violent behaviours indicate that the person may be more likely to resort to violence, especially if the current circumstances are similar to those in which the past violence occurred.
- *Direct questions about relationships to the person*: "Have you worried that _____ will hurt someone?"; "Has _____ ever hurt you?"
- *Direct questions for the person*: "What is the most violent thing you have done?"; "Do you ever feel you might physically hurt someone?"; "What is the closest you have come to hurting someone?"
- *Apprehend for hospitalization.*

Red Flags

- Words or actions that indicate an intent to cause bodily harm to another person
- Threats or intentions are specific to a person
- The individual is agitated, angry, and appears explosive
- Engaging in or intends to engage in irrational, impulsive, or reckless behaviour

USE OF FORCE

Although mental illness is often associated with violence in popular culture, the link between mental illness and violence is not well supported by research evidence.[10] Interactions between the police and those with mental health illness are common, and an area of concern is that the use of force is excessive in these interactions.[4] This includes handcuffing, injuring, and an unnecessary use of force to restrain. Experiencing excessive force from police has a substantial negative influence on how people perceive law enforcement,[4] and this can trigger an unwanted escalation in interactions with persons experiencing mental illness in particular, since the fear of force is worsened with symptoms such as paranoia. An expectation of heightened danger on the part of officers may contribute to the escalation of violence in the encounter and the need to respond with physical force.[5] In addition, people with mental illness may experience higher levels of police force due to their increased tendency to resist arrest.[5] When assessing the probability of violence, keep in mind that mental illness is not a static condition, that people with diagnoses are not symptomatic all the time, and that mental health symptoms are typically not physical or verbalized.[7] The authority for police to use force, pursuant to the Criminal Code of Canada, is one that is intended to be used only when all else fails—and other force options have been exhausted or the situation requires a quick response.[10] In other words, the progressive application of increasing force from communication, to soft-control tactics, to hard control tactics, to use of weapons, is not always required. Once on the scene, police respond accordingly to suspect-persons if they pose an immediate danger to anyone, which may involve an immediate escalation of using hard control tactics, conducted energy weapon, or, at a rare extreme, lethal force, depending on the situation. On the other hand, progressive use of force may not be appropriate in mental health crisis situations if the person does not pose any immediate danger. Rather, a continued calm and patient response using only communication or soft control tactics is appropriate, regardless of length of time, as long as the situation poses no risk to the officer or bystanders.

Factual knowledge about the real relationship between mental illness and present danger is critical when weighing the presenting situation and then applying discretion to avoid escalation of often delicate situations.[10] Some police officers spend insufficient time at the lower end of the continuum (being patient and verbally communicating) before escalating to a "higher" level (the use of physical force).[10] Disciplinary measures, including segregation or solitary confinement, can be highly traumatic and cause breakdown or psychosis for a person with mental illness.[9] This supports the idea that inappropriate responses worsen a situation rather than resolve it.

Approaching a Person Experiencing a Crisis

When approaching individuals in crisis, it is important to ensure that you are approaching them in a way that allows them to feel safe. Because most police officers believe that disturbance calls are the most dangerous, it is common for police officers to approach these situations with the expectation of encountering a hostile person. An officer's response can aggravate adverse mental health symptoms. In all your decisions, constantly incorporate a risk assessment, or, in other words, common sense evaluation. Think safety for yourself first and then others.

Safety Scan
The first thing you must do when approaching a crisis is evaluate it to ensure the safety of yourself and everyone involved. Be alert, consistently evaluating the situation and level of safety for everyone involved, and be ready for any quick changes in behaviour. The individual is probably frightened or angry. If they are hearing voices and those voices are saying that the officer has come to punish or hurt them, they may turn against the officer without any apparent provocation. The person may exhibit a burst of extreme strength and may appear impervious to pain, especially if intoxicated with drugs. Like anyone in crisis, the individual is unpredictable and may not respond in the manner expected by the officer. Do not be dubious if the person has a sudden return to reality; the person can just as quickly return from crisis.

Introduce Yourself
Introduce yourself by saying, "Hi, my name is...." This is an important step, as it will allow the individual to feel a certain security and familiarity with you. Explain who you are, who others are, and who may arrive.

Ask Questions
Try to recognize any symptoms of potential mental illness and ask the individual questions about their mental state and feelings. Ask questions to obtain a good understanding of the situation and what the person is feeling.

Remain Professional
Remain professional by not responding to insults or aggressive talk, but do respond to other questions with short, simply-worded language so that the person can understand and does not feel ignored. Emotions play a large role in mental health breakdowns, and it is important to be sensitive about the person's emotional state even if you are not comfortable discussing emotions.

Body Posture and Facial Expression
Just as an overpowering attitude can be unsettling, overpowering body language is equally triggering. Be aware of aggressive body language: do not stand over a

sitting person, be softer and open your stance, and be at the same level as the person. Turning your body partially sideways with your gun back actually offers you safety because you can draw your gun quickly and it makes you a smaller target. Also, be aware of your facial expressions. Persons experiencing psychosis may find certain expressions threatening—high sensitivity to expressions of negative emotions has been found among schizophrenic persons in particular. Eye contact is important: listen compassionately rather than aggressively and dominantly, but do not stare. Do not exhibit nervous or aggressive behaviour, such as crossing your arms, pointing at the person, standing with your hands on your hips, or making abrupt or quick movements, for this will increase any perception that you are a threat.

Make a Plan and Follow It

The things that a person in crisis will say and do can spark emotion or test your patience; therefore, it is important to make a plan when you are thinking rationally and ensure that you follow it. Don't rush, for it is important to maintain a calm demeanour. Keeping calm will allow you to think more clearly and deal with the situation more effectively—and will also calm the person in crisis. Explain what is happening from your end, not in terms of the person's own experience but what you or others are doing to help them. If they are hearing voices, tell them that you cannot hear them, but that you understand that they do. It's okay to ask if they are hearing voices and what the voices are saying; this may help the person's anxiety.

Maintain Appropriate Space

As stated above, it is important to ensure that the person feels safe. In order to do this, make sure that you are maintaining personal space.

    a.   Intimate: under 18″
    b.   Personal: 18″ to 36″
    c.   Social: 3′ to 6′
    d.   Public: over 6′

The officer should remain in the social space; however, the appropriate distance is situational. The more threatened the individual feels, the more space they may need. Avoid touching the person and do not stand between them and an exit (but make sure that you have access to a safe exit); this reduces the perception of you as a threat. Be aware that not all unusual behaviour is danger-ous or violent. It is better to perform a safe, controlled containment and negotia-tion when no one else is at risk. If there are numerous officers, avoid surrounding the individual. Don't give them any reason to be suspicious of you. Move slowly and keep an appropriate distance.

Giving Directions

Give firm and clear directions using a gentle voice that conveys the image of calm self-assurance. It is necessary that you take charge of the situation, but you want to ensure that you are supplying the person with comfort, safety, trust, and compassion. It is important that the person know that you want to understand and help.

Speak simply, briefly, and move slowly. Often persons in psychosis are experiencing auditory hallucinations (hearing voices) and cannot hear or deal with more than short, simple statements or questions. It may be necessary to repeat yourself before the person can hear and understand you. Minimize unnecessary sensory input, such as noises and crowds, as these tend to confuse the person.

Ask permission and announce your actions; this way you avoid startling distressed individuals. They will feel less threatened if they are aware of what is going on. If they are fearful of your equipment, take the time to explain that you carry it to enable you to perform your job, which is to protect them and the public. Also, avoid handcuffing unless it's absolutely necessary. One of the main catalysts to physical confrontations between police officers and persons with mental illness is fear of the police uniform and equipment.

Give Choices

Developing a sense of working together is helpful in these situations, as it allows individuals to feel less threatened and more in control; you can achieve this by providing choices, when possible, to allow them a certain level of control. For example, if you are taking them to a hospital, you could ask them, "Do you want me to call or do you want mom to call?" These small choices will develop trust and calmness in your interaction with a distressed individual.

Allow the individual an exit so they can "save face." Making the person feel embarrassed for their actions can escalate the situation, so when possible give them the opportunity to exit the situation when it is safe to do so, and/or the opportunity to explain themselves.

Tips for Approaching a Person in a Crisis Situation

1. Get their attention first.
2. Identify yourself. "Hi, my name is...."
3. Evaluate the crisis—constantly.
4. If suicidal gestures are not apparent, ask the person about their intent.
5. A suicidal individual may attempt to have others kill them (suicide by cop). Note that a suicidal person may become homicidal.
6. Reassure them that you do not intend harm.
7. Be alert.
8. Be professional.
9. Don't take words or actions personally.
10. Make a plan and follow it—don't rush.
11. Remain calm, do not over react.
12. Maintain personal space.
13. Give firm, clear directions but use a gentle voice.
14. Explain that you are trying to understand and help.
15. Speak simply, briefly, and move slowly; repeat yourself if needed.
16. Ask permission.
17. Announce your actions before initiating them.
18. Develop a sense of working together.
19. Give choices when possible to allow a certain level of control.
20. If possible, allow the person an exit to let them "save face."

CRITICAL INTERVENTION AND EMERGENCY RESPONSE TO ABNORMAL BEHAVIOUR: AGGRESSIVE BEHAVIOURS IN EMERGENCY SITUATIONS

When responding to a situation where any type of response will elicit harm either to the individual or to others (because the person has already committed murder, is currently engaged in a crisis situation, or detests authorities), the police response must be more acute and controlling—whether or not it involves a person with a mental illness. Likewise, when a crime is being committed, the police must use the appropriate amount of necessary verbal and physical force until the situation is controlled. When all other non-violent interventions to de-escalate the situation have been exhausted (depending on whether the situation is high-stress or low-stress), it is the duty of the police officer to intervene appropriately in this situation to minimize or prevent any harm.

Each crisis situation a police officer comes across is different, and some techniques employed may not work effectively for everyone. The manner in which the police interact with individuals with a mental health crisis and the amount of time involved in responding to a call impacts the disposition, use of force, and safety of both the civilians and police.[29] Persons are often in crisis due to experiencing suicidal tendencies, extreme emotional turmoil or mood arousal, or psychosis, and these crisis situations require **de-escalation** skills to achieve a desired, non-violent outcome as well as to minimize any scrutiny or sanctions on the police officer.[30,31] Nonetheless, if the persons are acting aggressively and want to hurt others or themselves, at this point it does not matter what else is happening: the risk of harm and ensuring safety must be addressed first.

De-escalation techniques can be an effective intervention tool that not only helps individuals who are in crisis but also reduces police liability and injury.[31] When an officer applies de-escalation skills appropriately, the probability that he or she will effectively intervene in a crisis is increased and the need for using physical force is minimized.[31] In some scenarios, officers may find that the use of de-escalation techniques aren't effective in helping the individual in crisis and the situation may be escalating more rapidly. In these types of scenarios, officers must make the appropriate choices and possibly use other means to control the situation to ensure the safety of the person and others. When a crisis situation has escalated to the point of harm in any way, an officer may be compelled to use force or restraint to gain control of a situation.[31] A soft technique may be used by an officer to gain control over an individual who becomes abusive or resistant to verbal commands. This type of action generally includes grabbing, holding, and joint locks to restrain the individual.[31]

Containment by officers may also serve to neutralize the actions and intentions of the individual.[21] The tactic of time and distance during containment may allow an emotionally charged individual an opportunity to calm down and regain composure.[21] Police officers can use this means of controlling a situation in order to protect individuals from harming themselves or others. There is the option of using less lethal means of controlling the situation if an officer deems them appropriate. Less lethal measures refer to using pepper spray or a conducted energy weapon on the person. This strategy can assert control over the person without resorting to any lethal means of intervention.

There are also positions officers can form as a means of asserting control of the person without using force. This includes displaying the reference call by placing the hand on one's firearm without drawing it. Officers can also display an interview position when approaching the individual with their hands up and open with no intent of forming fists. This supportive stance can maintain safety for the officer and signify to the individuals that the officer is not going to physically attack them; meanwhile, they remain in control of the situation.

At any extreme moment during a scenario, officers can call for backup assistance and present a low ready position where their gun is out and ready to shoot. However, the majority of police officers don't have to fire their weapon even if it is out on scene. The use of deadly force is dependent upon both the unique circumstances of the incident and the particular decision-making strategies of the individual officer.[30] Officers in the field are taught to use only the amount of force that is reasonable and necessary to overcome resistance, prevent injury, and/or escape.[29]

When dealing with these types of emergencies, there isn't much time to do a diagnosis of the person. Officers are reminded that if one tactic does not work, they must be flexible and willing to adjust their approach.[29] Police officers must be prepared and good at immediately assessing if a situation is an emergency and, if so, what kind of measures must be taken in order to achieve a peaceful resolution. Intervening officers should always focus on the behaviours of the individual in crisis.[31] Officers should never take the individual's words or actions personally and should always remember that the person is in crisis.[31] Over- or under-exaggerated reactions by the officers on scene can come between their control of the situation and how they respond towards the person.

After the situation has de-escalated, communication with persons must change because they are now controlled and no longer a threat to themselves or others. They are most likely frightened from the intervention used. They may feel that you might hurt them again, especially if an officer has used force as a means to control the crisis at hand. Acting calmly, especially following de-escalation, can ensure that the situation for all on scene won't escalate further. The officer should always remain calm and speak slowly, using short sentences, to encourage communication throughout the entire incident and afterwards.

When the situation is completely over, police officers should provide the right resources and treatment options for the person, including a possible mental health examination at a local remand centre. Using an urgent care centre can greatly reduce wait times, allowing patrol officers to return to their duties in under 30 minutes.[29] In addition, urgent care centres have a host of services, provide linkages, and decrease involuntary hospitalizations.[29] However, if a person requires additional involuntary services, they may be transferred to long-term care facilities as needed.[29] Therefore, it is important for officers to make the best decision in the interest of the person as to where they may be transferred for treatment.

It is crucial for police officers to express and cope with any high emotions or stress they may have experienced during the intervention once the situation is officially over. The personal well-being of the police officers on scene is just as important as those of the person and others nearby. With proper training and practice, officers can learn from these experiences and apply what they have learned to more effectively de-escalate future crisis situations and help those who are experiencing a mental health episode.

Case Study: Evening Surprise

One evening while on duty, Officer Dalton Bellmond stopped a man for a provincial bylaw offence on an LRT platform. He was having a difficult time identifying exactly what was going on with this man; he suspected the man was under the influence of alcohol because his story was not lining up. He finished up with the male and handed him his paperwork. He reached for his notes, while the man took off his backpack and placed it on the bench beside him. Officer Bellmond heard something fall onto the bench, and as he looked over, he saw a black pistol lying there and the man reaching for it. All of a sudden, everything appeared to move in slow motion for him. In this moment, the realization that you may have to kill someone in the line of duty rushes to the forefront of your thoughts. Bellmond had had that talk with himself when he was hired on the force, just like all officers do, and now it was actually happening—the possibility was real: if the man got a hold of the gun, there would be no other choice. He immediately stepped forward into action, pushing the man away with one hand, grabbing the gun with the other, and disengaging four steps backwards while the man put his hands in the air. With his heart beating a million miles an hour, Bellmond called for backup and told the man not to move. Once his adrenaline started to come down, he examined the gun and realized it was a replica pistol that was incapable of firing an actual bullet—the man could have been killed over a fake gun. Bellmond believed he made the correct decision in this scenario, but it could have turned out otherwise. This experience changed the way Bellmond deals with backpacks. It was on his mind, troubling him, for weeks. Only after talking about the experience with friends and family was he able to come to terms with it. Expressing his thoughts and emotions offered a cathartic release from the stress of such a scenario.

Questions
1. What did Dalton do well?
2. What could Dalton have done better?

SUMMARY

Police interactions with individuals with a mental disorder should be handled in a different manner than encounters with the general population. Contact with persons experiencing mental illness is common, and officers are usually the first responders on the scene. First, scan your environment; your safety is the first priority, then everyone else's. Make sure you know your location and obtain as much background information as possible. Be aware of verbal, non-verbal, behavioural, and environmental cues that signify the person is presenting symptoms of mental illness. The person may be hearing voices, interacting with objects that are only visible to them, or be confused and/or unaware of their surroundings, and there may be eccentric decorations or an unusual amount of trash lying around. When approaching, keep a safe distance—safe depends on the context: if the person is threatening self-harm, you must stay closer; if they're threatening harm to you or others, stay further away to avoid provocation. When speaking, talk calmly and slowly. Rather than be authoritative, treat the individual humanely and with respect, develop a sense of collaboration, and always seek to de-escalate the situation when possible—mental health episodes are not permanent states and do not define a person.

REFLECTION QUESTIONS

1. What are the steps to an environmental safety scan?
2. What are 10 cues indicating that a person may be experiencing a mental health episode?
3. What are the differences between hallucinations and delusion? How should your response differ depending on the psychosis presenting?
4. Give five examples of when individuals risk endangering themselves and five for when they pose a risk to others.
5. Describe the best behaviours to practice when attempting to de-escalate situations with persons presenting mental illness.

REFERENCES

1. Ruiz J, Miller C. An exploratory study of pennsylvania police officers' perceptions of dangerousness and their ability to manage persons with mental illness. Police Quarterly. 2004 Sep;7(3):359–71.
2. Livingston JD. Contact between police and people with mental disorders: a review of rates. Psychiatric Services. 2016 Apr 15;67(8):850–7.
3. Helfgott B, Hickman M, Labossiere A. A descriptive evaluation of the Seattle Police Department's crisis response team officer/mental health professional partnership pilot program. International Journal of Law and Psychiatry. 2016 Jan-Feb;44:109–22.
4. Brink J, Livingston J, Desmarais S, Greaves C, Maxwell V, Michalak E, et al. A study of how people with mental illness perceive and interact with the police. Calgary: Mental Health Commission of Canada; 2012. Available from: https://www.mentalhealthcommission.ca/sites/default/files/Law_How_People_with_Mental_Illness_Perceive_Interact_Police_Study_ENG_1_0_1.pdf
5. Lamb HR, Weinberger LE, Gross BH. Mentally ill persons in the criminal justice system: some perspectives. Psychiatric Quarterly. 2004 Jun 1;75(2):107–26.
6. Short TB, MacDonald C, Luebbers S, Ogloff JR, Thomas SD. The nature of police involvement in mental health transfers. Police Practice and Research. 2014 Jul 4;15(4):336–48.
7. Canadian Mental Health Association, BC Division. Police and mental illness: increased interactions. 2005 Mar.
8. Brown SG, Daus CS. Avoidant but not avoiding: the mediational role of anticipated regret in police decision-making. Journal of Police and Criminal Psychology. 2016 Dec 1;31(4):238.
9. Boyce J, Rotenberg C, Karam M. Mental health and contact with police in Canada, 2012. Juristat: Canadian Centre for Justice Statistics. 2015 Jan;1:1.
10. Reavley NJ, Jorm AF, Morgan AJ. Beliefs about dangerousness of people with mental health problems: The role of media reports and personal exposure to threat or harm. Social Psychiatry and Psychiatric Epidemiology. 2016 Aug;51(9):1257–64.
11. Lurigio AJ, Harris AJ. Mental illness, violence, and risk assessment: an evidence-based review. Victims & Offenders. 2009;4(4):341–7.

12. Crocker AG, Nicholls TL, Seto MC, Charette Y, Côté G, Caulet M. The National Trajectory Project of individuals found not criminally responsible on account of mental disorder in Canada. Part 2: the people behind the label. The Canadian Journal of Psychiatry. 2015 Mar;60(3):106–16.
13. Hakkanen H, Laajasalo T. Homicide crime scene behaviors in a Finnish sample of mentally ill offenders. Homicide Studies. 2006;10(1):33–54.
14. Assareh M, Rakhshani T, Kashfi SM, Rai AR. Homicide offending and its main determinants in patients with schizophrenia or bipolar mood disorders. Archives of Psychiatry and Psychotherapy. 2016;18(3):27–31.
15. Alnıak İ, Erkıran M, Mutlu E. Substance use is a risk factor for violent behavior in male patients with bipolar disorder. Journal of Affective Disorders. 2016 Mar 15;193:89–93.
16. Toftdahl NG, Nordentoft M, Hjorthøj C. Prevalence of substance use disorders in psychiatric patients: a nationwide Danish population-based study. Social Psychiatry and Psychiatric Epidemiology. 2016 Jan 1;51(1):129–40.
17. Kuypers KP, Verkes RJ, van den Brink W, van Amsterdam JG, Ramaekers JG. Intoxicated aggression: do alcohol and stimulants cause dose-related aggression? A review. European Neuropsychopharmacology. 2018 Jun 23.
18. Hanafi S, Bahora M, Demir BN, Compton MT. Incorporating Crisis Intervention Team (CIT) knowledge and skills into the daily work of police officers: a focus group study. Community Mental Health Journal. 2008;44(6):427–32.
19. Canada KE, Angell B, Watson AC. Intervening at the entry point: differences in how CIT trained and non-CIT trained officers describe responding to mental health-related calls. Community Mental Health Journal. 2012;48(6):746–55.
20. Meehan NC, Strange C, McClary M. Behavioral indicators during a police interdiction. Naval Research Lab Washington DC Information Technology DIV. 2015 May 1.
21. Canadian Mental Health Association. Study in blue and grey: police interventions with people with mental illness: a review of challenges and responses. Canadian Mental Health Association/Association canadienne pour la santé mentale, BC Division; 2003.
22. Murphy JJ. Beyond a split second. An exploratory study of police use of force and use of force training in Canada. Simon Fraser University; 2014.
23. Public Safety Canada. Promising practices in policing substance users: a handbook of integrated models and practices. Ottawa: Public Safety Canada; 2012.
24. Watson A, Swartz J, Bohrman C, Kriegel L, Draine J. Understanding how police officers think about mental/emotional disturbance calls. International Journal of Law and Psychiatry. 2014;37:351–8.
25. Hoffman R, Hirdes J, Brown G, Dubin J, Barbaree H. The use of a brief mental health screener to enhance the ability of police officers to identify persons with serious mental disorders. International Journal of Law and Psychiatry. 2016;47:28–35.
26. Morabito M, Socia K, Wik A, Fisher W. The nature and extent of police use of force in encounters with people with behavioral health disorders. International Journal of Law and Psychiatry. 2017;50:31–7.
27. Coleman T, Cotton D. Police interactions with persons with a mental illness: police learning in the environment of contemporary policing. Mental Health and the Law Advisory Committee: Mental Health Commission of Canada; 2010 May.
28. Barlow DH, Durand VM, Hofmann SG, Lalumière ML. Abnormal psychology: an integrative approach. In: Hunter D, editor. 5th ed. Toronto: Nelson Education; 2018.

29. Dempsey C. Beating mental illness: crisis intervention team training and law enforcement response trends. Southern California Interdisciplinary Law Journal. 2017;26(2):323–40.

30. Parent R. The police use of deadly force in British Columbia: mental illness and crisis intervention. Journal of Police Crisis Negotiations. 2011;11(1):57–71.

31. Oliva JR, Morgan R, Compton MT. A practical overview of de-escalation skills in law enforcement: helping individuals in crisis while reducing police liability and injury. Journal of Police Crisis Negotiations. 2010;10(1/2):15–29.

CHAPTER 11

Police Response to Crisis Involving Suicide Risk: Strategies for Suicide Intervention and Prevention

Jennifer A. A. Lavoie, *Wilfrid Laurier University*

Scott Blandford, *Fanshawe College, Wilfrid Laurier University, Retired Officer*

LEARNING OBJECTIVES

1. Understand the suicide rate in Canada, its legal status, and the factors that elevate suicide risk
2. Understand the reasons for increased suicide rates among Indigenous Peoples in Canada
3. Deconstruct the various suicide myths
4. Recognize and evaluate the warning signs of suicide risk
5. Learn practical strategies to respond to crisis situations involving risk for suicide, including approach, intervention, and post-interaction strategies
6. Understand and describe the special case of "suicide by cop"

INTRODUCTION

The suicide rate for Canadians is 11.5 per 100,000, based on a 2013 report from Statistics Canada (released in 2017).[1] Males are more likely to die by suicide, whereas females are more likely to survive an attempt.[2] Specific populations such as Indigenous communities are particularly vulnerable to suicide, with rates 3 to 10 times the national average.[3,4] Police officers are often called to the scene when a person is engaging in suicidal behaviour. Knowing how to effectively identify warning signs and intervene in situations of potential suicide is vital. This chapter discusses risk factors for suicide, including gender, age, culture, and mental illness. A model for practical suicide intervention strategies for police officers is provided, including approach, intervention, and post-interaction strategies. Relevant law and officer options for dispositions are outlined. The Evan Jones case (2010) involving the police shooting death of an 18-year-old man threatening suicide is used as a case study, and the situation of "suicide by cop" is discussed. The chapter concludes with the importance of follow-up with the person and family, as well as officer self-care in the aftermath of suicide.

SUICIDE RATE AND LEGAL STATUS IN CANADA

Suicide is the act of taking one's life voluntarily and intentionally. On average, approximately 4,000 Canadians commit suicide every year.[1] Suicide is the second leading cause of death among all young people aged 15-34 years old in Canada; however, contrary to common belief, the suicide rate is not highest among adolescents.[2] Rather, suicide is highest among those in mid-life. Men are more likely to die by suicide than women. For every suicide, there are about 20 other people who attempt it.[5] Suicides are thought to be under-reported due to the associated stigma or shame.

Suicide and attempted suicide were considered a criminal offence in Canada before being decriminalized in 1972. Counselling or aiding a person to die by suicide continues to be prohibited under section 241 of the Canadian Criminal Code (herein referred to as the *Code*).[6] However, physician-assisted suicide was decriminalized in 2015 to exculpate doctors participating in physician-assisted death—but only in the case of competent adults who have a grievous and irremediable medical condition that causes enduring and intolerable suffering, and who consent to termination of life (section 241 (2) of the *Code*).[6]

SUICIDE RISK FACTORS

Suicide is a complex phenomenon that is not usually triggered by a single cause.[5,7] Often, it is a combination of multiple factors and circumstances that contributes to the decision to end one's life. People who have suicidal ideation experience immense emotional pain;[7] these individuals generally have overwhelming feelings of despair and hopelessness. They feel helpless, believe their pain will never stop, and reason that ending their life is the only way to relieve their suffering.[7] The following table presents suicide **risk factors** categorized into three domains: (1) individual-level risk factors, (2) community-level and relationship risk factors, and (3) societal-level risk factors.[5]

Table 11.1: Suicide Risk Factors

INDIVIDUAL-LEVEL RISK FACTORS	
Prior attempt	The strongest indicator of future suicide risk is a history of one or more prior suicide attempts.
Demographic	Suicide risk increases with age. Middle-aged Canadians between 45 and 59 years have the highest suicide rates. Men are more likely to die by suicide; women are more likely to attempt suicide.
Mental illness	Most people who commit suicide have a mental illness. Not all people who have a mental illness are suicidal, and not all people who carry out suicide have a mental illness. Suicide risk varies depending on disorder type. Mood disorders (e.g., depression, bipolar disorder), anxiety disorders, substance use disorders, schizophrenia (particularly in the early years of the illness), and personality disorders are associated with increased risk. Those with more than one mental disorder have a higher risk of suicide.
Substance use	Intoxication through use of alcohol or other substances is common in suicide. Use of multiple substances, as well as withdrawal from addictive drugs, can trigger suicidal behaviour. Prolonged use of sedatives, hypnotics, and anti-anxiety drugs increases suicide risk.
Psychosocial stressors	Recent, significant stressful life events heighten suicide risk. This includes interpersonal loss, financial hardship, job loss, legal proceedings, illness, or major transition.
Physical illness	Chronic pain and illness (e.g., cancer, HIV/AIDS, diabetes), particularly in those over age 60, is a risk factor.
Genetic and familial	Family history of suicide where the loss is devastating, or causes shame or guilt, increases risk for a bereaved person. Family history of mental illness or abuse also elevates suicide risk.
Access to lethal means	Possession of firearms, direct access to lethal doses of medications, poisons, pesticides, heights, or other means elevate suicide risk.
COMMUNITY-LEVEL AND RELATIONSHIP RISK FACTORS	
Disaster	Incidence of natural disaster, civil conflict, and acts of war increase suicide risk due to negative consequences to health, well-being, basic needs, and security.

continued

Vulnerable group status	Discrimination of groups leading to continuous stress due to rejection, stigma, or loss of freedom elevates risk (e.g., LGBTQ2, migrants, prisoners, bullying victims). Stresses of acculturation and dislocation of groups such as Indigenous Peoples and refugees is also a risk factor.
Trauma	Experience of trauma, violence, and abuse increases stress, triggering suicidal behaviour. Childhood trauma, including sexual, physical, and emotional abuse, neglect, or parental loss or separation, increases risk.
Isolation	A sense of isolation and lack of social support—feeling disconnected from a close social circle—elevates suicide risk (particularly among the elderly).
Relationship problems	Relationship conflict (e.g., separation/divorce), violence (e.g., domestic violence), discord (e.g., child custody disputes), or loss (e.g., partner's death) can elevate suicide risk.
SOCIETAL-LEVEL RISK FACTORS	
Stigma about suicide	Stigma against people who seek help for suicidal thoughts and behaviours, mental illness, or substance use problems reduces likelihood of connecting to care. Stigma discourages family and friends from providing support to a person contemplating suicide.
Health care barriers	Barriers to timely and effective health care to address physical and mental illness contributes to suicide risk.
Media	Inappropriate media reporting that sensationalizes suicide (e.g., glamourizing celebrity suicide, reporting detailed information of methods used) can incite "copycat" suicides among vulnerable persons. The Internet is a key source of information about suicide containing easily accessible sites that may enable suicide.

Note: Adapted from Canadian and World Health Organization resources [5,7,8]

INDIGENOUS PEOPLES AND SUICIDE

In April 2016, the Attawapiskat First Nation on remote James Bay in northern Ontario (home to about 2,000 residents) declared a state of emergency after being overwhelmed by a wave of over 100 attempted suicides during an eight-month period.[9] Particularly startling in this incident was a thwarted suicide pact among 13 Indigenous adolescents, the youngest of the group being only nine years of age.[10] The national media coverage of this suicide crisis highlighted the elevated suicide risk within Indigenous communities in Canada. Indigenous populations have a disproportionate suicide rate, being three times that of the general public.[3] Indigenous youth are particularly at risk, with a suicide rate five to six times higher than non-Indigenous youth.[11] Suicide rates vary across Indigenous groups. For example, most First Nations in BC have comparatively low rates of suicide;[3] in contrast, the Inuit in Northern Canada experience suicide rates 10 times the national average.[4]

The National Inuit Suicide Prevention Strategy[4] reported that risk factors for suicide among members of Inuit communities include the following: historical trauma (impacts of colonialism, relocation, residential schools), familial factors (intergenerational trauma, family violence, history of family suicide), community distress (social and economic inequalities, poor education and housing, lack of access to health services), traumatic stress and childhood adversity (witnessing or experiencing physical or sexual abuse), acute stress or loss (death of loved one, isolation), and mental distress (mental illness, substance use, self-harm). Recommendations have recently been made by the Standing Committee on Indigenous and Northern Affairs[3] to prevent suicide in Indigenous communities. Strategies include a focus on self-determination and reconciliation, as well as improving social, economic, and cultural determinants of health (e.g., housing, childhood development and education, community centres for healing and cultural renewal). Mental health services recommended by the committee include an Indigenous-specific mental health framework and enhanced service delivery and aftercare. Clearly, these recommendations reflect the complex and multi-faceted approach required to address the suicide crisis among Indigenous populations.

DEMYSTIFYING SUICIDE

There are a number of inaccurate beliefs about suicide that influence how people respond to suicide crises. The following are common myths about suicide, followed by a factual explanation summarized from national and international mental health organizations.[5,12]

> *Myth: Talking about suicide will give a person the idea or encourage suicide.*
> Reality: Asking individuals if they are having thoughts of killing themselves will not make them suicidal. Rather, talking calmly and non-judgementally about suicide can be a relief to a person who is feeling isolated. Talking about suicidal feelings can provide individuals with alternative options, time to reconsider their decision, and can consequently reduce the risk of an attempt.
> *Myth: Suicide is sudden and happens without warning.*
> Reality: Suicide is usually a process, not a singular event. While some suicides are unpredictable, the majority of suicides are preceded by verbal

or behavioural warning signs. Knowing the indicators of suicide may help prevent a death.

Myth: Suicidal people are determined to die.

Reality: Suicidal people experience tremendous emotional pain and are often ambivalent about living or dying. They do not necessarily wish to die: they want to end their pain. Access to timely emotional support can prevent suicide.

Myth: Once suicidal, a person will always be at risk for suicide.

Reality: Elevated suicide risk is usually situation-specific and short-term. The overwhelming desire to escape from pain can be relieved when the problem or stressor is eliminated. While suicidal thoughts may return, such thoughts are not permanent. Learning effective coping strategies to manage stressful situations can be helpful.

PRACTICAL STRATEGIES FOR POLICE RESPONSE TO CRISIS INVOLVING SUICIDE RISK

Officers play a key role in crisis intervention for people at risk for suicide and act as gatekeepers to connect them to mental health services as necessary. While every situation is unique, knowing practical strategies for approaching a person at risk for suicide, including recognizing warning signs, could prevent death.

Warning Indicators of Suicide

People who die by suicide often give prior indication of their intentions. Consider as a group the risk factors for suicide described in table 11.1, as well as the following cues of impending suicide compiled from mental health resources.[12-14]

Assessing Danger to Self

Evidence of Self-Abuse
- Assess if the suicide attempt involves a weapon.
- Determine if the person is injured or currently attempting suicide.

Potential for Self-Injury
- Determine if the person has the means to harm themselves.

- *Confirm if the person is talking about suicide or left a suicide note.* Statements of suicidal intent, even those in a sarcastic or joking manner, are a strong indicator of potential for suicide. Research has shown that out of every 10 persons who kill themselves, eight have given definite warning.
- *Identify if the person has a specific suicide plan.* Studies have indicated that most people who die by suicide have made a deliberate plan to do so. The more specific and realistic the plan, the greater the potential for suicide.
- Observe if the person *exhibits gross neglect for their personal safety* or is at risk of receiving serious injury.
- *Establish if the person has made a previous suicide attempt.* Within the adult population of the United States, approximately 80% of the people who kill themselves have made at least one previous suicide attempt. People who have made a highly lethal attempt are more at risk for subsequent suicide than those who have attempted it using a method of low lethality.
- *Verify if the person has recently consumed any drugs or alcohol.* Persons who are under the influence of drugs or alcohol often do not think rationally. They are more likely to become anxious and depressed, and they become less inhibited. Because of these effects, they present a serious potential for suicide.

Red Flags

- *Assess if the person appears depressed.* This is one of the most common indicators; approximately 60-79% of all suicides are committed by depressed persons who exhibit some of the following signs of depression: extreme sadness or crying, apathy, loss of appetite, unusually slow reactions, difficulty concentrating, sleep disturbance, emotional flatness, tension and agitation or withdrawal, pessimism, emotional outbursts, hopelessness, desperation, and loss of self-esteem.
- *Determine if the person has experienced a major life change or loss.*
- *Confirm if the person has medical problems.* Intense pain and suffering, and/or loss of independence, income, or dignity can all lead to depression, and in turn to risk of self-harm.

continued

- *Assess if the person seems hopeless.* Hopelessness is a stronger indicator of suicide intent than depression alone. Statements indicating hopelessness include "there is nothing to look forward to," or "there is no way to make things better."
- *Verify if the person sees suicide as the only option.*
- *Determine if the person has established end-of-life plans.* Giving away possessions and making sure dependents are cared for (confirming life insurance policy, putting personal affairs in order) are signs of intent.
- Expressing intent to die by suicide, suicidal thoughts, or having a suicide plan.
- Lack of interest; withdrawal from friends, family, and previously enjoyed activities; ending relationships or commitments.
- High level of irritability, aggression, rage, anxiety, emotional outbursts, mood swings, impulsivity, and increased substance use and risk taking.
- Loss of energy, loss of appetite, changes in sleep pattern.
- Polarized thinking (seeing situations in absolutes; e.g., if they fail at one thing, they fail at all things).
- Demonstrate and express a preoccupation with death, intent to die by suicide, or have suicidal thoughts.

Specific Strategies for Suicide Risk Assessment

If an officer is responding to a call involving a potential suicide, he or she should ask questions that evaluate the warning signs of suicide to determine the imminence of suicide risk (e.g., the person has made a plan, has acquired the available means, and has the intention to die). Sometimes the immediacy of the risk is clearly apparent (e.g., the person is standing on the precipice of a bridge or has a firearm pointed at their head). In situations where the risk is not clear, officers should ask directly about suicide (e.g., "Are you thinking of killing yourself? Are you having suicidal thoughts?"). Follow up by asking if the person has made any preparations, such as planning how, when, or where they would kill themselves. Determine if they have acquired the items they need to carry out the act (e.g., medication, weapon) and whether they have made arrangements for when they are deceased (e.g., care for children or pets). Officers should also inquire about prior suicidal behaviour and if there was a resource that helped the person in the past in resolving their crisis.

MODEL FOR SUICIDE INTERVENTION

As first responders, police officers are often faced with situations that unfold quickly, are dynamic, and often emotionally charged. To assist police officers in responding to a call for service involving a person threatening to harm themselves, and sometimes others, a three-stage process, as illustrated in figure 11.1, is presented. The first stage (Approach) occurs prior to the officer(s) arriving on scene, with the initial call for service intake generally involving a police dispatcher speaking directly with an involved person or witness. In the second stage, (Interaction) the officer(s), fully aware of their legal authority, begins to plan their

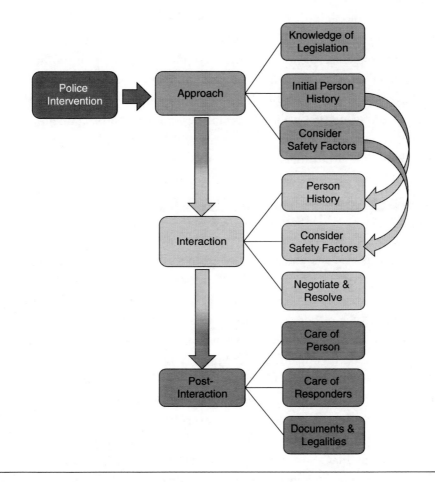

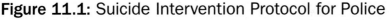

Figure 11.1: Suicide Intervention Protocol for Police

Source: Authors' original work—Jennifer Lavoie and Scott Blandford.

approach to the scene and initial interaction with the individual. Upon arrival, the officer(s) continues to build the profile of the person, while ensuring safety for all involved. Through communication and de-escalation strategies, the officer(s) attempts to negotiate a peaceful resolution to ensure the proper disposition and care of the person. The third stage (Post-Interaction) ensures the aftercare of the person, family members, other involved persons, and any first responders who may have been physically or psychologically affected by the crisis. The completion of documentation, legal requirements, and a debrief of the incident to identify learning points for future interventions concludes this stage.

Approach Phase

Knowledge of the Legislation
It is incumbent upon all police officers to have a comprehensive knowledge and understanding of the related legislation and legal authorities when dealing with persons with suicide risk, or mental illness more broadly. Police officers are a key source of referrals to mental health and emergency services. To be effective gatekeepers, officers must be knowledgeable about their local mental health legislation and the criteria for involuntary assessment and treatment. Legislation relative to the apprehension of persons with mental illness is governed by each province's and territory's mental health act (MHA) (e.g., section 17 of the Ontario MHA,[15] section 28 of the BC MHA;[16] see chapter 15 for a discussion). Common criteria across these acts to authorize apprehension by police are that the person must 1) present a danger to themselves or others, and 2) have a mental illness. Officers should understand how their local mental health system carries out legislated mandates and how to co-ordinate with other agencies (such as paramedics, community mental health services, and emergency departments) to streamline emergency referrals. Officers must be cognizant of legislation protecting the privacy of personal information (e.g., Freedom of Information and Protection of Privacy Act[17] (FIPPA)) when sharing information with mental health services, family members of the person in crisis, or other parties.

Other pieces of legislation officers must consider in responding to suicide crises where the person is uncooperative, requires de-escalation, or represents an imminent threat to safety, are those governing the use of force. The primary objective of such measures is preservation of life. When police officers are legally authorized, they may use as much force as necessary and reasonable to accomplish their purpose, as laid out in section 25 of the *Code*.[6] The National Use of Force Framework[18] (NUFF) provides guidance for officers to respond with a justified level of force (i.e., where force is sanctioned by law, the officer has reasonable grounds to use force, so long as the force is not excessive). Officers' decisions to use force is based on their subjective assessment of situational factors (e.g., time and distance from the threat) and the person's actions and perceived means, intentions, and opportunity to carry out harmful acts.

Notably, officers who perceive that they are less threatened by a person are less likely to use their firearms in a potential use-of-force situation and, instead, are more likely to try alternative tactics such as de-escalation strategies.[19] Addressing the prejudicial attitudes with officers—that people with mental illness are significantly more dangerous or unpredictable than the general public—may decrease inappropriate use of force with people in mental health crises.[20] Further, it is valuable to train officers to recognize that in some situations, traditional police tactics that are effective with most persons—such as the police challenge of "Stop, Police!"—may not be as useful with people who have impairments in rationality or cognition.[21] Given the potential for tragic outcomes during police responses to mental health crises, a thorough understanding of the NUFF, relevant legislation, and comprehensive training are the best strategies when dealing with these incidents.

Gather History

Generally, the first point of contact with the police will be through a police dispatcher in response to a call from a concerned person (e.g., a family member, bystander, or external agency) or in some cases, the persons in crisis themselves. The collection of background information at this point is critical and should be relayed to responding officers as the incident continues to unfold. Some of the questions that should be asked by the dispatcher will determine the following: if the individual is taking medication as prescribed, is being treated by a health care service, is under the influence of substances, and the existence of reported injuries. The dispatcher should also inquire whether the person has a history of violence or police contact, if the person is presently armed or has access to a firearm, and whether the person is in a public/open area or is barricaded. This initial intake of information will begin to shape the police officers' initial response, and in many situations, particularly those involving multiple officers attending, the dispatcher will remain engaged updating information and coordinating as necessary.

Consider Safety Factors

In responding to any call for service, the police officers' primary concern is the safety of not only the person, but all persons that could be involved, including the public and the officers themselves. Once officers are dispatched, they need to begin planning a tactical approach and plan of action to follow. Additional checks via their records management system to identify previous involvement with the person, any firearm or weapon history, and consideration of additional first responders (e.g., fire services, paramedics, joint response crisis teams as available) should be conducted on-route to the scene. Where public safety would not be impacted, consideration should be given to the need for lights and sirens upon approaching the immediate scene, as these may escalate the anxiety of the person. Upon arrival, efforts should be made to isolate and contain the person; family members and other civilians should be evacuated for their safety. A simple acronym to keep in mind upon approach and in the interaction phase is ICEN: *Isolate* the person; *Contain* them so they do not go mobile; *Evacuate* civilians and bystanders for safety; and *Negotiate* with the person towards a peaceful resolution.

Interaction Phase

Continued Gathering of History

Communication with the person, family members, and any other witnesses on scene is key to enhancing the officer's assessment of the situation. An officer should be designated to communicate with the person towards a peaceful resolution, while another officer should be tasked with gathering information from family members and witnesses. Questions for the family members or witnesses that are informative include the following:

- Has the individual acted dangerously towards self or others?
- Has the individual threatened or attempted the use of violence or suicide?
- Does the individual have access to weapons?
- Has the individual recently experienced a traumatic/upsetting experience?
- Does the individual have a history of mental illness?
- Does the individual take medication or have any physical impairments?

These types of incidents are often dynamic, so officers must continue to reassess, be alert, and adapt their response. This continuing evaluation includes suicide assessment through initial observations and examining how the person responds to direct questions. For example, the officer should evaluate whether the person is intoxicated, in possession of any weapons, is positioned so as to cause immediate harm to themselves or others (e.g., edge of bridge/balcony, standing on a railway track or in traffic), or intends to harm themselves. If suicidal gestures are not apparent, the officer should ask the person directly about suicidal intent. The key to this phase of interaction is to continue to build a profile of the person.

Safety Factors on Scene

As officers arrive at the scene, they should be alert to the possibility of suicidal behaviour as well as the risk of danger to others and themselves. Be aware that suicidal individuals may become homicidal or may attempt to force an officer to respond with force to kill them. Crisis situations are unstable and can change suddenly. As a result, officers should be vigilant and continuously evaluate the situation as it unfolds. Safety is a paramount concern. A seemingly low-risk situation can become lethal in an instant.[22] Every effort should be made to remove any lethal means accessible to the person. Consider both de-escalation and other use-of-force techniques to disarm a person holding a weapon (see chapter 10 for a discussion of de-escalation). As a general rule, officers should clear the scene of non-involved persons and family members should not be allowed to interact with the person. Until the complete set of circumstances is known, it is possible that family members were a contributing factor in initiating the crisis situation. In situations involving armed, barricaded persons, officers should set up containment perimeters. It is important to make all reasonable efforts to maintain control of the situation and to prevent the person from going mobile (i.e., leave the scene) or moving or positioning themselves where officers lose control of the situation. For example, do not allow the person to move to a room where they can then barricade themselves and escalate the situation. It is important to maintain visible and physical control of the person.

"Suicide by cop" (SbC) is a term describing a situation where a person deliberately engages in behaviour posing an apparent threat of serious injury or death, with the intent to compel law enforcement officers to respond with deadly force to resolve the crisis.[22-24] In these scenarios, the officers themselves may be threatened, or the person may place a third party (e.g., intimate partner, child) at risk by threatening them or taking them hostage. A review of SbC incidents in Canada and the United States found that SbC scenarios tended to involve younger (early 30s) white males with histories of mental illness, substance use problems, domestic violence, and prior suicide attempts.[24] This review found that most SbC situations involved a person armed with a weapon, usually a loaded firearm; in fewer instances, a person feigned or simulated weapon possession. SbC situations also tended to be spontaneous, highly dangerous for involved police officers, and result in high person lethality. Many police intervention strategies are not effective with SbC persons, including less-lethal responses, physical restraints, or communications focused on dropping the weapon. Verbal communication focused on resolving the person's problems has shown some promise.[24] In these situations, when no other persons in proximity to the person are in danger, it is advisable for officers to contain the person and wait for a tactical response, negotiator, and/or additional resources.

Negotiate and Resolve

Upon arrival on scene, there should be one officer identified as the lead contact person. This officer will be responsible for directly communicating with the person, notwithstanding the arrival of supervisors or other ranking officers. The goal of this lead officer is to establish a **rapport** (initiate and engage in communication) with the person in order to come to a resolution. The presence of the initial police officer plays a large role in setting the tone of the situation. As the situation develops, this lead officer may change as trained negotiators arrive, but it is critical that there be only one officer speaking to the person at a time to enhance clearer communication and reduce confusion.

When able, officers should attempt to engage the person in a calm dialogue to identify the root cause of the distress. Officers should demonstrate empathy to express concern, try to *relate to the experience*, and *provide reassurance* ("It sounds like you've been through a lot. I'm here because I want to help you"). Making *"I" statements* is preferable to "we" statements when referring to the police, especially if the suicidal thoughts intersect with paranoia or psychosis, where "we" may represent an entity in the person's delusions or hallucinations. Normalizing the situation and conveying that suicidal thoughts are not unusual in depression may allow the person to feel less stigmatized. Emphasize the temporary nature of the feelings the person is experiencing and how proper treatment can help the person overcome those feelings.

It is important to be respectful and listen non-judgementally. Encourage the person to talk without expressing shock or condemnation. Do not dismiss the person's behaviour as manipulative or attention-seeking; all suicide attempts or expressed ideas of suicide must be taken seriously. Do not sermonize, argue, or tell the person to "just forget about it."[14] The person may attempt to change the focus and move the discussion in another direction; the officer must deflect these comments and keep the focus on the situation ("I appreciate that, but ...; maybe so, but...).[25] **Active listening** is an effective verbal strategy to buy time and intervene to reduce the person's emotions and increase rationality. Active listening requires officers to fully concentrate on what is being said, demonstrate they are listening, and respond in a manner to ensure mutual understanding. Some key principles include reinforcing communication by paraphrasing, mirroring, summarizing, emotion-labelling, and open-ended questions.[26] It is important to keep communication simple, talk slowly, and be patient. Recognize that a person in crisis may need time to understand and respond to your questions and commands.

The **Behavioural Influence Stairway Model** (BISM)[27] is a more recent model of crisis negotiation that emphasizes the relationship-building process between the officer and the person in order to facilitate behaviour change, culminating in a successful resolution. Using active listening skills as a basis throughout the process, officers progress sequentially through stages of building three main foundations: (1) empathy, (2) rapport, and (3) behavioural influence, at which time a relationship is developed, thus enabling behavioural change (e.g., surrendering).[26] Officers can train to use BISM through role playing.

Officers should explain and inform the person of what their options are by being honest and upfront. Offer them alternatives and mutually explore their options (e.g., "What else could you do right now to make yourself feel better?"). Empower the individual in crisis with choices ("What would you like to bring with you to the hospital?" or "Do you want us to give you a ride to the hospital?" or "Would you like to ride with your brother?"). Offer them realistic hope ("We do have to go to the hospital now, but I'll get a hold of your family and let them know where you are.").

In the event that a suicide attempt occurs, immediate medical intervention is required if the person has serious injuries, has overdosed on medication or illicit drugs, or has swallowed a toxic substance.[14] Assess vital signs and apply resuscitation as appropriate. Where relevant, attempt to find out what and how much the person has ingested so that appropriate and timely treatment can be administered. Take unused pills and empty bottles to emergency services to assist in verifying the medication ingested. Contact the person's next of kin and communicate what has happened. Obtain further information about the person's history and medication. Assess how to help the relatives and be mindful to avoid making them feel guilty.[14] If transfer to a medical facility is unnecessary, lethal means should be removed and officers should ensure referral to alternate mental health care for treatment and follow-up. Mental health care referrals should be made outside any necessary medical treatment for physical injuries. If family members are present, they may be emotionally distraught by the circumstances. Provide compassion and support to those affected.

Available Dispositions

Potential resolutions to a situation involving suicide risk should be guided by officer discretion and their assessment of the situation, and can include the following:

1. *Apprehend under provincial/territorial mental health legislation.* If the person meets mental health legislation criteria, apprehend the individual and transport them to a hospital for involuntary assessment. **Apprehension** results in either involuntary commitment where the person is admitted for treatment, or unconditional release in the event that the person is not admitted because they do not meet hospital admission criteria as assessed by a physician.

2. *Referral to mental health services.* If the individual does not appear to meet mental health legislation criteria for apprehension, officers should still consider recommending voluntary hospitalization, mental health treatment, and/or community resources. The officer can provide the person with accessible contact information to crisis lines, emergency services, and mental health and addiction programs in the area. As such, officers should have up-to-date knowledge of the mental health services available locally, and how to access them in an emergency. Where appropriate, officers can engage the help of relatives and friends on scene to work towards a resolution in the best interest of the person.

3. *Arrest.* If the officer believes the person has committed a concurrent criminal offence or other offence, the officer may arrest the person and take them into custody (e.g., domestic assault, trespassing). Consideration might be given to mitigating the disproportionate criminalization of persons with mental illness when arrest (and charging) is used in cases of non-violent offences (i.e., nuisance offences). In the interest of public safety, where a suspect has committed a violent crime, police service policies direct that the officer shall not consider voluntary or involuntary hospitalization as a substitute for criminal charges.

4. *No further police action.* If the person presents no risk of harm to self or others, and no offence has been committed, the officer may decide that no further action is required.

All Possible Police Dispositions

- Apprehend for involuntary commitment under provincial/territorial mental health legislation
- Referral to mental health services (voluntary treatment/community programs)/Consult a mental health professional
- Arrest
- No further police interaction
  - Disengage/Unconditional Release
  - Release to families or care provider

Post-Interaction

The goal of the interaction phase is to gain the voluntary compliance of the person in order to have them receive the necessary assistance from a mental health practitioner to resolve their crisis. This may involve on-scene Crisis Intervention Training (CIT) teams or transportation to a medical facility. In the case where a person has died by suicide, the case may be treated as an investigation.

Care of Person in Crisis

Once a person has been apprehended under the MHA, the law requires that they be transported to a medical facility for examination by a physician. It is generally accepted that this means forthwith, but this action can often become complicated if the person has committed a criminal offence. Priority must be given to the physical and mental health of the person, and most police organizations have policies and protocols in place related to the transportation and security of apprehended persons. Officers should follow up with the person. People with mental illness are likely to have repeat encounters with police;[28] thus, a follow-up might head off future crises. The physical, emotional, and psychological health of involved victims, witnesses, and family members must also be attended to with tact and compassion.[14]

Care of Responders

In some situations, such as those that involve violence, the first responders can be emotionally affected. For example, a person may commit suicide prior to or during interaction with the police. Suicide by cop or a suicide that occurs while officers are present can be particularly traumatizing for all those present.[24] First responder organizations must ensure that processes and supports are in place to foster the physical, emotional, and psychological health of first responders. Activities could include debriefs of major incidents, counselling, or a break from work routines (see chapter 13 for a detailed discussion).

Documentation

Police officers must document the facts of the incident and their actions. The proliferation of social media and camera phones has placed greater scrutiny upon an officer's actions, and the need to ensure an accurate, detailed record of the incident is critical. Along with individual officer notes and reports, many police organizations require completion of Use of Force reports, mental health screeners, and the wearing of body cameras during encounters. The aftermath of these types of incidents may range from no further police involvement to coroner inquests or criminal trials. Detailed documentation will serve the police officer well in these situations and potentially provide protection from civil and criminal liability.

Case Study: Evan Jones

In the summer of 2010, 18-year-old Evan Jones was living with his family in Brantford, Ontario, and was struggling with mental illness and substance use problems.[29] The first evidence of Evan's drug use was in January 2009, when he was found to be in possession of cannabis. Evan completed a community addiction treatment service through a pre-charge diversion program. In June 2010, Evan was admitted to a local hospital's mental health unit for a suicide attempt following Tylenol ingestion. He was diagnosed with depression and addiction to cocaine, opiates, and alcohol. Evan ran away several times from hospital and was later involuntarily re-admitted when he was found on a busy highway asking police to shoot him. In July, Evan was admitted to a withdrawal management program but left two days later. Evan reported that he wanted help to become healthy and return to school but was frustrated with the available treatment programs.[29-31]

Evan's behaviour began to escalate in mid-July when he was arrested for shoplifting a chocolate bar. In early August, Evan became intoxicated and got into a fistfight with his brother, prompting his mother to call police. When officers arrived, Evan got into a scuffle and was charged with assaulting an officer. Police brought him to the hospital to treat an injury received while fighting; however, his mental health issues went untreated despite officers observing Evan banging his head against the partition in the cruiser, claiming to be psychotic, and displaying paranoid behaviour.[29-31]

A few weeks later, on August 25, 2010, Evan returned home intoxicated, agitated, and yelling. Concerned that her son would hurt himself, Evan's mother called police from outside the home. Two police officers arrived at the residence and found Evan standing on the front porch waving two large knives. Officers attempted to talk Evan down, repeatedly asking him to drop the knives. Evan demanded the officers shoot him and placed both knives to his throat. Evan then went back inside the house. Officers had received information that Evan's sister and two-year-old niece were inside the house in an upstairs bedroom. Two officers kicked down the locked front door and two other officers entered from the back door, confronting Evan in a hallway. Evan ignored the officers' commands to put down the knives. The lead officer pepper sprayed Evan in the eyes, but this failed to deter him. Evan charged at the officers with a cleaver and threw a knife at them. The lead officer fired five shots at Evan, striking him several times and killing him.[32]

At the time of his death, Evan had high levels of alcohol in his system as well as traces of cocaine. In May 2012, the officer who shot Evan was cleared of any wrongdoing by Ontario's Special Investigations Unit (SIU). The coroner's jury made 26 recommendations that frontline officers receive mandatory training on issues concerning people in crisis, and that the Ministry review Ontario's **use of force framework**, tactical communication standards, and the use of the police challenge.[32] In January 2015, the SIU took the rare step of re-opening this investigation after the officer involved in the shooting claimed criminal responsibility for Evan's death.[33] The SIU affirmed their previous conclusion and ultimately cleared the officer of misconduct.

Questions

1. Which risk factors for suicide were present in the case of Evan Jones?
2. Which warning signs of suicide were present?
3. If you were one of the officers responding to this incident, what are the most important factors you would need to consider at the Approach, Intervention, and Post-Interaction phases?
4. What aftercare options would you consider for the family and officers involved in this incident?

SUMMARY

Today in Canada about 11 people will die by suicide.[7] Suicide is a complex phenomenon and is generally the result of the interplay between numerous individual-, community- and relationship-, and societal-level risk factors. Some risk factors include gender, age, culture, and mental illness. Many Indigenous communities are particularly vulnerable to suicide and possess unique and overlapping suicide risk factors that must be addressed. Police officers are often called to assist a person engaging in suicidal behaviour. Accurately identifying and assessing warning signs, such as having a suicide plan and access to lethal means, is imperative to intervention. A three-stage model for practical suicide intervention strategies for police officers was described: approach, intervention, and post-interaction strategies. Legislation and officer options for dispositions (e.g., apprehension) were outlined. The Evan Jones case[29] illustrated the tragic outcome of a "suicide by cop" scenario.

REFLECTION QUESTIONS

1. Think about at-risk groups of people in your own community. Identify resources that are available in your community to respond to these groups. As a police officer, how would you leverage these resources? Are the resources adequate to manage the risk?

2. What is the difference between apprehension and arrest? When might you prioritize mental health care over criminalization?

3. Practice role-playing in which you use active listening skills to understand a partner's dilemma. Are there phrases you can use to build empathy and rapport with a person in distress?

4. Helpful online resources for suicide in Canada include the Canadian Association for Suicide Prevention (CASP), the Canadian Mental Health Association (CMHA), and the Centre for Addiction and Mental Health (CAMH). Visit one of these websites and identify current issues related to suicide prevention.

REFERENCES

1. Statistics Canada. Suicide and suicide rate, by sex and by age group [modified 2017 Mar 9; cited 2017 June 20]. Available from: http://www.statcan.gc.ca/tables-tableaux/sum-som/l01/cst01/hlth66d-eng.htm

2. Health at a Glance. Suicide rates: an overview. Ottawa: Statistics Canada [Internet]; 2015 [cited 2017 June 20]. Cat no. 82–624-X. Available from: www.statcan.gc.ca/pub/82-624-x/2012001/article/11696-eng.htm

3. Mihychuk, M. Breaking point: the suicide crisis in Indigenous communities. Report of the Standing Committee on Indigenous and Northern Affairs. Office of the Speaker of the House of Commons, Canada. 2017 [cited 2017 Sep 1]. Available from: http://www .ourcommons.ca/Content/Committee/421/INAN/Reports/RP8977643/inanrp09/ inanrp09-e.pdf

4. Inuit Tapiriit Kanatami. National Inuit suicide prevention strategy [Internet]. 2016 [cited 2017 Apr 17]. Available from: https://www.itk.ca/wp-content/uploads/2016/07/ITK-National-Inuit-Suicide-Prevention-Strategy-2016.pdf

5. World Health Organization. Preventing suicide: A global imperative [Internet]. 2014 [cited 2017 July 28]. Geneva, Switzerland. Available from: http://www.who.int/ mental_health/suicide-prevention/world_report_2014/en/.

6. Criminal Code, R. S. C., 1985, c. C-46.

7. Canadian Association for Suicide Prevention (CASP). Understanding [Internet]. 2017 [cited 2017 July 28]. Available from: https://suicideprevention.ca/understanding/

8. Centre for Addiction and Mental Health (CAMH). CAMH Suicide prevention and assessment handbook [Internet]. Centre for Addiction and Mental Health, Toronto. 2015 [cited 2017 July 28]. Available from: https://www.camh.ca/en/hospital/health_information/a_z_mental_health_and_addiction_information/suicide/Documents/sp_handbook_final_feb_2011.pdf

9. Rutherford K. CBC News, Attawapiskat declares state of emergency over spate of suicide attempts [Internet]. April 9, 2016 [cited 2017 Apr 27]. Available from: www.cbc.ca/news/ Canada/Sudbury/Attawapiskat-suicide-first-nations-emergency

10. "Attawapiskat suicide crisis: police break up suicide pact between 13 youths." The Canadian Press [Internet]. April 14, 2016 [cited 2017 Apr 17]. Available from: www.huffingtonpost.ca/2016/04/12/attawapiskat-suicide-pact_n_9671298.html

11. Royal Commission on Aboriginal Peoples. Choosing life: special report on suicide among Aboriginal people. 1995.

12. Canadian Mental Health Association (CMHA), Toronto. Suicide and youth [Internet]. 2017 [cited 2017 July 27]. Available from: http://toronto.cmha.ca/mental_health/ youth-and-suicide/

13. Hoffman R, Putnam L. Not just another call ... police response to people with mental illnesses in Ontario [Internet]. Toronto. 2004 [cited 2017 July 28]. Available from: http://www.pmhl.ca/webpages/reports/Not_Just_Another_Call.pdf

14. World Health Organization. Preventing suicide: a resource for police, firefighters and other first-line responders. World Health Organization. Department of mental health and substance abuse [Internet]. Geneva, Switzerland; 2009 [cited 2017 July 28]. Available from: http://www.who.int/mental_health/prevention/suicide/resource_ firstresponders.pdf

15. Mental Health Act, R. S. O. 1990. Government of Ontario [Internet]. Available from: https://www.ontario.ca/laws/statute/90m07#BK14

16. Mental Health Act, R. S. B. C. 1996. Chapter 288. BC Laws [Internet]. Available from: http://www.bclaws.ca/civix/document/id/complete/statreg/96288_01#section28

17. Freedom of Information and Protection of Privacy Act, R. S. O. 1990, c.F31.

18. The Canadian Association of Chiefs of Police. A national use of force framework [Internet]. Ottawa; 2000 [cited 2017 Sep 11]. Available from: http://www.cacp.ca/ cacp-use-of-force-advisory-committee-activities.html?asst_id=199

19. Parent R. Crisis intervention: the police response to vulnerable individuals. The Police Journal: Theory, Practice and Principles. 2007;80(2):109–16.

20. Godfredson JW, Ogloff JRP, Thomas SDM, Luebbers, S. Police discretion and encounters with people experiencing mental illness: the significant factors. Criminal Justice and Behavior. 2010;37:1392–1405.

21. Iacobucci F. Police encounters with people in crisis. an independent review conducted by The Hon. Frank Iacobucci for Chief of Police William Blair. Toronto: Toronto Police Service; 2014. Available from: http://www.police_encounters_with_people_in_crisis_2014.pdf

22. Miller L. Suicide by cop: causes, reactions, and practical strategies. International Journal of Emergency Mental Health. 2006;8(3):165–74.

23. Kingshott B. Suicide by proxy: revisiting the problem of suicide by cop. Journal of Police Crisis Negotiations. 2009;9:105–18.

24. Patton CL, Fremouw W. Examining "suicide by cop": a critical review of the literature. Aggression and Violent Behavior. 2016;27:107–20.

25. Blandford S. Tactical communication for police officers. Trainer. 1997;12(2):37.

26. Van Hasselt VV, Romano SJ, Vecchi GM. Role playing: applications in hostage and crisis negotiation skills training. Behavior Modification. 2008;32:248–63.

27. Vecchi GM. Crisis communication: skills building in an online environment. Unpublished manuscript. Quantico, VA: Behavioral Science Unit, FBI Academy; 2007.

28. Markowitz FE. Mental illness, crime, and violence: risk, context, and social control. Aggression and Violent Behavior. 2011;16:36–44.

29. Ruby M. "Son was 'crying for help'," Brantford Expositor [Internet]. May 2, 2012 [cited 2017 Apr 2]. Available from: http://www.brantfordexpositor.ca/2012/05/02/son-was-crying-for-help

30. Ruby M. "'I thought I was going to die': Hill on video." Brantford Expositor [Internet]. May 8, 2012 [cited 2017 Apr 2]. Available from: http://www.brantfordexpositor.ca/2012/05/07/i-thought-i-was-going-to-die-hill-on-video

31. Ruby M. "Evan Jones: portrait of a troubled teen," Brantford Expositor [Internet]. May 9, 2012 [cited 2017 Apr 2]. Available from: http://www.brantfordexpositor.ca/2012/04/30/evan-jones-portrait-of-a-troubled-teen

32. Office of the Chief Coroner. Evan Thomas Jones Inquest (May 11, 2012). Queen's Printer for Ontario.

33. Special Investigations Unit. SIU reopens investigation into Brantford fatal shooting. Case Number 10-OFD-178 [Internet]. [cited 2019 Jan 20]. Available from: https://www.siu.on.ca/en/news_template.php?nrid=2160

CHAPTER 12

Mental Health Services and Special Intervention Teams

Debra Jellicoe, *Forensic Assessment and Community Services, Alberta Health Services*

Tanya Anderson, *MacEwan University*

LEARNING OBJECTIVES

1. Discuss the intersection between mental health and policing
2. Describe integrated units of policing and health
3. Discuss theoretical models of offender management
4. Outline consultative partnerships to respond to persons with mental health concerns

INTRODUCTION

In some ways, it can seem as though there is an oppressive wall between policing and mental health. Police officers may be leery of what they deem the "touchy-feely, hug-a-thug" types, and mental health clinicians can be protective and defensive regarding persons who have mental illnesses. Competing goals of the protection of the public versus individual privacy and treatment can be at odds. Years of different and at times rigid approaches to dealing with similar individuals have put a distance between the two systems. However, when the focus becomes narrowed to one individual, a common goal becomes apparent: the preference for this person to achieve a healthy, pro-social life. The respective fields are beginning to see how coming together can better achieve that goal. The silo mentality to offender management has not been effective in creating meaningful, positive, long-lasting change.

Case Study: Charlie's Battle

Police officers receive multiple calls regarding an adult man who has stolen items from convenience and liquor stores in close proximity to one another. Based on the area and a basic description of the individual, they already suspect Charlie, well-known to the police for committing mischief and theft crimes. Police find Charlie, who is in possession of the items reported missing. He is intoxicated and belligerent. Charlie is arrested and held in police cells. Upon sobering, Charlie is apologetic and regretful. He mentions that he lost his job that day and believes that he will now lose his apartment. He is eventually remanded to jail. While in jail, Charlie is assessed by mental health professionals and diagnosed with depression and alcohol abuse. He is placed on medication and encouraged to see his community addictions counsellor. When Charlie is released from jail, he has lost his housing and stays at a men's shelter. He has no means of getting to a pharmacy to refill his prescription or to attend his counselling appointment. Charlie feels disappointed and hopeless with his life and with himself. He fears for his safety at the shelter and takes a hoot of meth from another patron. He enjoys the numbness and soon starts using more frequently. Meanwhile, Charlie's addiction counsellor logs another failed appointment in her notes. She has seen Charlie for years but has been unable to make gains in treatment due to his sporadic attendance. She was recently more encouraged when Charlie secured employment and housing, until she heard that he had been arrested again. She is uncertain how his life is proceeding in between sessions.

Questions

1. Develop a plan of care that describes the steps you would take to help Charlie and with which services.
2. How would you set and measure goals with Charlie?

There are different means by which police officers and mental health professionals can work together. Previous chapters have demonstrated how using behavioural and mental health approaches can be beneficial for police officers in dealing with individuals with mental illnesses. Police officers can receive training about mental health disorders to help gain a broader sense of the motivations and issues underlying the more difficult behaviours. This chapter focuses on the integration of policing units and mental health professionals, in particular on how creating these partnerships can more effectively manage specialized populations.

Many shifts in practice and policy across organizations typically occur in response to adverse incidents. This is also true of the shift in the world of policing when integrated teams are added to respond to mental health crises. Across North America there have been many tragic incidents involving police and individuals experiencing a mental illness or mental health crisis. These incidents have given rise to a desire to find more effective ways for police to respond to calls involving mental illness. The interactions between police and people who are experiencing a mental health crisis are only increasing, and there is evidence showing that police are often the first point of contact with these individuals.[1] There have been several different models developed and implemented, which have demonstrated various levels of effectiveness.[2] The police departments that have developed responses to mental health calls have implemented strategies that fall into three general models: 1) police-driven response with police officers specially trained in understanding mental health crisis, 2) mental health-driven response with mobile teams of mental health professionals, and 3) officers paired with mental health professionals who respond to calls together. Although each model is perceived to be effective, there is a slightly higher perception of effectiveness for the combined team of professionals and police officers.[2]

An example of the first model is the crisis intervention team (CIT) based on the Memphis Model.[3] This was developed following a police shooting of an individual with a history of mental illness. In the Memphis Model, police are trained specifically to respond to crisis situations. These officers are dispatched to assist the general patrol membership when dealing with individuals experiencing a mental health crisis. The training they receive allows the officers to de-escalate the situation and assess the appropriate next steps. Part of this program includes partnerships with local mental health authorities.[4] Agreements have been made so that if the CIT officers determine that further assessment by mental health professionals is imperative, there is a point of access into the health system. Collaboration between law enforcement and mental health providers in this model has attempted to address the tension that often occurs when the attitudes of these two groups differ.[4] This model has been acknowledged as a best practice by CIT organizations; however, there has not been enough research to declare this model as being evidence-based practice.[4]

Although in the second model the intervention is driven by mental health professionals, there is still a relationship between the teams and local law enforcement.[2] The teams vary in how they operate based on the local health authority. The teams are an immediately accessible resource to police dealing with individuals who are in the midst of a mental health crisis.

The third model of intervention team has been implemented across Canada as specialized police units known as a Police and Crisis Team (PACT). In Edmonton, the provincial health authority partnered with Edmonton Police Service (EPS) and created the first team in 2004. Prior to the implementation of this team, the mental health-driven response was the only resource being used. This method neither fully met the needs of either organization, nor did it offer the best response to the individuals in crisis. Due to this gap, the partnership was formed and a memorandum of understanding (MOU) was developed that allowed the two agencies to work together within the confines of the Health Information Act (HIA) and the Freedom of Information and Protection of Privacy Act (FOIP). Now the mental health response team and PACT work in conjunction.

PACT is a truly integrated response team. There are several teams comprising a sworn police officer employed by EPS and a trained mental health therapist employed by the local health agency. The mental health therapists comprise a multidisciplinary group of psychologists, clinical social workers, registered psychiatric nurses, and registered nurses specialized in psychiatry. Each team member has clearly defined roles. The police officer is primarily responsible for public safety and investigating complaints to police. Officers assigned to PACT receive on-the-job training in mental illnesses, engage with persons at calls with an increased sense of empathy, and de-escalate crisis situations. The mental health therapist is responsible for the assessment of an individual at a police call. This assessment focuses on mental status, the presence of symptoms of mental illness, and risk to the person and the community. Working together, the team evaluates the risk and how to best respond to the situation. The goal is to stabilize individuals who are experiencing crisis—in the community and in their own homes. There are times when the level of risk present or the level of decompensation in the person's mental health is so significant that the police officer will apprehend the individual experiencing crisis under the Mental Health Act (MHA).[5] This apprehension is completed to facilitate further assessment and treatment of the person, even if they are unable or unwilling to participate in this process voluntarily.

PACT responds to calls that are generated directly to the police emergency/911 line, the police general service line, and to calls generated through the mental health system. These calls may be placed by someone in crisis or by someone concerned for an individual in crisis. The team will deal with individuals experiencing anything from a situational crisis to a psychiatric emergency. Sometimes the officer will have to manage criminal and legal matters at a call, and this is always balanced with discretion in trying to understand and respond to the mental health crisis in progress. These calls may also involve substance addiction issues to which the team is also trained to respond.

One of the goals of the development of PACT was to decrease repeat calls for service, but this outcome is impossible to measure. What has been measured in Edmonton is an increase in the number of cases where individuals were diverted from being taken to the hospital. There have been several additional benefits to this new team. There has been a reduction in the time that police officers have spent waiting with individuals in hospitals when apprehension under the MHA has been required. PACT members play a key role in ongoing education with patrol members and the police service as a whole, which has led to more positive and efficient outcomes for crisis calls. They also assist in facilitating productive communication between police officers and the professionals working in the health system. Two of the focused recommendations from the Mental Health Commission of Canada in 2014 were to increase the education about and understanding of mental illness and crisis situations,[6] and this has also helped decrease the stigma surrounding mental health.[6] These positive outcomes have been beneficial to the police service, the health authority, and especially to those in crisis.

As demonstrated with PACT, some police and mental health collaborations are fully integrated (i.e., crisis teams that pair law enforcement and mental health administrators on the same team). Since the implementation of combined units such as mental health crisis teams, the groundwork has been laid to continue and expand this collaboration. Other countries, notably England, have had similar approaches and programs for years.[7] Forensic psychologists can offer theories and research on a wide range of criminal behaviour and offender management, which can, in turn, help shape police practices. As noted in Chapter 8, psychologists often complete risk assessments on sex offenders. More recently, there has been an increase in police officers being trained with risk and threat assessment tools. It is hoped that a similar rollout can occur with offender management. There has also been a shift to intelligence-led[8] or evidence-based[9] policing.

RISK NEEDS RESPONSIVITY MODEL

The most widely followed and researched model of correctional assessment and rehabilitation is the Risk Needs Responsivity (RNR) model, developed by Don Andrews and James Bonta.[10-13] The model began with the three titled principles and others were added with continued research.

The **Risk Principle** stipulates that criminal behaviour can be predicted and that the intervention should match the intensity of the risk level. Criminal behaviour is best predicted by employing validated risk-assessment instruments. When assessments are completed in a reliable and sound manner, they offer a comprehensive overview of the offender's risk level and risk factors. This information is then used when recommending treatment or intervention strategies. If an offender is assessed to be at a low risk to reoffend, then minimal interventions should be offered, as this may interfere with the pre-existing pro-social aspects that have contributed to the low risk. For example, if low-risk offenders are placed in a violence-prevention group with high-risk offenders, they become exposed to antisocial peers, thereby increasing their risk. Further, if individuals risk losing their jobs to attend the program, then their pro-social activities are also being jeopardized. Therefore, most resources and interventions should be directed at the population that has the highest risk to reoffend. Offenders assessed as being at high risk for spousal assault should be placed in a high-intensity treatment program and receive intensive supervision.

The **Needs Principle** focuses on the risk factors and the criminogenic needs of the offender that have been found through research to be most linked to criminal reoffending. Bonta and Andrews outlined "The Central Eight" criminogenic needs, consisting of the following:

1. Criminal History. Reflects early onset and duration of criminal behaviour. It is the only historical factor.*
2. Antisocial Personality Pattern. Encompasses a set of attributes such as egocentricity, opposition, impulsivity, adventurous, and pleasure-seeking.*
3. Antisocial Cognition. Outlines thoughts and beliefs that support criminal behaviour, such as disrespect for authority, attributing a high reward for crime, and justification for actions.*
4. Antisocial Associates. Socializing with criminal peers who hold similar values and attitudes is linked with recidivism. This need also includes isolation from pro-social peers.*

5. Employment/Education. Recognizing different points of time for everyone, this need focuses on performance and commitment to positive industries as well as the interpersonal relationships within them.
6. Family and Marital Circumstances. Reflects the support, quality, and level of satisfaction with the offender's closest interpersonal relationships.
7. Substance Use. Considers both past and present difficulties with alcohol or drug use and how that use has impacted different domains of the offender's life.
8. Leisure/Recreation. Having interests and involvement in activities that ally with criminal pursuits while having high amounts of unstructured time is associated with increased recidivism.

Note that the needs with an asterisk are also denoted as "The Big Four"; out of all eight criminogenic needs, they are the most correlated with recidivism. These needs are targeted in rehabilitative and supervisory efforts.

The **Responsivity Principle** is evidence that for rehabilitation to be most effective it must be responsive at a general and a specific level. At the general level, Bonta and Andrews prescribe social learning theories that suggest cognitive and behavioural approaches are effective means to bring about change. Reinforcement, modelling, and teaching practical skills are also encouraged strategies. At a specific level, interventions should be tailored to the offender's ability and learning style. For example, offenders with cognitive impairments should be placed in programming that is modified for such deficits. The Responsivity Principle is also where non-criminogenic needs may become important. It may seem as though certain needs were omitted from the Central Eight, such as mental health; however, studies have shown that mental health disorders are not linked with general reoffending. For instance, treating offenders' depression without targeting their antisocial attitudes, negative peers, and unemployment will be less effective in reducing their recidivism. However, these needs can be addressed by viewing them as impediments to addressing their criminogenic needs. If offenders have low motivation to engage in sexual offender programming, focus can first be placed on increasing their internal drive so that they are more amenable to treatment.

There are 13 other principles that guide this model, starting with three overarching ones. The first principle speaks to having respect for the person and context; approaching offenders and professionals in a just, decent, humane, and ethical manner. This can seem obvious, but many offenders face stigmatization and obstacles, especially as they attempt to reintegrate into the community.[14] The second overarching principle supports the notion that programs should be based on solid psychological theories, and to accomplish this the authors recommend a general personality and social learning theory. The third overarching principle is about enhancing the need for crime-prevention services. The model supports that focusing on decreasing crime victimization can be a goal held not only by correctional organizations, but also by community agencies.

The remaining principles highlight additional clinical principles (e.g., structured assessment, professional discretion) and organizational principles (e.g., community-based approaches, establishing core staff practices such as strong relationship skills, and having support for training and consultation from management).

COLLABORATIVE UNITS OF POLICING

There has been a developing partnership between Edmonton's forensic mental health clinic and the EPS, as demonstrated in the Memoranda of Understanding that formalizes the commitment to the collaboration. One example is the relationship between the EPS' Behaviour Assessment Unit (BAU) and Alberta Health Services' Forensic Assessment and Community Services (FACS).

FACS is a forensic mental health community clinic that provides services to individuals involved with the criminal justice system. Services include assessment, individual or group therapy, psychiatric and nursing services, as well as a day program for individuals with severe mental illness. Clients of FACS are largely those before the court for sentencing (court-ordered assessments), ones deemed Not Criminally Responsible, and those serving a period of probation.

The BAU is a unit of the EPS dedicated to conducting risk assessments and monitoring high-risk violent and sexual offenders that may be the subject of recognizance orders issued under Sections 810.1 and 810.2 of the Criminal Code of Canada,[15] long-term supervision orders, bail recognizance orders, or probation orders. These offenders are often being released from prison at the end of their sentence, on their Warrant Expiry Date. As a result, the Correctional Service of Canada does not supervise them, unlike those released on parole. Further, there are minimal established resources and supports in place to help them navigate re-entry into the community.

There is a common goal for the BAU and FACS to assist offenders as they re-integrate into the community and build pro-social lives. Adopting a framework to guide decision-making for treatment and supervision needs assists this goal.

Following the RNR Principles, it is recognized that high-risk offenders identified by the BAU require intensive and comprehensive services to optimally address their criminogenic needs. The BAU and FACS have established a partnership in which a multiagency approach is utilized in managing the risk of such offenders. RNR has been found to be a useful and effective means of case planning.[16] The combination of supervision, treatment, and responsivity principles are utilized as a means of attempting success for the offenders in the community. Emphasis is placed on the criminogenic factors that have been identified by the risk assessment completed by the police. Treatment may include psychiatric medication, group therapy, individual therapy, or occupational therapy. Families of the offenders, social agencies, and community corrections may also become part of the treatment team.

Effective communication is essential among the treatment team and frequent case conferences are held. Issues related to consent and confidentiality are thoroughly discussed, both with the offenders and between the agencies. The treatment team can provide clinical insight into the offender's mental health, progress in treatment, and response to supervision. The police officers can provide information from home visits and discussions with employers or family members that illustrate a broader view of the offender—compared to traditionally relying on self-report in therapeutic relationships. Moreover, police officers have access to services such as surveillance teams and more invasive supervision methods (e.g., searching offenders' homes and electronic devices) that can then be used as a topic within a treatment context. In addition to offender-specific work, psychologists at FACS provide consultation to the BAU to assist in questions related to diagnosis, assessment, or general risk management.

Crisis Negotiation

Another area in which the police can seek mental health consultation is with their emergency response/negotiation team. Most police agencies are connected with forensic psychologists and psychiatrists who can offer advice and information regarding mental health issues that could arise during the crisis. Crises could comprise various incidents, such as attempted suicides, barricades, or hostage-takings. Psychologists can serve different roles but are most often there as a consultant or participant-observer.[17] They provide clinical information and may recommend certain approaches. Communication is generally indirect, and psychologists rarely take a central role in the negotiation.[11] The individual characteristics of the consulting psychologist are integral to the success of this partnership. While many factors can contribute to this success, a noted area is mutual acceptance.[18] Mutual acceptance starts with an understanding of each side's roles, functions, and responsibilities. Psychologists must respect the structure and organizational make-up of police services and adjust their practice to the police setting. Likewise, police officers must expand their boundaries to allow for the contributions of the psychologist. As with most teams, it can take time and effort to develop sufficient credibility and acceptance, but once achieved, psychologists can offer a significant contribution to the process.

Case Study: Samuel

Samuel is a 31-year-old Indigenous man being released from a medium-security prison at the North Slave Correctional Centre in Yellowknife after serving seven years for aggravated assault, property damage, and theft. Throughout his incarceration, Samuel was involved in muscling, fights, and trading contraband. He participated in programming but was noted to only engage in a superficial manner. Given his poor institutional behaviour, his parole was denied and he was held until his Warrant Expiry Date. He was referred for a section 810.2 order. He was assessed and determined to be at high risk of reoffending violently. It was noted that his significant risk factors included antisocial associates, antisocial cognitions, unemployment, and marital problems. It was also noted that he has a history of gang affiliation, which has been a factor in his offence behaviour. Samuel has multiple convictions for drug-related charges and assaults. His index assault was perpetrated against his common-law partner and involved him severely assaulting her, smashing her belongings, and taking her car. Police documentation also notes prior violence against girlfriends and women that never resulted in formal charges or convictions. Samuel has had a conflicted relationship with his family. He was physically and sexually abused as a child and was placed in foster care on multiple occasions. He holds a great deal of resentment towards his parents and authority figures. Upon meeting with the police, he presents as suspicious and angry. After some rapport has been established, he expresses that he does not want to return to jail and is tired of that life.

Questions
1. Identify risk factors that seem to be apparent for Samuel.
2. Outline which factors should be targeted first.

3. What are some strategies you could use to increase his responsivity?
4. Identify what community agencies you would like to connect with in planning for Samuel.
5. What potential warning signs do you notice indicating that Samuel is likely to reoffend?

SUMMARY

More individuals with mental health problems continue to become involved with law enforcement and the criminal justice system than previously recorded. As such, there is an increasing need for police agencies and mental health professionals to work together. The combined expertise of each discipline can provide a more comprehensive and consistent approach to offender management and rehabilitation. The ultimate goal is fewer victims and the greater well-being of the larger community. Success in collaboration has been demonstrated with units such as PACT as well as the partnerships that have been developed informally. As both fields move towards more integrated units, it is hoped that partnerships between police and mental health administrators can be expanded and solidified.

REFLECTION QUESTIONS

1. Describe the major concepts and components of the Risk Needs Responsivity model.
2. What are key components of integrated partnerships?
3. What are the benefits of integrated partnerships for policing? Provide an example.

REFERENCES

1. Adleman J. Study in blue and grey: police interventions with people with mental illness: a review of the challenges and responses [Internet]. 2003. Available from: https://cmha.bc.ca/wp-content/uploads/2016/07/policereport.pdf
2. Williams DM, Steadman H, Borum R, Veysey BM, Morrissey JP. Emerging partnerships between mental health and law enforcement. Psychiatric Services. 1999;50(1):99–101. DOI: 10.1176/ps.50.1.9
3. CIT Center. Memphis Model [Internet]. [cited 2018 Jan 16]. Available from: http://www.cit.memphis.edu/overview.php?page=2

4. Watson A, Fulambarker A. The crisis intervention team model of police response to mental health crises: a primer for mental health practitioners. Best Practice in Mental Health. 2012;8(2): 71.

5. Mental Health Act, R. S. A. 2000, c M-13.

6. Coleman T, Cotton D. TEMPO: Police interactions: A report towards improving interactions between police and people living with mental health problems [Internet]. 2014 June. Available from: https://www.mentalhealthcommission.ca/sites/default/files/TEMPO%252520Police%252520Interactions%252520082014_0.pdf

7. Annison H, Bradford B, Grant E. Theorizing the role of "the brand" in criminal justice: the case of integrated offender management. Criminology and Criminal Justice. 2015;15(4):387–406.

8. Levi M, Maguire M. Something old, something new; something not entirely blue: uneven and shifting modes of crime control. In: Newburn T, Peay J, editors. Policing: Politics, Culture and Control. Oxford: Hart Publishing; 2012.

9. Dawson R, Stanko B. Implementation, implementation, implementation: insights from offender management evaluations. Policing. 2013. [cited 2017 Sep 17]. Available from: DOI: 10.1093/police/pat015

10. Andrews DA, Bonta J. The psychology of criminal conduct. 5th ed. New Providence, RI: Matthew Bender & Company; 2010.

11. Andrews DA, Bonta J. Risk-Need-Responsivity model for offender assessment and rehabilitation. Her Majesty the Queen in Right of Canada. 2007.

12. Craig LA, Dixon L, Gannon TA, editors. What works in offender rehabilitation: an evidence-based approach to assessment and treatment. Chichester, UK: John Wiley & Sons; Public Safety of Canada; 2013.

13. Holliday SB, Heilbrun K, Fretz R. Examining improvements in criminogenic needs: the risk reduction potential of a structured re-entry program. Behavioural Sciences and the Law. 2012;30:431–47.

14. Moore K, Stuewig J, Tangney J. Jail inmates' perceived and anticipated stigma: implications for post-release functioning. Self and Identity. 2012;1–21.

15. Consolidation Criminal Code, R. S. C., 1985, c. C-46. 2017 [Internet]. August 27 [cited 2017 Sep 11]. Available from: http://laws-lois.justice.gc.ca

16. Gossner D, Simo T, Rector B, Ruddell R. Case planning and recidivism of high risk and violent adult probationers. Journal of Community Safety and Well-Being. 2016 Aug;1(2):32–43.

17. Super JT. Forensic psychology and law enforcement. In: The handbook of forensic psychology. 2nd ed. Hess AK, Weiner IB, editors. New York: John Wiley & Sons; 1999.

18. Hatcher C, Mohandie K, Turner J, Gelles MG. The role of psychologist in crisis/hostage negotiations. Behavioral Sciences and the Law. 1998;16:455–72.

CHAPTER 13

Mental Health of Police Professions and First Responders

Patricia L. Schuster, *ECSS Psychological Services, Concordia University of Edmonton*

Graham E. Ross, *ECSS Psychological Services*

LEARNING OBJECTIVES

1. Recognize the variety of mental health issues that affect police officers
2. Describe the impact of compromised mental health on the police officer, family, and work
3. Execute understanding of interventions and treatments that are utilized (can be used to maintain mental health and can be used to address significant mental health issues when they occur)
4. Understand some of the challenges in providing mental health services to police officers
5. Apply knowledge of what resources are available within some organizations to promote mental health

THE SPECTRUM OF MENTAL HEALTH

When thinking about mental health issues or listening to media reports of events where the perpetrator was known to have compromised mental health, the emphasis is frequently on the diagnosis or the negatively portrayed illness. Reports stating "the shooter was bipolar" or "she was known to suffer from depression" are common. Even the Diagnostic and Statistical Manual of Mental Disorders, fifth edition (DSM-5), has a focus on deficit or compromised functioning.[1] A focus on mental health, rather than illness, first requires that we understand the full concept of mental health. Read the next three questions, then stop and develop your own response. What is mental health? How would you define it? How do you know if someone has good mental health? Now that you have developed your answers, compare them with the paragraph below.

According to the World Health Organization (WHO), there are some key facts related to mental health:

> Mental health is more than the absence of mental disorders. Mental health is an integral part of health; indeed, there is no health without mental health. Mental health is determined by a range of socioeconomic, biological and environmental factors. Cost-effective public health and intersectoral strategies and interventions exist to promote, protect and restore mental health.[2]

The fact that mental health is seen as more than the absence of mental disorders is important. Just because individuals are not diagnosed with a mental disorder does not necessarily mean they are emotionally and mentally healthy. The WHO goes on to state, "Mental health is a state of well-being in which the individual realizes his or her own abilities, can cope with the normal stresses of life, can work productively and is able to make a contribution to his or her community."[2] As can be seen, there is a positive and proactive dimension to mental health. This level of functioning enhances an individual's ability to successfully engage with the world, and this includes police officers.

When mental health is compromised, according to the WHO, "interventions exist to promote, protect and restore mental health."[2] The rest of this chapter will examine the unique areas that challenge and tax a police officer's mental health, outline areas of vulnerability, and explore interventions that can be effective in restoring individuals to previous levels of functioning.

MENTAL HEALTH ISSUES

Before discussing issues specific to police and first responders, there are issues common to individuals who are engaged in shift work, independent of vocation. The National Sleep Foundation[3] has indicated that shift work has been linked to a number of physical ailments (i.e., increased risk of cancer, metabolic problems, heart disease, ulcers, gastrointestinal problems, obesity). Others listed concerns with fatigue, decreased attention, and disrupted metabolic processes.[4] Fatigue is also equated with a decrease in safety. This becomes critical when thinking of police officers and other first responders who are required to be alert and functioning optimally to make split-second decisions that impact the lives and safety of others and themselves. There is also an increased risk of mental health problems (i.e., depression) and sociological issues (i.e., feeling out of sync with family and friends).[3]

Therefore, shift work is known to negatively impact safety, productivity, and physical health. What about cognitive abilities? Shift work has been associated with chronic impaired cognition, especially memory.[5] The loss of cognitive power is stronger for those who have worked shifts for over 10 years, and it is known to take five years after leaving shift work for an individual to fully recover cognitive functioning. This is an area that could impact police officers and other first responders in a significant way, given the nature of their duties.

With respect to identifying symptoms of mental disorders, a recent survey of Canadian Public Safety Personnel (PSP) provided some data.[6] PSP personnel were defined as correctional workers, dispatchers, firefighters, paramedics, and police officers, and people in these positions are exposed to potentially traumatic events through work. There were 5,813 participants (32.5% female) who responded to the survey. Just over 15% of participants reported current symptoms consistent with one mental disorder, and just under 28% reported more symptoms related to multiple mental illnesses. This is widely due to their exposure to potentially traumatic events increasing the risk for developing additional mental disorders. Many specific disorders were discussed, some of which will be covered in this chapter.

It should be noted that internationally the estimates of mental disorders among PSP range from 10% to 35%. Within the Canadian Armed Forces, 14.9% of currently active personnel met criteria for a mental disorder within the past year, whereas 44.5% of the PSP sample reported symptoms consistent with at least one mental disorder.[6] By comparison, according to Statistics Canada, the rates for lifetime mental disorders in Canadians 15 years and older is under 22% for substance use disorders, and less than half of that for mood and anxiety disorders.[7] Table 13.1 details the presenting symptoms of mental disorders in the two branches of police officers (municipal/provincial) and the RCMP as found in Carleton et al.'s survey.

With respect to the two policing groups, it was suggested that some of the differences in presenting mental disorder symptoms could be attributed to the fact that municipal/provincial police may have more access to supports consistent with urban deployment and are often deployed in pairs. Members of the RCMP are often in rural areas, relocate frequently, and tend to be deployed alone. It was also noted that women were more likely than men to report mental disorder symptoms; however, this was only statistically significant for the

Table 13.1: Frequencies of Positive Screens for Recent Mental Disorders

AREA	% OF TOTAL SAMPLE	% OF MUNICIPAL/ PROVINCIAL	% OF RCMP
PTSD (PLC-5)*	23.2	19.5	30.0
Major Depressive Disorder (PHQ-9)*	26.4	19.6	31.7
Generalized Anxiety Disorder (GAD-7)*	18.6	14.6	23.3
Social Anxiety Disorder (SIPS)*	15.2	10.0	18.7
Panic Disorder (PDSS-SR)*	8.9	5.9	12.0
Alcohol Use Disorder (AUDIT)*	5.9	5.8	3.9
Any other self-reported mood disorder[a]	1.7	-	1.6
Any positive screen for a mood disorder[b]	29.0	21.3	34.7
Any positive screen for an anxiety disorder[c]	30.3	23.7	37.3
Any positive screen for any mental disorder[d]	44.5	36.7	50.2

Source: (adapted from Carleton et al.)[6]
*Various instruments (in parentheses) completed by the participants
[a]Self-reported information regarding any previous mood disorder
[b]Positive screen for mood disorder (self-report plus positive PHQ-9)
[c]Positive screen for anxiety disorder plus self-report Obsessive-Compulsive Personality Disorder
[d]Any positive screen

firefighter and municipal/provincial police groups. In the general population, women are also more likely than men to report mental disorders.

Positive and supportive relationships increase resilience in mental health,[8] and individuals who are married or common-law are significantly less likely to screen positive for mental health disorders than individuals who are single or separated, widowed, or divorced.[6] PSP individuals who are older and with more years of service tend to report more mental health disorders, but across all areas of policing, positive screens were much higher than diagnostic rates for the general population.

Policing has numerous mental stressors, and there appear to be two primary work-related dimensions that cause stress for officers. The first dimension is organizational stressors found in bureaucracy, policies, lack of support from superiors, a sense of inequality, being second-guessed, diminishing resources, or seemingly impossible workloads.[9,10] This can result in officers feeling they have little control over their work environment. RCMP frontline personnel report that an authoritarian leadership style, lack of support from management, impossible workloads, and diminishing resources are issues that decrease morale and increase stress.[9]

The second dimension is operational stressors, where experiencing verbal aggression from the public, high-risk situations, traumatic events, stigma, and abuse, for example, increase officers' stress.[10] Increased stress results in increased mental health issues, which in turn impact areas such as sick leave and productivity. It has been found that the operational stressors are important to police officers and can be associated with mental health issues—nearly all the operational stressors are positively correlated with poorer mental health.[11]

Post-Traumatic Stress Disorder

As police officers and first responders are regularly exposed to unusual and violent circumstances involving significant trauma and death, it is not surprising that they are at greater risk for Post-Traumatic Stress Disorder (PTSD). Depending on the research, there can be a wide range of the estimates of PTSD in police officers, from 17.7%[11] to 19.5% in municipal and provincial police,[6] to 30% in the RCMP.[6] Regardless of the exact number, when comparing the lifetime risk for PTSD for the general population in the United States (8.7%) to police officers, it is clear that the percentage of affected police officers is much greater than in the general population. Furthermore, estimates in other countries for PTSD in the general population are less than a tenth of the United States'.[1]

Evidence also suggests that long-term police officers who have been continuously and repeatedly exposed to trauma are more likely to suffer PTSD as they move through their career.[12] Those experiencing PTSD symptoms suffer from a wide variety of psychological issues that impact their functioning in every major life aspect, especially in relationships, work performance, physical adeptness, and emotional and cognitive ability. PTSD is a significant mental health issue that can involve symptoms and act comorbidly with other mental health problems. Some of the known symptoms and mental illnesses associated with PTSD include hyperarousal/hypervigilance, depression, anxiety disorders, sleep problems, irritability, increased substance use, suicidal ideation, and, in some cases, domestic violence.[12] American police officers in urban settings have been found to have PTSD symptom prevalence rates of 13%, which has significant implications for morale, absenteeism, occupational health, early retirement, and family functioning.[13]

The symptoms of PTSD, especially hyperarousal and hypervigilance, have a significant impact on first responders. This can result in increased fearfulness or defensiveness, which in turn can lead the individual to be less trusting and more reactive. The person's reactions can be emotional, physical, or both. The individual may behave more aggressively, which can be expressed verbally or physically, and there is a cascading effect in that increased levels of arousal can impact officers' judgements, leading them to overreact. Behaviours associated with overreacting and other effects of PTSD can create further isolation for officers at a time when more involvement and support are required. Personal areas (e.g., identity, self-confidence, decision-making) and interpersonal areas (e.g., family, work relationships) can be impacted, leading to increased anxiety, sleep disturbance, depression, and/or suicidal ideation. In many ways, untreated PTSD sets the stage for a negative spiral, where one's mental health becomes increasingly compromised over time, reducing one's ability to function at work and at home.

SUICIDE

"More police officers die by their own hand than are killed in the line of duty."[14]

Police officers share some aspects of suicide risk with the public; however, there are dimensions of suicide unique to this group. The suicide rate for law enforcement personnel is two to three times that of the general population. Additionally, three times as many police officers kill themselves than are killed by criminals; "this makes suicide the single most lethal factor in police work."[14] There is some suggestion that the rate of police officer suicide might even be higher than reported, as some deaths not ruled suicide could be, but they are often not reported out of deference to the officers. The suicide rate among RCMP members is about half that of other agencies, and officer suicide rates in other countries are higher than in any Canadian agency.[15]

Some of the predisposing factors with respect to suicide are related to toxic police culture; for example, all-or-nothing thinking, self-reliance, and a sense of infallibility. For police officers, shame is often a worse emotion than fear. There is also a cognitive dissonance, where officers believe they should be able to handle things on their own while simultaneously needing approval.[9] Another artifact of the culture is that police are trained to act decisively, which is an asset in a work environment but a liability when contemplating suicide. Acting decisively does not give one the luxury to explore all the options, which increases the risk. Another major risk factor is that police have ready access to weapons and, in contrast to most gun owners who do not carry a weapon at all times, police officers do. It is noteworthy, however, that police officers use a variety of means to end their lives other than weapons. Therefore, although carrying a weapon may increase officers' risk, it is not the only lethal means at their disposal.[14]

In a Canadian study with respect to PSP and suicide, three dimensions of suicide were examined: ideation, planning, and attempts.[16] It was found that up to 47% of PSP reported lifetime suicidal ideation, with a wide range of self-reported attempts. These individuals were noted to have less fear of death, more compromised social supports, increased sleep issues, and access to weapons, which increases the risk for death by suicide.

Past-year suicidal ideation is more common in young officers, and those who are single, separated, widowed, or divorced have higher rates of suicidal ideation than those who are married or common-law.[16] Risk is also higher among those with less formal education. Municipal police report the lowest rates of past-year and lifetime suicidal ideation, and police reported the lowest rates of past-year and lifetime suicidal behaviour of any PSP.

Higher rates of depression, PTSD, and substance abuse possibly contribute to the higher rates of suicidal behaviours in PSP.[12] Organizational stressors are also contributing factors. Women as a group differ from men, both as officers and in the general population, in that they are more likely to report lifetime ideation, plans, and attempts. Workplace access to weapons is a risk factor for women but not for men.[16] Stigmatization of mental illness is often seen as a significant barrier to individuals seeking help for mental health concerns, which could also be considered a risk factor in some environments—particularly police departments.

DOMESTIC VIOLENCE

Awareness of domestic violence has increased significantly over the past number of years for both the general public and for police officers.[12] Domestic violence is now viewed as an area requiring significant attention and intervention. The estimated rate of **officer-involved (self-reported) domestic violence** ranges from 4.8% to 40% committing some form of offence to a partner. The results of one study reported an average rate of 21.2% of officer-involved domestic violence (OIDV), twice the rate of the general population.[17] In Florida, law enforcement officers' alcohol abuse and PTSD rates influenced rates of self-reported domestic violence, indicating a strong association among these variables.[12] Officers with PTSD are found to be four times more likely to report physical violence, and officers with hazardous drinking tendencies are also four times more likely to act violently. In addition, dependent drinkers are eight times more likely to report being physically violent with an intimate partner.

There are several dimensions to OIDV that are unique when compared to domestic violence in the general population; for example, officers are trained to control situations and command authority. When this approach is used with intimate partners, it can result in significant trauma, physical and emotional. Officers are also exposed to a variety of trauma while at work; this increases stress levels and emotional reactivity, which can lead to dysregulated behaviour at home. Officers also have ready access to firearms, which can exacerbate a potentially violent situation with an intimate partner.

There are barriers to reporting OIDV that are also unique. If a victim turns to law enforcement for assistance, it is likely that the investigating officer knows the victim's abuser. Moreover, while the locations of shelters that are available to victims are generally unknown to abusers, police are aware of their locations. These factors can make victims more anxious and less likely to report incidents. Lastly, if the crime is reported and officers are convicted, given the laws in most US states, the officers would lose their jobs, as in many states, those convicted of domestic violence are banned from carrying a weapon, and there are no exceptions for police officers. This is a factor that victims have stated reduces the likelihood of their making a formal complaint. In fact, in states that have implemented mandatory arrest policies, there was a 4.5% decline in reporting domestic violence rates.

SUBSTANCE ABUSE

Although a few police officers may use a variety of illicit substances, the primary focus of research into substance use appears to be related to alcohol use/abuse, perhaps because the drug is legal and generally socially acceptable. Alcohol use and PTSD are associated with three areas: critical incidents, coping, and social stressors.[18] Given that policing is a stressful occupation, officers must use coping methods—both positive and negative (maladaptive). Alcohol use is seen to be a maladaptive coping mechanism. This is difficult for some individuals to recognize, as it is socially acceptable, and, in some police cultures is an expected and legitimate means of dealing with stress.[12] Most police officers are not at risk for alcohol problems, but 16.8% are drinking at a harmful level, 1% at a hazardous level, and 0.4% have possible alcohol dependency.[19] Interestingly, officers drinking at a harmful level drink mostly with friends, while the hazardous group mostly drinks with co-workers. Those most likely to drink at these levels are officers who are young, white, single, and work the day shift.

Police officers have high rates of alcohol consumption and die from alcoholic liver disease at twice the rate of the general population. One American study estimates that 11% of males and 16% of females engage in at-risk levels of alcohol use.[20] Over one-third of officers' report binge drinking, and 3.4% of males and 3.7% of females report consuming over 28 drinks per week.

Eighteen percent of males and 16% of females report significant issues with lifetime histories of negative social and interpersonal consequences with respect to alcohol use. Police officers are more likely to be involved in binge drinking compared to the general public, with females being two to three times more likely. Lower education is correlated with greater alcohol use in males but not females, and workplace stress has not been found to predict drinking levels; however, workplace stress has been known to result in less alcohol consumption for females.[20]

Stress from organizational issues is known to result in compromised mental health and other negative outcomes.[10] When individuals are exposed to stressors, their adaptive coping strategies and thinking patterns are negatively impacted. This can lead to utilizing maladaptive coping strategies that further compromise functioning; with respect to maladaptive coping strategies, it has been found that **escape-avoidance coping** (e.g., failure to discuss emotions, failure to seek professional assistance, social withdrawal, self-criticism) is the most serious issue. Additionally, police subculture may encourage maladaptive coping, resulting in more negative outcomes.[10]

Alcohol use is positively and significantly related to PTSD symptoms,[12,17] and is related to sex, age, and time spent in policing—younger males and those with fewer years in policing are more likely to report problematic drinking. Alcohol use is also significantly and positively related to negative coping and social stressors. Interestingly, critical incidents are connected to alcohol use. However, coping mediates the relationship; therefore, officers who learn positive coping strategies do not experience a significant correlation between alcohol use and exposure to critical incidents. Furthermore, social stressors are not significantly associated with alcohol use.[17]

A significant association between alcohol use and subjective work-related traumatic distress and PTSD avoidance symptoms has also been found. To a lesser degree, personal relationship distress and depression can be associated with alcohol use. It is likely that alcohol use is a form of self-medication.[10]

RESOURCES AND COPING

The overall objective for police officers, like those in the general population, is to maintain their mental health and to be able to adequately cope with the various stressors that are encountered in daily living. Police officers encounter threats to their mental and physical health more frequently than the general population; therefore, they may require some additional supports and interventions. The World Health Organization notes that mental health is more than the absence of mental disorders, and that there is no health without mental health.[2] The RCMP has stated, "An organization's most valuable resource is its employees."[21] To that end, the RCMP has developed a mental health strategy that includes Employee Assistance Programs (EAPs), peer support, wellness days, and critical incident stress management; they have also implemented the use of in-house psychologists and health services personnel. Although it is easier to recognize a physical injury, mental health cannot be ignored and is of equal importance to physical well-being. The impetus of the RCMP's mental health strategy is to enhance the health of its employees, not just maintain it.

As an organization, the RCMP recognizes that maintaining good mental health presents some challenges in policing. The lack of knowledge with respect to psychological health can lead to reluctance among officers to talk about mental health. There are two aspects involved: first, a fear that disclosure will negatively impact one's career; and second, the stigma associated with psychological issues and what it means for an officer to need and/or access support. Mental health issues are a reality and are known to have a significant impact on the vitality, creativity, motivation, and commitment of officers, and poor mental health can lead to reduced productivity, staff turnover, and increased use of sick leave and health benefits.[9,20] The RCMP notes that about 38% of long-term sick leave is for mental health. In 2012, 55.4% of RCMP public service employees were being treated for mental health problems.[21]

It is important to support the mental health of police officers.[12] The areas of alcohol abuse, PTSD, depression, suicidal ideation, and domestic violence require additional strategies to intervene effectively. Intervention can occur through additional training, wellness programming, and policy development. The most difficult challenge is in changing the common drinking culture supported in law enforcement. As it is supported by most of the institution, it is difficult for officers to view drinking as a problem. It is recommended that when training is provided, the focus should be directly on officer (rather than civilian) drinking and how it affects the officers' health, families, and careers.

Despite the clear need to support police officers with substance abuse issues, findings from a 2018 United States study found only two out of 110 law enforcement agencies offered substance use services. The services were offered through direct linkages to regional outpatient and inpatient substance use programs (covered by health insurance plans). One agency offered closed Alcoholics Anonymous meetings for the region's police officers and firefighters.[21] In most police organizations, there are few targeted programs or supports to assist police officers with substance use issues. Therefore, it is imperative for law enforcement agencies to address this issue more directly through education, wellness programs, peer support, and formal linkages with substance abuse community resources that ensure confidentiality and do not penalize officers for identifying their drinking problem and accessing support.

With respect to PTSD, training and education are available as well as the use of EAPs.[12,20] EAPs are typically short-term, free for employees, based on self-referral, and confidential, and they provide mental health support through trained professionals (e.g., psychologists, clinical social workers). Services are provided in a variety of ways—face-to-face, telephone, or e-mail—so that the needs of each employee can be met efficiently.[22] EAPs can be in-house (i.e., run within the law enforcement agency) or external to the agency. This is an important variable, as the perceived confidentiality of such programs significantly impacts usage. This is particularly true in police agencies, where the stigma of mental health problems and their treatment remains high.

Wellness programs can help foster positive coping strategies for officers, which in turn impact their mental health. Those who use positive coping mechanisms have better outcomes than those who use maladaptive or negative coping methods. As has been stated, police culture supports some of the negative coping methods, such as avoidance and drinking; however, there is also some support for more positive methods, such as exercise.

There are two stages in assisting officers to enhance how they cope with stress or trauma. The first is to increase awareness that some responses to stress will lead to better outcomes than others. The second is to train, or assist, the officers to learn the new strategies (e.g., meditation) until they have developed a level of proficiency. Each of these can be accomplished in a variety of ways, including mental health programming and initiatives, wellness programming, peer support programs, individual therapy, and family therapy. In addition, policies

Table 13.2: Forms of Coping with Stressors

COPING MECHANISMS	
POSITIVE	NEGATIVE
• Meditation • Exercise • Physical self-care • Healthy eating • Good sleep habits • Talking to others • Engaging in hobbies • Pursuing interests • Relaxing and restorative activities (e.g., spiritual or creative ventures) • Establishing and maintaining healthy social relationships • Spending time with family • Belonging to organizations of interest • Volunteering	• Alcohol use • Drug use • Avoiding support • Disengagement • Failure to discuss emotions • Not seeking professional help • Overeating • Promiscuity • Isolation

can be developed to support mental health at an organizational level (e.g., wellness days, restorative sleep policies).

HEALTHY SOCIAL AND FAMILY SUPPORTS

Connection to healthy supports (e.g., friends, family, other officers) is essential to mental health. Officers who feel connected and engaged with their supports do better in their work and personal lives, and positive social support reduces the impact of traumatic experiences.[23,24] Given police officers' exposure to ongoing stressors and trauma, this type of connection is crucial to their mental health and well-being. Those who are better able to deal with work-related stressors have fewer negative outcomes and fewer negative behaviours.[18] The fact that officers work shifts can make developing or maintaining social connections, even with family, difficult, meaning support from the organization is imperative for officers.

Immediate social support from work peers is extremely important following any traumatic event. Many agencies have developed protocols to assist officers and ensure that they receive peer support.[24] Additionally, it is important for the officers to reach out to their work peers and personal support network to talk to them about their experiences, which can be encouraged through programming and peer support. As many officers who have experienced trauma turn to alcohol to assist them in managing their hyperarousal, this is an area where mindfulness training and substance abuse intervention can be helpful.

Further pertaining to traumatic events, cognitive appraisal during and following the trauma has been found to positively influence stress and coping. Individuals who perceive a traumatic event as time-limited, without negative global future implications, were less likely to develop PTSD.[25] This suggests that cognitive-behavioural interventions immediately after the traumatic event may assist officers in preventing the development of PTSD.

EFFECTIVE TREATMENTS FOR POLICING PROFESSIONS AND PTSD

From a mental health perspective, some officers will require a specific trauma treatment protocol beyond what is typically offered through an EAP. For those experiencing PTSD symptoms, treatment protocols have been developed to ameliorate the symptoms. Three common intervention protocols are cognitive processing therapy (CPT), exposure therapy (ET), and eye movement desensitization and reprocessing (EMDR).

CPT is a 12-session PTSD treatment that is conducted individually or in groups. It is designed to assist individuals in processing their emotions and confronting their beliefs about the traumatic incident and its effect on their life. It is a cognitive-based therapy that has undergone rigorous scientific clinical trials and that helps an individual make sense of the traumatic incident(s).

ET, which comprises 9 to 12 therapy sessions for PTSD, has been thoroughly and scientifically tested and shown to significantly reduce PTSD symptoms. It is a cognitive-behavioural individual treatment that targets multiple trauma-related difficulties by encouraging individuals to confront the traumatic memory by repeatedly telling the story to a therapist. This challenges the things in their lives that individuals are avoiding due to fear. The individuals are then assigned homework to encourage them to practice confronting these things.

EMDR is a structured form of psychotherapy that has the individual focus on external stimuli, such as a moving visual object (i.e., the therapist's finger), sound, or light, while remembering the traumatic incident; the intention is to increase positive ideas. Some research supports the use of EMDR with other treatments.

It has been noted that many of these treatments are underutilized, especially in law enforcement populations.[26] Individuals in one study, with varying trauma histories, expressed a preference for the type of intervention in which they would like to participate. Most of the participants stated a preference for Exposure or CPT treatments for PTSD over other interventions, such as EMDR. This suggests that it is important for law enforcement organizations to provide their members with direct information and support regarding evidence-based treatments for PTSD, as this may increase the likelihood that they will access treatment and benefit from it.

Properly prescribed and administered medication can also be helpful in treating mental health problems (i.e., depression and anxiety disorders), as well as in ameliorating some of the symptoms of PTSD. When examining the psychobiology and psychopharmacology of PTSD, optimal pharmacological interventions were identified.[27] Acute trauma is best treated by medications that reduce autonomic arousal, such as benzodiazepines or clonidine. If PTSD has already developed, first-line treatment should involve either a Selective Serotonin Reuptake Inhibitor (SSRI) or a tricyclic medication. In the event that a more complex trauma symptom profile (including aggression, impulsivity, and self-destructive behaviour) develops, a second drug, either an anticonvulsant, mood stabilizer, or benzodiazepine, is recommended. Such medications, in conjunction with psychotherapy, can significantly reduce the symptomology and assist the individual in resolving trauma symptoms.

ADDRESSING SUICIDE

Suicide, a major mental health issue among police officers, requires law enforcement agencies to implement suicide prevention programs, which is a more complex issue than at first appears. Many police organizations are engaged in efforts to promote wellness and prevent suicide. In a survey of 110 law enforcement agencies, four types of services were offered: minimal (an EAP), basic (mental health, critical incident response procedures, and training), proactive (in-house mental health care, embedded chaplains, substance misuse programs, peer support, screenings, or health and wellness programs), and integrated services (mental health services integrated into day-to-day operations).[28] However, most services did not have specific programs for suicide prevention, but rather focused on promoting employee mental health. It was stated that identifying officers at high risk through means other than self-report, such as utilizing a peer or an embedded chaplain, or using screening programs (e.g., administrative data or number of exposures to traumatic incidents), was a controversial issue. There were concerns these approaches could be perceived as punitive (i.e., peers reporting on each other) or could be inaccurate (i.e., too many false positives identified).

Addressing suicidality among police officers is best accomplished using a multi-pronged strategy that includes a variety of programs that target different areas. Such programs raise self-awareness and promote self-care, identify those at risk, facilitate access to quality care, provide quality care, and restrict access to lethal means.[28] Training programs can facilitate self-awareness regarding mental health issues and promote self-care by dealing with topics such as symptoms of mental health problems, sleep disturbances, responsible drinking, and promoting positive family relationships. Although methods used to identify officers who are at risk for suicide are quite controversial, it is necessary to have a system in place; one strategy to best accomplish this may be by providing debriefings right after the critical incident occurs, involving fellow officers, mental health staff, and peer support personnel. It is important to have several of these debriefing sessions, both individually and in groups, as recent literature indicates that single-session group debriefings are not effective.[28] With respect to facilitating access to and providing quality care, this can be accomplished through peer support programs, in-house mental health counselling, EAPs, and external referral sources (including private psychologists, psychiatrists, suicide prevention agencies and crisis lines, and reputable substance abuse programs).

There is also a place for individual, and at times marital, therapy for officers and their families. This often extends beyond the EAP format, especially if the EAP is designated short-term. Individual therapy provides support for officers, allowing them to address specific issues related to stressors, either organizational or operational. Marital therapy allows officers to attend with their partners and address issues that may be influencing the marriage or family.

Case Study: Words of Wisdom from a Veteran Officer

A Canadian active-duty female police officer, with over 20 years of service and who has recovered from PTSD, was interviewed. She was exposed to a traumatic incident while on duty approximately 15 years ago when her police cruiser was hit head-on by a stolen truck, driven by a male high on crystal methamphetamine, during a police chase. She and her partner suffered physical injuries and she was subsequently diagnosed with PTSD and eventually also with depression, anxiety, and panic attacks.

Over the past 15 years she has been engaged in many legal battles involving criminal offence with respect to the stolen truck, and two litigations initiated

continued

by herself with Workers' Compensation Board, all of which were very stressful. During this time, she resumed modified-duty work on at least seven different occasions, all resulting in further medical leaves due to PTSD symptomology.

Early on in her recovery, during a three-year long-term medical leave, she became hopeless and suicidal to the point where she had a plan; fortunately, she did not complete it, as her intimate partner intervened, and she received help from her family doctor. She indicated that her inability to work and the lack of support from her peers and supervisors in the police agency were major contributors to her poor mental health throughout this time. After her recovery from suicidal ideation, she returned to work and was able to sustain employment for short periods of time (up to one year), but the depression and anxiety would return increasingly, and she would go back on medical leave. This pattern continued throughout four more attempts to return to work.

In 2015, 12 years after her traumatic event, the police organization began to offer greater supports for officers with mental health issues (i.e., peer support program, in-house psychology, and a re-integration program for officers returning to work). She participated in these programs, which created a major turning point, as she began to recover. During her 15 years of dealing with PTSD, she has participated in numerous treatments, including long-term individual therapy with several psychologists (eventually participating in EMDR and CPT), worked with different psychiatrists who prescribed a variety of medications, peer support groups, PTSD retreats, and most recently a work re-integration program.

She has successfully returned to work for the past two years and is currently providing peer support to fellow officers diagnosed with PTSD. She has effectively dealt with the trauma related to her police work, as well as her childhood sexual abuse. In addition, she has resolved her issues related to the lack of support and betrayal she suffered during the past 15 years as an injured police officer and reports that she is now happy, probably for the first time in her life. She has many stories of incidents involving her peers and supervisors not supporting her in her healing journey or assisting her in successfully returning to work. She indicates that the following treatments were pivotal in her recovery: EMDR, CPT, the re-integration program, peer support groups, and her successful return to work.

This officer exemplifies resilience and courage in the face of great adversity. In discussing her journey, she identified some things that she believes new police officers should know before they enter law enforcement. Specifically, she strongly advises new recruits to understand that mental health is extremely important, and that although there is a stigma regarding metal health in police agencies, this is getting better. She urges new police officers to do the following:

Self-Health Checks
- MOST IMPORTANTLY—self-care needs to be a priority—have a system in place before you begin your police work and maintain it!
- Know the signs and symptoms of mental health problems (depression, anxiety, panic attacks, suicidal ideation, PTSD) before you get on the job and try to notice when they occur in yourself or your colleagues.
- Have a good support system in place before you start the job.
- Watch for sleep disturbance and nightmares and talk to somebody about this.
- Be open. Talk to your co-workers and give fellow officers a chance to talk about their critical incidents.
- Do debriefings—they help.
- Don't push counselling away.
- Don't be afraid to ask for help.

Questions
1. What are effective treatments for trauma?
2. How do you manage your stress?
3. If you began experiencing PTSD symptoms in your life, what approaches would you use to deal with it?

SUMMARY

The expression mental health is all-encompassing and captures many dimensions of a person's functioning. A diagnosis is not necessary to be struggling with mental health. Police and first responders more often than other professions experience mental health concerns and other health-related issues due to the nature of their work. First responders experience a higher likelihood of PTSD in addition to substance use disorders, mood disorders, and anxiety disorders. Officers with substance use issues have a higher death rate due to liver diseases. These stressors, especially if not treated, lead to a high proportion of suicide among police and first responders in comparison to other career professions. In addition to mental health issues, first responders who commit suicide also typically tend to have access to a weapon and are not in relationships.

Because mental health issues do not occur in isolation, work stress extends to home life. Many mental health concerns such as PTSD have shown a higher incidence of domestic violence. One factor that builds resiliency and coping among police and first responders is maintaining a high level of mental health functioning. This involves seeking therapy when experiencing mental health symptoms as well as living a healthy lifestyle and enjoying healthy relationships. It is possible to achieve better mental health functioning through resources and education, but often stigma deters police from requesting help. Effective treatments for officers include CPT, ET, and EMDR. Some health checks to enhance mental health functioning and decrease suicide ideation include making self-care a priority, knowing mental health signs and symptoms, having a strong social support system, watching for sleep disturbances, engaging in debriefings, not being afraid to ask for help, and engaging in counselling.

REFLECTION QUESTIONS

1. Identify three statements by the WHO about mental health.
2. What are three common reasons individuals in policing may avoid reporting their mental health issues?
3. List five positive and five negative coping strategies for stress.
4. Give a brief definition and explanation of the processes behind CPT, ET, and EMDR.
5. What steps should you follow after experiencing a traumatic event?

REFERENCES

1. American Psychiatric Association. Diagnostic and statistical manual of mental disorders (DSM-5). American Psychiatric Pub; 2013 May 22.
2. World Health Organization. Mental health: strengthening our response [Internet]. 2018 Mar 30 [cited 2018 May 30]. Available from: http://www.who.int/news-room/fact-sheets/detail/mental-health-strengthening-our-response
3. National Sleep Foundation. Living and coping with Shift Work Disorder [Internet]. 2018 [cited 2018 May 30]. Available from: https://sleepfoundation.org/shift-work/content/living-coping-shift-work-disorder
4. Price M. The risks of night work [Internet]. 2011 Jan [cited 2018 May 30]. Mon on Psych 42(1):38. Available from: http://www.apa.org/monitor/2011/01/night-work.aspx

5. Marquié J, Tucker P, Folkard S, Gentil C, Ansiau D. Chronic effects of shift work on cognition: findings from the VISAT longitudinal study. Occup Environ Med. 2014 Nov;72(4):258–64.

6. Carleton R, Afifi T, Turner S, Taillieu T, Duranceau S, Lebouthillier D, et al. Mental disorder symptoms among safety personnel in Canada. Can J Psychiatry. 2018;63(1):54–64.

7. Statistics Canada. Rates of selected mental or substance use disorders, lifetime and 12 month, Canada, household population 15 and older, 2012. Canadian Community Health Survey (CCHS)-Mental Health. Ottawa: Government of Canada; 2012.

8. Afifi T, MacMillan H, Taillieu T, Turner S, Cheung K, Sareen J, et al. Individual- and relationship-level factors related to better mental health outcomes following child abuse: results from a nationally representative Canadian sample. Can J Psychiatry. 2016;61(12):776–88.

9. Perrott S, Kelloway E. Scandals, sagging morale, and the role of ambiguity in the Royal Canadian Police: the end of a Canadian institution as we know it? Police Pract Res. 2011;12(2):120–35.

10. Chopko B, Palmieri P, Adams R. Associations between police stress and alcohol use: Implications for practice. J Loss Trauma. 2013;18:482–97.

11. Arial M, Gonik V, Wild P, Danuser B. Association of work related chronic stressors and psychiatric symptoms in a Swiss sample of police officers; a cross sectional questionnaire study. Int Arch Environ Health. 2010;83:323–31.

12. Oehme K, Donnelly E, Martin A. Alcohol abuse, PTSD, and officer-committed domestic violence. Policing. 2012;6(4):418–30.

13. Robinson HM, Sigman MR, Wilson JP. Duty-related stressors and PTSD symptoms in suburban police officers. Psychol Rep. 1997;81(3):835–45.

14. Miller L. Police officer suicide: causes, prevention, and practical strategies. Int J Emerg Ment Health. 2005;7(2):101–14.

15. Loo R. Suicide among police in a federal force. Suicide Life Threat Behav. 1986;16(3):379–88.

16. Carleton R, Afifi T, Turner S, Taillieu T, Lebouthillier D, Duranceau S, et al. Suicidal ideation, plans, and attempts among public safety personnel in Canada. Can Psychol [Internet]. 2018 Feb 8; advance online publication. Available from: https://web-a-ebsco-host-com.ezproxy.aec.talonline.ca/ehost-pdfviewer/pdfviewer?vid=6&sid=a884b205-e17f-4360-9261-8f007cf1a97f%40sessionmgr4008

17. Mennicke A, Ropes K. Estimating the rate of domestic violence perpetrated by law enforcement officers: a review of methods and estimates. Aggress Violent Behav. 2016;31:157-64.

18. Menard K, Arter M. Police officer alcohol use and trauma symptoms: associations with critical incidents, coping, and social stressors. Int J Stress Manag. 2013;20(1):37–56.

19. Lindsay V. Police officers and their alcohol consumption: Should we be concerned? Police Q. 2008;11(1):74–87.

20. Ballenger J, Best S, Metzler T, Wasserman D, Mohr D, Liberman A, et al. Patterns and predictors of alcohol use in male and female urban police officers. Am J Addict. 2010;20:21–9.

21. Royal Canadian Mounted Police. RCMP Mental Health Strategy (2014-2019) [Internet]. 2014 Sep 05 [cited 2018 May 30]. Available from: http://www.rcmp-grc.gc.ca/fam/strat-eng.htm

22. Government of Canada. Information for employees – Employee Assistance Program (EAP) [Internet]. 2017 Jul 24 [cited 2018 May 30]. Available from: https://

www.canada.ca/en/health-canada/services/environmental-workplace-health/
occupational-health-safety/employee-assistance-services/information-employees-
employee-assistance-services.html

23. Kirschman E. I love a cop: What police families need to know. Revised ed. New York: Guilford Press; 2007.

24. McCormack L, Riley L. Medical discharge from the "family," moral injury, and a diagnosis of PTSD: is psychological growth possible in the aftermath of policing trauma? Traumatology. 2016;22(1):19–28.

25. Ehlers A, Clark D. A cognitive model of posttraumatic stress disorder. Behav Res Ther. 2000;38(4):319–45.

26. Becker CB, Meyer G, Price J, Graham M, Arsena A, Armstrong D, et al. Law enforcement preferences for PTSD treatment and crisis management alternatives. Behav Res Ther. 2009;47(3):245–53.

27. van der Kolk B. The psychobiology and psychopharmacology of PTSD. Hum Psychopharmacol Clin Exp. 2001;16(Suppl1):S49–64.

28. Ramchand R, Saunders J, Osilla KC, Ebener P, Kotzias V, Thornton E, et al. Suicide prevention in U. S. law enforcement agencies: a national survey [Internet]. J Crim Pol Psychol. 2018 Apr 12 [cited 2018 May 30]. Available from: https://link-springer-com .ezproxy.aec.talonline.ca/content/pdf/10.1007%2Fs11896-018-9269-x.pdf

PART III

Special Topics

This part of the book discusses current trends and issues in policing. Policing and mental health is understood through historical perspectives, post-arrest processes, treatment management, and reflections on experience and informal recommendations.

CHAPTER 14

The History of Policing and Indigenous Persons in Canada

Daniel J. Jones, *University of Huddersfield*
Peter Jensen, *Elizabeth Fry Society*

LEARNING OBJECTIVES

1. Understand the history of Indigenous people in Canada and the origins of addiction and crime
2. Understand the interrelationship between trauma, mental health, and crime
3. Learn about the overrepresentation of the Indigenous population in the criminal justice and child welfare systems
4. Identify the dynamics of gangs in Canada
5. Understand bias awareness and strategies to reduce the challenges between police and the community
6. Identify aspects of healing and health promotion through the medicine circle

CANADA'S CRIMINAL SYSTEM

The separation of families, de-culturation, and physical and sexual abuse that Indigenous persons experienced in Canada from the late 1800s to the mid-1900s have stripped away their identity. Those are some of reasons Indigenous persons today struggle with trauma, addictions, gang associations, and poverty.[1] In other words, previous psychological suffering has rippled through and pervaded the mental health of the current generation of Indigenous persons.[2] Indigenous persons have higher rates of substance use and mental disorders than non-Indigenous persons in Canada.[3]

A strong, societal impact, both financially and emotionally, occurs when one segment of a population struggles with substance use and criminal behaviour. The economic burden of substance misuse in Canada, excluding tobacco and cannabis, is estimated to be $27.2 billion annually.[4] Likewise, the cost for law enforcement to respond to substance related matters in Canada is an estimated $5.4 billion.[5]

There have been proportionately more instances of alcohol consumption (without drugs) on the day of the crime among offenders incarcerated for committing violent crimes, including assault (38%), murder (31%), or sexual assault (30%), than any other crime,[6] with 40% of detainees attributing their crime to substance use.[7] Alcohol is legal in Canada and considered a part of the social fabric, yet is considered to be responsible for more crime than any other factor, constituting 40% of all police calls.[7,8] It is often easy to rationalize criminal activity as being only a part of the streets, when, arguably, it begins inside our own homes and neighbourhoods.

The Correctional Service of Canada (CSC)[9] expenditures in 2016 totalled approximately $2.4 billion. In 2015-16, it cost an average of $116,000 to maintain an offender in a CSC institution, whereas it was $31,000 in the community. During 2015-16, CSC was responsible for an average of 22,872 offenders, including 14,639 in custody at federal institutions and 8,233 supervised by the CSC in the community. Who are in Canadian correctional facilities today? What is the connection between incarceration, mental illness, and trauma? The dynamics of how a person ends up in a correctional facility is complex, but there seems to be underlying factors regarding who is incarcerated and who is not. Socioeconomic factors and demographics (including ethnicity), as well as personal bias, play a role.[10]

The offender population at the federal level is becoming more diverse, as evidenced by the decrease in the proportion of Caucasian offenders from 62.8% in 2011-12 to 58.8% in 2015-16.[9] Between 2011-12 and 2015-16, the Indigenous population increased by 16.6%.[11] According to the 2016-17 Canadian Census Poll,[12] Indigenous people represent the second largest ethnic group of the federal incarcerated population, at 27%, while being only 4.1% of the total Canadian population. These numbers are a staggering overrepresentation of the Indigenous community. A better understanding of why Indigenous populations in the corrections system are growing is required. To do this, we must go back in Canadian history and find a recurring theme, and it seems that psycho-emotional trauma may be at the root of why so many Indigenous people are in our corrections facilities and child welfare system today.[1]

CANADA'S HISTORY WITH INDIGENOUS PERSONS

The history of colonization in Canada is one that is now well-known and talked about; however, this has not always been the case. A historical root of an Indigenous issue today occurred when fur traders socially interacted with Indigenous populations—often using alcohol as a medium or in trade for fur and animal skins. Some nations, according to one source, produced weak beers or other fermented beverages, but only for ceremonial purposes. For the most part, Indigenous populations throughout North America did not consume alcohol before the arrival of Europeans in the fifteenth and sixteenth centuries. The introduction of distilleries by Europeans to make far more potent alcohol made the substance readily available to different nations and could not be effectively countered through social, legal, or moral guidelines to regulate its use in time.[13] The prolonged psycho-emotional pressures caused by the stress in the transition of North Siberian Indigenous populations to sedentary and non-traditional work in the mid-twentieth century have significantly contributed to the spread of alcoholism[14]—a similar situation has occurred for Indigenous Peoples in North America.

With colonization came the residential school system. This was a system that enabled the assimilation of the Indigenous population into European society, a process that was, in essence, cultural genocide. Many people speak of this issue as if it were from the distant past; however, the last residential school closed in 1996, making the topic far more recent than many Canadians once believed. The Truth and Reconciliation Commission (TRC)[15] saw seven events begin nationally as a class action lawsuit in 2007 and end in 2012. The TRC was able to shine a light on the dark past of residential schools and make it a priority to teach Canadians the true history of the nation.

Another historical issue that is now coming to light is the concept known as the **Sixties Scoop**. This was another attempt to assimilate Indigenous children into Western society by apprehending children and putting them up for adoption for mostly Caucasian families—under the guise that the system felt Indigenous children were not being adequately cared for. There is currently a class action lawsuit in place for the Sixties Scoop.[16]

The history of Indigenous Peoples in Canada is one that is very challenging to summarize. One piece of legislation that must be discussed is the

Indian Act, established by the federal government to address issues pertaining to the Indigenous population.[17] This legislation allowed for residential schools, the loss of Indian status if an Indigenous woman married a white man, determined voting rights, and much more. The interesting fact about the Indian Act is that it is the only racialized piece of legislation still in force, with amendments, in the world.

RELATING INDIGENOUS HISTORY TO CANADIAN POLICING

As we move through time in Canada, we cannot ignore the impact of colonization and its impact on the relationship between Indigenous Peoples and law enforcement. Police were the agents of the state responsible for removing children from their homes to take them to residential schools. These children were taken, placed in the schools, robbed of their culture, and when they returned home they could no longer communicate with their families. The unfortunate reality is that some never returned home: either they were used as a labor force or died in the residential school system.

The concept of vicarious trauma is of some significance, as it relates to Indigenous Peoples. **Vicarious trauma** is often spoken about in relation to the effects of trauma on counsellors following countless hours of listening to their clients speak about trauma they have endured.[18] For Indigenous populations, it is the trauma experienced by the loved ones and family of individuals who have experienced the cultural genocide of the residential school system.[18]

Police had a role in the Sixties Scoop, which resulted in yet another government-led initiative that pitted police against the community in a traumatic and adversarial way. Police may not have directly caused the trauma faced by individuals in residential schools or who were part of the Sixties Scoop, but police were the gatekeepers who introduced Indigenous families to the multi-generational trauma.

Unfortunately, the police continue to act as agents of the state, as they incarcerate members of the Indigenous community and assist Child Welfare in apprehending children. The overrepresentation of Indigenous people in both these systems continues to lead the conversation between police and the community, interactions that sometimes involve distrust and uncertainty.

Spotlight: Kari Thomason, SNUG

I had a very bad night last night. Pretty much like most nights with a few exceptions. The truth is I'm grateful to still be mentally all here. I'm wired and desperately need to forget the fact that hours earlier I was raped. Later on I was robbed and then got busted for talking to a wanna-be-john (an undercover police officer). What put the cap on the needle was when I had my miscarriage in a desolate and dirty back alley. All alone, sad and confused. There is a part of me that makes me believe I deserved it all. I chose to say yes to a hoot of cocaine, I chose to pull a trick. I need to run from the excruciating sadness, emptiness, fear, and shame I feel within me right now. ~ Charlene Johnson[19]

In the world of a sex trade worker, a bad date or bad night equates rape and violence. SNUG is a harm-reduction, trauma-informed program that assists individuals involved in the sex trade. SNUG coordinator Kari Thomason's usual shift starts late at night so she can check in with her "girls" and "guys" throughout the night in the streets in addition to conducting john bust operations with the police. In one night, she connects to about 25 women, men, and transgendered individuals to provide immediate assistance for safety planning, guidance, and support before bad dates happen and after bad dates occur. SNUG staff works to meet all individuals where they are in their journey and works hard to help individuals see their self-worth. The SNUG team builds positive, non-judgemental relationships with high-risk individuals who are marginalized and stigmatized in the communities. Individuals involved in the SNUG program often suffer from complex trauma and feel the effects of intergenerational trauma. Because SNUG staff works from a trauma-informed, harm-reduction approach, the team is able to provide guidance for individuals to exit the sex trade and help end the intergenerational cycle of abuse and trauma. SNUG provides ongoing supports to individuals and can assist with food, clothing, basic needs, counselling, advocacy, addictions guidance, emotional support, and a variety of community referrals to secure further support and services.

Kari has been honoured with numerous community awards and featured in documentaries by *The Fifth Estate*, *CTV*, *BBC*, and *CBC*.

INDIGENOUS OVERREPRESENTATION IN THE CRIMINAL JUSTICE AND CHILD WELFARE SYSTEMS

The concept of overrepresentation in these systems can be directly linked to the historical trauma experienced by the Indigenous population. In the last 10 years, corrections have reported a 53% increase in the incarceration of Indigenous people in Canada.[12] This overrepresentation is also related to the victimization of the Indigenous population. An Indigenous person is seven times more likely to be murdered in Canada than a non-Indigenous person, and two to three times more likely to be the victim of assault, sexual assault, or robbery.[20,21] An RCMP inquiry into missing and murdered Indigenous women showed that from 1990 to 2016, 16% of all murdered women in Canada were Indigenous.[22] This is a gross overrepresentation, as Indigenous women comprise only approximately 4.3% of the population.[23]

In 2011, Indigenous children under 15 comprised 7% of all the children in Canada; however, they represented 48% of all the foster children in the country.[24] Tragically, history repeats itself from residential school to foster care, group homes and prison, where the police are seen as the system's agents who take away the freedoms of Indigenous people. This massive overrepresentation indicates a deeper underlying issue of victimization and trauma. This trauma at a young age contributes to many issues in adulthood, such as a broken identity, mental health issues, addiction, ongoing victimization, criminality, and gang association.

GANG PHILOSOPHY

A **gang** is a group of three or more individuals existing for at least one month who engage in criminal activity on a regular basis that benefits the gang—along with gang representation by colours, tattoos, and an insignia symbol.[25]

Gang violence is a serious concern across Canada. When we try to define what a gang is, we often respond with adjectives such as criminal, violent, teenage, armed, and so on. However, there are numerous misunderstandings about what gangs are, how they attract new recruits, how to deal with gangs at the community level, and how members can escape the gang lifestyle. From a community perspective, street gang violence is not directed at the public—in most cases violence is a result of attempts to settle financial scores between rival gangs.[25]

A number of studies have tried to identify the primary motivations for joining a street or prison gang. Some of these reasons include a search for identity and belonging—family problems may push young people into gangs that promise excitement, loyalty, protection, and a "substitute family" that offers a near-endless supply of money, drugs, and sexual partners to its members.[26] Other psychosocial factors include exposure to crime, family members already in gangs, histories of sexual or physical abuse, and a lack of success in other areas of life (e.g., school).[27] These factors, and others not listed, seem to be prime motivators as to why an individual would want to choose a lifestyle affiliated with gangs.

Gang life, for many, seems glamorous and attractive from the outside; however, this notion is soon replaced by the sombre reality on the inside. The typical gang member spends a considerable amount of time "hanging out," looking for excitement and regaling members with past war stories. Gang and non-gang youth found that gang members were significantly more likely to hang out, attend parties, cruise, and fight when contrasted with their non-gang counterparts.[28]

Indigenous-based street gangs are the purest form of street gang in the Canadian context. **Indigenous-based gangs** identify with Indigenous culture and have a high population of persons of Indigenous descent. The history of these gangs can be traced to the early 1980s, with humble beginnings in Winnipeg, Manitoba. The necessity or need for belonging to something was a strong driving force in these early gangs, which mostly began by committing small crimes and eventually graduated to robbery, drug trafficking, and murder. There is a strong argument that oppression, bias, and systemic racism in multiple systems assisted these gangs in recruiting and retaining membership. From the 1980s to the present, there have been ebbs and flows in gang activity in Canada, but there has been consistent activity in prison settings. The overrepresentation of Indigenous persons incarcerated in Canadian facilities has led to a strong recruiting ground. Gang recruitment is done through senior members convincing recruits that they are oppressed, constantly stereotyped, and manipulated. Recruits are quick and eager to conform to gangs in order to secure safety, belonging, and status. Indigenous street gangs identify themselves with colours and often wear them on track suits, hoodies, ball caps, and bandanas. The bandanas are referred to as rags and are a sign of membership in the gang. In addition to gang colours, various tattoos are utilized to depict gang membership and affiliation.

Indigenous street gangs are loosely structured organizations, and there are several ways to increase one's standing within the groups; one of them involves how long you are "down for the group," which means how long you have been around. Another factor is what kind of an earner you are for the gang; basically, how much money you make by criminal means. Doing federal prison time is also a way to establish oneself in the gangs. The structure and culture of these organizations make it very difficult for police, as gang members are reluctant to speak to police in any official capacity. If you cooperate with the police, you become an informant or a rat, and in the street and prison subculture, a rat is the lowest form of criminal. The nature of criminality and the expectation of criminal behaviour in these organizations, coupled with the opportunistic nature of violent criminality, make infiltration and investigations a challenge for police agencies.

Many Indigenous children are born into families associated with gangs. Young children often join gangs in early adolescence because their parents struggle with addiction issues and are absent—siblings often join gangs to financially provide for their family members, and gang culture is something they are familiar with.[2,9] Deciding to leave a gang is often not easy. Respondents in one study suggest that environmental supports play a large role for those who wish to leave or have left a gang. The provision of information about funding options for education and employment programs and support programs (e.g., counselling, mentorship, and job search) is critical.[2,6] Ideally, anyone wishing to leave this kind of lifestyle is encouraged not to return to this same toxic environment. However, that becomes a difficult predicament, as it involves numerous factors, such as peer pressure, relationships, employment status, racialized oppression and stigma, a lack of healthy choices as a result of undiagnosed mental disorders, poor education, and addiction-related problems.[2,9]

Case Study: Gang Honour

On November 25, 2017, at approximately 3:00 p.m., Russel entered a small Winnipeg mall with his friends Ashley and Dakota. Once inside, they headed over to the payphone where Ashley made a call. While all three were standing there, Brandon started to walk past the group and Russel made a comment. A verbal confrontation erupted between Brandon and the other three. Brandon pulled a knife out of his pocket, stepped back, and flashed the Indian Posse gang sign. The verbal confrontation continued to escalate and Brandon stepped back a bit further—pulling a sawed-off rifle from his bag. Brandon loaded the firearm and pointed it at the group of three.

Russel became even more verbally aggressive with Brandon, daring him to shoot. At this point, Brandon came right towards the group, more specifically towards Russel, levelled the firearm, and fired a single shot, hitting

continued

Russel in the forehead and killing him instantly. Previous to this incident, Brandon had not been identified by the Winnipeg Police as a member of Indian Posse or any other Indigenous gang. He was unknown to police, but stated he was representing Indian Posse during the incident and because of gang code could not back down.

Questions
1. What gang dynamics played a role in this incident and influenced Brandon's behaviour?
2. Other than gang involvement, what other factors play a role in this incident?

HEALING: A BALANCED LIFESTYLE

Many impoverished people lose hope, become angry, or simply give up.[29] Emotional trauma, including inter-generational trauma, being disconnected from others by displacement, identity loss, and family break-ups seem to be major triggers for the addiction and underlying mental illnesses found in Indigenous communities today.[1]

When an individual, group, or community is traumatized, humans still try and maintain connections and bonds with others. This seems to be hard-wired in us—after all, human beings are social animals. Usually, socioeconomically deprived areas will see gangs appearing in various communities. The implementation of gangs may be another way of connecting and bonding with others, but it also produces adverse and negative consequences for the individuals involved and the community at large.

A key principle for maintaining a healthy mental state is a balanced lifestyle. This is extremely important for personal growth, for continuity in maintaining/forming healthy relationships, and for overall wellness, which incorporates mental, physical, emotional, and spiritual dimensions. The concept of the **Medicine Wheel** has been used by North American Indigenous cultures for hundreds of years. According to some cultures, the universe is always trying to maintain a state of harmony and balance, and these include polarities (e.g., day and night, the seen and unseen). Life cycles (i.e., baby, youth, adult, and elder) signify the cycles of the four seasons and the four directions, showing intricate and connected dimensions in all areas of the world and life. This model also illustrates the four directions of human growth—the emotional, mental, physical, and spiritual[30]—with the addition of a social circle.

The Emotional Quadrant:
- Love, control, acceptance, understanding, discipline, privacy, relationships, etc.

Examples include "having control over my feelings," and "accepting that I may have some bad days."

The Mental Quadrant:
- Thoughts, ideas, concepts, habits, education, training, etc.

Examples include breaking old habits and forming new ones, or gaining a better education for a better quality of life.

The Physical Quadrant:
- Air, water, food, shelter, rest, fitness, safety, intimacy, a nurturing environment, etc.

Examples include fostering intimate relationships with others for emotional well-being, or leaving a toxic environment to start a better life and form new relationships.

The Spiritual Quadrant:
- Reconnecting to cultural roots and questioning why we are here, and the meaning of life

Spirituality is distinct from religion (although the two domains may overlap). It focuses on connecting to higher powers, building self-esteem, creating healthy boundaries, making connections with others, and pursuing goals. In order to embrace a life free of drugs, alcohol, or other behavioural addictions, individuals must begin to change their thinking by what may be called a gaze inward. A gaze inward often begins by asking yourself a question: Why am I always engaging in this kind of behaviour? In attempting to answer this question, we must understand the word's true implications. This may be achieved by reconnecting with family (roots) and personal values and replacing hopelessness with faith.[31] Becoming honest allows us to show our vulnerabilities. When we foster illusions of grandeur—an absence of fear, pain, or suffering—we sweep all our issues under a rug and continue to self-medicate, resulting in what may be referred to as a **spiritual malady**, a condition that eventually consumes our entire being.

At the centre of these four quadrants is another smaller circle representing balance. To create a balanced lifestyle, we need to incorporate all the quadrants listed above to achieve a life free from addiction or negative-producing behaviours. Having too much or too little of any quadrant in our lives will upset this balance.

The Social Circle:

An expansion of this wheel involves adding a circle around the entire wheel to represent social support, including a continuity of health care and additional resources to draw upon. Examples include love, care, and respect from family, friends, and professionals, as well as respect from the larger community. This also involves removing negative language and stigma around substance use in order to create positive discussions. These discussions and the removal of stigma may, for example, include expanding and integrating with health-promoting organizations such as Recovery Day, National Addictions Awareness week, and Mental Health Awareness week. This is an excellent opportunity for those afflicted with mental and substance use disorders to go out and use their voice to raise awareness, support, and remove the stigma attached to addiction and other mental disorders. Over the past few years, numerous First Nations such as the Wapekeka, Attawapiskat, and Cross Lake have declared a state of emergency due to the vast number of attempted and committed suicides over a short period of time in communities of 400, 2,800, and 6,000 members, respectively.[32] Within these small communities, there have been approximately 300 suicide attempts and 23 suicides, the youngest being a nine-year-old, within a one-year span. One factor that brings resiliency to the community is the notion of family, belonging, and love, especially when welcoming a newborn. A baby symbolizes a fresh start, hope, and love, and gives meaning to individuals, as they are now responsible for caring for another human being.

The social circle can also be represented by learning new skills, for example playing an instrument, and physical well-being through groups, for example running clubs, playing softball, rock-climbing, etc. Spiritual growth may also be enhanced through taking yoga or art classes. All these areas expand out from the Medicine Wheel to form other connections for a better-balanced lifestyle. For people afflicted with mental health disorders, there is a wide range of support groups to join, sharing stories of strength and hope and passing those along to others.

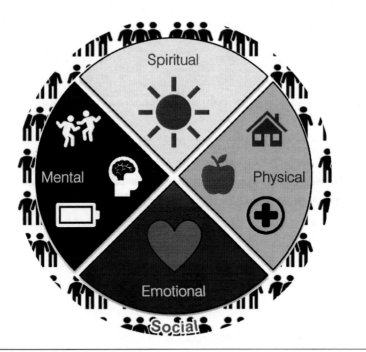

Figure 14.1: Medicine Wheel

Source: : Indigenous Culture – creation is original authors work – Peter Jensen and Uzma Williams.

Case Study: Troubled Beginnings

Dason's early childhood was not perfect, but, regardless, he was happy and had a mom who loved him and provided for him and his sister Cheyenne, who was three years older. The way Dason's mom was able to provide was through turning tricks and selling drugs, and, because of this, Dason clearly remembers that when he was eight the police came to take him and his sister away. The two were initially placed in foster care together, and the pair went from home to home and both suffered physical, sexual, and mental abuse. While this was happening, Dason's mom turned to addiction, as did his sister. By the age of 11, Dason and his sister were separated because she had run away and began living on the streets. When his mom was murdered when he was 13 years old, Dason's life hit rock bottom. He became involved in addiction, crime, and violence. During the next six years, his sister was always in and out

continued

of the hospital due to her addiction to alcohol and other drugs. At one point, Dason began turning his life around and was working to change it. Unfortunately, it was at this time that Cheyenne died of an overdose at the age of 24. Dason once again hit rock bottom and began associating with a gang. He describes a darker side of himself and of gang life by relating how older gang members would send him on jobs to collect drugs, giving him money, drugs, and praise. Later, he started living on the streets, sleeping at other peoples' houses on floors and sofas. Other people would always be coming and going, bringing drugs and taking them. Dason confesses that he was "scared, angry, and broken," but he had to put on a good front and show no fear. When he was committing a crime, he often would just react for his own security. He recounts how his mental health deteriorated and he has attempted suicide multiple times.

Question

1. How can the Medicine Wheel be used to heal Dason in each quadrant, and also the social circle?

BIAS AWARENESS IN POLICE COMMUNICATION

Implicit biases (conscious level) and **explicit biases** (unconscious level) exist for everyone. Our life experiences, our perceptions, and the environments in which we are raised, as well as media influences and the socialization of our significant and generalized others, impact our biases. For police, some bias is developed prior to becoming officers, while some can be developed or further confirmed based on what we see and hear on a daily basis.

Some police agencies have policies against discrimination and stereotyping; unfortunately, such policies pose difficulties because everyone has biases. What is necessary is bias awareness. Police officers must maintain a level of neutrality to be effective at their jobs. This neutrality offers the possibility of looking for and determining the truth while seeking justice. Every story has three sides: that of the complainant or victim, that of the offender, and the thin line in the middle: the unbiased truth.

When police communicate with Indigenous individuals, neutrality must come through. There is already a potential bias against the police for being agents of the state that have for so long had a negative impact on the community.

The concept of social othering arises for the Indigenous population, and as such their members often experience bias and racism in day-to-day life, making these individuals more acutely aware of when they are being treated unfairly. Communication using neutrality—without prejudgement and with a genuine desire to arrive at the truth—is of the utmost importance. The only way the police can be a neutral, effective investigative body is to start by being aware of biases.

EXPLORING HOW TO REDUCE THE CHALLENGES BETWEEN POLICE AND THE COMMUNITY

The history of colonization, residential schools, the Sixties Scoop, and overrepresentation of Indigenous people in the criminal system create a barrier for Indigenous people to seeing the police as legitimate power holders. This barrier has a definite impact on offending behaviour as well as victimization. Tom Tyler and colleagues'[33-35] research on police legitimacy shows that if the police are seen as a legitimate power holder, people offend less and are more inclined to report victimization. Although it is impossible to undo the harm done to Indigenous Peoples, the police must prove they are not the same agents they were when colonization began.

Hundreds of years of interactions have created this tumultuous relationship, and now the relationship must be restored. The only way to accomplish this is through open and honest communication between the Indigenous community and the police. Police must first and foremost have an understanding of the issues that the community faces as a result of history. This includes trauma, vicarious trauma, Fetal Alcohol Spectrum Disorder, poverty, etc. Failing to understand these and other issues can only result in failed relationships.

One of the constant failings of police agencies in communicating with communities is their tendency to tell people what to do to be healthy, rather than to ask the community what they require to be supported. In communicating with community groups or individual members, it is vital to ask the question, "What do you need from the police?"

The Indigenous community is often considered a vulnerable population, and delving into the statistics on victimization and predation confirms that vulnerability. One of the key concepts in communicating with vulnerable people and populations is to allow them to see your vulnerability, and this can be done at the individual or organizational level. When speaking one-on-one to a person in crisis, it is acceptable for police officers to share a situation that exposes their own vulnerabilities to the individual. From an organizational perspective, it is necessary to expose police vulnerability to increase trust with communities. With Indigenous Peoples, admitting that the police played a significant role in the trauma of their community opens doors to communication, as in many ways the issue is a shared one.

In order to effectively communicate with Indigenous people, there must be a genuine desire on behalf of the police to actually communicate. The historical impacts of a system that has not been honest or forthcoming with the Indigenous population is well known. Failing to genuinely acknowledge and express issues will cause further deterioration of the relationship, rather than build it up.

SUMMARY

The history of Indigenous communities in Canada is one of trials and tribulations that have caused significant issues in dealing with the police and the justice system for too many years. Indigenous people from coast to coast face significant historical and cultural challenges that often lead them to come into contact with the justice system.

All addictions and crime-related behaviours have a history attached to them. There are stories behind each act of what society views as deviant behaviour. Many of these stories are steeped in trauma, poverty, and isolation. The alarming number of Indigenous individuals being apprehended and incarcerated in correctional systems has a significant and staggering effect on the population. Indigenous populations over time have higher levels of incarceration, in part because of the federal government's implementation of the residential school system (est. after 1880) and continued segregation through the Indian Act of 1876, and because Indigenous cultures have been marginalized or swept away by the dominant culture's laws, languages, and technology, adding to the assimilation process. All these events have, over time, precipitated what we see today: widespread poverty and isolation for many Indigenous cultures (and other marginalized groups) throughout Canada. The police are often the agents of the state; they take away the freedom of the individual based upon criminal investigations, or they assist child welfare agents in removing children from the home. The socioeconomic impact on Indigenous and other groups has produced psycho-emotional trauma—a major symptom of mental illness, including addiction, which we see today.

Society's attitudes and perceptions of the dysfunctional side of its culture need to change in such a way that we can begin to replace fear with trust, hopelessness with hope, hatred with love, and a pinch of compassion thrown in as represented in the Medicine Wheel.

REFLECTION QUESTIONS

1. What attempts at reconciliation has the Canadian government made with Indigenous Peoples? Have these efforts been effective? Discuss.
2. What are some key causes that perpetuate intergenerational trauma?
3. Considering the high representation of Indigenous people in gangs and working in the sex trade, how can culture be used for them to understand and break out of these life cycles for the sake of future generations?
4. How would you incorporate the Medicine Wheel to understand others and assist in their healing?

REFERENCES

1. Gone JP. Redressing First Nations historical trauma: theorizing mechanisms for Indigenous culture as mental health treatment. Transcultural Psychiatry. 2013 Oct;50(5):683–706.
2. Fournier S, Crey E. Stolen from our embrace: the abduction of First Nations children and the restoration of Aboriginal communities. Douglas & McIntyre; 1997.
3. Boyce J, Rotenberg C, Karam M. Mental health and contact with police in Canada, 2012. Juristat: Canadian Centre for Justice Statistics. 2015 Jan;1:1.
4. Etches V. Addressing substance misuse in Ottawa: Ottawa Board of Health [Internet]. March 18, 2013 [cited 2018 May 28]. p. 4–5. Available from: http://ottawa.ca/calendar/ottawa/citycouncil/obh/2013/03-18/report%20c.pdf
5. Rehm J, et al. The cost of substance abuse in Canada 2002. Ottawa: Canadian Centre on Substance Abuse (CCSI); 2006 March. p. 1–12.
6. Brochu S, et al. Drugs, alcohol, and criminal behaviour: a profile of inmates in Canadian federal institutions. Forum on Corrections Research: Focusing on Drugs and Alcohol. 2001 Jan;13(3).
7. Payne J, Gaffney A. How much crime is drug or alcohol related? self-reported attributions of police detainees. Trends and Issues in Crime and Criminal Justice. 2012 Jun(439):1.
8. Shore K, Lavoie JA. Exploring mental health-related calls for police service: a Canadian study of police officers as "Frontline Mental Health Workers." Policing: A Journal of Policy and Practice. 2018 Apr 5.
9. Correctional Service Canada. CSC statistics – key facts and figures [Internet]. [cited 2018 June 2]. Available from: http://www.csc-scc.gc.ca/publications/005007-3024-eng.shtml
10. Sartorius N. Iatrogenic stigma of mental illness: begins with behaviour and attitudes of medical professionals, especially psychiatrists. British Medical Journal. 2002 Jun 22; 324(7352):1470–1.
11. Public Safety Canada. Corrections and conditional release statistical overview (see figure C9) [Internet]. 2016 [cited 2018 June 5]. Available from: https://www.publicsafety.gc.ca/cnt/rsrcs/pblctns/ccrso-2016/index-en.aspx#c9

12. Malakieh J. Adult and youth correctional statistics in Canada, 2016/2017 (Table 5). [Published 2018 June 19; cited 2018 June 29]. Catalogue no. 85-002-X [Internet]. Available from: https://www150.statcan.gc.ca/n1/pub/85-002-x/2018001/article/54972-eng.htm

13. Beauvais F. American Indians and alcohol. Alcohol & Research World. 1998; 22(4):253–9.

14. Savchenko M, Bokhan N, Plotnikov E. Analysis of alcohol dependence in Indigenous Peoples in Northern Siberia. Archives of Psychiatry and Psychotherapy; 2015. p. 14–20. DOI: 10.12740/APP/58735

15. Truth and reconciliation Canada. Honouring the truth, reconciling for the future: summary of the final report of the Truth and Reconciliation Commission of Canada. Winnipeg: Truth and Reconciliation Commission of Canada; 2015.

16. Brown v. Canada (Attorney General), 2018 [cited 2018 June 30]. ONSC 3429 (CanLII) [Internet]. Available from: http://canlii.ca/t/hsm3g

17. Indian Act, R. S. C. 1985 c I-5 [cited 2018 June 30] [Internet]. Available from: http://canlii.ca/t/5333k

18. Hackett C, Feeny D, Tompa E. Canada's residential school system: measuring the intergenerational impact of familial attendance on health and mental health outcomes. J Epidemiol Community Health. 2016 May 11;70(11).

19. Nowlan B. Intervention through interdiction: Project "SNUG" – a collaborative, community initiative in Edmonton, Alberta designed to permanently remove women from street prostitution using law enforcement, intervention and education. 2007.

20. Brennan S. Violent victimization of Aboriginal women in the Canadian provinces, 2009. Juristat: Canadian Centre for Justice Statistics. 2011 Jan 1:1D.

21. Boyce J. Victimization of Aboriginal people in Canada, 2014. Juristat: Canadian Centre for Justice Statistics. 2016 Jun 28:1.

22. Royal Canadian Mounted Police. Missing and murdered Aboriginal women: a national operational overview; 2014.

23. Arriagada P. First Nations, Métis and Inuit women. Statistics Canada; 2016.

24. Turner A. Living arrangements of Aboriginal children aged 14 and under. Statistics Canada/Statistique Canada; 2016.

25. Eurogang consortium. In: Wortley S, Identifying street gangs: definitional dilemmas and their policy implications. Public Safety Canada; 2012.

26. Chalas DM, Grekul J. I've had enough: exploring gang life from the perspective of (ex) members in Alberta. The Prison Journal. 2017;97(3):364–86. DOI: 10.1177/0032885517705312

27. Muller RT. The trauma and mental health report [Internet]. [cited 2018 June 4]. Available from: https://www.psychologytoday.com/us/blog/talking-about-trauma/201308/poverty-broken-homes-violence-the-making-gang-member

28. Yearwood D, Hayes R. Overcoming problems associated with gang research: a standardized and systemic methodology. Journal of Gang Research. 2000 Summer;7(4):1–8.

29. VICE. The aboriginal gangs of Winnipeg [Internet]. 2011 July 11 [cited 2018 June 29]. Available from: http:// https://www.vice.com/en_ca/article/4w74eq/the-aboriginal-gangs-of-winnipeg-141

30. Coyhis D. The red road to wellbriety: in the Native American way. Colorado Springs: White Bison; 2002.

31. Nechi Training, Research and Health Promotions Institute. Student manual: CAT 2,5,6. St. Albert, Canada. 2010. Revised 2013.

32. First Estate. Cross Lake: this is where I live [Internet]. April 7, 2017. [cited 2018 June 29]. Available from: Nechi Training, Research and Health Promotions Institute. Student manual: CAT 2,5,6. St. Albert, Canada. 2000, 2010. Revised 2005, 2011, 2013.
33. Tyler TR, Huo Y. Trust in the law: Encouraging public cooperation with the police and courts. Russell Sage Foundation; 2002 Oct 10.
34. Mazerolle L, Antrobus E, Bennett S, Tyler TR. Shaping citizen perceptions of police legitimacy: a randomized field trial of procedural justice. Criminology. 2013 Feb 1;51(1):33–63.
35. Sunshine J, Tyler TR. The role of procedural justice and legitimacy in shaping public support for policing. Law & Society Review. 2003 Sep 1;37(3):513–48.

CHAPTER 15

NCRMD Legal and Ethical Issues

Courtney J. Hunt, *Forensic Psychiatry, Alberta Hospital Edmonton*

John R. Reddon, *Department of Psychology, University of Alberta and Forensic Psychiatry, Alberta Hospital Edmonton*

Andrew M. Haag, *Alberta Health Services, University of Alberta Psychiatry Department*

Salvatore B. Durante, *Alberta Hospital Edmonton*

LEARNING OBJECTIVES

1. Explain the origins and evolution of the Not Criminally Responsible on Account of Mental Disorder (NCRMD) defence in Canada
2. Understand the NCRMD legal process and the factors affecting it, including the review board process
3. Differentiate between absolute discharge, conditional discharge, and custodial detention
4. Report the characteristics of NCRMD offenders and the factors affecting recidivism rates and treatment among NCRMD offenders
5. Recognize the implications of the recent Bill C-14 on NCRMD cases
6. Describe the ethical concerns that have been raised about NCRMD cases

INTRODUCTION

In Canada, section 16 of the Criminal Code declares that "no person is criminally responsible for an act committed or an omission made while suffering from a mental disorder that rendered the person incapable of appreciating the nature of and quality of the act or omission or of knowing that it was wrong."[1,2] This defence is referred to as **Not Criminally Responsible on Account of Mental Disorder** or the NCRMD defence. Due to the intersection of the mental health system and the criminal justice system regarding the NCRMD defence, it is important that individuals working in the criminal justice system understand the NCRMD population, the origins of the defence, and the process that goes along with claiming that defence. Due to a recent deinstitutionalization movement in Canada, persons with mental illness are becoming overrepresented in the criminal justice system, and, thus it is becoming even more important that criminal justice workers such as police officers obtain an in-depth understanding of the individuals who have both criminal justice issues and mental health system needs.[2]

ORIGINS AND EVOLUTION OF NCRMD IN CANADA

The NCRMD defence has been present since 1843, when the House of Lords in England responded to the M'Naghten case.[3] There are multiple spellings for M'Naghten, but we have chosen this particular one.[4,5] Worldwide, the insanity defence has been present in some form for much longer than 1843. For instance, it was not acceptable to hold offenders with a mental illness criminally responsible under Roman law, and custody was used as a safety measure rather than as a punishment.[6] In Europe, a call for a standardized and generalized theory of insanity as a defence from criminal liability was called for in the twelfth century and three main tests were developed in the nineteenth century to diagnose insanity for legal reasons.[4] These tests included the good and evil test, the wild beast test, and the right and wrong test. However, it was in England in 1843 that Daniel M'Naghten, intending to shoot the British prime minister, shot and killed the prime minister's secretary, Edward Drummond.[6] M'Naghten was subsequently acquitted by reason of insanity using the right and wrong test. This led to the presentation to the Court of five questions to determine insanity by the House of Lords, which ultimately resulted in the M'Naghten rules becoming the modern basis for the definition of insanity as a legal defence.[6]

In Canada, there have been several major reforms of the NCRMD defence.[7] Bill C-30 was passed in 1992, in response to R. v. Swain,[8] which ruled that indefinite detention of NCRMD offenders was unacceptable, making it a more attractive option to defence teams.[7,9,10] In 1999, the ruling of the Supreme Court in R. v. Winko[11] held that detention of persons found to be NCRMD can only be established when the NCRMD accused is found to pose a significant threat to society; otherwise the NCRMD accused is entitled to receive an absolute discharge.[10] In 2011, the Supreme Court ruled in the case of R. v. Bouchard-Lebrun[12] that a substance-induced psychosis is not eligible for a defence of NCRMD. It should be noted that this interpretation of self-induced intoxication is consistent with section 33.1 of the Criminal Code[13] that also addresses this issue. The most recent changes to the NCRMD defence have resulted from Bill C-14, the *Not Criminally Responsible Reform Act*, receiving royal assent in 2014. The four major changes that have resulted from Bill C-14 will be discussed later in the chapter.

LEGAL PROCESS OF NCRMD IN CANADA

Once an individual has been found to be NCRMD, the case must be reviewed by a forensic mental health tribunal known as a **Criminal Code Review Board** (RB).[14] Review boards can be defined as "independent tribunals established to determine dispositions of accused found unfit to stand trial or NCRMD."[15] They must take into consideration case law and the Criminal Code of Canada when making their disposition, with an ultimate goal of simultaneously protecting both the safety of the public and the rights of the individual found to be NCRMD.[14] RB hearings are held at least once a year to determine a disposition that is most appropriate for the accused.[14,16] The three dispositions that are available to RBs to consider in their decision-making process are custodial detention, conditional discharge, and absolute discharge, each of which will be explored in more detail in the next section.

From the time of the initial verdict, a review board must hear a case within 45-90 days.[7] In making their decision, RBs have access to multiple sources of information, including charge information, trial proceeding transcripts, victim impact statements, criminal and clinical histories of the NCRMD accused, risk assessment tools, diagnoses, results of psychological and neurological tests, results of laboratory tests, social assessments, the person's family history, and a recommendation by a hospital.[7,10] Each RB must comprise at least three to five members, two of which must be a chairperson who is a practicing or retired judge and a psychiatrist. The remaining members can be a psychologist, a social worker, or a lay person from the public.[7,14] Many factors are considered by the members of the RB when deciding on a disposition, and it has been found that static factors (e.g., gender, psychiatric history, severity of the offence) are more likely to influence the decision of the RB early in the process, while dynamic risk factors (e.g., non-compliance with RB decision or with medication, or suicidal ideation) have more of an influence later in the process.[16] The factors that influence the RB's decision have been found to fall into one of three categories: the NCRMD accused's behaviour, mental health, and reintegration into society.[17] Some of these factors include the threat to the safety of the public, the clinical need of the individual, and the chance of rehabilitation of the NCRMD accused.[14] After all available information and contributing factors have been considered, the RB then decides on the disposition that best protects both the safety of the offender and of the public.[14,16]

While participants have considered the review board process respectful and fair, some offenders have expressed concerns with the process. These concerns include feeling that their participation was constrained, that excessive forms of punishment were used, and that there were tensions among the various interests of the multiple parties involved.[14] Victims have also made complaints against the process, stating that there is a lack of justice and that they are the "forgotten party" in the system.[18] Both the well-being of the NCRMD accused and the victim must be considered when deciding on a disposition, and thus it is important that victims feel as if their voices are being heard in the review board process. Some ways of increasing the participation of victims in the process include delivering information to the victim quickly, maintaining respectful communication with criminal justice personnel when interacting with victims, ensuring that information is readily available, and ensuring the implementation of restorative justice measures throughout the process, such as the use of victim impact statements.[18]

DISPOSITIONS IN NCRMD CASES

There are three dispositions for review boards to choose from when deciding on a verdict for an offender who has been found to be NCRMD: 1) custodial detention, 2) conditional discharge, and 3) absolute discharge.[1] **Custodial detention** refers to a disposition whereby the offender will be detained in an area of custody, such as a psychiatric hospital.[16] When offenders receive the disposition of **conditional discharge**, they are released with the stipulation that they comply with certain conditions.[16] For instance, offenders may have to live in a specified place, abstain from the consumption of alcohol or drugs, follow specific treatment recommendations, and/or abide by travel restrictions.[17] **Absolute discharge** of an NCRMD offender means that the offender can be fully released from custody with no conditions or legal restrictions.[16] Under Section 672.54 of the Criminal Code, the review board must take into consideration "the need to protect the public from dangerous persons, the mental condition of the accused, the reintegration of the accused into society, and the other needs of the accused."[1,15] Deciding on a disposition is not a straightforward task, and review board members must take a multitude of factors into consideration when making their final decision.

Dispositions tend to be referred to review boards in approximately 82.2% of cases, and despite the presence of at least three to five other members on the board, psychiatrists tend to have the most influence on the disposition decision.[19] All members of the RB must take into consideration several factors when deciding on a disposition. One of the factors playing a role in the disposition process is whether the offence was violent. For instance, it has been found that offenders who committed nonviolent offences are more likely than sexual or violent offenders to receive an absolute discharge.[19] There are multiple risk assessment tools that can be used to measure risk for violence, including actuarial estimates based on historical risk factors, and tools, such as the Historical-Clinical Risk Management (HCR-20), that use static and dynamic risk factors to assess the risk of short-term violence.[20] Factors that have been found to decrease the likelihood of an absolute or conditional discharge include a higher number of past offences, a diagnosis of a psychotic spectrum disorder, and a more severe index offence.[19] The use of risk assessment tools throughout the review board process affects the disposition, as it has been found that using a structured risk assessment throughout the process results in a higher likelihood of the offender receiving a conditional discharge.[16]

CHARACTERISTICS OF NCRMD OFFENDERS

Both those who have been involved in the criminal justice or have mental illness system face stigma and prejudice.[21] Therefore, it should come as no surprise that NCRMD offenders who intersect the mental health and criminal justice systems face misperceptions and stigmas from various areas of society. These misperceptions cross into the judicial system and can affect the attitudes jurors have towards offenders who are attempting to use a NCRMD defence in court.[21] These misperceptions have been found to be especially true for offenders diagnosed with a substance abuse disorder who make up approximately one-third of NCRMD offenders.[22] Thus it is clear that the typical profile and characteristics of an NCRMD offender are not common knowledge.

Because every individual offender is different, it is not accurate to say that all NCRMD offenders share the exact same characteristics. However, studies have found characteristics that tend to be common among NCRMD offenders. For instance, the following characteristics tend to be shared by mentally-disordered accused: severe mental illness resulting in previous hospitalizations, a tendency to be treatment resistant or non-compliant, the presence of Fetal Alcohol Syndrome/Fetal Alcohol Effects (FAS/FAE) or other neurodevelopmental issues, adverse childhood experiences, substance abuse, intoxication at the time of the offence, and substance abusing parents.[10] It has also been found that less than 1 in 10 NCRMD offenders have been accused of homicide, many have had no prior contact with the criminal justice system, less than 1 in 10 are homeless, few are in supervised residences, and NCRMD rates are far lower for the Indigenous population than general rates in the criminal justice system.[23,24] Women also have low rates of NCRMD offending, and make up only 15.6% of the NCRMD population.[22]

The NCRMD patient population has been compared to several other populations who are involved in both the mental health and criminal justice systems, including the **Mentally Ill Prisoner** (MIP) population and the **Incarcerated Severely Mentally Ill** (I-SMI).[25,26] The main difference between the NCRMD population and the MIP and I-SMI populations is that those in the NCRMD population are not seen as being criminally responsible for the offence, while those in the other populations have been held criminally liable and are incarcerated as punishment for their offence. When compared to the MIP group, NCRMD patients were found to be less assaultive, less self-destructive, and to have lower rates of polysubstance abuse and psychopathic traits, suggesting that the NCRMD group may be easier to manage than the MIP group.[25] Both groups were also found to have different factors that predisposed them to violence.

When compared to a group of Incarcerated Severely Mentally Ill individuals, NCRMD offenders were found to be more likely to experience bipolar disorders or schizophrenia, while the I-SMI offenders were more likely to experience psychotic/delusional disorders not otherwise specified (NOS) or major depression.[26] NCRMD offenders were also found to have more schooling, fewer violent and non-violent crimes, fewer self-aggressive behaviours, and a lower prevalence of Cluster B personality disorders (borderline, narcissistic, histrionic, antisocial) and psychopathic traits. Comparisons between NCRMD offenders and offenders who have criminal culpability for their crimes show a clear distinction between NCRMD offenders and other offenders with a mental illness.

Along with the characteristics of the offenders themselves, the nature of the offences that NCRMD offenders typically commit has also been studied. Only 1 in 10 NCRMD offenders is accused of an offence involving a homicide or an attempted murder, despite the high level of media coverage of such cases.[23] Two out of three offences were found to be against the person, with a family member the most likely victim of such offences.[23] Of these offences against the person, half were found to be assaults and half included minor assaults, property offences, and other non-violent violations of the Criminal Code.[23]

Serious violent offences such as homicide, attempted murder, and sexual offences are rare among the NCRMD population, with less than one in 10 offences committed by an NCRMD offender representing a sexual or violent offence.[24,27] Despite the rarity of such offenders, they do exist and have characteristics that are distinct from the rest of the NCRMD population. NCRMD offenders accused of homicide have been found to be less likely to have comorbid conditions and have the lowest rates of recidivism.[27] Offenders accused of a sexual offence were found to be predominantly male, have higher rates of past offences and recidivism, and a higher likelihood of violent recidivism and a violent past.[27] As with other NCRMD offenders, the victims of serious violent offences are likely to be family members of the offenders rather than strangers.[27]

RECIDIVISM RATES AND TREATMENT

While recidivism rates may be higher among those who have committed non-violent offences,[27] it is important that all NCRMD accused are offered the appropriate treatment to lower their risk of recidivism in the future. The National Trajectory Project (NTP) in Canada found that the three-year recidivism rates in British Columbia, Ontario, and Quebec were 17% following the index offence that led to the NCRMD verdict, 20% following a conditional discharge, and 22% following an absolute discharge.[28] It should be noted that the recidivism rates among NCRMD offenders after discharge are significantly lower than the recidivism rates among general offenders and inmates with a mental disorder who were not found to be NCRMD.[28] Studies have identified multiple factors that affect risk of recidivism, including criminal history, psychiatric diagnosis, and the nature of the index offence that led to the NCRMD ruling,[28] with criminal history remaining one of the most important factors.[16] Substance abuse and a prior conviction have been found to increase risk of recidivism,[22] and those who committed a more serious crime are less likely to reoffend than those who committed a less serious crime.[28]

Despite the low rates of recidivism among the NCRMD population, individuals who reoffend after discharge are nevertheless a significant problem. It has been found that NCRMD offenders who are re-hospitalized after discharge are more likely to be younger, diagnosed with a schizophrenia-spectrum disorder, have engaged in a concerning behaviour since the hearing, and are less likely to have a diagnosis of a personality disorder.[17] Similarly, those who were detained after discharge were found to be more likely to have had a psychiatric history before the NCRMD hearing.[17] While rates are extremely low, recidivism also happens among offenders who committed a serious violent offence, with sexual offenders having a higher rate of general and violent recidivism than other violent offenders.[27]

While there are factors that increase risk of recidivism, there are also multiple factors that play a role in lowering recidivism risk. These factors fall into three main categories: demographic, psychosocial, and mental health factors.[16] The demographic factors associated with success include being Caucasian, being employed, and being married.[16] The psychosocial factors include having a minimal criminal history as well as a minimal level of violence prior to the offence.[16] The primary mental health factor associated with minimizing likelihood of recidivism is the adequate provision of mental health services to NCRMD accused;[16] therefore, it is crucial that such offenders be offered treatment as part of their recovery plan regardless of their disposition.

One common aspect of the trajectory of NCRMD individuals through the RB system is readmission into a treatment facility after they have already been discharged. Reasons for readmission tend to be the presence of questions regarding an offender's ability to receive adequate treatment in the community or the offender's use of alcohol or drugs after discharge.[29] When people are readmitted to the hospital after discharge, their stays tend to be brief and preventative in manner, lasting for only a few days or a few weeks at a time.[29] Patients may also voluntarily readmit themselves to a hospital; this is evidence of good judgement and self-management on the part of the individual and does not represent failure.[29]

Among those who receive treatment after an NCRMD verdict, schizophrenia tends to be the most common diagnosis, along with a variety of other diagnoses such as personality disorders and substance abuse.[29] Among Canadian NCRMD patients in treatment, 30% to 45% were found to have had prior contact with the criminal justice system for minor offences, two-thirds were found to have prior hospitalizations, and 35.4% were already in a treatment program before they committed the index offence that led to their NCRMD verdict.[29] Men and women have been found to have different needs when it comes to treatment, with women more suited to community levels of treatment after discharge and presenting with fewer criminogenic needs than men.[30] Thus, female NCRMD offenders may be more successful with less intensive therapy than male NCRMD offenders, as well as benefit from different management strategies.[30] The motivational influences behind an offender's actions have also been found to have important treatment implications for violent offenders who are diagnosed with a serious mental illness.[3] Understanding the motivational

influences behind an NCRMD accused's actions helps in distinguishing between actions that are driven by symptoms and actions that are driven by other
factors such as anger, lust, and poverty.[3]

Treatment among NCRMD offenders is not always successful, and outcomes
such as recidivism and fatality can occur. The fatality rate among NCRMD offenders has been found to be quite high, with the reasons for such high rates
possibly being an increased prevalence of unhealthy lifestyle behaviours, side
effects of psychotropic medications, and poor access to mental health services.[31]
To reduce patient fatality and create more successful treatment programs for
NCRMD offenders, treatment services should offer better follow-up care as well
as better organized services that focus on the complex factors contributing to
patient fatality and recidivism, instead of trying to narrow in and focus on a
single cause.[31]

IMPLICATIONS OF BILL C-14 ON NCRMD IN CANADA

In 2013, Bill C-14, also known as **The Not Criminally Responsible Reform
Act**, was passed in Canada and made several major amendments to the NCRMD
defence.[7] This bill was met with much controversy and criticism, as it has major
implications for the NCRMD defence in Canada. The NCRMD defence is
already misperceived by the public, as high-profile cases such as that of Vince Li
can exacerbate the negative aspects of the NCRMD defence, causing the public
to believe misperceptions, such as the idea that offenders are released very early,
that many are faking their condition to obtain a lighter sentence, and that the
defence is overused.[7] The "tougher-on-crime" approach of Bill C-14 may partially be the result of the media's inaccurate portrayal of individuals with severe
mental illness as being violent;[28] therefore, it is important that the implications
of the Bill be fully understood.

The influx of immigrants into Canada from numerous countries is an additional complexity for the criminal justice system.[32-34] Immigrants generally
come from different cultures with different values and languages—often with
varying degrees of exposure to trauma.[32,33] This is evidenced by the documented
association between migration and serious mental illness.[34] Moreover, immigrants may be deported for their crimes without subsequent treatment for their
trauma and/or other mental disorders.[32,33]

The amendments created by Bill C-14 can be divided into three main categories: 1) the alteration of the wording of review board dispositions, 2) the
creation of a high-risk designation, and 3) changes in the involvement of victims

in the process.[2,9,35] In terms of the wording of dispositions, "least onerous and least restrictive" has been replaced with "necessary and appropriate," and the safety of the public has been stated as being the "paramount consideration" of the defence, with the well-being of the offender a secondary concern.[2,7,35] The new **high-risk accused** (HRA) designation may be based solely on the index offence of the accused, ignoring other factors that may contribute to risk of recidivism.[7] This designation is meant for NCRMD offenders convicted of a serious personal-injury offence of a violent nature and is meant to protect the public from potentially dangerous offenders.[7] Offenders with this designation are not eligible to receive the conditional discharge or absolute discharge dispositions and are limited to detainment in a hospital setting.[7] The Bill also aims to increase the involvement of victims in NCRMD cases through several measures, including notifying victims of the offender's residence after discharge and the consideration of victim impact statements in court or review board hearings.[7]

Aside from the area of Bill C-14 that promotes victim involvement, most of the amendments have been met with criticism and controversy.[7] Mental health organizations, including the Canadian Psychiatric Association, were not consulted during the drafting process of the Bill, and existing evidence does not support the idea that Bill C-14 will improve the safety of the public.[7] Criticisms of the Bill include the following: it does not address the provision of adequate mental health services to prevent such offences from occurring; the new HRA designation may deter defendants from using the defence; the provisions may decrease the safety of the public; and the HRA designation may impinge upon offenders' rights and freedoms under the Charter.[7]

In terms of the future implications of Bill C-14, the HRA designation has been argued to be potentially problematic for NCRMD accused.[7] The HRA designation does not accurately reflect recidivism risk because there is more to the risk of recidivism than the index offence alone. Hence, the HRA designation may impact treatment delivery and inadvertently prevent offenders from receiving the appropriate treatment.[7] The HRA designation also limits the access of offenders to community supports and a review board's disposition options, leaving them only with the option of custodial detention, limiting the freedom of the offender.[22] The "tougher-on-crime" approach may not only limit the freedom of NCRMD accused, but may also support misperceptions that already exist regarding the NCRMD defence, thus promoting negative attitudes towards offenders diagnosed with a mental illness.[35] The media already falsely portrays people with mental health disorders as being a violent population, and Bill C-14 may only exacerbate these existing misperceptions, further disadvantaging offenders found NCRMD and limiting their access to treatment. Therefore, it should come as no surprise that Bill C-14 has not been met with a high degree of support and has prompted much criticism and controversy.

ETHICAL CONCERNS SURROUNDING NCRMD

Several arguments have been made against insanity defences in general, as a response to the ethical issues that surround the nature of the defence. Gerben Meynen addresses nine of these arguments in his book *Legal Insanity: Explorations in Psychiatry, Law, and Ethics*.[36] The first argument he addresses is that assessing a past state of mind is too difficult because mental state changes over time, and it is impossible to go back in time and assess the state of mind of offenders while they were committing the offence. Meynen counters this by stating that though it may be difficult, it is done all the time in both psychiatry and law. One may also argue that **expert testimony** (i.e., qualified professional) is indirect and only complicates legal judgement. However, Meynen counters that expert testimony is used in law constantly and is not confined to insanity cases. Another argument is that claiming an insanity defence is only for the rich, as most defendants will not be able to afford to use the defence in court. Meynen counters that while this may be true, financial resources will benefit a defendant in any area of the law, not simply in insanity cases. There is also the issue of whether the partiality of the mental health experts providing testimony affects the case, as the professional may be biased in one direction or the other. While this is a real concern, Meynen argues that it can be prevented with the proper implementation of professional ethics, training, and health law. It can also be argued that the criteria of insanity defences are under debate and, therefore, the defence is not well-established enough to be viable in court. Though this may be true, Meynen states that this is not a valid argument, for many areas of criminal law are under debate.

Along with these arguments that criticize the legal basis of insanity defences, Meynen discusses arguments that relate more to the defendants using the defence rather than to the legal processes of the defence itself.[36] For instance, many are concerned that the use of the insanity defence undermines deterrence of crime, as offenders may believe they can get away with a crime by claiming the defence. However, as Meynen points out, there is no clear empirical support for this claim, and even if it proves to be the case, the defence likely also results in an increase in the belief of the fairness of the legal system. Similarly, it has been argued that defendants who deserve to be held responsible for their crimes may fake psychological symptoms to avoid legal punishment. However, successful insanity defences are so rare that it is unlikely many defendants are getting away with faking their symptoms, and psychiatric professionals should be able to detect signs of faking. There is also the issue of the insanity defence creating stigma among the offenders who claim the defence and the mentally ill population in general. While Meynen agrees that stigma is a very real issue, he does not believe that this argument provides sufficient grounds to get rid of the defence, as mentally ill populations face stigma from other areas as well. Lastly, many critics argue that the insanity defence is "too rare to be worth the trouble," but the real issue is the fairness of the legal system and not the defence's rarity.[36] While Meynen believes that the above arguments lack sufficient empirical evidence to support removing the defence from the legal system, he also believes that they are valid criticisms; therefore, efforts should be made to understand these areas of weakness and make sure they are taken into consideration.

Along with these arguments against the insanity defence, Meynen also addresses several ethical concerns that surround the insanity defence in all its forms, including Canada's NCRMD defence. These concerns include remembering the boundary between psychiatry and law, who should carry the **burden of proof**, what the standard of proof should be, and the issue of reliability of the defence.[36] Regarding the boundary between psychiatry and law, it is important to understand that insanity is a legal term and the defence is legal in nature, not medical.[35] Therefore, it is important that an insanity defence act as a bridge between psychiatry and law, allowing psychiatric professionals to stay away from the legal domain.[36] The burden of proof shifts between legal systems, with some jurisdictions placing the burden of proof on the defendant and some on the prosecution. It is important to remember that the burden of proof that refers to which side must prove that an NCRMD verdict is called for can appropriately be placed on the defendant only if the defendant is competent to stand trial.[36] There is also the issue of **standard of proof**. For instance, should it be proven "beyond a reasonable doubt," or "by clear and convincing evidence?" Meynen believes that the standard of proof should not be as rigid as "beyond a reasonable doubt," but instead be "by a preponderance of the evidence." Lastly, a major ethical issue surrounding the insanity defence is its level of reliability. Therefore, as reliability is an issue with all insanity defences, all measures should be considered that could increase this reliability.[36] For instance, some believe that assessing offenders' knowledge and appreciation of their offence can be more reliably tested than their ability, or lack thereof, to control the actions that led to the offence.[36]

Case Study: Joe's Breakdown

Joe is a 39-year-old male who lives in Cape Breton. Joe was noted to have nearly died at birth due to hypoxia. Joe's parents are divorced and both abuse intoxicants. Joe's mother was once hospitalized for "involutional melancholy" for two months. Joe has one sister that he has not seen in years. He sees his parents about twice a year. He does not like his step-father. Joe was first hospitalized at the age of 18 for two weeks with a diagnosis of schizophrenia. After this discharge, Joe was re-hospitalized on five occasions for as long as four months. Joe's employment history has been sporadic. Joe has, however, maintained employment for the past year on a part-time basis at a bottle recycling facility. He needs support from social services to ensure that his rent is paid on time. Joe has been incarcerated on five occasions for the following offences: (1) indecent exposure (public urination), (2) assault, (3) public mischief (running naked in the street screaming that the aliens are coming), (4) failure to appear in court, and (5) failure to comply with recognizance.

One day Joe was walking in downtown Cape Breton. Joe was hearing voices that told him to smash a window in order to prevent the apocalypse. After smashing the window, Joe stood at the scene and screamed that Satan was around the corner. A passerby told Joe to "shut up." Joe got mad and struck the passerby. Joe was charged with mischief in relation to the window and assault for striking the passerby. Police that were on bicycle patrol in the downtown area arrested Joe almost immediately after his striking the passerby.

Questions

1. What biopsychosocial factors in Joe's life have negatively impacted his mental health?
2. Would Joe be eligible for an NCRMD defence for the charge of mischief?
3. Would Joe be eligible for an NCRMD defence for the charge of assault?
4. If you were the arresting officer, what kinds of observations would be important for you to note?
5. What programming/support/treatment would be optimal to assist Joe in avoiding recidivism?

SUMMARY

The NCRMD defence refers to individuals who are Not Criminally Responsible on Account of Mental Disorder, and the Criminal Code of Canada states that "no person is criminally responsible for an act committed or an omission made while suffering from a mental disorder that rendered the person incapable of appreciating the nature of and quality of the act or omission or of knowing that it was wrong."[1] Insanity defences have existed around the world in some form since Roman times, and the NCRMD defence has been present in the United Kingdom since 1843 and in Canada since 1867. Review boards comprise at least three to five members who must decide on a disposition for offenders who have been found to be NCRMD; dispositions include 1) custodial detention, 2) conditional discharge, and 3) absolute discharge. The NCRMD defence and insanity defences in general involve ethical issues; therefore, it is important that the weaknesses of the defence be understood and considered when making amendments to the defence. Bill C-14 is one such amendment and, while its goal is to protect the public, the Bill has mainly been met with criticism from professionals in psychiatry and law. Because those in the police force are part of Canada's criminal justice system, it is important that individuals working in this field understand the NCRMD defence, its legal proceedings, and its implications for the criminal justice system in Canada.

REFLECTION QUESTIONS

1. What is a review board and what are the three dispositions that are available to review boards when dealing with an NCRMD case?
2. What are some of the factors that review boards must consider when making a disposition in an NCRMD case?
3. What is Bill C-14, and what are some of the major implications of the Bill on NCRMD cases in Canada?
4. What are some of the ethical issues surrounding the NCRMD defence in Canada and other insanity defences around the world?
5. What are some of the misperceptions regarding the mentally ill population in general and those who are found to be NCRMD?
6. What is the major difference between offenders found NCRMD and mentally ill offenders who are incarcerated?

REFERENCES

1. Criminal Code, R. S. C., 1985, c. C-46.
2. Crocker AG, Nicholls TL, Seto MC, Côté G. The national trajectory project of individuals found not criminally responsible on account of mental disorder in Canada. The Canadian Journal of Psychiatry [Internet]. 2015;60(3):96–97. Available from: https://www.ncbi.nlm.nih.gov/pmc/journals/2444/
3. Penney SR, Morgan A, Simpson AI. Motivational influences in persons found not criminally responsible on account of mental disorder: a review of legislation and research. Behavioral Sciences and the Law. 2013;31:494–505. DOI: 10.1002/bsl.2067
4. Diamond BL. On the spelling of Daniel M'Naghten's name (reprinted from Ohio state law journal 1964 vol 25 no 1). Daniel McNaughton: his trial and the aftermath. UK: Gaskell Books; 1977. p. 86–90.
5. Schneider RD. The lunatic and the lords. Toronto: Irwin Law; 2009. p. 29.
6. Hallevy G. The matrix of insanity in modern criminal law. Switzerland: Springer International Publishing; 2015.
7. Lacroix R, O'Shaughnessy R, McNiel DE, Binder RL. Controversies concerning the Canadian not criminally responsible reform act. The Journal of the American Academy of Psychiatry and the Law [Internet]. 2017;45(1):44–51. Available from: https://www.ncbi.nlm.nih.gov/pubmed/28270462
8. The case of R. v. Swain [Internet]. 1991. Available from: https://www.canlii.org/en/ca/scc/doc/1991/1991canlii104/1991canlii104.html
9. Schneider RD. The mentally ill: how they became enmeshed in the criminal justice system and how we might get them out. Research and Statistics Department of the Department of Justice, Canada. 2015.
10. Steller S. Special study on mentally disordered accused in the criminal justice system. Catalogue no. 85–559. Ottawa: Statistics Canada. 2003. 33 p.
11. The case of R. v. Winko [Internet]. 1999. Available from: https://www.canlii.org/en/ca/scc/doc/1999/1999canlii694/1999canlii694.html
12. The case of R. v. Bouchard Lebrun [Internet]. 2011. Available from: https://www.canlii.org/en/ca/scc/doc/2011/2011scc58/2011scc58.html
13. Criminal Code, R. S. C., 1985, c. C-46: Section 33.1: Self-induced intoxication [Internet]. p. 51-2. Available from: http://laws-lois.justice.gc.ca/eng/acts/C-46/section-33.1.html
14. Livingston JD, Crocker AG, Nicholls TL, Seto MC. Forensic mental health tribunals: a qualitative study of participants' experiences and views. Psychology, Public Policy, and Law. 2016;22(2):173–84. DOI: 10.1037/law0000084
15. Crocker AG, Nicholls TL, Seto MC, Côté G, Charette Y, Caulet M. The national trajectory project of individuals found not criminally responsible on account of mental disorder in Canada. Part 1: context and methods. The Canadian Journal of Psychiatry [Internet]. 2015;60(3):98–105. Available from: https://www.ncbi.nlm.nih.gov/pmc/journals/2444/
16. Crocker AG, Nicholls TL, Charette Y, Seto MC. Dynamic and static factors associated with discharge dispositions: The national trajectory project of individuals found not criminally responsible on account of mental disorder (NCRMD) in Canada. Behavioral Sciences and the Law. 2014;32:577–95. DOI: 10.1002/bsl.2133
17. Wilson CM, Nicholls TL, Charette Y, Seto MC, Crocker AG. Factors associated with review board dispositions following re-hospitalization among discharged persons found

not criminally responsible. Behavioral Sciences and the Law. 2016;34:278–94. DOI: 10.1002/bsl.2220

18. Quinn J, Simpson AIF. How can forensic systems improve justice for victims of offenders found not criminally responsible? The Journal of the American Academy of Psychiatry and the Law [Internet]. 2013;41(4):568–74. Available from: https://www.ncbi.nlm.nih. gov/pubmed/24335331

19. Crocker AG, Charette Y, Seto MC, Nicholls TL, Côté G, Caulet M. The national trajectory project of individuals found not criminally responsible on account of mental disorder in Canada. Part 3: trajectories and outcomes through the forensic system. The Canadian Journal of Psychiatry [Internet]. 2015;60(3):117–26. Available from: https://www.ncbi. nlm.nih.gov/pmc/journals/2444/.

20. Crocker AG, Braithwaite E, Côté G, Nicholls TL, Ceto MC. To detain or to release? Correlates of dispositions for individuals declared not criminally responsible on account of mental disorder. The Canadian Journal of Psychiatry. 2011;56(5):293–302. DOI: 10.1177/070674371105600508

21. Mossière A, Maeder EM. Juror decisions in not criminally responsible on account of mental disorder trials: effects of defendant gender and mental illness type. International Journal of Law and Psychiatry. 2016;49:47-54. DOI: 10.1016/j.ijlp.2016.05.008

22. Baillie P. A valuable (and ongoing) study, the national trajectory project addresses many myths about the verdict of not criminally responsible on account of mental disorder. The Canadian Journal of Psychiatry [Internet]. 2015;60(3):93-95. Available from: https:// www.ncbi.nlm.nih.gov/pmc/journals/2444/

23. Crocker AG, Nicholls TL, Seto MC, Charette Y, Côté G, Caulet M. The nationally trajectory project of individuals found not criminally responsible on account of mental disorder in Canada. Part 2: the people behind the label. The Canadian Journal of Psychiatry [Internet]. 2015;60(3):106–16. Available from: https://www.ncbi.nlm.nih.gov/pmc/ journals/2444/

24. Haag AM, Cheng J, Wirove R. Describing the not criminally responsible population in Alberta's history: sociodemographic, mental health, and criminological profiles. Journal of Community Safety & Well-Being. 2016;1:68–74.

25. Sreenivasan S, Kirkish P, Shoptaw S, Welsh RK, Ling W. Neuropsychological and diagnostic differences between recidivistically violent not criminally responsible and mentally ill prisoners. International Journal of Law and Psychiatry. 2000;23(2):161–72. DOI: 10.1016/S0160-2527(99)00040-0

26. Dumais A, Côté G, Larue C, Goulet M-H, Pelletier J-F. Clinical characteristics and service use of incarcerated males with severe mental disorders: a comparative case-control study with patients found not criminally responsible. Issues in Mental Health Nursing. 2014;35:597–603. DOI: 10.3109/01612840.2013.861885

27. Crocker AG, Seto MC, Nicholls TL, Côté G. Description and processing of individuals found not criminally responsible on account of mental disorder accused of "serious violent offences." Research and Statistics Department of the Department of Justice, Canada. 2013.

28. Charette Y, Crocker AG, Seto MC, Salem L, Nicholls TL, Caulet M. The national trajectory project of individuals found not criminally responsible on account of mental disorder in Canada. Part 4: criminal recidivism. The Canadian Journal of Psychiatry [Internet]. 2015;60(3):127–34. Available from: https://www.ncbi.nlm.nih.gov/pmc/ journals/2444/

29. Luettgen J, Chrapko WE, Reddon JR. Preventing violent re-offending in not crimi-
    nally responsible patients. International Journal of Law and Psychiatry [Internet].
    1998;21(1):89–98. Available from: https://www.ncbi.nlm.nih.gov/pubmed/9526718

30. Nicholls TL, Crocker AG, Seto MC, Wilson CM, Charette Y, Côté G. The national tra-
    jectory project of individuals found not criminally responsible on account of mental
    disorder. Part 5: how essential are gender-specific forensic psychiatric services? The
    Canadian Journal of Psychiatry [Internet]. 2015;60(3):135–45. Available from: https://
    www.ncbi.nlm.nih.gov/pmc/journals/2444/

31. Fazel S, Fiminska Z, Cocks C, Coid J. Patient outcomes following discharge from secure
    psychiatric hospitals: systematic review and meta-analysis. The British Journal of Psy-
    chiatry. 2016;208:17–25. DOI: 10.1192/bjp.bp.114.149997

32. Pain C, Kanagaratnam P, Payne D. The debate about trauma and psychosocial treat-
    ment for refugees. In: Simich L, Andermann L, editors. Refuge and resilience: promoting
    resilience and mental health among resettled refugees and forced migrants. Springer;
    2014. p. 51–60.

33. Joseph AI. Deportation and the confluence of violence with forensic mental heath and
    immigration systems. London: Palgrave Macmillan; 2015.

34. Kokona A, Tarricone I, DiForti M, Carra E. Cannabis, migration and psychosis. In:
    Handbook of cannabis and related pathologies. Academic Press; 2017. p. 79–88.
    DOI: 10.1016/B978-0-12-800756-3.00010-7

35. Maeder EM, Yamamoto S, Zannella L. Putting negative attitudes on the agenda? Not
    criminally responsible reform act publicity and juror decision-making. International Jour-
    nal of Law and Psychiatry. 2016;49:154–9. DOI: 10.1016/j.ijlp.2016.08.010

36. Meynen G. Legal insanity: explorations in psychiatry, law, and ethics. Switzerland:
    Springer International Publishing; 2016.

CHAPTER 16

Letters to Policing Professionals

Kyle L. Klein, *Concordia University of Edmonton*

In this chapter, we conclude the book with a compilation of letters from individuals with mental health struggles or family members who have loved ones who struggled with mental disorders. These individuals have had interactions with the law and would like to share their past experiences. The participants describe their own mental health condition and how it played a role in their interaction with policing services and police officers. These individuals explore what went well, what could have gone better, and what did not go well in their dealings with the law. These letters can be used as a reflection to provide an understanding of and empathy with people impacted by mental health. They can also provide advice on how to interact with individuals when problems arise.

LETTER 1

Dear Reader:

My name is Leif Gregersen. I currently work for the Schizophrenia Society as a "lived experience" presenter of information about mental illness and I have written two books about my journey from being a very ill young man to being a middle aged success story (insofar as one can be considered a success when they have a chronic mental illness). I have been diagnosed with bipolar disorder, schizoaffective disorder, and anxiety. Though the more serious side of my illness is well controlled with medications, I still have to deal with side effects of medications and a mind that is not completely balanced.

In my work with the Schizophrenia Society, I am called upon to speak to each new class of Police Recruits. I think part of the reason I was chosen to present to these people is that I spent three years in the Air Cadets and then 15 plus years as a security guard. I have had several brushes with the law while I experienced mental health episodes.

My illness, undiagnosed, was the worst when I was 18. One day, my best friend came and picked me up to give me a ride and for some odd reason I was talking nonsense and laughing at things that weren't funny. For some reason, though I had never done them much at all, I was also saying that I needed to "get some drugs." My mind at the time had fooled me into thinking that drugs were a natural and essential part of fitting in, and the reason I hadn't had many friends or girlfriends was that I hadn't used them.

My friend took me to the local hospital, where two police officers held me while I was given an injection of major tranquilizers, and then I was taken to a psychiatric hospital. At this time, I was so far gone that I honestly feel the police officers couldn't have done anything other than what they did. It may have been nicer if they had told me what type of medication I was being injected with and where I was being taken, but it simply didn't happen. I can't say whether these officers had a poor opinion of people with mental illnesses or not. I can say it was extremely distressing to be taken to a place I had never even had an inkling of and being locked into a place that was almost hellish in nature.

After a few short weeks of treatment, I responded well to medications and left the hospital. Sadly, I didn't take my medications and there was little to no follow-up when I went home. A few days later, amidst a few other situations, I got into a fight in school and was taken to the school office. I was non-compliant with the school administrators, who didn't understand why a person who had no history of fighting in four years of high school would suddenly "snap" in this way. Two RCMP officers arrived shortly and told me to come with them. I had enough knowledge of the law to realize that this meant I was under arrest and had planned to leave quietly. The problem came when I was taken out in the hall and there in front of me were dozens of students, all peers, silently watching me being taken out of my school. My heart cried out from the very pits of my soul that things were going to end for me this way, and I knew all hope of saving face was gone. I pushed, yelled, and fought the two officers all the way down that hallway. If only they had somehow found a way for me to leave with my dignity, so much grief could have been avoided.

I don't count myself as perfect, or those RCMP officers as wrong. I was taken to get the help I needed, but for me to be pulled out of my school, locked away for months, put on debilitating amounts of tranquilizers, and repeatedly punished like a rat in a cage in Alberta Hospital—it was enough for me to want to end my own life.

So, one of the things I would like police to understand is that a couple of kind words, a little bit of reassurance that a psychiatric patient is still a human being, can go a long way. About a year and a half after the previous incident, I found myself living in Vancouver. I was ill at the time, had been off my medications, and was in a terrible state. I was staying at a traveller's hostel, where I rented a bed and I had a dream so real and disturbing I thought that in some way it had really happened. I went for a walk to clear my head and delusional thinking hit me from every direction. These interruptive thoughts told me I wasn't a human being, I was a robot, that I wasn't in Vancouver but in a replica of Vancouver in the future, and that all I had known and all the people I had cared about were long gone. Part of me desperately wanted help, and the other part of me wanted to walk to the Lion's Gate Bridge and jump into the icy water 100 feet below. I had no idea at that point how to get help and I was incredibly ashamed about my mental illness.

What I finally did was to phone the police and tell them I thought someone had put hallucinogenic drugs in my food. That was the only way I could avoid being blamed for being just another mentally ill person. The cop that responded was a very nice guy, and he took me to a hospital where I got help for my illness.

In another incident however, while working as a security guard, a woman with a severe mental illness came up to me, afraid someone was chasing her, and I tried to help. The police were in pursuit of her and I witnessed one officer take her down with a full football tackle when he could have just taken a few more steps and restrained her with much less chance of injury.

A few weeks ago, I was going to a hospital to visit a family member and I ran into a police officer who remembered me from his training class. He was an incredibly nice guy and told me that just that day alone he had responded to two mental health calls and that he couldn't believe how much what I and my co-workers told him had helped him to do his job. If I were to make a suggestion, I would say that guest speakers with lived experience in mental illness should be utilized in every police cadet class and criminology course in this country: it really could do a lot of good.

Overall, what I feel that police need to do when faced with a person with a mental illness is, of course, if they are a danger to themselves or others, handcuff them, but it should be emphasized that they are certainly not any lower form of human life and should not be mistreated or dehumanized. They should be spoken to and one should try to relate to them, give them confidence that they are going to get help, not punishment.

There is also something that I try to address carefully if I can when I speak to police cadet classes. I like to try and say that it is extremely important to re-humanize and respect people with mental illnesses because they are not just strange faces out there thrown at random in our path. Police cadets are a group of people who will suffer more than their share of mental illness. It is very common for police, who are under a great deal of work strain, to develop Post-Traumatic Stress Disorder, alcoholism, depression, and many other illnesses inherent to their line of work. And when I end my lecture to the class, I always love to quote the dispatcher from one of my favourite old cop shows, "Hill Street Blues": "and hey—let's be careful out there."

Sincerely,
Leif

Leif is the award-winning author of 10 books, including two memoirs of his battle with mental illness. Contact Leif at www.edmontonwriter.com

LETTER 2

Dear Reader,

I am a person who has been living with a mental disorder for most of my life. I was diagnosed with bipolar disorder in my twenties (15 years ago now), which has given me time to reflect on incidents and situations that have happened to me throughout my life. I have always wondered how my mental health "breaks" or "episodes" could have been dealt with better by me and by professionals.

Looking back now there's one incident that stands out in my mind. I was 17 and very confused about life. I acted out a lot and couldn't understand why my mood was so unstable. I attended high school and was a very distant person. Mental illness wasn't always as upfront and acknowledged as it is nowadays—even though there is still a long road ahead. Also, not knowing that you have a mental illness and acting out the way I had, made me question my sanity in this situation. Anyway, I was having an episode and got asked to leave class. I started pacing the halls, angry and confused, questioning why this was even happening in the first place. The constable at our school approached me and started asking me what I was doing, why I was in the hallways, and why I was walking up and down looking at lockers. I felt so attacked, mainly because of his attitude, tone, and manner. I tried to explain I just needed space. I just needed my own time when irritated and emotional. I'm sure it just came off as somebody trying to make excuses or the ramblings of some big kid that just got caught. I didn't know how to take how he was talking to me, but I did understand he was doing his job. I understand that now, as a 35-year-old, but when you're 17 and a police officer starts confronting you, assuming that you're doing something wrong or plotting something, my response was defensive. I had an irrational fear of getting arrested, thrown in jail, and all other things that go through your mind as a young kid, similar to what you mostly see as negative experiences through the media, all of which made this situation worse.

He asked me to leave the school grounds. Being defensive for no reason, I said no. So he said that if I didn't comply, I would be removed from the property by force and expelled. I remember looking at him confused, wanting to explain that I was a student here and what I really needed was someone to talk to. I shouldn't have had to leave; I just needed a minute to get myself together. I was distraught with anger. I felt hurt that somebody who was supposed to be a protector or somebody you're supposed to go to for help was almost turning their back on me. I truly believe that if he had said, "Come to my office, let's figure out why are you feeling this way," things would have gone a lot differently that day. Unfortunately, for the rest of my school life, I was very standoffish with this constable of course, due to a rebellious teenage chip on my shoulder. How dare he judge me and make me feel like a delinquent, I thought, when all I was doing was trying to clear my mind. However, part of that is my fault because I had no idea what was going on mentally either. Again, it wasn't until my twenties that I was actually diagnosed with a mental disorder. Once you understand what's going on in your head and you deal with it either medically or by talking it out with somebody, you can start to feel more normal and more relaxed. I really hope that anybody who has to deal with a 17-year-old or a 50-year-old with a mental illness like bipolar disorder will know how to approach them. The person should be more understanding and figure out ways of addressing these issues without coming off as being aggressive or judgemental.

Sincerely,
Maria

LETTER 3

Dear Reader,

I was contacted first by my brother's friend early in the day asking me if I had spoken to my brother or knew his whereabouts, as the news was reporting that there had been a shooting, two bodies had been found, and footage of his home was being aired. I immediately started to scream and cry and called my sister-in-law, who said she would bring my parents, both of them elderly, to meet me at my brother's home. I arrived first and, worrying over my 80-year-old father who has diabetes, high blood pressure, and a host of other health-related issues, I ran up to the police and told them I was the sister and this home was in fact in my name. The police stated that they could not release any information about the bodies that were identified in the home and we were not able to go in. I begged the police officer to please tell me if it was my brother's body that was found in the home, as my elderly parents would be here any minute and it would be too traumatic for them if they did not know what had happened. The police refused, just repeating that they could not give any information at that time.

When my parents did arrive, my father was very emotional and things escalated. He was shouting at the police to allow him into his son's home to see his son. At one point my father pushed a policeman to get him out of his way and the policeman actually pushed my 80-year-old father back rather roughly. I wish the police had been more sympathetic and compassionate, especially when dealing with my father.

After waiting in our vehicles for some time, we were instructed to go to the police station. At the station, my other brother and I were both interviewed by detectives regarding my brother, but again while we wept, they would neither confirm nor deny whose body had been found. After answering all their questions, we were sent home and told to wait until they could confirm the identities. We returned home and sat in shock and disbelief, and every hour I continued to call the detective, asking if she could provide a confirmation. In our hearts, though, we already knew, especially with all the questioning centred around my brother. It was after midnight when the detective called to say she was very sorry but that my brother was one of the bodies that had been identified. Coming in person to confirm his death, even though it was in the middle of the night, would have been much better than a phone call informing us of one of the worst pieces of news in our lives.

In the days following, we had very little support from the Canadian Police Service. While we understood that they cannot share information that would compromise any leads in solving the case, I would contact them and ask for updates but was told absolutely nothing, not even words of hope or reassurance. I began to think that because my brother was well-known to the police, his death was not taken as seriously as a regular civilian death would be. You see, my brother had antisocial personality disorder. From a very young age, he began a criminal path and had convictions consisting of drug trafficking, carrying a concealed loaded and restricted firearm, and violent assaults, among many others. Most of his teenage years and adult life were spent in prison.

The day after the shooting, one of the contacts called to advise us that the cat in the home needed to go. For now, they had barricaded it in the basement, but we had only until the end of day to come and take it if we were planning on finding it a new home. While grieving for my brother, we had to scramble to find someone to take the cat and were able to pick it up from outside the home.

We were not allowed access to the home until five days later, and when we entered, it was in complete disarray, the scene of a murder with blood splatters on the wall, the mattress and carpet soaked in blood. My family and I have been quite traumatized in having to clean up the room where my brother and his girlfriend were murdered. I recall the mattress was still wet because it was soaked in their blood. While it may not be a current practice, I wish the police had had professionals clean up the bedroom where he died.

Victim services came out once, but when I called them for a particular reason, my calls were not returned. Time passed and unless it was me reaching out looking for any updates, I hardly heard from anyone from the Canadian Police Service.

I have respect for police, but they showed a clear lack of empathy during his investigation, so my final recommendation is a hope that police will be more emotionally responsive when dealing with family members who have just lost a loved one.

Karina

LETTER 4

Dear Reader,

Of all my experiences, my brother's death has had the most profound impact on my life. While I lost my brother in 2013, I think of him daily and it takes all my strength to tell his story because of the pain and sorrow that his loss brings.

My brother, Amir, and I grew up in a high-conflict home, often with only the bare essentials in the fridge. We didn't have much at all in our childhood, with our parents being on social assistance, but we had each other. My mother has emotional issues and my dad has organic brain damage, so our home was broken from the start.

My brother began struggling with severe clinical depression when he was 12 years old. Bullied at school, he began hanging out with the "bad" kids, where he fit in. Soon enough, his need for belonging, love, and friendship turned to more organized crime, especially by having other family members well vested into organized crime. The turning point in his life came when one of his best friends was murdered at 16 years old. At this point, Amir spiralled completely downwards, and he didn't care much for his own life from this point forward. He began engaging in more unlawful, risk-taking behaviours and with very dangerous people. At about 15 years old he was in and out of jail and his mental health further deteriorated. While there was no official diagnosis other than clinical depression, I have a hunch he struggled with a psychosis, and this was especially apparent when he was under stress because he stated time to time that he heard voices—and all the while not once did anyone reach out to talk to him about or help him with his mental health, including myself. I realize this now only in hindsight.

By his early 20s, crime was all he knew. His only saving grace was that he tried to do well in school, but he struggled, perhaps because he felt alienated or had difficulty concentrating because of his mental health issues. About the third time he got arrested, I remember being very sad but having a moment of realization that at least he is safer in jail than he is on the street, and all of a sudden there was a sort of relief.

When he was out of jail, he was often on house arrest. Especially while he was on house arrest, I did not worry about him having to leave at night and thinking if that is the last time I would see him. So, I would like to take this opportunity and thank the police for making him safe against himself and others, even though he was in jail or house arrest, he was at least alive and monitored. My last conversation with my brother occurred a couple days after he was released from house arrest. I asked him to stay out of trouble because every time he finished house arrest it was only a matter of months before he was back in jail since the police would constantly monitor him. Sadly, he was murdered at the age of 25, days after the last time he finished his last house arrest sentence.

I hope his story helps you realize that in the grand scheme of everything you do as police professionals, it is for the right reasons, especially when working towards the betterment of your profession. His favourite story of law enforcement that he brought up over and over was about a police officer who brought him a sandwich while he was in court. He spoke kindly of this police officer for many years because of the compassion the officer had showed. So, when times get tough and people are constantly belittling you with cusses and insults, please don't take it to heart. Know that you are doing your job, and everyone is thankful for you, including the family members of the perpetrators (and deep inside perhaps even the perpetrators). Thank you for your service and for letting me have my brother longer than I would have, had he not been supervised by police through all his struggles and troubles.

Uzma

GLOSSARY

Absolute Discharge: The offender can be fully released from custody with no conditions or legal restrictions. Under Section 672.54 of the Criminal Code of Canada, the review board must take into consideration "the need to protect the public from dangerous persons, the mental condition of the accused, the reintegration of the accused into society, and the other needs of the accused."

Accurate Diagnostic Skills: Investigating a problem prior to responding and attempting to treat it by gathering information from sources and taking time to deliberate before taking action.

Active Listening: A skill that emphasizes full attention and accurate listening by demonstrating interest and encouraging continued speaking.

Acute Stress Disorder (ASD): Characterized by the development of severe anxiety, dissociation, and other distressing symptoms that occurs within a month of exposure to a traumatic stressor such as witnessing a death.

Addict: Pejorative and stigmatizing label given to those who consume excessive amounts of psychoactive substances.

Addiction: A biopsychosocial condition that considers physical dependency, psychological dependency, and the social context of drug use, including the user's environment and culture. Can lead to a disorder that is progressive and chronic, that may compel the user to continue the use of the drug despite adverse biopsychosocial consequences caused by its use.

Adolescence-Limited Category: Involvement in crime is temporary and limited to one's adolescent developmental period. Comprises 95% of adolescents who are delinquent and is therefore considered normative rather than pathological.

Antidepressants: Pharmacological drug treatment options most commonly administered to treat unipolar depression.

Antipsychotic Medications: Medications that attenuate or eliminate psychotic symptoms; also called neuroleptic medications.

Antisocial Personality Disorder (ASPD): Pattern of disregard for, and violation of, the rights of others.

Apprehension: A disposition whereby the police officer takes into custody a person who is perceived to be experiencing a mental illness and an apparent risk to themselves or others and transports them to a mental health facility for evaluation by a physician.

Asexual: Individuals without an identified sexuality.

Asphyxiophilia: A subtype of sexual masochism disorder that involves sexual arousal related to the restriction of breathing.

Attention Deficit Hyperactivity Disorder (ADHD): A neurodevelopmental disorder marked by an inability to focus or concentrate, hyperactivity, and impulsive behaviour.

Avoidant Personality Disorder: Pattern of social inhibition, feelings of inadequacy, and hypersensitivity to negative evaluation.

Be "for" the Individual: Being "for" the individual does not mean you agree with them, only that you are taking their perspective seriously.

Behavioural Activation: A newer psychological treatment for depression that aims to decrease avoidance from social situations and increase involvement in activities shown to improve mood.

Behavioural Assessment: Measuring, observing, and systematically evaluating (rather than inferring) the client's thoughts, feelings, and behaviours in the context and situation.

Behavioural Influence Stairway Model (BISM): A recent model of crisis negotiation that emphasizes the relationship-building process between the officer and the person in order to facilitate behaviour change, culminating in a successful resolution.

Biopsychosocial Approach: Combined influence of biological, psychological, and social factors.

Bipolar Disorder (BPD): A mental disorder recognizable by cycling periods of mania and depression. Bipolar I involves mania and often depression; whereas, Bipolar II involves hypomania and depression.

Borderline Personality Disorder: Pattern of impulsiveness and instability in interpersonal relationships, self-image, and affect.

Burden of Proof: The obligation of the prosecution to provide evidence that will prove the claims made against the defendant in a trial.

Care: The serious attention or consideration applied to doing something correctly to avoid damage or risk.

Catatonia: An extreme exacerbation or lack of motor responsiveness to the external environment characterized by minimal or no movement, expressiveness, or communication.

Central Nervous System (CNS): Encompasses structures within the skull and spine called the brain and spinal cord, which are complex nerve tissues that control the activities of the body.

Chief Complaint: A precise statement describing the symptom, condition, diagnosis, problem, or other reason for an encounter with a medical professional.

Circumstantiality: Person talks all around an issue but never gets to a logical end or point.

Clarification: Ensures aspects of information have been divulged clearly and accurately by using open-ended and close-ended questions properly.

Clinical Assessment: Systematic evaluation and measurement of psychological, biological, and social factors in a person presenting with an apparent possible psychological disorder.

Clinical Interview: A tool or inventory that helps health practitioners and researchers make an accurate diagnosis of a variety of mental illnesses. There are two common types: structured clinical interviews and clinical diagnostic interviews.

Closed-Ended Questions: Questions a person can answer with a simple yes or no and can often seem like an interrogation that the interviewer is conducting, rather than a dialogue. Used to clarify contradictions and obtain specific information.

Cognitive Behavioural Therapy (CBT): A form of psychotherapy that attempts to change maladaptive patterns of thoughts, emotions, and behaviours.

Cognitive Processing Therapy (CPT): A form of cognitive behavioural therapy consisting of 12 sessions to treat trauma by assisting individuals with processing their emotions and confronting their beliefs about the traumatic incident and its effect.

Cognitive Impairment: Inability to perceive accurately or reason correctly about the outside world.

Collaborative Problem Solving: A psychosocial treatment approach that emphasizes shared responsibility and decision making between the client and the therapist. Collaborative problem solving focuses on improving the fit of the person with the demands of the environment and addressing skill deficits such as flexibility, adaptability, frustration tolerance, and problem solving.

Comorbidity: Two or more co-existing mental health disorders.

Compassion: Showing kindness to others when they are experiencing hardship.

Conditional Discharge: Individuals are released from custody with the stipulation that they comply with certain conditions. For instance, the offender may have to live in a specified place, abstain from the consumption of alcohol or drugs, follow specific treatment recommendations, and/or abide by travel restrictions.

Conduct Disorder (CD): A consistent pattern in childhood and adolescence that violates the basic rights of others or violates societal norms or rules. Commonly precedes antisocial personality disorder.

Confidentiality: The professional expectation that information about an individual will be treated with respect and that accessing or disclosing it will only occur in the proper course of your duties.

Continuum of Care: The range of treatment services provided to those, for example, with varying levels of addiction, from harm reduction to detoxification to community-based and residential treatment.

Coprophilia: Paraphilia characterized by sexual arousal to feces. May involve the individual performing the act on the partner or having the partner defecate on the individual.

Cortisol: A stress hormone produced by the adrenal cortex.

Criminal Code Review Board (RB): Independent mental health tribunals established to determine dispositions of the accused found unfit to stand trial or NCRMD.

Crisis Intervention Training: A multi-disciplinary approach that teaches officers about mental illness, substance abuse, verbal and non-verbal techniques, and risk assessment for responding and deescalating a mental health crisis.

Critical Incident Stress Debriefing (CISD): A group debriefing conducted within two to seven days after traumatic event exposure. Provides participants with social support, a sense of meaning, and mastery of the event—helping to facilitate symptom relief. CISD is only one component of CISM.

Critical Incident Stress Management (CISM): An individualized treatment that allows the individual to process and defuse the emotions tied to a work-related serious incident such as a traumatic event.

Cross-Dependence: The use of different drugs interchangeably in preventing withdrawal symptoms.

Custodial Detention: Refers to a disposition whereby the offender will be detained in an area of custody such as a psychiatric hospital.

Cyclothymic Disorder: Type of bipolar disorder characterized by periods of mild depression alternating with brief periods of hypomania.

De-escalation: Officers attempt to negotiate a peaceful resolution to ensure the proper disposition and care of the person.

Deinstitutionalization: The reallocation of people with disorders and disabilities from institutions and the provision of community-based accommodation and services.

Delirium: Rapid onset of confusion, typically about time, place, or memory, or an acute change in awareness of the environment, or a change in level of consciousness.

Delusion: Abnormality in thought content in which there is a fixed but false belief.

Dementia: A state of mind characterized by constant and worsening confusion about time, place, memory, and awareness of oneself and the environment.

Dependability: Refers to being reliable and following through with promises.

Dependent Personality Disorder: Pattern of submissive and clinging behaviour related to an excessive need to be taken care of.

Depressants: Psychoactive drugs that slow the body's metabolism and the functioning of both the central and peripheral nervous systems leading to changes in thought, affect, mood, and behaviour, include alcohol, antihistamines, barbiturates, benzodiazepines, inhalants, and solvents.

Depression: A disorder marked by intense feelings of sadness, which can present as irritability.

Diagnosis: In the realm of medicine and psychopathology, a determination or identification of the nature of a person's disease or condition, or a statement of that finding.

Diagnostic and Statistical Manual of Mental Disorders, 5th edition (DSM-5): Manual used by health care professionals in North America as the guide to the diagnosis of mental health disorders; containing descriptions, symptoms, and other criteria for diagnosing mental disorders.

Dialectical Behaviour Therapy (DBT): A form of treatment that involves reflection and education in which the individual learns about the disorder and themselves, including triggers and self-management.

Differential Diagnosis: Alternative diagnosis that explains the observed symptoms or patterns of the mental health disorder.

Dignity: Valuing the worth of an individual.

Disorganized Thinking: Abnormality in thinking process. The inability to logically sequence the thinking process.

Do No Harm: An ethical principle emphasizing a non-manipulative and non-exploitive approach.

Drug Abuse: Refers to any instance of drug administration that is disapproved of by the society in which it occurs and is often legally prohibited or restricted.

Drug Dependency: Consists of two distinct but connected processes—physical and psychological—that are perceived as necessary for the user, corresponding to addiction.

Drug Misuse: Refers to improper or inappropriate use of any drug (legal or illegal) and includes periodic or occasional use of either a social or a prescription psychoactive drug.

Dynamic Risk Factors: Factors that can increase the risk for an individual to re-offend. Dynamic factors, in contrast to static factors are often changeable within the person and as a result targeted as part of treatment. Examples include attitudes about sexual offending, social rejection, and negative emotionality.

Emotion Dysregulation Theory: Regarding criminality, proposes that antisocial behaviour and aggression arise in conduct disorder through abnormalities in neurobiological circuits involved in regulating negative emotions and processing environmental cues.

Empathetic Listening: A key feature of active listening that centres on the kind of attending, observing, and listening needed to develop an understanding of individuals and their world, and that is highly effective for interviewing.

Empathy: Relating to others and understanding their perspectives as fully as possible. In other words, it is "the individuals' social radar through which he or she senses others' feelings and perspectives and takes an active interest in their concerns."

Endogenous Depression: Occurs due to the presence of certain genetics or internal stressors and therefore is sometimes referred to as biologically based depression. Symptoms are physical in presentation, such as psychomotor disturbances and psychosis.

Escape-Avoidance Coping: Refers to modifying behaviour based on trying to avoid or escape particular emotions or thoughts. Examples include failure to discuss emotions, failure to seek professional assistance, social withdrawal, and self-criticism.

Etiology: Causes or origins, especially of disease or disorders.

Exhibitionism: Exposure of genitals to a non-consenting person—including fantasies and sexual gratification within this context.

Exogenous Depression (reactive or neurotic): Depression is considered to occur as a result of negative life stressors or traumatic event and is therefore a reaction to the environment.

Expert Testimony: Testimony in a trial provided by highly qualified individuals in their respective fields.

Explicit Biases: Refers to the attitudes and beliefs individuals possess about a person or group at a conscious level.

Exposure Therapy: Reintroduce individuals to the traumatic event that precipitated their trauma. The participant is often gradually reintroduced to the most intense event or stimulus.

Eye Movement Desensitization and Reprocessing (EMDR): Form of psychotherapy in which the client is asked to recall traumatic images while generating a bilateral sensory input, such as hand-tapping or side-to-side eye movements.

Fetal Alcohol Spectrum Disorder (FASD): Prenatal alcohol exposure that results in a wide range of brain abnormalities, such as intellectual disabilities, learning disabilities, impulsivity, behaviour disorganization, and physical abnormalities.

Fetishism: Consistent sexual urge, desire, interest, and arousal from the use of non-living objects to achieve sexual gratification

Frotteuristic Disorder: Rubbing genitals against a non-consenting person—including fantasies and sexual gratification within this context.

Gang: A group of three or more individuals existing for at least one month who engage in criminal activity on a regular basis that benefits the gang—along with gang representation by colours, tattoos, and an insignia symbol.

Gender Identity: The self-perception of one's gender.

Genuineness: Not overemphasizing the role you are in, avoiding defensiveness, and being open. Allows one to be authentic, honest, and sincere.

Grandiose Ideas: Pertains to the individual expressing an unrealistic sense of superiority.

Hallucination: Visual or audio experience of a sensory perception with no external stimuli present—seeing or hearing something that is not there.

Hallucinogens: A distinct family of psychoactive drugs that disrupt the messages being perceived in the central nervous system. These psychoactive substances produce radical changes in a person's mental state by creating a disconnect between the physical world and the user's perception of the physical world leading to sensory hallucinations. Members of this family of drugs include LSD, mescaline, and psilocybin.

High-Risk Accused (HRA): Component of the amendments made to Bill C-14. Designation based solely on the index offence of the accused, ignoring other factors that may contribute to risk of recidivism. This designation is meant for NCRMD offenders convicted of a serious personal-injury offence of a violent nature, and is meant to protect the public from potentially dangerous offenders.

Histrionic Personality Disorder: Pattern of excessive emotionality and attention-seeking.

Hypomania: A less severe form of mania, distinguished from mania due to its lack of psychotic features.

Hysteria: Label given to unexplained physical complaints. The term hysteria has been largely replaced by the term somatization.

Ideas of Persecution: Individuals believe they are being harassed or threatened.

Implicit Biases: Refers to the attitudes and beliefs individuals possess about a person or group at an unconscious level. The unconscious attribution of particular qualities to another individual.

Impulsivity: Recklessness and risk-taking without consideration of consequences.

Incarcerated Severely Mentally Ill (I-SMI): Individuals who suffer from a mental disorder held criminally liable for their actions and incarcerated as punishment for their offence. I-SMI offenders are more likely to suffer from psychotic/delusional disorders not otherwise specified (NOS) or major depression than individuals found NCRMD.

Incoherent Speech: Words that do not fit together.

Indicated Intervention Strategies: Similar to tertiary prevention strategies. Aimed at persons in whom prodromal symptoms of antisocial personality disorder are already present but who do not yet have the disorder fully developed.

Intelligence Testing: A series of tasks designed to measure one's capacity to make abstractions, to learn, and to deal with novel situations.

Intergenerational Trauma: A collective trauma that crosses generations and is associated with ineffective or maladaptive child-rearing practices, low socioeconomic status, and criminal behaviour.

Interpersonal Development: Relating to relationships or communications between people.

Interpersonal Psychotherapy (IPT): Treatment approach that emphasizes resolution of relationship stressors such as role disputes in marital conflict or forming relationships in marriage or a new job.

Interpretation: A communication strategy that helps to clarify and build rapport by checking that one's understanding is correct.

Invasive Treatments: Neurostimulation therapies that target the brain and spinal cord to relieve pain or restore function. Includes vagus nerve stimulation (VNS) and deep brain stimulation (DBS) and requires implantation of a pulse generator or electrodes, respectively, into specific areas of the brain.

Language Aptitude: Understanding and relating to others (empathy), a capacity to listen (active listening), and non-judgement.

Legal Cynicism: Refers to the perception that the police are corrupt, unjust, and unresponsive; in other words, there is a lack of police legitimacy.

Life-Course-Persistent Category: Adolescents who persist with offending will continue to engage in antisocial behaviour throughout adulthood and across different circumstances, with many receiving a diagnosis of antisocial personality fisorder as adults. Represents only 5% of males and is marked by significant impairment across different life domains.

Loose Association: The combination of unrelated or abstract topics.

Major Depressive Disorder (MDD): major depressive episodes include symptoms such as feeling sad, diminished interest in previously enjoyed activities, and significant weight loss or gain. MDD is diagnosed when it is not better explained by other disorders and there has never been a manic or hypomanic episode.

Malingering: When a person intentionally pretends to be ill for an incentive such as being acquitted of a crime.

Malleus Maleficarum: "The Hammer of the Witches," book published in 1487 by two Catholic monks that dominated thinking for approximately 250 years. The book authorizes the torture of persons who were thought to be witches or possessed by demons.

Mandated Programs: Non-voluntary participation in a treatment where the person must complete the program.

Mania: Extreme state of euphoria or elevated mood characterized by sustained periods of psychosis or extreme/exaggerated behaviours.

Masochism: Involves the suffering or pain being inflicted upon the self.

Medication Adherence: Extent to which patients take medication as prescribed.

Medicine Wheel: A model used by North American Indigenous cultures. According to some cultures, the universe is always trying to maintain a state of harmony and balance. The model in this book illustrates the four directions of human growth—emotional, mental, physical, and spiritual—with the addition of a social circle.

Mental Hygiene Movement: A movement characterized by a desire to protect and provide humane treatment for persons with mental health illnesses.

Mentally Ill Prisoner (MIP): Individuals having been held criminally liable and who are incarcerated as punishment for their offence. When compared to the NCRMD group, MIP patients were found to be more assaultive, more self-destructive, and to have higher rates of polysubstance abuse and psychopathic traits.

Mindfulness-Based Cognitive Therapy (MBCT): A modified form of cognitive therapy designed to treat depression. The main focus is the practice of mindfulness and utilizing tools such as meditation and breathing techniques to break away from negative thought patterns that lead to depressive episodes.

M'Naghten Standard: Standard of insanity defined by the case of *Regina v M'Naghten* (1843) that became the accepted rule in Canada, England, and the United States. In today's interpretation of the standard, (1) the accused must have been suffering from a mental disorder, and (2) the individual must not have known at least one of two things: the nature and quality of the act and that what he or she was doing was wrong. That is, inability to understand that an act is wrong can be sufficient even if the accused understands the act itself. Because the second element requires determination of the accused's thinking, the M'Naghten standard is referred to as a "cognitive" test of insanity.

Mobile Crisis Response Teams: Partners police departments with experienced mental health professionals to better address the needs of persons experiencing mental health.

Monoamine Oxidase Inhibitors (MAOI): For example, Marplan, Nardil. These drugs inhibit the enzyme monoamine oxidase that breaks down monoaminergic neurotransmitters, such as dopamine, norepinephrine, and serotonin, in the presynaptic cell. Therefore, there are more monoamines available to be released into the synapse, resulting in more binding to receptors triggering action potential.

Moral Reasoning: A thinking process with the objective of determining whether an idea is right or wrong.

Narcissistic Personality Disorder: Pattern of grandiosity, need for admiration, and lack of empathy.

Necrophilia: Pathological desire to engage in sexual activity with dead bodies.

Needs Principle: Part of the Risk-Needs-Responsivity theory that focuses on the high risk factors and the criminogenic needs of the offender, which have been found to be linked to criminal reoffending.

Negative Symptoms: Withdrawal, flattened emotions, decreased mood (affect), lack of spontaneity, and decreased energy and motivation.

Neuroplasticity: The ability of the brain to form and reorganize synaptic connections, especially in response to learning or experience following injury.

Neurostimulation Treatments: Involves the use of electrical or magnetic stimulation applied externally or internally to specific areas of the brain. Neurostimulation treatments can be invasive (internal) or non-invasive (external).

Noninvasive Treatments: Neurostimulation treatments that include transcranial direct current stimulation (tDCS), magnetic seizure therapy (MST), and repetitive transcranial magnetic stimulation (rTMS).

Non-Judgemental: Being accepting of others and not passing moral judgement.

Non-Mandated Programs: Programs that individuals attend of their own free will.

Nonsensical speech: Unclear speaking or inability to communicate an idea.

Non-Shared Environmental Factors: Individual potentially contributory influences such as delinquent peers, individual, social and academic experiences, sexual abuse, or sustaining an injury (e.g., a head injury) that may contribute to antisocial behaviour.

Not Criminally Responsible on Account of Mental Disorder (NCRMD): Section 16 of the Criminal Code of Canada declares that "no person is criminally responsible for an act committed or an omission made while suffering from a mental disorder that rendered the person incapable of appreciating the nature of and quality of the act or omission or of knowing that it was wrong."

Nurture: Refers to all the environmental variables that impact who we are, including early childhood experiences, social relationships, and surrounding culture.

Obsessive Thoughts: Individuals are preoccupied with obsessions, whether death, germs, guilt, or a person, and are unable to properly function due to these obsessive thoughts.

Obsessive-Compulsive Personality Disorder: Pattern of preoccupation with orderliness, perfectionism, and control.

Officer-Involved Domestic Violence (OIDV): When police officer families experience violence in the home. Officers with post-traumatic stress disorder are more likely to report physical violence, and officers with hazardous drinking tendencies are also more likely to act violently.

Open-Ended Questions: Questions that prompt an unstructured response from the individual, providing rich, detailed responses.

Opioids: Sub-group of CNS depressants that slow central nervous system activity and mask pain, leading to changes in thought, affect, mood, and behaviour. Members of this sub-group include codeine, dilaudid, fentanyl, morphine, opium, and oxycontin.

Oppositional Defiant Disorder (ODD): Characterized by mood issues, defiant behaviour, and vindictiveness. ODD involves intense emotional experiences (e.g., rage).

Over-Inclusiveness: Excessive and irrelevant detail, making it difficult to reach a logical end.

Pansexual: Individuals attracted to all genders.

Paranoid Personality Disorder: Pattern of distrust and suspiciousness such that others' motives are interpreted as malevolent.

Paraphilia: Sexual urge, desire, interest, and gratification in deviant sexual activities.

Paraphrasing: Involves expressing the meaning of what the individual is saying using different words to achieve greater clarity.

Patience: Refers to our capacity to tolerate difficult situations without getting upset or angry. It is waiting, watching, and knowing when to act.

Pedophilic Disorder: Involves sexual arousal to children.

Peritraumatic Factors: Factors that arise during the event. These risk factors include the severity and duration of the trauma, interpersonal violence (such as being attacked), dissociation during the event, feelings of helplessness, and being a perpetrator or witness to atrocities.

Perpetuating Factors: Factors that serve to maintain a particular disorder.

Persistent Depressive Disorder (PDD): Diagnostic sub-category of depressive disorder characterized by chronic, mild depressive moods that persist for two or more years in adults.

Personality: Typically refers to consistent patterns of thinking, feeling, and behaving, and is thought to be relatively stable over time.

Personality Disorder: Inflexible, rigid, long-lasting traits and characteristics of personality that cause dysfunction and distress in an individual's daily living in terms of behaviours, thoughts, and feelings.

Personality Inventories: Self-report questionnaires that assess personal traits by asking respondents to identify descriptions that apply to them.

Physical Dependence: Physiological state of cellular adaptation occurring when the body becomes so accustomed to a psychoactive drug that it can only function normally when the drug is present.

Plasticity: Adaptability of an individual to change in their environment.

Police Legitimacy: Pertains to the public's perception of police ethics and professional conduct that impacts a person's likelihood to obey law enforcement. Representation of justice that the community feels will be provided when it reports something to the police (or, conversely, a lack of police legitimacy is the belief that nothing will be accomplished).

Positive Symptoms: Presence of symptoms that should be absent, such as delusions or hallucinations.

Post-Traumatic Factors: Factors that contribute to the development of post-traumatic stress disorder after the event has occurred. These include social support after trauma exposure, development of ASD, access to clinical intervention, physical injuries, subsequent negative events, substance use, litigation, and feelings of guilt and shame.

Post-Traumatic Stress Disorder (PTSD): A reaction to an adverse event that exceeds one's available coping mechanisms.

Precipitating Factors: Events or situations that trigger or cause a given disorder.

Predatory Aggression: Otherwise known as instrumental aggression. Violence that is accompanied by little arousal. The violence is emotionless, planned, and purposeful.

Predisposing Factors: Any conditioning factor that influences both the type and the amount of resources that the individual can elicit to cope with stress. It may be biological, psychological, genetic, or sociocultural.

Pressured Speech: A form of unusual speech patterns where individuals express urgency when they speak.

Pre-Traumatic Factors: Pre-existing vulnerability or exacerbating factors that contribute to the impact of the traumatic event.

Prevalence Rates: The frequency of a disorder in a population at a given point or period of time.

Primary Mood Disorder: Classification of the mood disorder is based upon age of onset and family history of the individual. Important distinction in creating a treatment plan.

Privacy: An individual's right to choose the time, circumstance, and extent of their personal information being shared with or withheld from others. A basic human right in the Charter and an essential part of human dignity and freedom.

Privilege: A legal concept that addresses an individual's right to withhold information from you or any other legal proceedings.

Probing: Involves asking for deeper and more in-depth information by frequent use of phrases, such as "tell me more" or "please explain." Our interpretations are only hypotheses; they are not facts.

Prognosis: Course of the disorder and future outlook.

Proper Attitude: Being engaged, empathetic, patient, and non-judgemental.

Psychoactive Drug: Includes either a chemical not naturally found in the body or a normal body chemical that when administered alters both the central and peripheral nervous systems leading to changes in thought, affect, mood, and behaviour.

Psychodynamic Therapy: An approach to therapy used by Sigmund Freud, which emphasizes that behaviour is controlled by unconscious forces of which we are unaware.

Psychoeducation: Psychological education about mental health disorders, monitoring of symptoms and moods, substance abuse, medical adherence, and creating a relapse prevention plan.

Psychological Dependence: Occurs when a drug becomes so important to a person's thoughts or activities that individuals believe they cannot manage without it.

Psychological Disorder: Psychological dysfunction within an individual associated with distress or impairment in functioning and a response that is not typical or culturally expected.

Psychological Tests: Process of administering, scoring, and interpreting psychological assessment.

Psychopathology: Both the scientific study of psychological abnormality and the problems faced by people who suffer from such disorders.

Psychopathology Inventories: Measures that identify mental health symptoms and behaviours that are abnormal and characterized by specific disorders.

Psychopathy: Observable behaviours and personality traits that include a lack of affect and callous, superficially charming, irresponsible, deceitful, manipulative, and socially deviant traits. Termed 'moral insanity' in the 1800s.

Psychopharmacology: A branch of psychology concerned with the effects of drugs on the mind and behaviour.

Psychosis: Serious mental disorder involving symptoms such as thought disorder, hallucinations, etc.

Psychotherapy: A treatment using talk therapy with individuals or groups.

Rapport: A harmonious dialogue or relationship that reflects respect, trust, empathy, and mutual respect.

Reasonable Flexibility: Being fully present in the moment and changing or persisting in behaviour based on what the individual situation affords, to a reasonable degree. In other words, when we remain rigid in every situation, we are unable to fully assess each situation as it requires and often limit our outcome possibilities.

Recidivism: The tendency of a convicted criminal to relapse into criminal behaviour and re-offend violently, non-violently (for example, parole violations), or sexually.

Residential Schools: Placement of Indigenous persons in schools separated from their families in an attempt to assimilate Indigenous children into

European culture. Only English and European cultural values were taught, which resulted in a generational loss of Indigenous languages and cultural practices.

Respect: The regard for the feelings, wishes, rights, and traditions of another individual.

Responsivity Principle: An aspect from the risk-needs-responsivity model specifying that rehabilitation is most effective when it is sensitive to the learning style, motivation, and abilities of the person.

Risk Factors: Factors that exacerbate a particular, high-risk outcome. Can be organized into 1) individual-level risk factors, 2) community-level and relationship risk factors, and 3) societal-level risk factors.

Risk Principle: Stipulates that criminal behaviour can be predicted and that the intervention should match the intensity of the risk level.

Sadism: Receives pleasure from inflicting/seeing the physical or psychological suffering of another person.

Schizoid Personality Disorder: A pattern of detachment from social relationships and a restricted range of emotional expression.

Schizophrenia: A mental illness in which the hallmark is chronic psychosis. Positive symptoms are hallucinations and delusions. Negative symptoms include disorganized thinking and disorganized behaviours.

Schizotypal Personality Disorder: A pattern of acute discomfort in close relationships, cognitive or perceptual distortions, and eccentricities of behaviour.

Secondary Mood Disorder: Mood disorder that develops as result of a medical disease such as Parkinson's or a non-affective psychiatric condition (for example, schizophrenia).

Selected Intervention Strategies: Otherwise known as selected prevention strategies (an idea similar to secondary prevention). Applied to people who are at risk of developing a disorder or who may show early signs of it.

Selective Serotonin Reuptake Inhibitors (SSRI): For example, Prozac, Zoloft. They block reuptake of serotonin into the presynaptic cell, thus leaving more serotonin available in the synapse to bind to receptors and trigger action potentials.

Self-Awareness: Defined as "an accurate appraisal of a given aspect of one's situation, functioning, performance, or of the resulting implications."

Sexual Identity: Refers to the biological aspects of a person's sexual characteristics. An individual's sex includes their chromosomes, hormones, and sexual genitalia.

Shared Environmental Factors: Shared environmental influences that are risk factors for antisocial behaviour, such as poor supervision from parents, single-parent households, antisocial parents, siblings who are delinquent, parental conflict, harsh discipline, neglect, large family size, and having a young and/or depressed mother.

Sixties Scoop: An attempt to assimilate Indigenous children into Western society by apprehending them and putting them up for adoption to mostly Caucasian families—under the guise that the system felt Indigenous children were not being adequately cared for.

Social Modelling: Refers to one person presenting certain behaviours that elicit a similar response from the person. For example, if a police officer presents a hostile mood, the person will also demonstrate hostile traits and behaviours, so if the officer wants to create conditions of calmness and openness, then the officer must exhibit these qualities.

Socioeconomic Status: The social standing or class of an individual or group; often measured as a combination of education, income, and occupation.

Solution-Focused Therapy: A goal-directed collaborative approach to psychotherapeutic change that places emphasis on present circumstances and hope for the future rather than on past problems.

Somatogenic Hypothesis: The idea that psychopathology is caused by biological factors.

Standard of Proof: Proof beyond a reasonable doubt. The degree of evidence necessary to establish proof in legal proceedings.

Standardization: Process of establishing specific norms and protocol for a measurement technique to ensure it is used consistently across measurement settings. This includes instructions for administering the measure, evaluating its findings, and comparing these to normative/reference data for large numbers of people.

Static Risk Factors: Factors that can increase the risk for an individual to re-offend. Historic in nature and rarely changes. Examples include the number of prior criminal offences, and age of first offence.

Stigma: Relates to societal disapproval or rejection associated with a person's attributes or behaviour that marginalizes the individual.

Stimulants: Psychoactive drugs that increase the activity of both the central and autonomic nervous systems, particularly the sympathetic portion of the Autonomic Nervous System leading to changes in thought, affect, mood, and behaviour. Members of this family include cocaine, amphetamines, methamphetamine, nicotine, and caffeine.

Substance Use Disorders: Use of drugs or alcohol, or other substance use that interferes with an individual's functioning, such as occupation or relationships.

Suicide by Cop: A method of suicide in which a person deliberately behaves in a threatening manner to provoke a police officer into using lethal force.

Summarizing: Large chunks of information are aggregated into a concise statement.

Tactical Skills: Using language to instruct, inspire, and openly communicate rather than constrain situations.

Teachable Moments: Where the police have an opportunity with every interaction to erode or build legitimacy—and every effort should be taken to increase legitimacy.

The Not Criminally Responsible Reform Act: Bill C-14 was passed in 2013 in Canada and made several major amendments to the NCRMD defence.

Transgender: An umbrella term encompassing all individuals with a discrepancy between their gender and biological sex.

Transvestic Disorder: Involves sexual arousal paired with cross-dressing, that is, dressing in clothing opposite to one's sex. The cross-dressing can vary from one article of clothing to an entire wardrobe. It should be noted that there can be individuals who cross-dress but do not meet the criteria for the disorder, as the clothing is not part of their sexual excitement.

Traumatic Brain Injury (TBI): Results from a violent blow to the head or body causing brain injury and dysfunction.

Trephination: A prehistoric form of surgery possibly intended to let out evil spirits; it involved chipping a hole into a person's skull.

Tricyclics (TCA): Antidepressant medications such as Tofranil and Elavil.

Trust: The belief in the reliability, truth, ability, or strength of someone or something.

Unipolar mood disorders: Characterized by extreme depressed mood such as major depression and that causes marked functional impairment with no episodes of mania or hypomania.

Universal Intervention Strategies: Primary prevention strategies for antisocial personality disorder or other disorders that are directed at the general population.

Urophilia: Paraphilia characterized by sexual arousal to urine. May involve the individual performing the act on the partner or having the partner urinate on the individual.

Use of Force Framework: Developed to assist in the training of officers. Used as a reference when making decisions and explaining police actions with respect to the use of force.

Validation: Establishes that the individual's feelings are reasonable.

Values: A set of practical criteria for making decisions in human service professions.

Verbatim Playback: Re-stating what individuals are saying, in their exact words.

Vicarious Trauma: Indirectly experiencing trauma by hearing stories of victims who have experienced trauma, often impacts therapists or family members.

Volitional Impairment: Inability to exert adequate control over one's behaviour.

Voyeuristic Disorder: Viewing of a non-consenting person, typically through a window, with interest or sexual arousal including fantasies and sexual gratification.

Withdrawal: Physical, mental, and emotional impacts that a person experiences when they do not consume the drug that they are addicted/dependent upon.

Word Repetition: Unusual speech patterns that often include frequently stating the same words and phrases or using rhyming words and phrases.

Word Salad: A part of disorganized speech and thought where the person combines random words and phrases together.

Zoophilia: Paraphilia involving sexual arousal to non-human animals.

EDITOR BIOGRAPHIES

Daniel J. Jones, PhD (ABD), completed his Master's degree at the University of Cambridge in Applied Criminology and Police Management, and he is currently completing his Doctorate in Philosophy at the University of Huddersfield in Criminal Justice. Daniel has been a police officer for 21 years, with his father, brother, uncle, and cousin also serving in police organizations. Daniel's interest is in promoting police legitimacy and community trust as well as fair Indigenous representation in the legal system. Dan is a sessional instructor at the University of Alberta in the Sociology Department, and provides special lectures around the globe on policing.

John R. Reddon, PhD, received Bachelor of Arts, Bachelor of Commerce, and Master of Science degrees from the University of Alberta and then received a Doctor of Philosophy from the University of Western Ontario. Since 1983 he has been ensconced at Alberta Hospital Edmonton (AHE, a psychiatric and forensic facility). In 1983 he began his tenure at AHE in the Department of Neuropsychology and Research; in 1992 he transitioned to the Clinical Diagnostics and Research Centre at AHE; and since 2008 has been in Forensic Psychiatry at AHE. Since 1995 he has also been an Adjunct Professor of Psychology at the University of Alberta (U of A). His focus at AHE and the U of A has been applied research, program evaluation, and training in support of assessment and treatment in the forensic and mental health areas with children, adults, and the elderly. To date he has published 130 journal articles and book chapters.

Uzma Williams, PhD, graduated with a Bachelor of Arts from Concordia University of Edmonton, a Master of Science from the University of Alberta, and a Doctor of Philosophy from McMaster University. Uzma's doctorate work explored patterns of participation, service need and use, and family-centred care of families using rehabilitation centres. Uzma is a sessional instructor at MacEwan University in the Department of Public Safety and Justice and at Concordia University of Edmonton in the Psychology Department. Uzma and her husband Chris have two children, Joseph and Eva, and live in St. Albert, Alberta.